RENEWALS 458-4574

DATE DUE

JUL 1 9			
7-26-97			
DEC 1 2	.		
AUG 1 2	.		
NOV 0 9 200?			
GAYLORD			PRINTED IN U.S.A

The Library Administration Series

Lowell A. Martin, General Editor

Planning Library Buildings and Facilities

From Concept to Completion

RAYMOND M. HOLT

Scarecrow
Library
Administration
Series
No. 9

The Scarecrow Press, Inc.
Metuchen, N.J., & London
1989

British Library Cataloging-in-Publication data available

Library of Congress Cataloging-in-Publication Data

Holt, Raymond M., 1921–
  Planning library buildings and facilities : from concept to
completion / by Raymond M. Holt.
      p.   cm. — (Scarecrow library administration series : no. 9)
  Includes bibliographical references.
  ISBN 0-8108-2203-2
  1. Library planning.   2. Library buildings.   3. Library
architecture.   I. Title.   II. Series.
Z679.5.H65   1989
022'.3—dc20

                                              89-10947

CONTENTS

LIST OF FIGURES

PREFACE

THE PLANNING or replanning of a library building is often the high point—or low point—of a librarian's career. For the administrator who successfully combines function and design and environment, the finished structure is a fitting monument to the individual's imagination, judgment, and persistence. Thousands and thousands of users will benefit over the years, and in the process will have a little extra sense of the rightness of the world. But librarians who are confused or carried away with pet enthusiasms or dominated by architect or higher authority will have to live with the result for the rest of their lives. In this case the thousands of users will silently curse whoever did it this way.

As building consultant, Ray Holt has been through the process literally scores of times. He and his wife, Sarah, constitute a team that has advised on library buildings large and small, new and remodeled, and the imprint of their work can be seen across the land. We were fortunate at Scarecrow Press to get their time and attention between projects to set down what will be the definitive work in the field.

This fits the pattern of the administration series of Scarecrow, the production of volumes that bring the experience of seasoned administrators to librarians confronted with the whole range of problems inherent in service institutions. The series started with the legal basis for such institutions, went on through organization, communication, finance, public relations, and related topics, and now deals with the building itself. A volume on policy planning is also nearing completion.

Besides rich experience, Ray Holt brings an organized mind and clarity of expression to this presentation. And he is practical: Note the down-to-earth section on construction, note the appendixes right down to questions to be presented to the architect and how to calculate space for specific functions.

Before long we must replace past generations of library buildings. Here is a guide to that future.

Lowell A. Martin
Series Editor

ACKNOWLEDGMENTS

*I*N WRITING THIS BOOK, *I must acknowledge a deep indebtedness to all who have labored before me in this same field beginning with those monumental librarians Joseph L. Wheeler and Keyes D. Metcalf. Their significant and enduring contributions to the literature on library buildings are still basic to acquiring a working knowledge of the library planning and building process.*

Acknowledgment is also gratefully made to the gracious cooperation of Cynthia Ripley, AIA, of Ripley Associates, Architects & Planners of San Francisco, and Jane Light, Director, Redwood City Public Library, for making available the numerous architectural drawings illustrating chapter 14. Without such drawings, this key chapter on plan review would not have been possible.

Finally, I wish to express my deepest appreciation to my wife and partner, Sarah, for her unfailing encouragement, thoughtful contributions, and careful proofreading of the text. Her unflagging efforts have made this volume possible. Without her enthusiastic endorsement and continued participation, this book would never have been attempted, let alone completed.

INTRODUCTION

COPING with change is an everyday challenge for librarians. When those changes result, as they frequently do, in demands for new facilities, practical assistance is needed. The librarian must understand both the process and the consequences of facility planning if he or she is to provide the necessary leadership. Unfortunately, there is little in the way of a professional training ground other than experience itself. Yet, the opportunity for gaining such experience is limited. Even the literature on planning library buildings is somewhat circumscribed and, to some extent, dated. This is of little comfort to the librarian who must suddenly grapple with the problem of running out of space.

Learning by doing, while it can be an effective teacher, can also be expensive. Most facility planning decisions are for the long haul and have large dollar signs attached. Moreover, the consequences of facility planning decisions are almost certain to affect library users, services, staff and, by no means least, the operating budget. The chances of making serious mistakes decrease markedly when the librarian understands the facility planning process and appreciates the gravity of the manifold decisions which must be made.

Library facility planning is further complicated by the fact that the librarian, even though playing an essential role, must depend upon the talents and labor of design professionals and share the decision-making with others as the project advances. Maintaining leadership and direction under such conditions is often confusing and difficult, especially when the process itself is unclear. Too often, librarians who are intimidated by this or preoccupied by other responsibilities are tempted to limit their participation. This tendency may be encouraged by the assumption that little can go wrong when design professionals and other responsible people are involved. Such complacency is bolstered on occasion by a feeling of inadequacy stemming from a lack or familiarity with facility planning. All too often, librarians who have minimized their participation have a rude awakening when the project is finished and its avoidable shortcomings become apparent.

A text on library facility planning can no more substitute for experience than a text on any other subject. Yet, born of our own experience with scores of projects, this volume attempts to provide an array of practical information which the librarian can use in preparation for personal involvement. It is pragmatic and, to the degree possible, describes facility planning in a sequential manner from needs assessment through construction. Knowing the limitations on the librarian's time, it is assumed that most will read those portions of greatest immediacy, rather than read the volume from cover to cover. In this sense, this is more a handbook than a textbook, although there is a logical sequencing and development of information.

Finally, the overriding goal of this volume is to provide a source of solid, realistic and functional information which will enable the librarian to participate fully in the facility planning process. Since there appear to be more similarities than differences in planning both academic and public library facilities, it is hoped that the volume will be of general use; librarians in school, institutional and special libraries may also find help here. To the degree that this text contributes to improved library facilities, it will be deemed successful.

Raymond M. Holt
Raymond M. Holt and Associates
Del Mar, California

PLANNING LIBRARY BUILDINGS AND FACILITIES

1 BASIC PHASES OF THE LIBRARY FACILITY PLANNING PROCESS

PLANNING for adequate library facilities is one of the most challenging opportunities a librarian is likely to face—and perhaps the least familiar. For this reason, it is important to understand the basic phases of the library building planning process and the scope of each phase. Whether the project involves the remodeling of an existing library building, an expansion of the building by means of an addition, the conversion of a structure originally designed for another purpose, or an entirely new facility, a similar process involving the same phases will be encountered. The chapters of this book have been organized to follow the progression of these phases and the purpose of this first chapter is to briefly describe their scope.

The exact role of the librarian in a building project will depend upon many factors. In most instances, the librarian will be the primary resource person, regardless of what other responsibilities he or she may have. However, with few exceptions, the library's governing body will retain the responsibility for major decisions. Few things are likely to contribute more to a building project's success than a clear-cut chain of command that unequivocally establishes the location of decision-making authority.

Of course, library building projects do not follow identical schedules. Therefore, the phases may overlap or be treated in a different sequence. Sometimes, one or more phases may be abbreviated or even skipped. For instance, a gift of funds or of a site will eliminate the funding or site-selection phase. If a building formerly used for some other purpose unexpectedly becomes available for use as a library before a formal review of requirements has been made, the needs assessment study may be unnecessary. However, most librarians are apt to encounter most, if not all, of the following project phases.

Generally speaking, the major project phases and their major elements are:

Phase 1: Fact Finding

1 / Needs Assessment
2 / Evaluation of Options

Phase 2: Planning

1 / Preparation of the Building Program
2 / Funding
3 / Selection of Design Professionals and the Project Team

Phase 3: Architectural Development

1 / Conceptual Design
2 / Schematic Design
3 / Design Development
4 / Construction Documents

Phase 4: Interiors and Furnishings

1 / Furniture and Equipment Layout
2 / Casework Design
3 / Furniture and Equipment Selection

Phase 5: Construction

1 / Bidding and Award of Bid
2 / Site Work and Foundations
3 / Construction
4 / Finishing

Phase 6: Occupation, Orientation, and Evaluation

1 / Moving
2 / Orientation
3 / Post-Occupancy Evaluation and Remedial Work

The remainder of this chapter provides an overview of these basic elements in the planning and building process and indicates how they relate to the usual facility schedule. Later chapters will consider these subjects in much greater detail and indicate some of the parameters of the librarian's role. Each element is an essential part of the facility planning process, the aim of which is to provide for the efficient and effective delivery of library services. The librarian who has an understanding of the entire process is more likely to be able to fulfill the key role which he or she needs to play.

The ensuing presentation assumes that the reader is interested in following the course of a library facility project from the outset to its ultimate conclusion. For those who have had prior experience with facility planning, or whose projects are already beyond this initial point, the review will serve as a framework for these major steps and provide a coherent perspective that may otherwise be lost in the maze of inherent details.

Phase 1: Fact Finding

The first inkling of a future building project often begins with the librarian's perception that the existing library facility is lacking in some regard. It is the purpose of the fact-finding phase to document such perceptions and convert them into a program of action. While the actual point at which building projects begin differs widely and may often be too amorphous to recall with any certainty, each beginning is like a different door opening into the same maze of future steps.

Few library projects emerge full-blown overnight. Most have a long genesis, commencing, for instance, with the shadowy perception that space is running out, overcrowding is beginning to occur and functions and services can not be properly accommodated. Between this first premonition of inadequacy and the initial formal step in the planning process there may be a long interval. During this period awareness, often accompanied by frustration, slowly increases as the evidence continues to mount.

Needs Assessment

The purpose of the fact-finding phase is to convert all of these bits and pieces of suspicion and reality into incontrovertible testimony regarding the facility's shortcomings. These facts, in turn, can be used to support a plan for taking necessary action.

While most librarians will have to take the initiative in deciding to enter the data-gathering phase, an in-

creasing number of agencies is providing motivation through requiring library participation in an ongoing Capital Improvements Plan, often know as the CIP. The purpose of most CIP plans is to project capital needs for a period of five or so years as a means of dealing with major capital needs in a logical and consistent manner. In effect, the library joins other departments of the academic system or governmental agency in estimating space and other facility-related needs for several years in advance. After evaluating these needs and other aspects, the officers of the agency or academic institution evaluate the responses and place the requests in a queue according to priority. Participation in the CIP process sometimes forces the librarian to confront the realities of the library's facility requirements in an orderly way. Even though the data for the CIP program may be brief and formalized, it may be enriched and strengthened by using some of the fact-finding techniques characteristic of Phase 1.

No matter how horrifying or desperate your library facility needs may seem to be to you, the librarian, they are not likely to be so obvious to others. The question, "Is a new, remodeled, or expanded library building really necessary at this time?" must still be answered with firm and convincing facts and figures. What may be obvious deficiencies to you are likely to require specific identification and amplification for those who hold the decision-making power. The process of gathering, analyzing and presenting this information is known as needs assessment.

Usually, needs assessment involves at least the following steps, which are applicable to both academic and public libraries:

1/ Analysis of community need for library resources and services;
2/ Projections of growth for collections, seating, staff, and other components;
3/ Consideration of current developments in library service delivery which are apt to affect future space needs;
4/ Anticipation of changes in the organization and management of library services and staff;
5/ Addition of any new services or accommodations, such as meeting rooms.

Data should be carefully gathered from reliable sources and documented wherever possible. Because this information will be used as the basis for convincing others of the library's space needs and will later be used in conjunction with the preparation of the building program, it is imperative that the data be sound.

During the needs assessment process, visits by library staff to other libraries should be initiated. Such visits will often trigger recognition of otherwise unnoticed conditions and needs, as well as provide a valuable frame of reference. Additional background is also available through perusal of library literature. In many cases, needs assessment may merit retaining a library consultant who is familiar with the process to help gather and analyze data and to assist in preparing the report. Such a person may bring a new perspective and make certain that all of the important aspects are covered.

When the needs assessment study is completed, the results should be assembled into a well-written report with an executive summary. The manner of presentation is an important element in making the needs assessment study persuasive. Full use should be made of graphics, for instance. One cautionary note: scare tactics must be avoided, no matter how desperate the library's plight. Information on the condition of the library building, for instance, should be restricted to a factual and unemotional recital of facts, backed up where necessary by reference to authoritative sources. Creating the needs assessment study is the first in a long series of cumulative steps and deserves to be handled with full awareness of its importance. The lack of an adequate needs assessment study has caused many a library project to flounder or to incur long, frustrating delays.

The needs assessment process is discussed in greater detail in Chapter 2.

Evaluation of Options

The second part of the fact-finding phase is aimed at evaluation of the options for resolution of the library's space needs as established in the needs assessment study. The major options are usually limited to one of the following, or some combination thereof:

1/ Remodel the existing library building without adding any new space;
2/ Expand the existing facility and remodel portions or all of the building;
3/ Convert to library use a structure originally designed for another purpose;
4/ Design and construct an entirely new library facility.

All too often, library facility planning begins with the assumption that only one or two of these options exist. This preconception can blind library officials to other solutions which may be more favorable. For instance, it may have been assumed for many years that an addition to the original structure offers the only logical response to future space needs. Such a presumption may have overlooked the poor condition of the existing structure, severe site constraints or a bad location. To avoid wasting time, effort and money in pursuing an ill-conceived solution of this kind, all possible options should be considered during the fact-finding phase. This requires gathering information and reporting it in such a manner that comparisons can be made in order to select the most practical and cost-effective solution.

The evaluation of options also involves establishing criteria by which each of the possible solutions can be impartially compared. Since data will still be far from complete and unlikely to represent input from professionals such as architects and engineers, the librarian will be required to employ certain assumptions. A conscientious comparison of the pros and cons of each option should indicate the most cost-effective course of action.

Further discussion of methods for presenting options, evaluating their merits and making the ultimate choice is presented in Chapter 3.

Phase 2: Planning

The planning phase, which has the preparation of the building program as its chief product, usually does not begin until the library's space needs have been accepted along with approval of a particular solution for meeting space demands. Bringing about this consent is one of the more difficult tasks facing the librarian and requires a variety of political skills as well as patience. However, once the solution has been chosen, no time should be lost in actively entering the planning phase. An awareness of what that phase includes will be most helpful to the librarian attempting this transition.

Depending upon the agency involved, the sequence of the planning phase tasks will vary. However, because of its importance as the project's basic document, preparation of the building program should receive the highest priority in planning. When planning begins without a building program, serious deficiencies often complicate matters later on.

The Building Program

When properly developed, the building program is the most important and useful tool that the librarian and other project team members have at their disposal. Its primary function is to provide all of the information about the library that the architect and interior designer need for their work. This includes space requirements, functional relationships, and a host of other details. By analyzing the amount of space necessary for individual portions of the collections, services, and operations, the needs of individual areas as well as the total space needs of the library are verified. The process of preparing the building program enables the librarian and staff to identify potential operational problems and to work out solutions. Finally, the building program becomes the primary source book for the design professionals as well as a checklist for guidance during subsequent stages of the project such as the review of drawings and specifications.

The building program covers every facet of the library, from its major collections and services to details on the organization of procedures, work flow, and user needs. Desired esthetics and environmental conditions must be specified in order to provide the design professionals with indications of how the building should feel to those using it and working in it. This step includes information on lighting, acoustics and general decor. Any areas devoted to a particular age group, a special collection or service should be clearly identified and described. Projections of future space needs and the areas of the library on which they are most likely to have an impact must be presented to help the architect arrive at a design which can successfully accommodate growth.

Program data, after they have been accumulated, must be put into written form—usually a combination of narrative text, tables and figures. A detailed table of contents or a full index is needed to provide easy access to the program details. Because the building program represents the best chance for establishing the basic elements of the library building's design, its importance can hardly be overemphasized. When completed, the building program should be officially accepted by the governing body and later incorporated into the architect's contract as the basis for design.

The building program and its preparation are described in greater detail in Chapter 4.

Financing the Project

Sometime during the early stages of planning, the question of funding will require resolution. In some instances, funds will already have been accumulated by one means or another. Other institutions and governmental agencies may have an established process for securing the necessary monies. A sizable number, however, will have to decide on a source for funds.

Various facets of funding, including the librarian's role in this process, are discussed in Chapter 11.

Assembling the Project Team

The final task to be accomplished during the planning period is choosing the team that will be responsible for the project. The "Project Team" concept, though not always officially recognized or used, has developed over the past several decades as a means of bringing together those most vitally concerned with a particular building project. In the case of a library building, the project team is likely to include most, if not all, of the following:

1/ The Client's representative
2/ The Librarian
3/ The Library Consultant
4/ The Architect
5/ The Interior Designer
6/ The Building Contractor (after the construction contract has been awarded).

As an essential member of the team, the librarian must understand how the team is organized and what each person is responsible for during the course of the project. In fact, of all the team members, the librarian's role may vary the most from one situation to another, ranging from that of client's representative and convener to honorary advisor. Since the librarian will be intensively involved with the team and its activities for a period of several years, the responsibility that such membership confers is not to be taken lightly. The larger the role assumed by the librarian, the greater the commitment in time and energy.

Obviously, one key to the success of the project lies in the selection of the respective team members. While their professional qualifications and experience are major factors to be considered, the team's ability to produce a successful project will be determined to some degree by the compatibility of the individuals. Therefore, the choice of each team member is of considerable significance and justifies a systematic search. Procedures for the task of selecting team members, and especially the architect and interior designer, should be formulated well before the need for hiring occurs. Whether this task evolves on the librarian, or not, it is important for the librarian to understand how the selection process can best be structured to obtain optimum results. Chapter 5 has been devoted to describing the roles of the project team members and the processes for their selection.

On many projects, the design professionals, the librarian and other designated individuals form the Project Team. This may be a formal arrangement but it is more likely to be informal in nature. The Project Team concept has grown out of the need to assure broader participation during the design process. A full understanding of the Project Team concept and how it operates is necessary for the librarian seeking to make the most of his or her participation. Chapter 6 is concerned with the Project Team, its organization and management, with emphasis upon the librarian's role.

Phase 3: Architectural and Interior Development

The conclusion of the planning phase is usually marked by the choice of the project team members. With the design professionals chosen and the other project team members in place, the process of translating the building program into drawings and specifications can begin.

Architectural and Interior Design Phases

The architectural and interior design phases are often considered the most interesting, as well as the most crucial part of the project. Seeing the image of a building materialize from the words of a building program is a rewarding experience that team participants anticipate with pleasure and excitement. For the librarian, it is a reward for the interminable hours spent in bringing the project to this point.

While architects may differ in their approach to any specific project, the period of architectural design and development will normally encompass the following phases:

1/ Conceptual Phase (often combined with Schematics)
2/ Schematic Design
3/ Design Development
4/ Construction Documents

As this terminology implies, the process proceeds from general concepts to the final drawings and specifications that the building contractor will follow in constructing the facility. The same stages occur whether the project involves the remodeling of a library or an entirely new facility. Understanding this process and what is involved at each stage will enable the librarian to function effectively as a project team member.

While few will argue the importance of architectural design, it is usually the design of the library's interior spaces which have the most impact on users, staff and operations. Therefore, the librarian must have a good understanding of how the interior design will evolve.

Good interior design, like good architectural design, begins with the building program. The librarian must therefore incorporate information into the program which will be useful in the design of the interiors and the selection of furniture and equipment. This involves describing the atmosphere to be achieved in each space, including lighting and acoustical requirements. It does *not* mean selecting colors and the like, all too often considered to be the basis for interior design.

Because interior design is so crucial, responsibility for interior planning should be established before the design professionals are selected. Because interior and architectural design must be closely coordinated to achieve a unified whole, some architectural firms provide interior design services through their own staff. However, because of the high degree of specialization required in the design of interiors, including the selection of furniture and equipment, a separate professional group known as interior designers has evolved in recent years. Whether it is preferable to use such a specialist or to depend upon the architect's skills is a question that the librarian must deal with. There are numerous pros and cons which require consideration.

In any case, once selected, the person responsible for the interiors becomes an integral part of the project team and should begin serving in that capacity immediately. The scope of work assigned the interior designer must be carefully defined and coordinated with that delegated to the architect. Otherwise, conflicts may arise to complicate matters. Usually the interior designer will be held responsible for the layout of furniture and equipment, design of casework, selection of furniture, equipment, floor and wall coverings, graphics and signage; the interior designer will also work with the architect in selecting the proper lighting system. If the project includes art work, the interior designer should act as an advisor in the selection of appropriate pieces and in designing suitable niches, hanging spaces, lighting, etc.

Interior design has added significance because of its eventual impact on library operating costs, particularly for custodial services, maintenance and repair, and in time on replacement. Using an interior designer with a good track record in these areas will pay dividends in the future.

Each of the phases of architectural & interior design and development, and their implications for the librarian, are described in Chapter 7.

Phase 5: Construction

Although the librarian and library staff will have little direct involvement in the construction of the library building, a knowledge of what the construction phase entails can be helpful. Knowing the normal course of events during construction enables the librarian to anticipate the evolution of the building and to coordinate the scheduling of plans for moving and adapting to the new facility. In many instances, there may be a limited amount of direct involvement through the review of addenda or change orders required to alter certain aspects of construction or to remedy a situation not anticipated during design. Reviewing shop drawings for casework will be one of the tasks normally required of the librarian.

The major phases of construction following the award of bid include: 1/ site work, 2/ raising of the structure, 3/ enclosure, and 4/ completion of finish work. Given a full understanding of the construction process the librarian can follow its course in an intelligent manner and help interpret progress to others. Understanding will also result in a greater appreciation of the building as being the end product of many trades closely coordinated by the contractor.

Because the construction process has become so involved, the librarian needs to comprehend the role of those who may be retained by the client to oversee the project, such as the clerk of the works or construction manager. When and under what circumstances the librarian may visit the construction site is another subject to be understood.

The construction phase and the librarian's role therein are further described in Chapter 8.

Phase 6: Occupation, Orientation, and Evaluation

Completion of construction inaugurates the final phase of the building project: occupation, orientation, and evaluation. While it is apparent from the day a building project is conceived that the library will eventually need to move into the remodeled, expanded or new facility, planning is often inadequate. Preparations for moving and for the changes in operations which the move-in may require should begin long in advance of the event. Moving and orientation plans will be conditioned to some extent by the nature and size of the project and the amount of change involved in the organization of collections and services. A very large addition or a new building may entail more planning than is required for a small expansion or minor renovation. On the other hand, major remodeling projects are almost certain to require a succession of moves, each potentially disruptive and time-consuming. Learning how to handle these situations is a part of the librarian's preparation for moving.

Plans for moving will depend on what is to be moved, how far it must be transported and what conditions will be involved. These variables require careful attention to details and to consideration of optional courses of action. The counsel of moving experts and the experience of other librarians will be helpful.

Planning for orientation is akin to anticipating the effect of the arrival of an infant will have on a family. Unfortunately, planning for orientation is seldom given much thought, even though the new surroundings will have a variety of impacts on library routines as well as on library users and staff. To avoid the often awkward and confused state of affairs that moving sometimes creates, a program of orientation for staff and users is necessary. The goal is to help each person become familiar with the building as rapidly as possible, so as to speed effective use of the library's resources. A dynamic orientation program will help everyone realize the full benefits of the new facility and lead to a higher level of user and staff acceptance.

The first weeks and months of occupation constitute a shake-down period for the building. Despite the best efforts of the architect, interior designer and construction crews, some things are bound to go wrong. Because the library staff is likely to be the first to detect and report these events, the librarian must know how to proceed. A carpet seam breaks, a roof leaks, a piece of HVAC equipment malfunctions, an electrical outlet doesn't work, a leg breaks on a chair—these and many more minor crises may develop which the librarian must be ready to handle by knowing whom to call.

Before the new project has been occupied for very long, the librarian will begin to understand and appreciate it in a new way. This should result in a realistic post-occupancy evaluation by the end of the first year. Attention should be called to both the advantages and the blemishes that have become evident. Remedial action can then be suggested wherever it is called for.

The major facets of occupation, orientation and post-occupancy evaluation are discussed in Chapter 9.

Other Aspects of Planning Facilities for Library Service

The remainder of the text is devoted to particular aspects of planning for library buildings that the librarian may encounter, including site selection, funding, space planning, and the special problems related to remodeling, additions and conversions. They will add depth to the librarian's knowledge of the planning and programming process whether these factors are directly involved in a particular project or not. A brief description of these chapters follows.

Site Selection

When a building project involves a new structure, site selection will probably be a part of the process. Location is a crucial factor in usage, whether the library is an academic or a public one. For the librarian, site selection often marks the first stage—and possibly the first skirmish—of the long campaign to make a new library building a reality. Therefore, the librarian must be fully prepared to evaluate the potential of locations proposed for a library facility.

Site selection is apt to create wide interest; it is a subject about which many people have an opinion, informed or otherwise. This is particularly true for public libraries, though locating academic library buildings does not always occur without debate. Knowing what the site selection process entails and the interest it is likely to create should alert the librarian to the major issues and pitfalls that may arise.

Over the years, certain criteria have emerged out of library experience which can be applied to site analysis. When these are used, the possibility for choosing a desirable location improves considerably. A knowledge of the criteria and perseverance in adhering to them will do much to overcome opposition. Interestingly enough, while the general public is likely to acknowledge that a librarian and library staff are best prepared to create the building program, a surprising number of non-librarians are confident that they are in a better position to choose the site—even if they seldom or never darken the doors of the library! Few library issues become obscured faster or to a greater depth by irrational thinking, extraneous arguments and irrelevant facts than site selection. To counteract any emotional outburst which may threaten the success of the project, the librarian must maintain a calm demeanor and be prepared to explain every proposed site with effective reasoning. This is the purpose of Chapter 10.

Funding

The role of the librarian in securing funding for library building projects has been described earlier in this chapter as a part of the project process. Few building project issues are more frustrating, or can cause more delay, than the resolution of funding. "How much is the project going to cost?" and "Where's the money coming from?" are two very fundamental questions, almost certain to be raised at the mere mention of the library's need for more space. While obtaining the actual funds is not likely to be the personal responsibility of the librarian, knowing how to arrive at a project cost estimate and understanding when this estimate should be made are incumbent upon the librarian. Further, it is important that the librarian understand such things as: 1/ basic cost factors involved in a building project; 2/ major funding sources and how they can be utilized, and 3/ what implications a library building project will have on the future operating budget.

A cost estimate can be made in a variety of ways depending upon circumstances and the degree of accuracy desired. If possible, the estimate should not be made until sufficient information is available to establish the size of the project and any special requirements. This usually means that the needs assessment study must be completed, and possibly the building program also. If funding for the project is established prior to the time that these documents are available, the square footage of the building and/or the quality of its furnishings and equipment will be predetermined before the actual amount of space and other needs of the library can be ascertained. This is one of the primary reasons why so many library buildings run out of space long before they should.

The first task is to assemble a list of all items to be funded, including site, site preparation, construction, furnishings and equipment, and professional fees. Once the square footage of the project has been determined, along with any special requirements, an intelligent estimate can be made based on current costs. If necessary, an architect can be asked to assist in bringing this information together. Where projects are very involved, a professional construction cost estimator's services may be warranted.

To locate funding sources, the librarian can often begin with local institution or government officials in the field of finance. They are often well informed about current resources. In these days of "creative financing" it may be necessary to consult a financial specialist knowledgeable about new or less commonly used methodologies. For public libraries, the state library is sometimes a good resource for information on how other libraries are securing funds for their projects.

In addition to determining project costs, it is important to estimate the impact of a building project on future operating costs, including, but not limited to, moving expenses, utility costs, personnel, custodial services, and maintenance. The librarian will need to factor in the effect higher rates of use and larger areas of supervision will have on staffing. Preparing a budget for the move-in and for the first year of operation is a helpful exercise in this regard.

The funding of library projects is a vital issue discussed in greater detail in Chapter 11.

Space Planning for a Portion of the Library

There are times when a new facility, or even the expansion of an existing building, may not be an acceptable solution to the library's space needs. The timing may be wrong, funding not available, or the space deficiency too limited to warrant a full-scale building effort. Still, a solution may be needed to meet the needs of a particular service, collection or operation that is being crippled by space limitations.

Some potential space shortages can be predicted if the librarian is alert to the signs. If remedial action is begun when the warning first sounds, it may be possible to ward off more serious consequences. In any case, the librarian should understand the methodology of space planning, including techniques for analyzing space needs, arriving at reliable space requirements, determining alternatives and selecting a solution. It is equally important for the librarian to be aware of the steps involved in implementing space-planning decisions.

Space planning for different parts of the library requires attention to a variety of details. Dealing with a shortage of space for collections, for instance, is somewhat different from finding space for a new or enlarged public desk. Offices and workrooms present another range of requirements and solutions.

Space planning for different parts of the library is dealt with in some detail in Chapter 12.

Remodeling, Additions, and Conversions

For a variety of reasons, more and more libraries are meeting their facility problems by remodeling or adding onto an existing building or converting to library use a structure which was originally designed for another purpose. While the processes involved may be thought of as variations on the general new library building theme, each of these alternatives is different in some respects. Remodeling or expansion by means of an addition involves an immediate choice of either remaining in the building while work goes on, or making a temporary move to another structure. If the decision is to remain in the building, the librarian must anticipate a host of new problems ranging from the intrusion of workers, noise and construction debris, to temporary entrances and difficulty in securing the library premises. Construction crews, equipment and material stockpiles may usurp staff and public parking. Within the building the librarian will be deeply involved in scheduling the relocation of collections and services as work proceeds from one area to another. Maintaining effective public relations with library users throughout the project period is a special challenge.

If, on the other hand, the choice is to move to temporary quarters while construction is going on, a suitable building must be found. Some collections may need to be placed in storage, certain services may have to be curtailed, and library staff must be reorganized to meet the new service pattern. Public relations must aim at keeping library users aware of the moving schedule, acquainting them with the new location and encouraging usage during the interim.

Converting another building to library use creates a somewhat different, but every bit as critical, set of problems to be solved. In evaluating buildings that might be converted to library use, the librarian must be particularly aware of basic requirements. Here, compromise between what would be most desirable and what is reasonable and/or possible is a continuing struggle. The librarian must focus attention on basics such as floor loading capacities, floor-to-ceiling heights, column spacing, accessibility, and other fundamentals. Assistance is likely to be required from design professionals and engineers to assess certain aspects of the buildings available for conversion and to estimate costs for bringing them into conformance with current building codes as required by the local jurisdiction. Having a knowledge of this process should prove helpful to the librarian involved in a conversion project.

Some of the special concerns associated with remodeling, additions and conversions are discussed in Chapter 13.

Technique of Plan Analysis

The librarian's ability to read and interpret architectural drawings and specifications will be a major determinant in his or her effectiveness. This is an acquired skill which can be readily learned by most librarians with a bit of help and considerable practice. A variety of textbooks are available and there are extension classes in high schools and community colleges.

Plan analysis is basic in determining whether the concepts represented by blueprints and specifications accurately interpret the building program. While design professionals are usually conscientious in their attempts to help the novice understand drawings, work will be vastly facilitated if the librarian has developed a competency in this area. Team meeting sessions are seldom long enough to pursue all of the information the plans represent. The librarian must be able to do this alone. In addition, the librarian will need to interpret the plans to members of the staff and can answer questions only by knowing where to look for the information and how to read it from the drawings.

The first step is to understand how drawings and specifications are created, the various stages they go through on their way to completion, and what the different kinds of drawings portray. Reading drawings requires the use of an architect's scale so that dimensions can be read directly from the plans. This is an invaluable exercise for the librarian since it provides the square footage data for each area or room, which can then be compared with the building program's requirements. Similarly, understanding the drawings enables the librarian to compare their provisions with other building program requirements ranging from stack ca-pacities and functional relationships to the location and number of electrical outlets and sinks. The earlier that omissions and potential problem areas can be detected, the faster and easier they can be dealt with by the design professionals. The librarian's role in plan review is not unlike that of a watchdog who knows the territory better than any one else and who stands ready to challenge whomever and whatever intrudes on the integrity of the territory created by the building program.

Chapter 14 deals at some length with the techniques of analyzing drawings and specifications, although it is no way a substitute for texts on blueprint reading.

Summary

The purpose of this chapter has been to provide a brief overview of the processes involved in a library building project. This has been done by briefly summarizing some of the material to be found on these subjects in the remainder of this text.

While some readers may wish to peruse the rest of the volume in a fairly systematic way, it is assumed that many librarians will want to turn to particular chapters which address their particular situations. In either case this chapter should serve as a guide to the more detailed text which follows.

II NEEDS ASSESSMENT

LIBRARY building projects do not begin spontaneously. They are usually the end result of a concerned effort to inform officials of conditions and needs that have arisen over a long period of time. Those who stand by, quietly hoping that someone will recognize the library's plight and then take appropriate action, usually have a long, if not interminable, wait ahead of them. The librarian has a very special responsibility to analyze, document and present the need for proper facilities. Otherwise the user community suffers undue disadvantages, collections are placed at risk and library staff productivity drops while unit operating costs rise.

When space runs out or adverse conditions prevail in the library, the tool needed by librarians to make a cogent presentation of relevant facts is the Needs Assessment Study. It is the precursor to the consideration of alternatives discussed in Chapter 3 and, later, the preparation of the building program as presented in Chapter 4. It is the purpose of this chapter to describe the needs assessment study and the process used in its formulation. More detailed information can be found in a search of library literature.[1]

The needs assessment process is the vital "first step" in facility planning. Because it lays the foundation for a long-term solution to the library's facility requirements, the needs assessment study must be soundly based and well articulated. Both the information and arguments presented should be carefully documented; emotional appeals are usually less effective. The librarian should take full advantage of the fact that the needs assessment study provides the proper forum for focusing attention on both space limitations and physical conditions which adversely effect users, collections and staff. A thorough investigation of library needs will often gain attention and action where less intensive and forthright efforts have failed.

Librarians are sometimes reluctant to call attention to their facility's shortcomings, fearing that to do so may reflect badly on their administrative ability to "make do" or that other adverse inferences may be made by officials. For those with such concerns, it should be pointed out that most facility deficiencies do not arise overnight, nor are they the result of any one person's actions. Rather, space deficiencies are most often the end result of long-term development of collections, the addition of new services, an increase in the number of users, technological changes, and growth in the number of staff required to handle the larger and more complex user needs. Likewise, deficiencies in the building's structural, mechanical and electrical systems are probably the outgrowth of years of service, obsolescence, and the passage of time which has brought new and mandatory requirements such as access for the physically handicapped and more stringent building codes. Designs of library buildings constructed more than a very few years ago did not begin to anticipate the changes that have occurred in collections and services, user demands, communications technology, and staffing.

Needs assessment must be pursued along two paths: 1/ determination of space deficiencies, and 2/ identification of shortcomings in the building's structural, mechanical and electrical systems. The goal is to develop persuasive evidence of present and future space needs and to provide confirmation of any serious problems in the existing building. This task can be all the more difficult if adverse conditions have existed for so long that they are taken for granted by users, staff and officials alike. Breaching this apathy is not always easy, or comfortable. Librarians are also likely to face competition with the directors of other facilities which, for one reason or another, have achieved greater visibility. Where serious structural or other building defects affecting safety are encountered, the librarian may hesitate to call attention to them for fear of being accused of using scare tactics. Further, pointing out long-standing building deficiencies may be seen by some librarians as a potential source of embarrassment: what if someone should ask why remedial work was not called for at an earlier time? Such concerns must be set aside if the needs assessment study is to be an honest statement of fact.

The needs assessment study approach remains valid even in those situations where the institution or govern-

13

mental agency involves the library in some form of long-range planning such as a Capital Improvements Program (CIP). Data furnished by the needs assessment study is likely to be much more detailed and revealing than that required for such efforts. In fact, the needs assessment study is sometimes used to break out of the mold cast by too-rigid CIP efforts. The answers such a study provides have many uses.

Who Should Make the Needs Assessment Study?

While the librarian may prepare the needs assessment study with no more than staff assistance in some cases, the results are apt to be more persuasive if the study represents the work of a group appointed for this purpose. The composition of the study group and their respective roles will vary according to the type of library involved and the institution or governmental agency responsible for the library. In some cases, the members may actively seek and share information. In other situations, the members will act more in an advisory capacity, spending time on review and evaluation of information gathered by the librarian and staff assigned to the project.

The Academic Library

A reasonably broad-based study committee should be formed to develop the academic library's needs assessment study. Once the study committee concept has been approved by the institution's administrators, the librarian should submit a list of nominees for the task force. While the faculty library committee might be used for this purpose, its composition and the interests of its members are not likely to represent the groups and disciplines on campus that are most related to the purpose of the study. Study committee membership should have representation from at least the following: the student body; library staff; planning office; maintenance staff; faculty; administration. Representation may also be given to library support groups. If the library director lacks experience in conducting such studies, or the time required, a knowledgeable library consultant should be retained to provide expertise and guidance.

Usually the library director will be responsible for organizing and managing the team and will serve as its chairperson. Committee members will look to the director for leadership and direction. In most cases, the library director will also carry the heaviest responsibility

for supplying the committee members with information. Some of this work, of course, will be delegated either to the library staff or to the library consultant, if one is retained. As with any other task force, membership must be restricted to the optimum number required for effective research and evaluation.

The Public Library

A properly constituted task force will also lend credence to a needs assessment study prepared for a public library. As with the academic study committee, membership should consist of representatives from certain facets of community life that may have a special stake in the library and/or be effective supporters of the study's conclusions. Composition and organization of the committee will depend to some degree on whether the library has a board of trustees. The following should probably be represented: the agency's governing body; library board of trustees; library staff; city or county building official; planning department; chamber of commerce or board of trade. Other members may be recruited from support groups such as the Friends of the Library or the PTA. A library consultant may be retained to assist the committee, especially if the study is extensive or complex. Such a person's broad range of experience will be a special resource. The library director will usually assume leadership of the task force, establishing roles for each member, setting agendas, calling meetings and enlisting staff assistance in assembling information.

The Needs Assessment Study Process

Before plunging in, the librarian and task force must share a clear concept of what the needs assessment study is to accomplish and how the information is to be gathered, analyzed and reported. The primary purposes of the study are to:

1/ Evaluate and document existing conditions, including space deficiencies;
2/ Convert space inadequacies into meaningful space requirements;
3/ Project space requirements to a pre-determined future date, 10, 15, or 20 years hence;
4/ Assess the existing library structure's ability to meet present and projected requirements; and
5/ Propose alternative means for achieving an adequate library facility.

It is the task force's responsibility to assemble, analyze and evaluate all data relevant to the library's space and facility needs. Usually this begins with the establishment of a broad line of investigation which addresses the basic areas of concern. Library staff and/or task force members then proceed to bring together pertinent information for study.

Before beginning work, task force members may wish to familiarize themselves with similar studies done by other libraries. They may also profit from visiting other libraries serving comparable academic institutions or communities. However, emphasis must constantly be placed on the imperative that the validity of the needs assessment study is dependent upon its being a genuine study of the *local* library. It must not be a paraphrase of some other library's findings. Preparing a needs assessment study is hard work, requiring time and dedication from all concerned.

Two pitfalls which can be encountered near the outset must be avoided. Both are the offshoots of wishful thinking for an easy way out.

First, someone is almost certain to assume that some formula exists which can reliably calculate library space needs, making a needs assessment study a matter of filling in a few blanks and using a calculator. Some formulas *do* exist, in both the academic and public library worlds, but unfortunately they are oversimplifications. Because they fail to recognize the individual differences among libraries and the community of users that each serves, these equations have contributed a good deal to the space shortages in many libraries today. Based on averages and limited understanding of the scope of contemporary library operations, these formulas do not consider most of the local factors which have a heavy impact upon academic and public libraries. Nor do they consider the extent of existing collections and areas of specialization which have such importance to the individual library. The "formula" approach to estimating library space needs must be avoided at all costs.

A second tempting theory assumes that libraries serving similar academic institutions or communities of comparable size will have nearly equal space requirements. Using this rationale, the local library's space needs can be easily determined by finding out how much space equivalent libraries contain. This simply is not true. The number of students and faculty on a campus is but one of many variables requiring consideration in the determination of library space requirements; the curricula, level of degrees awarded and many other factors have a profound effect on the library. Likewise, the public library's requirements are dependent upon far more than the number of people living within the service area. Demographics such as education levels, occupations, age and income distribution are important determinants in usage. Again, this attempted short cut is woefully shortsighted and will not provide an accurate picture of a library's true needs.

Determining the Present Space Deficiency

Usually the first task to be undertaken by the needs assessment study is to determine the amount of space required to properly house the library's existing collections, services, users and staff. These figures can then be compared to projected space requirements for the future. Though it is somewhat laborious, it is essential that this first step be taken and carefully documented since the figures will be the base for future calculations. A simple enumeration of collections, seating, equipment and work stations is required. A few hints on accumulating this information and converting it to square footage figures are provided below.

Collections

Collections occupy much of the space in most library buildings. A needs assessment study must determine how much space is presently used for housing materials of all kinds, and then estimate the amount of space that would be needed under optimum conditions for the same collections.

The book collection. Estimating the amount of space needed to house the book collection is usually a good place to start in the needs assessment process. What this will entail depends upon the accuracy and currency of library collection statistics. Unless an actual inventory has been taken recently, most collection statistics must be viewed with some skepticism. For the purposes of the needs assessment study, it is better to rely on an actual shelf estimate.

Estimating the number of volumes in the library is a laborious job, at best, but it should yield data that will be useful for some time to come. There is a difference, of course, between producing a shelf estimate and making an actual volume count—the latter being even more tedious. The shelf estimate, which is sufficient for needs assessment purposes, involves counting the volumes on two or three sections of shelving in each major classification or section where the dimensions of books may be a factor. Dividing this total for each classification or sub-group by the number of shelves in the sections counted will result in the number of volumes per shelf. This average per shelf can then be multiplied by the total number of shelves for each classification or sub-group. For example, assume that a count of volumes on the first three single-faced sections of shelving containing biography results in a total of 21 shelves holding 630 volumes, or an average of 30 volumes per shelf. If there are 385 shelves in the biography section, the total biography collection can be estimated as: $30 \times 385 = 11,550$ volumes. This process can be continued until the entire collection has been counted. Because the count is based on the books actually on the shelves, this methodology eliminates the necessity for making an allowance for books in circulation.

Determining how much space would be needed to properly house a collection of a given size is a matter of multiplying the optimum number of volumes by the number that can be shelved in one square foot. Here the librarian must make a choice, because the average number of volumes which will fit in one square foot varies depending upon how it is calculated.[2] Several of the more common figures are explained below. The rationale for whatever figure is used in the needs assessment study should be carefully noted.

Perhaps the most commonly used figure is 10 volumes per square foot. This figure appears widely in library literature. It is based on averages for 90-inch high, double-faced sections of shelving with three-foot aisles and transverse or access aisles at regular intervals. Further, the figure of 10 volumes per square foot assumes that each shelf will be two-third's full, leaving one linear foot for shifting.

Another figure can be derived from the generally used standard that sets the volume capacity of a double-faced section of 90″ shelving at 336 books—the maximum number that can be shelved leaving about 12–15% of each shelf as open working space. Dividing the 336 volumes by the 15 square feet occupied by the double-faced section of shelving produces an average of 22.4 volumes per square foot. However, this figure makes no allowance for transverse or other access aisles.

A third average used by some has been based on the 250-volume per double-faced section of 90″ shelving figure used by some bookstack manufacturers. Without providing access aisles, this amounts to 16.7 volumes per square foot.

So, depending upon the multiplier used, the volumes per square foot may range from 10 to more than 22! The prudent librarian will usually opt for one of the lower figures, since the inexorable growth of book collections in most libraries soon uses up all available space. This is the reason why the 10 volumes per

square foot is commonly used, at least for preliminary calculations at a time when there are still so many unknowns.

Estimating the amount of space presently occupied by the book collection requires the measurement of the actual space used for stack ranges, augmented by an approximation of space used for wall shelving and freestanding shelving scattered in the building. The measurement of stack space is a straightforward calculation of well-defined areas, multiplying the width of a space or a room by its length.

Determining the space presently occupied by wall shelving and free standing units is more complex since these tend to share space with other functions such as seating. The important thing is to be consistent and not account for the same space twice. Where the distance between shelving and a table is three feet or less, count only the dimensions of the shelving; i.e., a single-faced section of wall shelving would occupy 3 square feet, 1′ deep × 3′ wide. (The aisle space will be considered as part of the space for seating in later calculations.) If the distance between the face of the shelving and the edge of a table is more than 3 feet, include aisle space so that a single-faced section occupies 12 square feet and a double-faced section, 15 square feet. A floor plan or hand-drawn diagram of such areas will help immensely in producing fairly accurate figures and avoiding duplication.

Microforms. Space for microforms should be estimated in terms of the number of storage cabinets in use. Typically, each microfiche storage cabinet in a row will require about 10 square feet. A cabinet for rolls of microfilm will use 12 square feet. This provides space for the user to pull out the drawer and stand in front of it while retrieving materials. If microform materials are housed on shelving, then the number of sections should be counted, allowing 12 square feet for each single-faced section and 15 square feet for each double-faced section.

Other printed materials. Space requirements for other printed materials such as periodicals and documents must also be estimated. Because shelving practices vary as widely as do the materials in these collections, this space estimate may best be made by actual count and measurement.[3] Careful records should be kept of these measurements and calculations.

Pamphlet, picture, and map files. The amount of space required for pamphlet or picture files will vary somewhat depending upon dimensions of the file cabinets. However, on the average, a pamphlet file will require 10 square feet and a jumbo picture file, 12 square feet.

Topographic, aerial survey and other large-scale

maps are likely to be housed in flat drawer files commonly referred to as plan or blueprint files. While the dimensions vary, a typical file will require about 30 square feet.

Non-print materials. In many libraries, audio-visual materials pose a special problem when projecting space requirements. In part, this is because AV materials comprise the most volatile part of most collections. Philosophies of organization, usage and housing are often in flux. A basic decision must be made, for instance, as to whether the AV materials are to be distributed throughout the collection according to subject or concentrated in a single department. If the latter choice seems most desirable, should AV be combined with some other subject department, or be considered as a separate entity? The responses to these questions have obvious space implications. While some tentative efforts have been made to produce over-all space requirements for various types of AV materials, these have extremely limited application because such guidelines do not address these fundamental questions which have an impact upon space requirements.

Other questions revolve around the space implications of new formats and those which are still on the horizon. Concerns here are due in part to a lack of familiarity with new formats which may supplement or replace others. For instance, a current concern is the effect compact discs should be allowed to have on the long-playing record: total replacement? partial replacement? a duplicate collection of classics? Similarly, the advent of digital tape cassettes and high-definition television brings similar questions which must be resolved. Moreover, should the AV area contain future CD/ROM materials that will surely be available for instruction and entertainment? Is this the place for the library's offering of personal computers for in-house use? If so, how will programs be handled?

Public libraries, especially, have been increasingly prone to offer an array of non-print materials on a self-service basis. Is this a desirable practice in face of the high losses reported by some? What are the alternatives? Matters are further complicated by the variety of equipment offered by manufacturers to house AV materials. While some libraries house most, if not all, of their AV materials in some fashion on standard shelving, many utilize specialized display units ranging from bins to carousels. The capacity of each type varies from manufacturer to manufacturer, as does the amount of floor space required. The lack of standardization means that each library must choose the equipment it wishes to use before space estimates can be made.

Two other variables are also associated with space requirements for AV materials. The first of these in-

volves in-house use. One alternative is to provide audio-visual (wet) carrels with built-in playback equipment which the listener/viewer controls. Such carrels may be slightly larger than the standard study carrel and at least 30'–40' square feet should be allowed. Another method is the provision of listening/viewing stations with playback controlled from a central station adjacent to the AV services desk. There is less risk to equipment in this method, but more staff time is required. These questions related to equipment for in-house use also apply to CD/ROM and the personal computer.

Still more space must be allocated for AV materials in libraries which do not allow users to handle audio or video cassettes until they check them out for home use. Separate space must then be provided for the selection media and for the actual materials. Often this means that the empty cassette container is on display in the public area. When chosen for home use, the container is taken to the circulation desk where it is matched by number or other identification with the item housed there. In such instances, audio cassettes are most often housed in drawers, while video cassettes are more likely to be shelved as if they were books on reserve. While providing additional collection security, this method may result in a substantial increase in the space needed for AV materials and will have a profound impact on the space and configuration of the circulation desk.

From this brief review, it is obvious that estimating space for the non-print collection cannot be reduced to a formula. Decisions must be made as to the media to be represented in the AV collections, the size of those collections and how they are to be shelved. Other questions involve in-house use of materials. Once these choices have been made, it is necessary to identify the types of equipment to be used, their capacities, and the square-footage requirements per unit. The latter estimate must include circulation space for the user.

Miscellaneous items. If the library has other miscellaneous items in its collection, they should be accounted for and the amount of space needed to house them estimated.

Seating

The second major element to be calculated in the needs assessment study is seating for the users. Compared to estimating space for collections, this is easily done and the instructions are simple. While maintaining a careful record, count all of the seats in the library, keeping them in the following categories for future reference: seats at tables; lounge seats; seats at carrels; seats at index tables, catalogs, microform readers, computers, and other equipment. Multiply the total number of seats at tables and carrels by 25 square feet. Lounge seats should be estimated at 35 square feet each. Seating at index tables, catalogs, computers, microform readers, etc. should be multiplied by 30 square feet to allow for larger tables, equipment, etc. In public libraries, seating for children will require slightly less room: an average of 20 square feet per seat. These dimensions include an allowance for the chair, table, carrel or other piece of furniture with which they are used, and for primary circulation space around them.

Public Catalogs

The space required for the public catalog will vary slightly depending upon the dimensions of the cabinets in use. However, a general figure of 20 square feet per catalog case is sufficiently accurate for most estimating purposes. This allows for the catalog case and space for the user to pull out a drawer for consultation. It will be necessary to add to this any space provided for consultation tables.

During these years when libraries are converting to various forms of an automated or on-line catalog system, estimating space for the public catalog is a bit more complicated, since many libraries may maintain all or a portion of the card catalog while introducing the automated public access catalog. For computer stations or microform readers, assume each station will require at least 25 square feet including circulation space.

Public Desks

The space occupied by a public desk, especially the circulation desk, is often as much a product of architectural design as it is of the functions to be housed. In measuring the space now in use for public desks, include the actual desk or counter and a perimeter area of 3′ to allow for circulation, unless there are other clearly defined boundaries. When estimating space for future public desks, use a figure of 150 square feet per staff station: for a reference desk that may accommodate two librarians the space requirement would amount to 300 square feet; a circulation control desk with four stations would require at least 600 square feet. If a ready reference collection or data access computer station is to be incorporated into the desk, add space for these functions: 12 square feet for each single-faced section and 25 square feet for each terminal.

Staff Work Areas

Estimating space for staff work areas requires some knowledge of future staffing requirements, usually based on a long-range plan for the next 10–20 years. The process will be more accurate if a model staff organization chart is created so that staff can be allocated to various offices and workrooms. In some cases, academic libraries will need to use approved staffing formulas which determine the total staff allowed under given conditions of enrollment, etc.

Space estimates should recognize that many, if not most, staff offices and work stations will include a computer terminal and printer. (The sharing of terminals by staff is not expected to remain cost-effective in the future as equipment costs decrease and personnel costs continue to rise.) Automation is increasing the amount of square footage required for staff work stations and offices. Generally speaking, the needs assessment estimate should allow 60–100+ square feet for each work station or office. While this may appear generous to those used to very tight work spaces, it is well within the allowances used by most interior designers of office and workroom space. The fact that a worker may be provided a station of lesser size does not mean that productivity and job attitude are not adversely affected.

A special word about work stations for part-time employees. These are often forgotten in planning. Since productivity increases when there is adequate provision for individual work space, consider adding a work station for each position scheduled for half-time or more (excluding time spent on public desk duty).

Librarians who wish to save space and costs may want to consider the sharing of certain work stations. This procedure has been effective in certain commercial and industrial applications where there are two or more distinct work shifts. Whether it is applicable to libraries will depend upon the ability to schedule personnel in shifts that do not overlap. This may include weekends. Certain operations, such as technical services, appear to be more compatible with such a schedule than do others that are tied to public service hours. The obvious drawback to inserting this concept into the needs assessment study is that it reduces the space provided for staff, thereby setting a limit which may be difficult to live with if future conditions make the sharing of work stations unproductive or impossible for some reason.

Storage

While opinions vary on how much storage capacity a library should have, no one can reasonably doubt that some storage space is necessary. Unfortunately, in most situations it is about the first function to become over-crowded. Every closet and hallway then becomes a storage area, with predictably bad results. Quantifying a library's storage capacity will depend upon the individual library's size and collection goals as well as other factors. Every library seems to have a legitimate requirement for room to store pieces of furniture and equipment, displays, and other items in addition to collection materials. While there is no rule for estimating the amount of storage space needed, there seems to be ample justification for placing the estimate at somewhere between 5% and 10% of the library's usable floor space; i.e., a 30,000 net square foot library might require 1,500 to 3,000 square feet. If the need is greater than this, costs may support installation of compact storage shelving to double collection capacity. In most cases, 25% to 33% of the space should be left as open floor space for general storage, and the remainder shelved for collections.

Miscellaneous Functions

In addition to the functions described above, which are commonly shared by most libraries, many academic and public libraries will need to add space requirements for specialized functions. For instance, academic libraries must include space for study rooms, faculty offices, and similar activities. Both public and academic libraries need to account for conference rooms, public meeting rooms, shared staff spaces such as locker rooms and lunch rooms. Public libraries may require garage facilities for bookmobiles, outreach vans and other vehicles.[4] When calculating the amount of space actually needed for these miscellaneous activities, space for people in conference and meeting rooms can be estimated at 15'–20' square feet per person. Study rooms for individual graduate students will require about 40 square feet. Faculty study rooms are normally estimated as ranging from 60 to 80 square feet or more depending upon furnishings; assuming that computers are likely to be used in the future, a range of 80–100 square feet may be more adequate. Calculations for shared space depends on the number of staff using the lunch room at any one time. An allowance of 30 to 35 square feet per person will provide some space for lounge seating, chairs at tables and a kitchenette. If vending machines are used, add 20 square feet for each.

Totaling the Space

When all of the space calculations have been completed, it should be possible to create a table with head-ings representing the amount of space presently used for each item and the number of square feet the item will require if properly located. The difference between the totals for these two items will represent the current space deficit. Usually it is helpful to include a summary table that shows the deficit in terms of percentages for the major categories, such as collections, seating, etc. Although this represents only the first part of the needs assessment study, these tables should provide valuable insight into the library's space deficiencies.

Projecting Future Space Needs

The second step in the needs assessment process is to project the amount of space each library element will require to meet conditions expected at a future date—usually 10, 15 or 20 years hence. It is likely that the logical target year has already been predetermined by the planning office for the academic institution or governmental agency. While the life span of library facilities may be 25–50 years, or more, planning for more than 15 to 20 years substantially increases the margin for error; a look backward for that number of years is proof enough of the many unexpected and unpredicted twists and turns occurring in the path of progress. On the other hand, a period of much less than 15 years requires making choices which may be short-term in nature and not in total harmony with long-range events. One hedge is to use two or three target dates, with the expectation that adjustments can be made as changes occur.

As a basis for making reasonable projections, the academic librarian will need to enlist the help of the campus office for long-range planning to get reliable projections related to library service. For the academic library, this will include student enrollment and changes in the curricula, among other things. Conferences with deans and departmental chairs may be helpful in establishing possible trends in teaching styles, such as computer-assisted instruction, which may affect library use. If the college or university is located in a state which uses formulas for projecting the size of collection, staff and seating, make certain that the latest revision of these standards and formulas is in hand.

The public librarian will likewise want to contact the planning department responsible for the library's service area. In addition to the total number of people projected for a particular date, the librarian should become acquainted with demographic details such as age distribution, levels of educational attainment, personal income and occupational interests for the projected population. These are indicators as to the possible intensity of use.

Both academic and public librarians will need to consider how predicted changes in life style may affect library use. Similarly, technological progress must be considered, especially in terms of collections and information retrieval and dissemination. Here the librarian must lean heavily on the thinking of the "futurists" who devote themselves to describing the world of tomorrow. Their insights and predictions are valuable background for projecting library space needs. The accelerating explosion of knowledge, the revolution in communications technology and media, and societal evolution preclude librarians from making straight-line projections of space requirements.

Collections

Both the quantity and the format of library materials are expected to undergo profound change in the years ahead. Delivery systems will also affect collection development, as networking, bibliographic utilities, electronic data transmission, etc. mature and become commonplace. The amount of material kept "in house," as opposed to that secured from other sources, seems certain to increase. Still, print must be considered basic and the book format is expected to remain the library's fundamental stock-in-trade for the foreseeable future.

The methodology for projecting the collection size will usually involve a formula of some sort. This will vary from one type of library to another and from jurisdiction to jurisdiction. It is often helpful to estimate collection growth for target years 5, 10, 15, and 20 years hence, as a way of determining how rapidly space needs will grow as well as to provide intermediate check points.

In most instances, the librarian will need to balance collection projections against the hard reality of funding probability. The history of past funding levels exists in the library's own records of acquisitions; the institution or funding agency's office for planning or finance should provide some idea of future financial growth. Comparing these with the projections for collection growth may bring about some adjustment.

To illustrate this, assume that the projections for a given library will require a collection of 200,000 volumes ten years hence. This is double the present collection of 100,000 volumes. Simple arithmetic indicates that an accessions rate of 10,000 net volumes per year will be required to reach the goal. However, the library must also recognize that about 10% of the total collection is subject to replacement each year as new editions appear, books are lost in circulation and other

standard titles are worn out. When these 1000 replacement volumes are added to the 10,000 new titles, the library will need funds for 11,000 books a year. (Note that the number of replacement copies is apt to increase year by year.)

Looking at the previous five years or so, the librarian can determine whether such a rate of acquisitions is likely to be possible. If the pattern indicates otherwise, the librarian should discuss this with funding officials to determine what future funding limits are likely to be. The acquisitions rate can then be adjusted accordingly, along with the projected space requirements. This does not mean, of course, that the librarian should abandon collection goals justified by the projections. Indeed, every opportunity should be used to keep officials aware of the gaps created by inadequate funding.

For general collections subject to circulation, the total to be used for space calculations should be reduced by a percentage representing the volumes in circulation. If, for example, records indicate that an average of 18% of the non-fiction collection is in circulation, the total projected non-fiction collection of 160,000 volumes should be reduced by that percentage: 160,000 volumes less 18% (28,800) = 131,200 volumes. This is the number for which shelf space will actually be required when the non-fiction collection reaches 160,000 volumes.

The librarian must also make quantitative projections of other collection materials and their costs. This process is likely to raise many questions about the future that may not have been addressed previously. Policies on conversion of periodical back-files to microform, for instance, have a profound effect on both budget and collections space. Phasing in new audiovisual materials, and possibly discontinuing other formats, will likewise need consideration. How terminal access will be supplied for computerized instruction or other uses must be pondered. Will the library be developing special collections of any kind? Is the library's status as a document repository apt to change? These and similar questions should be raised to clarify the range and quantity of materials the library will have in its collections, 10, 15 and 20 years hence.

After the number of items have been estimated for the target years, a simple table should be prepared showing each type of material, the number of units presently in the collection and the number to be housed at each of the future dates. Sub-totals need to be provided for the major categories in the same manner used for the current collections earlier. Using similar equivalents, the amount of space required can now be projected; i.e., general book collection of 200,000 volumes @ 10 volumes per square foot = 20,000 square feet, and so on for each grouping of materials.

Seating

As with collections, there is no universally accepted means of estimating the amount of seating a library will require sometime in the future. This depends upon many factors that are difficult to predict. For example, the seating requirements for a research library are likely to be quite different from those of an undergraduate library; a central public library will have demands differing from those of a community branch. An academic library which is residential in nature will require more seating, generally, than a commuter college. Similarly, a public library easily accessible to the public will have need for more seating than one located in the heart of an urban core which is difficult to reach.

Calculations are further hampered by the fact that existing seating in most libraries is too inadequate to serve as a basis for estimating future needs. Looking at libraries serving similar populations can be helpful providing they have not had to compromise their seating goals and find the number of seats adequate.

Some libraries will find help in guidelines issued by state agencies, accrediting associations, etc. Unfortunately, these do not always reflect local conditions. Most public library formulas either include or are derived from work done in the 1930s and 1940s by the team of Wheeler and Githens.[5] A table in a later volume by Wheeler and Goldhor may be more helpful, though it is limited to the small public library.[6] Public libraries often resort to estimating the number of seats on the basis of so many per thousand people in the service area, although there is little consensus about what the ratio should be.

After the total number of seats has been estimated, the figure can be multiplied by 30 square feet to arrive at the estimated space required for seating. A slightly more precise way is to divide the seating between lounge seating and seating at tables, carrels, etc., then multiplying lounge seating by 35 square feet and calculating the remainder at 25 square feet. This will usually result in a slightly lower figure. In either case, the total space requirements should be set forth in an appropriate table.

Service Desks

Estimating the amount of space to be occupied by service desks requires consideration of how services are most likely to be provided 10, 15, or 20 years hence. While there is a trend toward self-service, there seems to be little expectation that the traditional service desks will be abandoned. Given the growth in collections, the greater diversity in media formats, and higher usage rates, the librarian will need to anticipate the number of possible service desks and their staffing requirements. A minimum of 150 square feet per public desk station should be allocated, with an additional 25 square feet for every terminal used.

Staff Offices and Workrooms

A projection of staffing requirements for the target years is required before an estimate can be made of the space needed for staff offices and workrooms. Crystal balls grow fuzzy the further off the target date; nonetheless the exercise is essential to the process. Although the use of automation for library operations is having an enormous impact on the work place, early indications are that the end result is more likely to be a shift in responsibilities than a gross reduction in numbers. While the number of staff required for technical services may be reduced by technology, this may be offset by an increase in the rate of acquisitions. In any case, there is likely to be greater demand for staff at the public service level. Each librarian will have to factor in his or her opinion of where such staffing trends will lead.

Regardless of the number of staff predicted, it seems that they will require larger work stations and offices to accommodate technology and managerial styles. Good office design will provide each worker a sense of personal control over the work station environment. Staff at the supervisory and managerial levels frequently require small conference tables in addition to their desks, credenzas, bookcases and terminal stations. It seems safe to assume that an estimate of 125–150 square feet per staff member will prove conservative when offices and work stations are actually designed, whether in traditional fashion or with the use of open office landscape furnishings.

Once the number of staff has been determined and their space needs estimated, the figures should be incorporated into a table. Sub-totals by department or other library division will prove helpful in future evaluations of the data. Incidentally, these calculations will be important in estimating operating costs in a new facility.

Special Space Requirements

Estimates of space required for any special areas of the library must be added to the previous figures. For instance, the academic library with an active reserve book program which requires its own distinct space should be calculated separately. Both public and academic libraries must consider programming spaces such as conference rooms, lecture halls, exhibit galleries and the like. These special purpose facilities and their support areas, such as an exhibit preparation room, may be nonexistent in the present library, but along with other items on the "wish list," they should be included in the needs assessment study. While their inclusion may not guarantee their realization, their absence is almost certain to exclude them from consideration later on.

Miscellaneous Equipment and Furnishings

Although their space requirements may not be great, some allowance should be made for furnishings and equipment not otherwise accounted for. Such items may include copy machines, atlas and dictionary stands, and display cases. Looking back over the needs assessment worksheets should enable the librarian to identify such omissions. The space needed for some of these items is shown in Appendix A. Each allowance must include the object and circulation around it.[7] When all of the miscellaneous items have been listed and space estimates made, a table should be created to carry this information forward into the needs assessment study.

Shared Staff Space

Besides the space required for staff offices and workrooms, library staff will also require space for certain shared purposes. Among these may be a staff lunch room, conference room, lockers, pigeonholes for mail, bulletin boards and other amenities. In larger libraries, a professional library may be included as well.

The staff lunch room should include seating for 25%–50% of the full-time personnel. Adequate kitchen facilities, space for vending machines, a dining area, and comfortable seating will be needed. A desirable addition to most shared space is one or more first aid rooms, also called quiet rooms or cot rooms, where a staff person or a member of the public can lie down in case of sudden illness. Such rooms require little space, 50–75 square feet being adequate. Once again, a table should be compiled to show the space required for shared staff facilities.

Delivery and Storage

Delivery and storage are two areas which often receive inadequate attention in needs assessment studies.

The delivery area needs to be large enough to provide space for receipt of shipments, preparation of shipments leaving the library, packaging, mail sorting, etc. The space needed will depend upon the frequency and volume of shipments as well as on the library's related procedures. For instance, an academic or public library with a consortium or system membership which includes daily shipments of interlibrary loan materials must recognize the impact this service has on delivery facilities. Further, a headquarters or central library with numerous active branches will use its delivery area heavily. Whether shipments are unpacked in the delivery area or in the department receiving them will have some effect on the size of the delivery room.

As noted earlier in this chapter, virtually every library requires two types of storage space: one for library materials and the other for open-floor storage of miscellaneous items. Storage needs are almost always greater than the space available. This often forces libraries to acquire off-site storage space which is both expensive and inconvenient. The needs assessment study provides the librarian with an opportunity to anticipate and provide for future storage requirements. These may include storage of less frequently used library materials, long back-files of newspapers, periodicals, and documents in hardcopy, gift books awaiting review for possible addition to the collections, material held for varying lengths of time to be used in stocking a new facility or to be transferred to another branch. Open floor storage is required for many things including items of furniture and equipment awaiting repair or transfer. Depending on the library, storage space will often run from 5–10% of the net square footage in the library building.

Summarizing Space Requirements

Thus far in this chapter, the objective has been to produce an estimate of net, or usable, square footage requirements. These must now be converted to gross, or total, square footages. Architects frequently use the term "assignable" for "net" or "usable" square footage since it is the space which can be assigned for specific library-related uses. Space which is required for the building's structure and operation but not available for specific library uses, such as corridors, toilet rooms, etc. is known as the "nonassignable area." The combination of assignable and nonassignable areas make up the total or gross square footage.[8] To arrive at the total or gross size of the building required, it is necessary to add an amount to the estimated net square footage. This amount, represented by a percentage figure, provides space for lobbies, stairwells, restrooms, mechanical equipment rooms, electrical and telephone equipment rooms, elevator shafts, duct shafts, pipe chases, enclosed corridors, custodial closets, and the structure's walls, columns, etc. Taken together, these functions occupy from 25%–35% of the total building.

Failure to include the nonassignable space in the summary of space requirements can have disastrous consequences.

For instance, assume that approval has been given for a 50,000-square foot building and funding secured for its construction. Too late the librarian discovers that no allowance has been made for nonassignable spaces. The needs assessment study failed to convert the 50,000 net square feet to gross square feet by adding a factor for nonassignable spaces. Instead of having 50,000 usable square feet, the library will contain 25–30% less, reducing the space available for library collections, users, services and staff to 32,500–37,500 square feet. Disaster!

The percentage of space that will be required for nonassignable functions will vary considerably from building to building depending on design factors and site considerations. A multi-storied building will usually have more nonassignable space because of additional room needed for stairwells, elevator shafts, ducts and pipe chases, etc. Using a figure between 30–35% is often justified in a multi-storied structure.

The conversion of net square feet to gross square feet requires a simple act of division, wherein the net square footage is divided by the percentage allowed for nonassignable space. Returning to the 50,000 net square foot example, a 30% nonassignable ratio means that the 50,000 square feet represents 70% of the total building. Therefore, the 50,000 square feet is divided by 70% to determine the gross square footage, resulting in a figure of 71,428 gross square feet. In other words, 21,428 square feet must be added to the 50,000 net square feet to arrive at the ultimate size of the building.

At this point, a summary table should be prepared to compare the amount of square footage presently available with that needed to meet requirements for the target years. This table should be prepared with considerable care since it will be a major tool in the campaign to satisfy the library's space needs. Translating the information into graphs may enhance contrasts and improve comprehension of the data. The amount of space justified in the needs assessment study is likely to represent the maximum that will be considered for funding. All the more reason, therefore, to take great care in assembling and presenting the data; any revision of the total square footage will probably be down rather than up.

Evaluating Building Deficiencies

Up to this point, emphasis has been placed on examining the space the library needs to meet present and future circumstances. A needs assessment must also evaluate any serious deficiencies in the present building. Librarians sometimes assume that such deficiencies are too obvious to require attention. This is not the case, however, for library users and staff alike often take even serious conditions for granted. It is the librarian's responsibility to investigate these shortcomings and indicate how they adversely affect library service or pose a threat to users, staff or the contents of the library.

Evaluating the physical condition of the library can be done in two steps. The first, taken by the librarian with staff assistance, is to compile an initial listing and assessment of shortcomings. The second stage involves professionals in the fields of architecture and engineering. These professionals will examine and evaluate the library building's structural, mechanical and electrical systems to determine their adequacy and to estimate costs of repairs, replacement, or other remedial action.

Site

This part of the needs assessment study should begin with a thoughtful evaluation of the site. Among the questions to be addressed are:

- Is the site appropriate for the library given its functions and clientele? How would usage change if the library were located elsewhere?
- Are there site constraints such as soils, a high water table, or neighboring land uses which might limit the expansion or construction of a new library building at this location?
- Are adjacent land uses compatible?
- Is the site easily and safely accessible to the maximum number of potential users?
- Are there inherent site constraints such as excessive traffic, poor orientation for windows or use of solar energy, strong wind venturi, or other conditions?
- Is there sufficient room on the site for expanding the library building, required setbacks, drives and parking?

Public libraries, especially, will seek answers to other questions, such as:

- Is the site located near or at the crossroads most frequently traveled by potential users of the service area?
- Does the site provide the library high visibility and easy identification?
- Are other facilities nearby generating traffic that might use the library?

Academic libraries may consider questions such as:

- Is the library related well to major arteries of campus traffic?
- How does the library site relate to campus residential and classroom facilities?
- Is the library reasonably located for use by students living off-campus and by extension class students, especially at night?

Preliminary Building Survey

The preliminary building survey involves a review of possible inadequacies that may bear further investigation by qualified professionals. As a first step, office records should be reviewed to determine whether or not there are elements that require more than routine maintenance and repair. A simple listing of building maintenance and repair records can sometimes add up to convincing proof of a basic inadequacy which might otherwise be forgotten. In this category are roof repairs, painting to cover up tell-tale signs of leaks in the ceilings and walls, repairs to plumbing, and replacement of electrical fuses caused by overload.

This initial effort should be followed by a systematic inspection of the building. Here, eyes, ears and all the other senses need to be attuned to possible deficiencies and their ramifications. Asking questions along the way is a good means for keeping alert to possible trouble spots. Here are a few:

- Do the physically handicapped have barrier-free access to all parts of the library, its collections, services, and user accommodations?
- Does the floor feel solid underfoot when loaded book trucks are rolled across it?
- Are there visible deflections in the floor, causing ranges of shelving to dip and rise?
- Are basement walls or foundations cracked?
- Does the roof leak? If so, under what conditions? Is wind a factor?
- Do walls show signs of cracks?
- Is there spalling (chipping or flaking) of foundations or walls?

- Are there visible cracks around windows or doors?
- Is there seepage or flooding in the basement or other areas?
- If ceiling beams or trusses are visible, do they appear twisted, bent or otherwise out of alignment?
- Are interior walls in good condition?
- Is the grout between bricks, cement blocks, or stonework crumbly, soft, and easily removed?
- Are outside walks and steps cracked and broken enough to become uneven?
- Are there signs of the building, or any portion thereof, settling?
- Does rainwater or snow melt drain off the roof and the site quickly?
- Do windows bind in their tracks when an attempt is made to open or close them?
- Do doors tend to sag, dragging on the floor and making closing difficult?
- Are there any signs of termites, wood rot, or other pestilence?
- Are ducts and pipes properly insulated with a non-asbestos material?
- Are there adequate floor drains in all restrooms to handle flooding when fixtures or pipes leak or break?
- Is it necessary to make frequent calls for repairs on plumbing?
- Are there enough electrical outlets to provide sufficient capacity for both present and projected needs?
- Are frequent complaints received from staff and/or public about inadequate lighting or glare?
- Do lights sometimes flicker and dim, seemingly without cause?
- How often do fuses burn out or breaker switches trigger themselves because of overloaded circuits?
- Is it necessary to use drop cords to reach equipment in offices and workrooms?
- Is the door or facing of the electrical panel board containing the fuses or breaker switches hot to the touch?
- Are utility bills considered equitable with those of comparable buildings?
- Is it necessary to consider whether or not electrical service is available when selecting new equipment?
- What provision has been made for emergency lighting and power?
- Does the HVAC system provide relatively even temperatures throughout the building?

- Are there persistent complaints of drafts from users or staff?
- Does the HVAC system transmit annoying vibration or noise through walls, floors or duct work?
- Do maintenance and/or HVAC services personnel complain about the lack of space in the mechanical equipment room?
- Is the number of toilet fixtures adequate for the traffic in the library?
- Do toilet fixtures, including water closets, lavatories, mirrors, paper dispensers and disposal units, meet standards for the physically handicapped?
- Are drains chronically sluggish, and do they require frequent cleaning?
- Does water supply and pressure remain fairly constant?
- Are there adequate drains in exterior stairwells, elevator pits, or low spots adjacent to the building?
- Are there features of the building which inherently create security or safety hazards?
- Is there an adequate fire detection system?

If the library is located in an area where winter brings snow and ice, certain other questions are pertinent:

- Does the library building seem to suffer from frozen water pipes more often than other structures in the area?
- Do avalanches of snow and ice threaten to fall from the roof or parapets onto people entering or leaving the library?
- Do roof drains tend to freeze, causing snow melt to stand on the roof?
- Is the HVAC system capable of maintaining the library at a comfortable temperature on the coldest days?

For libraries located in seismic zones 2, 3, & 4, which include significant parts of the United States from the west coast through the mid-west and the east, these questions should be addressed:

- Is shelving properly braced and secured?
- Is the building designed and constructed to meet current seismic requirements for its zone?

The regulations concerning access for the physically handicapped continue to be revised and may be made even more stringent by local regulations. Assessing a library building's conformance with such regulations involves consideration of more than the entrance and restrooms. The needs of those with impairments to sight and hearing must be considered as well as those temporarily handicapped by illness or accident. While the exact dimensions may vary slightly with the jurisdiction, the following questions might be typical:

- If it is necessary to climb steps to reach the library, is there a ramp or mechanical lift conveniently available outside the building to provide access for the physically handicapped?
- Are walks and ramps at least four feet wide?
- Do all ramps and walks to be negotiated by the physically handicapped have a slope not greater than one foot for every twelve feet?
- Do all ramps have handrails 30 to 32 inches high?
- Is there a level platform at least five feet long at 30-foot intervals?
- Is the entrance door at least 32 inches wide?
- Are all interior passageways at least 32″ in width?
- Are there sufficient toilet stalls for the physically handicapped and are they correctly dimensioned for wheelchair access?
- Do any door thresholds extend more than one-half inch above the finished floor or carpet?
- Is there at least one lavatory in each restroom mounted to provide 29 inches of clear space at the bottom of the apron, with a maximum fixture height of 34 inches?
- Is there at least one mirror and towel dispenser or hand dryer mounted at not more than 40 inches above the floor?
- Are the drinking fountains and public telephones mounted at a height convenient for the physically handicapped?
- Have international symbols been used to identify accessible entrances, toilet facilities, drinking fountains, telephones, apronless library tables, vehicle parking spaces, etc.?
- Are elevator controls, light switches, etc. mounted so as to be accessible to a person in a wheelchair?
- Are elevator panels containing controls and floor designations marked in braille and/or raised letters of sufficient size?
- Do bookstack aisle widths meet standards set by your state? (These range from 36″ to 42″ or more; check with your state officials.)
- Can a person in a wheelchair place books on top of the circulation counter without effort?
- Are emergency signals for evacuating the building both visual and aural?
- Can staff offices, workrooms and shared staff space be used effectively by a physically handicapped person?

Survey by Professional Architects and Engineers

Once the initial survey has been completed, the librarian is likely to have a list of shortcomings along with many unanswered questions about the causes and the seriousness of the findings. It is now time to ask for assistance from professionals such as architects and building engineers. Usually the first step is to review the findings with an architect, who can determine whether further expertise may be needed. Structural, mechanical and electrical engineers are among those most likely to be called upon to assist. Funds, of course, must be available for paying the nominal fees these specialists will require. The architect will probably assume leadership and may negotiate the cost of the services of any engineers that may be required.

This team may confine itself to further investigating and answering specific questions raised by the original survey. However, a more thorough approach, in addition to responding to the specific questions raised by the librarian, is to ask for a code compliance study. Such a study will compare the library's structural, mechanical and electrical systems with the requirements of applicable building codes. The resulting report should not only describe the deficiencies where non-compliance is detected; it may also provide a cost estimate for making necessary improvements to meet code requirements. In any case, the study should focus on the adequacy of the building to serve as a library facility for the next ten to twenty years.

A survey of this kind will take only a few weeks. The reports of the respective architects and engineers should be submitted in writing and include all findings and recommendations. There should be opportunity for an oral presentation and review before appropriate library and other officials. By going beyond the normal area of lay observation, the professional study provides an authoritative base for evaluating the condition of the library building in terms of its future use.

The Needs Assessment Report

Having assembled all the evidence, a formal report should be written. This needs to contain detailed information on all facets of the building as gathered during the needs assessment process. Space needs should be presented in the form of tables and graphs supported by narrative explanation and summaries. The evaluation of the building's condition needs to be presented in lay language, reinforced by reference to the reports of the professionals who surveyed the building. Because so much of the report will consist of details, it is important that a non-technical executive summary be included either as the opening chapter or as an attachment. Accuracy in conveying the findings is necessary because the final study will have extended use and will be the basis for establishing some of the building program requirements. Appendices should be used freely to augment and document the study. While needs assessment studies are not likely candidates for the best-seller list, they nonetheless have lasting value and their format and presentation deserve attention.

Summary

Having followed the general sequence of this chapter, the librarian will have amassed detailed information never before gathered concerning the library's space needs and the condition of the existing structure. The space needs of the library for the next 10, 15 and 20 years will be clearly delineated and compared with the space presently available. Having been carefully researched and documented, this information can be the basis for future action to provide the library with adequate space. With this study in hand, the librarian should be ready to proceed to the next step: "Evaluating the Options," which is addressed in Chapter 3.

Notes

1. See especially: "Needs Assessment for Academic Libraries," by Bob Carmack, and "Needs Assessment: The Point of Origin," by Raymond M. Holt, in *Planning Library Buildings: From Decision to Design*, edited by Lester K. Smith (Chicago: Library Administration and Management Association, American Library Association, 1986), pp. 1–42.

2. For a further discussion of calculating volumes per square foot, see: Keyes D. Metcalf, *Planning Academic and Research Library Buildings* (New York: McGraw-Hill, 1965), p. 395.

3. See Appendix A for estimated space requirements of various pieces of furniture and equipment.

4. Long out-of-print and out-dated, the classic public library planning guide, *The American Public Library* by Joseph Wheeler and Alfred Githens, was published in New York by C. Scribner's and Sons in 1941. It contains some of the basic concepts for public library design as well as methods for estimating space, some of which are no longer considered valid.

5. *Ibid.*

6. Joseph Wheeler and Herbert Goldhor, *Practical Administration of Public Libraries* (New York: Harper & Row, 1962), p. 554.

7. Appendix B shows how circulation space can be calculated.

8. For further discussion, see pp. 28–30 of *Measurement and Comparison of Physical Facilities for Libraries*. Ad Hoc Committee on the Physical Facilities of Libraries . . . (Chicago: American Library Association, 1970).

III EVALUATING THE OPTIONS

ARMED with the information provided by the needs assessment study, the librarian is now prepared to consider the various options for solving the library's facility requirements. These usually include some or all of the following:

- Do nothing
- Reduce space requirements
- Remodeling
- Expansion through an addition, with or without remodeling
- Design and construction of a new building
- Conversion to library use of a building originally designed for another purpose

In some instances the options may be limited, or even predetermined, by circumstances beyond the librarian's control. In other cases, all may be open for consideration. The purpose of this chapter is to discuss some of the major questions and issues that pertain to each option. Chapter 13 provides further information on remodeling, additions and conversions.

The "Do Nothing" Option

Sometimes, the ultimate and perhaps wisest decision is to "do nothing." Certain political, economic or other factors may make this the most realistic course to follow. However, doing nothing in the face of a documented need for improved library facilities is acceptable only after other alternatives have been given reasonable study. The choice to do nothing should be as deliberate and overt a decision as that of any of the alternatives. It is a decision that merits thoughtful discussion of the probable consequences of doing nothing as compared to accepting one of the other options. Will doing nothing result only in a postponement of action, or is the lack of action at this time tantamount to forfeiting opportunity for the foreseeable future? How will doing nothing affect library usage, operational costs and long-term growth? What will the psychological

effect of doing nothing be for users and staff? If other alternatives are passed over at this point, how long will it be, according to the needs assessment study, before the library's situation becomes so critical that action is mandatory? Is land that is presently available for an addition or a new building likely to be used for some other purpose if action is postponed? Are construction costs apt to rise to prohibitive levels if nothing is done now? These questions, along with others bound to occur, should be fully addressed. The reasons for the choice of doing nothing should be recorded, just as they should for any other overt action.

Reducing Space Requirements

If the needs assessment study shows that the library's space problem is due primarily to collection growth, the most logical option may be to reduce the amount of space occupied by library materials. This is a possible solution for the academic library serving a college or university where enrollment remains fairly stable year after year unless major changes are occurring in the curricula and academic program. Similarly, it may be the answer for the public library serving a stable population. Where such conditions prevail, and the library's space problem is created primarily by collection growth, reducing space requirements is certainly a viable option for consideration.

Shrinking the Collection

Discarding library materials is the most obvious means of reducing space requirements for the collections. Paying for additional building space to house materials no longer needed by the users does not make good sense. While many libraries follow a routine collection evaluation process, this may result in eliminating only a fraction of the titles that are eventually eligible for weeding. Certainly the new automated circulation systems provide an improved means for determining usage, which is often a key consideration. To meet accrediting guidelines for collection size, or to match other standards, libraries sometimes allow materials to accumulate and remain on the shelves longer than they should.

A thorough weeding job should begin with a re-evaluation of the library's collection goals and a revision of evaluation guidelines. A systematic weeding process should then be initiated to eliminate materials which do not meet the guidelines. A major weeding program is not inexpensive and the costs should be budgeted before the effort is launched. Getting materials off the shelf is but one of many steps that must be taken. Weeding will require a commitment of substantial staff resources for collection evaluation, review for possible replacement, the changing of bibliographic records and other tasks. The maturity of the collection, especially important to many academic and larger public libraries, can be adversely affected by an overly ambitious or improperly managed discard program. Yet it remains as a useful option for creating more space for some libraries.

In determining the viability of this approach, the librarian must raise, and answer, a number of questions. Some of these are:

- What percentage of the collection must be weeded to provide enough space for collection growth over the next 10, 15, or 20 years?
- Is it realistic to think that this amount of space can be recovered by the weeding project?
- What effect is the weeding program likely to have on the user?
- How will the scope and depth of the collections be changed by the weeding of this amount of material?
- Is there sufficient staff time available to plan and complete the project, including correction of bibliographic records, within a realistic timeframe?
- Does weeding represent a long-term solution to the library's space needs, or only a temporary respite?
- How will resorting to this alternative affect the library's chances for another solution later on?

Weeding is not the only collection control method, of course. Another involves participation in resource sharing networks, which enables the library to substitute the resources of other libraries for some of their own. Since most such networks assume that each library will continue to be responsible for the bulk of the materials necessary to handle normal requests, this may result in very limited space savings. The costs of such networking needs to be considered, as does the cost of expanded interlibrary loan services.

Perhaps the most common means of reducing collection space needs is to store portions of the collections away from the public areas, where narrower aisles or compact storage shelving can increase collection density. Materials stored in this manner may include long back-files of periodicals and documents as well as less frequently used books in the circulation and reference collections. Storage may be especially attractive if the library has a basement or other space that can be readily converted to this use. Use of compact storage shelving, though somewhat more expensive, will virtually double the capacity of a given space.

If there is no space within the library for storage, consideration may be given to using a suitable building elsewhere. The cost goes up, of course, if it is necessary to pay rent or to purchase a building. When an off-site building is used for storage, the costs and inconveniences associated with retrieval and the time-delay for users must also be weighed. Sharing storage space with other libraries is another option in some situations. Where regional or last-copy depositories are available, the library may find further possibilities for reducing collection space.

Librarians who find that their collection space is cramped by long back-files of newspapers, periodicals and/or documents may wish to consider the amount of space that might be saved through conversion to microforms. Whether this is feasible depends upon the amount of space to be recovered, the comparative cost of purchasing microforms and microform reader/printer equipment, and the expenses associated with their use, such as staff time. Before this decision is made, the librarian must also weigh the factor of possible user resistance to microforms. This is often a more attractive option for libraries with unbound collections of materials.

Depending on the amount of space that can be saved, any of these devices may be worth studying. If they provide only temporary relief, the librarian must make certain that this is understood and that the library's space needs will have to be addressed in some other manner in the future.

Recovery of Spaces Used for Non-Library Purposes

Space problems can sometimes be solved by incorporating areas in the same building which are currently used for other purposes. For instance, an academic library may share a building that contains classrooms, offices, or other facilities used for non-library purposes. A public library may have offices, a recreational center or other activities under the same roof. In many such cases, when the building was designed spaces of this kind were intended for future library expansion. Such combinations often begin as a temporary measure to satisfy more than one function, but the provisional nature of this occupation is often forgotten. The problem, of course, is to correlate the library's need for more space with the relocation of non-library facilities. A plan which anticipates library expansion into these spaces over the span of several years may be more realistic than the expectations of short-term action. Space captured in this manner by the library will follow the same path as remodeling and expanding by means of an addition.

Remodeling

When the needs assessment study indicates a limited requirement for additional space, remodeling can be a logical alternative. As used in this text, remodeling is meant to cover work concerned with space which is contained within the existing structure and does not require construction of additional space. Expansion of the library through an addition, with or without remodeling, is described in a later section of this chapter. Remodeling may or may not include renovation—which is more nearly synonymous with the term restoration, aimed at restoring the interior and exterior of the building to its original appearance. Unlike restoration, remodeling can significantly alter the interior spaces of the building and may change the exterior to some degree.

This chapter considers some of the pros and cons of remodeling as an option for meeting library space needs. The planning and process of remodeling is discussed in greater detail in Chapters 12 and 13.

One of the first questions to be answered is whether the remodeling of the library will require the building to conform to current building codes. In some jurisdictions, this requirement is triggered by the percentage of floor area involved; in other cases it may be determined by the percentage of a building's value represented by the proposed work. In older buildings, especially those in which little remodeling has been done previously, bringing the building's structural, mechanical and electrical requirements into conformance with applicable codes can be expensive, perhaps prohibitively so.

This possible hurdle deserves resolution very early when this option is under consideration.

Perhaps the next most pertinent question is whether or not the library's space needs can actually be met by remodeling. Obviously, the answer to this question can only be answered after comparing the amount of space needed and its purposes to the changes that might be made to the library. Are there rooms which can be enlarged by removing partitions? Is there a basement that is under-used or an attic that can be converted into usable space? Sometimes a large entry vestibule can be incorporated into the circulation area to provide more space. Moving an office or workroom to another location may permit expansion of seating or stack space. The opportunities will vary from building to building.

Existing Conditions

The present condition of the building's structural, mechanical and electrical systems will be a major factor in determining the wisdom of remodeling. If the needs assessment study has included reports from an architect and engineers on this subject, their recommendations should provide guidance. If such a study has not been made, then it should be undertaken (see Chapter 2) at this point. The possibility that major repairs or changes must be made on structural, mechanical and/or electrical systems can be costly and is sometimes a decisive factor when comparing this option with others.

Usable Space

Whether or not remodeling represents an effective option often depends upon how much usable space can be added and how useful this space will be. If the amount of space that can be gained is only a fraction of that justified by the needs assessment study, then serious questions should be raised about the advisability of remodeling. Likewise, if the space that can be created is not located where it is needed, the remodeling may produce more problems than it solves. A library cramped for seating space, for instance, may decide to remodel a basement presently used for storage, thereby converting it into a reference room. Such a proposal raises questions, however. As an example, the necessity for staffing public service desks on two levels, rather than one, will require more personnel. This will have long-term budget implications, adding two or more positions to the annual budget. Moreover, moving reference services, or for that matter any public service, to the basement requires installation of an elevator to meet regulations for access by the physically handicapped. The result is higher initial cost and further increases in the operating budget to cover elevator maintenance and insurance. Moving staff offices and workrooms to the basement from their present location on the second floor would solve neither the staffing nor the elevator problem. Unless the library can find a solution to this dilemma, it would appear that space available in the basement may not necessarily represent the best option.

Location

A decision to remodel usually results in the commitment of substantial funds. Officials and the public are then apt to assume that having spent this amount of money on the library, the remodeling represents a long-term solution to the library's facility needs. With this in mind, it is important that the library determine whether or not it is in the best interests of future users for the facility to remain at its present location. If not, the investment in remodeling may be a poor one.

Academic libraries, especially on older campuses, may find, for instance, that the construction of other facilities over the years has effectively separated the library building from major classrooms, residential facilities, or commuter parking. In such cases, even though the building may be sound, there may be reason to decide that the library should be relocated on a more convenient site, allowing the old library building to be converted to another academic use.

For public libraries, the issue is even more crucial because of the relationship between certain site characteristics and usage (see Chapter 10). If the present location has proven to be a good one and there are no visible forces at work likely to change this, then location need not be a factor, especially if there is ample land for any additions (including parking) that might be required later. On the other hand, a public library may find that its community has grown away from it. The library may no longer enjoy the virtues of easy access and high visibility, to name but two characteristics of a desirable location. Or, investigation may show that adjacent properties are no longer available for future expansion. Spending sizable sums on remodeling a poorly located library building is throwing good money after bad. Other options should then be considered.

Space Efficiency

Remodeling may have the potential for creating needed space, but will the new space be efficient? De-

pending on how they are to be used, some spaces are less efficient than others. For example, removing a partition to increase the size of a reading room may be advantageous. However, if the new room has changed from a rectangle to an "L" shape, supervision may become a problem requiring additional staff. Eliminating walls between a stack area and a former office or workroom may provide space for more shelving. But if this results in a series of alcoves, the logical sequential shelving of materials may be disrupted. Consideration of remodeling options should be preceded by planning which will conceptualize how the new spaces will be used. What the effect will be on the organization and administration of services and collections can then be determined.

The Physically Handicapped

In most instances, remodeling beyond the barest minimum will precipitate compliance with the regulations pertaining to access for the physically handicapped. Such access, as indicated in Chapter 2, can be much more involved than might at first be assumed. Assuming the needs assessment study has covered this point, the librarian will have an idea of the implications and costs which can be factored into the decision-making process. If such information is lacking, it is important that it be gathered.

Remodeling as a Stop-Gap Measure

Remodeling is sometimes an attractive stop-gap measure which can make existing conditions bearable and temporarily satisfy special needs without a large capital outlay. This is usually true if the necessary work is relatively uncomplicated and does not impinge on basic structural, mechanical or electrical systems, or trigger building code compliance requirements. Under certain circumstances, remodeling can make an existing library easier to live with while awaiting a more permanent solution. In some instances, remodeling can also provide opportunity for experimenting with a reconfiguration of functional relationships or the implementation of a new service pattern. Offices and workrooms may be remodeled to improve working conditions and staff productivity. Storage space may be found to relieve overcrowded shelves for a time. Remodeling the circulation area may give a face-lift to the library while providing improved conditions for the use of an automated circulation system. New lighting in a basement room may turn it into a more useful space. Such improvements are often advantageous providing that they do not substitute for, unduly postpone, or preclude a more permanent solution to the library's facility requirements.

Interim Conditions

Remodeling is likely to disrupt normal library operations. (Interim conditions are discussed in greater detail in Chapters 12 and 13.) The more extensive the remodeling, the greater the possibility of disruption and the longer the period of disorder. Before this option is adopted, the librarian should work with an architect or contractor to determine how the remodeling will affect library operations. What portions of the building will be out of use and for how long? What part of the collections will have to be shifted or stored temporarily? How disruptive will these moves be to the users and to the staff? Would the remodeling costs be lower and the schedule shortened appreciably if the library moved part or all of its functions to another building? If so, is there a suitable building available and what will it cost? Learning the answers to these and related questions, the librarian should assess the inconveniences to be imposed on the users and staff, including additional wear and tear on library materials. Knowing how the collections must be moved, stored or shifted, the librarian will need to estimate the cost for this work as well. These costs, both monetary and otherwise, are as much a part of the total as the actual price of the remodeling.

Costs

Remodeling is often looked upon as a conservative and economical approach to the solution of a library's facility requirements. However, as indicated in the foregoing paragraphs, there are many factors which may affect the cost-effectiveness of a given project. So many unknowns enter into estimating remodeling projects that costs frequently exceed initial estimates. In some cases, the remodeling cost may equal or even exceed that of a new building of similar size. After the remodeling concept has been agreed upon, an estimate of cost should be obtained from a competent source. Architects familiar with this kind of work can usually provide such an estimate, as can a building contractor specializing in remodeling. Having more than one estimate is helpful. If they are not reasonably close, it is important to discover why and obtain one or more additional estimates. Getting accurate information on project costs, including any expenses the library will incur

as part of the interim situation, is basic to the final evaluation of remodeling as a viable option.

Expanding and Remodeling the Existing Library

Space needs and other building deficiencies substantiated in the needs assessment study can often be met by expanding the existing structure. This usually includes partial or total remodeling of the original building. Some library buildings were originally planned so that they could be expanded either vertically or horizontally. If such plans exist, they need to be reviewed to determine whether they remain valid. Most of the questions related to remodeling are applicable to expansion through one or more additions. Besides, other factors also merit consideration.

Site Considerations

Assuming that the library's present location is satisfactory, a determination must be made as to whether there is sufficient land available adjacent to the building for the contemplated addition. The amount of land required will obviously depend upon the project. Where site constraints exist, consideration may be given to a multi-story addition, especially if the additions will adjoin a multi-storied library building. Other than the amount of land available, there are other vital questions to be probed. Will the site accommodate an addition of a size sufficient to meet the library's space needs? How will the geometry of the building, when the addition is completed, effect the distribution of collections and services, including staffing and supervision? What effect will the use of land for the addition have on off-street parking? How will the addition affect the possibility of other additions in the future? Does the addition complement the building and the site? These and other site-related questions deserve discussion as the project details are considered.

Space Efficiency

Additions vary in the usefulness of the space they create. Distances between related points may be improved, or they may be stretched too far to be effective. Some additions improve supervisory control while others create restrictions that result in a requirement for more personnel. Staff travel time from service desk to collections, etc. may increase dramatically, with frequently used materials less available. A multi-level addition may fragment collections, increasing travel time, provoking user frustration and creating supervision problems.

On the other hand, properly planned additions may help solve shortcomings in the original structure. Adequate space may be provided for crowded functions. Functional relationships may be improved. Obstacles to good supervision can sometimes be eliminated. By increasing their size or changing the geometry of their design, spaces can be made more pleasant and efficient. It is for the librarian to decide whether the net impact of the addition will result in space that is more efficient, or more burdensome.

Mezzanines

A special word needs to be said about creating mezzanines as a means of expanding a library building's capacity. There may be particular interest in such an addition where the original design contemplated a future mezzanine by increasing ceiling heights. Mezzanines are not uncommon in library buildings. However, that does not mean they are generally successful or desirable. Because they create a quantity of usable space without increasing the cubage (volume) of the building or altering the exterior appearance of the structure, mezzanines are sometimes favored by architects. But serious drawbacks are frequently associated with mezzanines.

Here are some of the most frequent complaints about mezzanines. Unless carefully designed, they often introduce new deficiencies in lighting and air handling. Because mezzanines usually have a minimum ceiling height, they may have a claustrophobic effect on users and staff. Supervision of the mezzanine area becomes a problem and extra staff may be necessary. Because mezzanines are almost always less popular with users, the collections located there are apt to be under-utilized. To conform to the requirements for access for the physically handicapped, the introduction of a mezzanine will require the addition of an elevator. In smaller libraries, where collections can be reasonably distributed on a single floor, the use of a mezzanine results in a loss of sequential continuity for shelving library materials. This, in turn, complicates self-service and is likely to increase the time required for re-shelving materials.

Mezzanines can also have an adverse affect on the architectural design of a building's interior space if it was not a part of the original concept. Inserting a mezzanine adds columns as well as a balcony floor with a railing to interrupt visual esthetics. If the building was not planned to incorporate a mezzanine, there are potential structural questions to be dealt with, such as the effect of column footings on the building's foundation. In most cases, the addition of a mezzanine will require major alterations in the HVAC system and new lighting. The supposed advantages of a mezzanine, or even the expansion of an existing one, often disappear under the weight of such shortcomings.

In spite of their many deficiencies, mezzanines may, under certain circumstances, warrant consideration. Usually, this means that the concept of the mezzanine was included as part of an original design providing for adequate ceiling heights, elevator access, and column footings. In such cases, the primary concern may be the provision of adequate supervision. Metcalf indicates that a mezzanine, "to be practicable from the cost point of view, must occupy at least 60% of the floor area."[1] Anyone seriously considering the construction of a mezzanine should consult the literature on library buildings.

Architectural Design Considerations

Unless it was a part of the original design, the construction of an addition is likely to change the appearance of the library building. What effect the addition will have depends to some degree on the nature of the addition. In Chapter 13, the most common addition forms are discussed in some detail. Usually the form depends upon the geometry of the original structure and the site. For instance, an addition to a rectangular building may form an "L", a "T", or simply extend the structure along one axis. An "L"-shaped building is likely to accommodate an addition that fills in the "L" or adds an "L" to the opposite end of the structure, creating a "U" shape. If the building is already "U" shaped, the addition may extend one of the wings or may fill in the "U". Whether the effect of the addition will be beneficial to the design is a matter best left to the architect to determine. Some architectural styles lend themselves to additions more readily than others. If the building was designed initially to receive an addition at a later date, the effect on esthetics has probably been foreseen and allowed for in the initial structure.

In most instances, the librarian will be well advised to have the assistance of an architect at this point. A few quick sketches by an experienced architect can provide alternatives showing the visual effect of the proposed addition, both inside and out. The architect can also speak to other relevant issues which might otherwise not be foreseen. Among these could be the effect the addition might have on the library's visual relationship with the site and with adjacent structures.

Engineering Systems

Depending upon the extent of the intended addition, it is almost certain to have an impact on the library's mechanical and electrical systems. An addition of any size at all is likely to require greater HVAC capacity than the existing system can provide. Whether the present mechanical plant can be expanded sufficiently, or whether it must be replaced by other equipment, or supplemented by a separate system serving only the addition, are legitimate questions that have cost and other implications. If the needs assessment study has shown deficiencies in the existing HVAC system, the construction of the addition should coincide with their corrections. Unless this was covered in the needs assessment study, the librarian should ask a qualified architect or mechanical engineer for assistance in evaluating the effect an addition might have on the HVAC system.

For most libraries an addition is almost certain to require a greater electrical capacity than the existing system can supply. If the extra capacity is minimal, it may be handled by augmenting the existing electrical panels. Greater demand may necessitate replacing the present electrical panels with panels of greater capacity, or providing panels dedicated to the addition. In some instances, electrical service to the library building may also need to be increased. Adding electrical capacity may require expansion of electrical equipment rooms or new space devoted to this purpose. When considering these implications, the librarian should determine how much unused capacity will be available for future use. Again, assistance should be provided by an architect or electrical engineer.

Like the electrical system, telephone lines will be affected by expansion of the building. Besides the lines needed for telephones serving the new space, wiring should be provided for future computer data transmission. If a substantial amount of new wiring and instruments results from the addition, it will probably be necessary to augment equipment in the telephone room. This may or may not be possible without enlarging the space it is in.

Remodeling

All of the issues raised in the previous section on remodeling are relevant to additions. For instance, it is almost a foregone conclusion that an addition of any size will necessitate bringing the entire building into conformance with building codes and requirements for the physically handicapped. Interim construction conditions may prove equally disruptive, including the impact of removing walls, etc. The likelihood of having to move a part or all of the library's collections and services to another building may be even greater. This poses questions about costs and disruption of services that should be included when determining the advisability of an addition.

Costs

As with other alternatives, the librarian must arrive at a cost estimate for the contemplated addition and remodeling. This can best be done when an architect has been involved sufficiently to provide a conceptual plan and cost figure. The librarian must add to the architect's cost estimate whatever amounts of money may be required by the library for continuing operations during construction, including the expenses of moving to and from temporary quarters if this should be necessary. While costs should never be the sole determinant for selecting one option or another, it remains a significant factor.

Conversion of an Existing Structure Originally Used for Another Purpose into a Library Building

Called by various terms, the conversion of an existing structure designed for a non-library purpose into a library building has become an increasingly popular option, especially for public libraries. This recycling has proven advantageous under certain conditions. However, the librarian must make certain that the structure proposed for library use is a suitable and viable one.

Consideration of this option assumes the availability of a suitable structure. Neither the "availability" nor the "suitability" of a building can be taken for granted, however. The librarian will want to proceed expeditiously to verify both of these conditions.

Availability

From time to time, buildings become vacant, or plans are announced for their being vacated that stimulate interest in converting them to library use. Vacancy does not mean that a building is necessarily available, however. The owner of the property may have very definite plans for the building or for the site. Before taking availability for granted, the librarian should work with the appropriate office in his or her institution or agency to determine the intentions of the owner. Caution must be used, for some owners, or their realty agents, may use such an inquiry as an opportunity to mount a campaign for the sale of their property, assuming they wish to dispose of it. This may cloud the objectivity of those who must decide whether or not the building is going to be suitable. If possible, the owner or owner's representative should provide the library with a written statement verifying whether or not the property is available and, if so, under what conditions.

Suitability

Given the space and other requirements expressed in the needs assessment study, the librarian should be prepared to study some of the attributes a building must have to be suitable for conversion to library use. The more technical details may require the assistance of a design professional. Buildings will vary widely in the amount and type of work required to convert them to library purposes. In some areas, bringing the building into conformance with all applicable codes will be almost mandatory. How critical this is will depend upon whether, when added to the purchase and other costs, the option of conversion remains competitive with other alternatives.

Location. Location of the building proposed for conversion is one of the first hurdles. Regardless of the success the previous occupancy may have had at this location, does the site meet the criteria for a library? Are neighboring land uses compatible with the library? What are the future plans for adjacent properties? This latter is a question of particular importance to public libraries considering properties that are a part of an urban redevelopment effort. The fact that a tenant has moved from a building may have been due to conditions that will prove as adverse to the library as it was to the prior occupant. Assistance in answering these questions should be sought from the planning and zoning department of the jurisdiction.

Before taking over another building on campus, academic librarians should give close attention to its relationship with classroom buildings, student residency facilities, and parking lots, if commuters make up a sizable percentage of the student body. Other applicable criteria to be weighed by academic and public libraries are presented in Chapter 10. How well the building scores on this question should be a major determinant.

Size. Knowing how much space the library needs, the librarian should be able to determine, from information available from the building's owner, whether the structure is large enough. Usually this will begin with comparing gross square footage figures. If the building appears to meet the library's space needs, then the librarian must examine the candidate structure more closely to see whether other factors adversely affect library use of the space. Given a library's need for 50,000 square feet, for instance, it will make considerable difference whether that amount of space is supplied in a two-story building or one of five stories.

A building that is not quite large enough may still qualify for consideration if the site and design make it possible to accommodate an addition that will make up the difference. The cost of such an addition and of the attendant remodeling must, of course, become a factor.

Occasionally the building under consideration contains more space than the library will need either initially or for the foreseeable future. The plethora of space need not, in itself, be considered a disadvantage. Under such circumstances, the library will need to consider how the excess space might be used. Academic libraries, for instance, may be happy to have it converted into classrooms or similar uses. Public libraries may find their governmental agencies can use the additional space for offices or other purposes. In some instances, public libraries may wish to consider the possibility of creating income property by leasing the surplus space for compatible retail, commercial or office use.

Structural concerns. Besides passing the tests for location and size, the building must meet certain structural requirements. While the old adage that anything is possible if there's enough money is still apt, some changes are likely to be prohibitive or impose unreasonable, if not impossible limitations on library usage. Floor load, for example, is critical. Most building codes place the requirement for library buildings at 125-150 pounds per square foot. This is considerably greater than the floor loads required for such types of buildings as hospitals and schools (40psf), offices (50psf), or retail stores and light manufacturing plants (75psf).[2] Ground floors usually qualify for the library's load requirements. However, other floors may not, including those constructed above basements. If the floor-load factor is unknown, and the local building department is unable to help, it will be necessary to consult an architect or structural engineer to determine the appropriate steps to be taken. Although floors can sometimes be reinforced to carry more weight, the process is expensive.

For buildings located in seismic zones 2, 3 and 4[3] it

will be necessary to determine what structural modifications may be required to meet current seismic regulations. The older the building, the more likely it is that the modifications will be significant. An architect or a structural engineer, again, should be called upon to help interpret the consequences of code compliance.

Inspection of the building should include determining whether load-bearing walls will interfere with library functions. Most buildings of the last several decades have minimized the use of interior load-bearing walls except where necessary to enclose a mechanical core or stairwell/elevator shaft. Older structures, depending upon their original use, may have interior walls which cannot be easily removed. If the interior load-bearing walls seem to form barriers to library functions, the librarian should take careful note of this as a distinct disadvantage, if not sufficient reason to rule out a prospective building.

Is the structural system such that much of the building is open and free of columns and load-bearing walls? Open floor space makes it easier to organize collections and services efficiently. Space that is unduly cut up, especially into irregular shapes, is very difficult to arrange. Some buildings have much more open space than others because they were designed for purposes needing sizable uncluttered areas.

Column spacing, or bay size, is another prime concern. Structures designed for libraries ideally have large bays so that long ranges of shelving can be accommodated without interruption. When designed for library purposes, the distance between columns is usually based on the three-foot module represented by a section of standard library shelving, or a five-foot module representing the space required for a double-faced section of shelving and a three-foot-wide aisle. (The module will vary depending upon aisle width: a four-foot aisle representing a six-foot module, etc.) Spacing between columns should range between twenty-one and thirty or more feet. The bay formed by four columns, or two columns and a wall, may be square or oblong in shape. By making a simple diagrammatic layout of the floor space showing the location of the columns, it should be possible to determine rather quickly whether the column spacing will be compatible with shelving. If shelving does not fit conveniently within the module, considerable space will be wasted and the capacity of the building adversely affected.

Multiple-storied buildings add questions of vertical access. Are there sufficient stairwells and elevators and are they located where they can be supervised? Do stairwells meet the code requirements for a public building in terms of width, stair rise and run, and landings? Replacing or adding staircases can represent an added expense as well as a reduction in space.

Floors. Besides satisfying the library's floor-load requirements, the condition of the building's floors is important. Wood floors should feel sturdy underfoot and show no signs of deflection. If flooring has been damaged, it may require repair or replacement before it can be carpeted. Cement floors should be smooth and level. Large cracks may indicate unstable conditions beneath the slab, poor slab construction, or settling of the building.

Floor-to-ceiling height. Another primary test to be applied to a candidate building is the distance between floor and ceiling. To provide adequate space for the distribution of light and air, ceilings should be not less than ten feet in height in public areas; nine feet is permissible in offices and small workrooms. Ceilings more than fourteen or fifteen feet high increase HVAC and energy requirements unduly and will have an adverse effect on energy bills. In most buildings, there should be about four feet or more between the ceiling and the slab or roof above, to provide space for HVAC ducts, wiring, piping for fire extinguishing systems, etc. Taken together, the distance between the floor and the slab or roof above should be a minimum of fourteen feet. If a building does not have this much floor-to-ceiling space, an architect will be needed to determine what alternatives there may be and what effect they will have on the library.

Roofs. The condition of the roof should also be of interest, since libraries abhor roofs that leak. If ceilings or walls indicate signs of leakage, beware. A person knowledgeable about roofing should examine the building and the roof to determine its condition. How sound is the roof and how long will it be before major repairs or replacement will be necessary? It is advisable to discuss the record of roof repairs with the roofing firm responsible for maintaining the roof, if this is at all possible. The firm's records will pinpoint trouble areas and potential future problems as well as provide important information about the age of the roofing material and other facts.

In looking at the roof, are there skylights or other openings which may be potential problems? Is the roof parapet so high that snow and ice may build up? Are the drains adequate for carrying off water from heavy downpours? Are the entrances and walks protected from avalanches of snow or ice accumulated on the roof? Do downspouts carry the water away from the building and sidewalks into storm drains? These questions, along with others, deserve consideration as part of the evaluation of the roof.

Mechanical and electrical systems. In the majority of instances, the mechanical and electrical systems will require major overhaul, replacement or augmentation to meet current building codes and library needs. This will depend somewhat on whether the needs of the previous tenant were simlar to those of the library. A building used for a supermarket, for instance, is not likely to have been provided with an extensive HVAC system, nor will there have been much reason for electrical outlets except those needed at the check-out stands. Lighting is often provided by rows of fluorescent fixtures matched to the spacing of the aisles in the store and will not coincide with the library's layout.

The cost of upgrading or replacing the mechanical and electrical systems is likely to be significant. Sometimes it may be more expensive than similar systems installed in a new building. This is particularly true if slabs must be cut for new duct shafts, or routed out for electrical conduit. If roof-mounted HVAC units are used, portions of the roof structure may have to be reinforced. Adding HVAC capacity may mean larger units of equipment than will fit in the existing mechanical equipment room(s), making it necessary to increase the size of these spaces. Similarly, additional electrical panels will probably be necessary to furnish sufficient power. Just because the building seemed to function well in terms of its former use does not mean that it will do so as a library without substantial modification of its systems.

Interiors

How much, if any, of the existing interior structure can be used for library purposes will depend upon the individual building. In most cases there will be a combination of removing partitioning here and erecting partitioning there to create needed office and workroom space, special purpose areas, etc. Knowing the functional relationships which are necessary to provide cost-effective service, the librarian must be careful not to accept compromises in the location of staff, collections and services, simply to utilize the existing layout. At the very least, the preparation of the interior space will probably require new floor coverings, paint or vinyl wall coverings, and ceiling materials. The cost of the remodeled interiors must be projected as part of the price to be paid for this option.

"Face Lifting"

Conversion of a building from one use to another often involves a certain amount of cosmetic treatment, or "face lifting," to enhance its visual appearance as a library. This may vary from a simple coat of exterior paint to extensive redesign of the building's facade.

Large show windows, for instance, may be partially replaced by walls to provide room for wall shelving. If it is a near-windowless building, it may be desirable to create openings to break up the monotony of the walls. The entrance must often be moved or modified to conform with the library's traffic and needs. Walks and landscaping may be added to provide a more attractive approach to the building or to soften a severe facade. Exterior lighting may be needed to improve personal security—especially if the building was not used much at night by the former occupant.

Future Additions

Where the existing building will require an addition immediately, or sometime in the future, to meet the library's space needs for the next 20 years, all of the questions relevant to additions noted in the previous section must be considered. If an otherwise desirable building can be expanded without serious consequence or expense, its usefulness and life expectancy is considerably enhanced. However, if the building can not meet the projected space requirements for at least the next twenty years, the property is probably a poor risk.

Costs

Establishing costs for a conversion project includes more variables than is so with most other options. If the property has to be acquired through purchase, a likely sale price must be provided. Then the costs must be estimated for remodeling and any addition that might be required. Usually, these costs will be most accurately assessed by an architect familiar both with the building in question and with the library's requirements. To these figures should be added the cost of moving the library's contents into the converted facility. When completed, the cost data can be used to make comparisons with the cost of other options.

Designing and Building a New Library Building

It is perhaps natural to assume that construction of a new library building is both the most advantageous and the most expensive option. Neither assumption is necessarily correct. Choosing to build a new library may mean relinquishing a prime location, for instance. Or, the much-appreciated ambiance of an older building may be lost. However, in many instances the advantages offered by a new building are likely to outweigh the disadvantages. If the alternatives involve both remodeling and an addition, or the conversion of a structure requiring substantial modification, the cost of a new building may be comparable, or even less. A new building always deserves consideration when the needs assessment study substantiates the need for major improvements and additional space. When the location of the existing library is no longer advantageous, a properly located new building may be the best solution.

Location

The option of building an entirely new structure to house the library provides an opportunity for considering the question of location. Where the present site continues to meet the criteria for a good location as discussed in Chapter 10, and offers adequate space, the new building may be constructed on the same site. Obviously, when this occurs the library must move into temporary quarters during the interim period of construction, which entails an added cost. If the site is inadequate, or does not meet site criteria, then the construction of a new library building offers the opportunity to relocate the library facility. Site costs sometimes force a library to choose between spending money for a better location or a larger building constructed on a less adequate site. When such a question arises, priorities must be clearly established and alternatives carefully evaluated. There is no guideline representing the desirable ratio of site cost to total project cost; local conditions are the determinants.

Architectural Considerations

A new library building project presents an opportunity to design a well-integrated and efficient facility. Desirable functional relationships can be achieved and adequate space can be provided for collections, services, users and staff. Future space needs can be anticipated by incorporating unfinished space in the building and/or by including provisions for future additions in the design. The new building will meet all current building code requirements including those concerned with access by the physically handicapped and energy conservation. The building's interiors can be designed to create an appropriate environment for the user, the staff and the collections. HVAC, electrical and communications systems can be designed to meet foreseeable needs. The design can relate the facility to its environment and to adjacent buildings. In spite of the fact that

every project involves some compromises, fewer will be made in the design of a new structure than in a building that already exists.

The design of an entirely new building provides the optimum conditions for accommodating automation, non-print media and other advances in library science. The technical requirements for computer main-frame rooms, video studios, media production, etc. can be handled with greater flexibility and, often, at a lower cost. The needs of both the present and the future can be more easily met in a new structure than in one which is remodeled, added on to, or converted from some other use.

Usable Space

The ratio of usable space, or building space efficiency, is apt to be significantly higher in structures designed for a particular purpose, such as a library. New library buildings generally have an efficiency factor of 70-80%, as compared to older buildings which may have a net to gross ratio of 50% or even less. Since the entire building must be heated, cooled, lighted and otherwise maintained, the cost per usable foot of floor space is substantially lower in the new structure. This is due to the fact that columns, load-bearing walls and other impediments to effective space utilization can be controlled somewhat more in the design of a new building than in the remodeling or expansion of an existing structure. The careful choice of locations for major functions can improve functional relationships among collections, services and staff. Vertical access requirements may be minimized by careful choice of which functions are to be located on which floor or level of the building. For instance, if a second floor is required to meet space needs, all public functions may be placed on the main level while staff offices and workrooms can be located on the second level.

The Process

The process for acquiring a new library building appears elsewhere in this text. Once the needs assessment study and building program are completed and a site selected, the design professionals must be designated (see Chapter 5). The evolution of the design will follow the sequence described in Chapter 7, followed by construction and occupation as presented in Chapters 8 and 9.

Costs

Once the gross square footage of the facility has been determined, the cost of a new building can be predicted with reasonable accuracy by a design professional acquainted with construction costs in the area. Such estimates are based upon current building costs for structures of similar size and complexity. (Chapter 11 contains further information on cost estimating.) The cost estimate should contain some allowance for contingencies. However, there are fewer surprises with the construction of an entirely new building than with the alternatives previously discussed, because the unknowns are more limited.

Disposal of the Existing Library Building

In many cases, the question of what to do with the existing library building becomes a major hurdle, if not a road block, in evaluating building options. Perhaps this should be viewed as a positive sign since it often indicates that the library, as represented by the building it occupies, has gained recognition and acceptance by its community—be it on a campus or in a town or city. To some people a new library building represents a threat to their sense of security since they look upon the existing edifice with nostalgia and affection. The librarian must anticipate such a reaction and prepare as carefully for the disposal of the existing building as for the coming of its replacement. Even those most familiar with the present building's shortcomings are apt to voice concern over its loss.

Of course there is no pat solution; one must evolve as appropriate for each situation. Where severe structural problems exist, it may be helpful to have the reinforcement provided by qualified engineers who can speak dispassionately to the nature of the deficiencies and the cost of remedial action. However, care must be taken in releasing such information to avoid accusations of "scare tactics" or a move to force the library to take drastic measures. Where the primary factor is inadequate space, the librarian should make every effort to demonstrate the lack of space, even if this means overcrowded shelves, seating replaced by shelving, and the carving of staff work areas out of former public space. Some libraries have had considerable success in changing public opinion by arranging for campus or community leaders to tour the library, acquainting them with every nook and cranny while explaining the library's needs. All available media should be fed news stories and feature articles describing the library's predica-

ment. Libraries may use films, slide shows or video cassette productions, as well.

Of course, there is no reason to assume that the old library must be torn down if it can be rehabilitated and converted to some other use. Library buildings often lend themselves to various academic, civic, cultural or commercial purposes. For instance, a campus library can be converted to much needed classroom space or to administrative or faculty offices. Perhaps it can be used for a student union building or even a storage facility. Old public library buildings have emerged as the homes of museums, art galleries, offices for community service agencies, and other public uses. Some have even been converted to commercial use, becoming attractive retail shops, boutiques, restaurants, etc. Possibilities such as these should be explored and then publicized to assure the public that the building can have a continuing life after the library moves to more adequate quarters.

Sometimes the library building is less a factor of concern than is the site it occupies. If the library is to be moved to a new location, disposition of the site may be the primary focus of public interest. In most cases, subsequent use of the site will not be determined by the library. However, the librarian should acquire a reasonably accurate estimate of its value, since this is sometimes magnified by the public opposing the library's move. A qualified appraiser may be required for this chore. The sale of library property is sometimes complicated by deed restrictions which commit the property to use for a library or for other public purposes. This is often a local legend, whether true or not. A careful reading of pertinent title documents is required and the assistance of an attorney may be necessary to interpret legal language. In rare instances, the library or its jurisdictional authority may have to resort to court action to clear the title so that the site can be disposed of in a normal manner.

The Historical Monument Building

Library buildings in some communities and on some campuses are considered to be historical monuments. This may stem from association with a local historical event or be due to architectural significance. Whether officially designated as a monument or not, many library buildings are looked upon as monuments because of their venerable years on the campus or in the community. This can complicate the librarian's job in dealing with the existing building.

If the building has actually been placed on a historical register, it is important to learn the exact rationale for its designation. Usually such a designation limits the available alternatives. Remodeling may be limited to restoration work which, in effect, may reduce rather than enlarge the available space for library use. Additions, if allowed at all, are apt to be strictly controlled. For the library wishing to leave the premises for another site and building, an alternate use for the building must be found which is compatible.

There is nothing intrinsically wrong with the library continuing to inhabit a historical monument providing there is adequate funding to complete restoration work and to provide the library additional space elsewhere, if necessary. Restoration work is often expensive and operating costs in many historical buildings are higher than they are in contemporary structures of equivalent size. Some academic institutions and governmental agencies are unwilling to accept the higher costs of renovation, operation and maintenance. In such instances, the librarian should carefully separate the provision of library materials and services from the image of the building it occupies: the library is *not* the building, it is the materials, services, staff and users that the building shelters. As simple as this may sound, it is a point missed by many who would commit the library to an eternity in an inadequate home simply because of a long association of one building with the library.

When public sentiment runs high over the historic monument syndrome, the librarian must avoid becoming entangled in this emotional web. This can be done by understanding the underlying causes of the controversy while concentrating on a careful analysis of the alternatives. Wherever there is reason to believe that the historical monument question will arise, it is imperative that the librarian encourage a careful and objective investigation of the alternatives before it becomes a public issue.

Evaluating the Options

During the course of formulating the options, one or two will probably appear to be the most advantageous. However, in order to avoid criticism it is important for the librarian to make an objective presentation of the data that have been assembled for each option before a conclusion is reached. Information must be presented in a manner that permits comparison. Use of a matrix, such as that shown in Appendix C,[4] has great value in this regard. Great care must be taken to avoid allowing the comparison to be made on the basis of price alone. Though costs must be considered as a major factor, it is

imperative that other data be given fair weight in the decision-making process.

While the conditions and figures in Appendix C are arbitrary, they serve to illustrate how the findings for various options might be presented to promote discussion and decision. Such an approach should help reduce emotional arguments by concentrating attention on key aspects. By placing the decision within a framework of determining what is the best option for the library over a twenty-year period, perspective is added to the factual data, and especially the cost analysis. What may appear to be the best short-term solution may turn out to be much less advantageous given a twenty-year perspective. In any case, Appendix C illustrates at least one way in which relevant information can be compared in an objective manner.

Handling the Final Decision

Regardless of which option may be chosen, it will probably be a newsworthy event. Recognizing this, the librarian should make careful preparations for the release of the information. This will usually mean preparing a news release detailing all of the supporting arguments in carefully worded language. If the choice among the options has been controversial, or has extended over a long period of time, extra care must be taken to keep the release factual. Where a considerable body of information has been assembled, a press packet might be created to include background information. Architectural sketches, site photographs, and other graphics where pertinent should be supplied as $8'' \times 10''$ glossy prints. The announcement of the final decision may, under certain circumstances, merit a press conference with media representatives invited to hear the formal announcement themselves and to have the opportunity to interview those responsible. Distribution of a press release and kit of information will be extremely helpful in such instances. For many projects, the announcement of the chosen solution often marks the first major step in the process of meeting the library's facility needs and should be used to the full benefit of the library.

Summary

This chapter has dealt with the steps required to assemble and evaluate information relevant to the various options a librarian may face in improving a library facility. Remodeling, expansion and remodeling, conversion of a structure originally designed for another purpose, and designing a new library building have been discussed. It should be emphasized that the option chosen will have far-reaching consequences for the library's operations for many years. Therefore, assembling complete and accurate information for each option is imperative. While the librarian will play a key role in this process, additional assistance is likely to be needed from a variety of design professionals, engineers and appraisers, depending upon the conditions represented by the options. The findings, when complete, must be presented in a clear and concise manner to promote unemotional consideration and decision making. Cost must not be the controlling factor. Announcing the final decision should be treated as a major event marking the first step made by the library toward improved library facilities for the campus or community.

Notes

1. Keyes D. Metcalf, *Planning Academic and Research Library Buildings* (New York: McGraw-Hill, 1965), p. 72.

2. *Uniform Building Code: 1985* (Whittier, California, International Conference of Building Officials, 1985), Table 23-A, p. 124. Librarians should consult the building code applicable to the area in which the building under consideration is located.

3. See applicable building code and any local zoning regulations.

4. See Appendix C, which shows an example of a matrix format for presenting options.

IV PREPARING THE BUILDING PROGRAM

At the heart of most successful library building projects is a carefully prepared written statement which is generally referred to as the building program. It is a primary means for communicating vital information to team members. Because of its importance, the librarian must be familiar with the purpose, the content and the process of preparing this statement. The detailed requirements described in the building program must be incorporated in the building design by the design professionals. A building program is equally important whether the project involves remodeling, an addition or a totally new library building.

This chapter has been divided into several major areas for easy reference: 1/ scope and objectives of the building program, 2/ the preliminary steps, 3/ the process of assembling information for the building program, 4/ writing the building program, and 5/ a list of topics for special consideration. To supplement this text, a detailed outline of topics to be covered by the building program is presented in Appendix D.

Scope and Objectives of the Building Program

The purpose of the building program is to provide the architect and the building engineers with information about the library and the requirements that must be met in the design of the library building in order to serve your institution or community. This primary objective should control the content and presentation. A well-written building program is an indispensable tool for every library facility project.

Objectives of the Building Program Statement

The primary objective, as indicated above, is to describe the purpose, functions, relationships and operations of a particular library in terms of its space needs, functional relationships, environmental requirements, and all other characteristics. Each area of the library must be covered in detail; the emphasis should be on describing what is needed to make the area function effectively and efficiently. Although dwelling on the future, the building program should include a brief history of the library and the buildings it may have occupied as a means of providing background to design professionals who may not be acquainted with the institution or community. When completed, the building program stands as the project source book, providing all essential information and guidelines.

The process of preparing the building program helps the library administrator to achieve a second objective, namely the identification of persistent problems and concerns in library organization and operation and the working out of long-term solutions. The building program must be based on a description of tomorrow's library—not that of today. Therefore, the future personnel organization, levels of staffing, numbers of service desks, numbers and types of departments, special collections, services and programs must all be addressed.

In academic libraries, particular note should be taken of the effect long-term trends will have on the library. Include such areas as anticipated changes in curricula, degree programs to be added or deleted, addition and/or deletion of departments, trends in the use of instructional materials and resources, and similar long-range academic goals. Describe patterns of library usage and how they may be changing, as well as collection development goals. Note any relevant facts from recent accreditation reports.

A similar list can be made for public libraries, where long-term trends are equally important. Factors that tend to drive public library services and collections, such as population numbers and demographic characteristics, should be noted. Indicate what changes are likely to occur in the population mix that will effect the library. Describe new media and services which are on the horizon and which must be anticipated in the new building. Indicate any plans for future extension services which may require library space for collections, staff, or equipment.

Regardless of the type of library, the librarians and staff must reckon with the implications of automation, non-print media, and other changes in library technology. The building program statement is not a document to be prepared overnight. It requires long hours of hard work, staff discussion and participation, decisions at the administrative level of the agency, institution or jurisdiction, and difficult choices by staff and the librarian. It is a time for dreaming, and a time for reckoning with reality; it is a time for philosophical discussion and a time for practical solutions. Taken as a whole, the period during which the building program is in preparation can well be the most creative time in the library's recent history. Resolving critical issues as part of the building program process will go a long way toward avoiding costly pitfalls and shortcomings.

Finally, as a third objective, the building program creates a checklist for use during the architectural design phase, described in the next chapter. As drawings evolve, it is imperative that the provisions incorporated in the architectural drawings be reviewed against the program in order to determine whether requirements are being met. While the drawings will contain some departures from the building program, these should come about as the result of conscious decision making. The earlier that divergence from the building program can be detected, the sooner necessary decisions and corrections can be made. Without the building program as a checklist, the librarian has nothing to document the needs of the library or to refer to when there is cause to believe that library requirements are not being met. For this reason, it is essential that the building program be incorporated into the architect's contract as a legal instrument of guidance.

Scope of the Building Program

Regardless of the type of library, the building program covers every facet of the library, from descriptions of its collections and services to details on the organization of work flow, handling of user traffic and routine operations. Flow diagrams, bubble diagrams representing functional relationships, and other means may be used wherever they can be effective in transmitting ideas, concepts and needs. The librarian must assume that the architect is not familiar with libraries and that the internal workings will be complex and confusing without the information provided by the building program. Use of library jargon should be avoided and all library terms defined. To illustrate, the word "circulation" is used by architects to describe the flow of people

and the space they require—not the procedures associated with borrowing library materials. Other terminology may be equally mystifying to the uninitiated. Even though an architect who has designed other libraries may have been chosen, these rules still apply to the building program. The architect may, indeed, understand other libraries, but not necessarily yours. Besides, there is nothing to say that others in the same firm working on the project will have equal familiarity with library requirements.

Besides the facts of space requirements and functional relationships, the building program must also deal with the esthetics and the atmosphere or feeling which is desired for the various parts of the project building. This includes general decor, lighting and acoustics. For lighting, indicate typical tasks that must be done in a given area and whether or not precautions need to be taken to avoid glare on microform reader screens or CRT monitors. Indicate acoustical needs in a similar manner by describing whether normal conversation is to occur, as at a circulation desk, or whether an area is to be limited to those desiring isolation from noise. Where offices and workrooms are concerned, note which must be designed to avoid transmission of conversations, etc. to adjacent spaces. Note those areas which merit special attention to decor and describe the effect to be achieved. However, avoid trying to tell the design professionals how that effect is to be achieved. Program writing requires the writer to clarify concepts and make careful use of language.

What the Building Program Should Not Do

The building program must concentrate on telling the architect *what* must be done, not *how* it should be done! The major contribution made by the architect to the project is skill in design. Therefore, the program should deal in concepts, information and data. No attempt should be made to draw floor plans or to use other devices to force a particular solution on the design professionals. In some instances, program concepts can be best conveyed, it is true, through diagrams which resemble floor plans in that they have certain dimensions and scale. However, these must still be presented as *diagrams* which the architect is expected to reinterpret to suit the evolution of the building's design. Some of the poorest examples of library buildings are those in which the library programmer failed to observe this admonition and used the building program as a means of substituting his or her design concepts for those of the architect. While hardly the chief cause of poor library design, it is one that can be avoided with a bit of care. (See Chapter 5 for further comments on the qualifications and role of the design professionals.)

Preliminary Steps

Before a building program can be written, certain preliminary steps must be taken. These are common to the preparation of the programs for most projects, regardless of size or type of library. It is usually best to take these steps consciously at the outset as a means of saving time and effort later on.

Who Should Prepare the Building Program?

The question of who should be responsible for the preparation of the building program is often an open one and should be resolved very early in the project. While the ultimate responsibility usually lies with the librarian, this task is sometimes delegated to someone else, with the librarian retaining the authority of final review and approval. Where sufficient experience and expertise is not readily available among staff members, a qualified library consultant may be retained for this as well as other project responsibilities. (See Chapter 5 for details on selecting a library consultant.) Among the advantages offered by the library consultant are: objectivity, familiarity with the process, experience gained from participation in other projects, and freedom from other library responsibilities.

Besides librarians and library consultants, there are others who prepare building programs. In fact, there is a small group of professional building programmers usually known as space planners. Design professionals such as architects and interior designers often offer programming as a part of their services. Considerable caution should be used in delegating the preparation of the building program to such sources, however. While they may understand building design in general, they seldom know much about library functions and operations. Many will emphasize their ability to accurately estimate space requirements. While this is important, it is eclipsed by the need to understand and project functional relationships—a task that requires much more than a superficial comprehension of library operations.

In any case, the person to whom the task of formulating the program is assigned must have several qualities, including analytical ability, skill in conveying ideas through the written word, a genuine interest in the project, an ability to see the forest as well as the trees, and the capacity to work well with the staff. Unless the project will require only a small program, as with some remodeling or simple additions, time for preparing the program will be a major concern. The person responsible, whether it is the librarian or some other staff member, will probably need to be relieved of at least a part of his or her normal duties to allow sufficient time for this task. Energy levels must be high because preparation of the building program is a creative task requiring concentrated effort including the ability to conceptualize, make decisions and prepare detailed information in a logically written format. The preparation of the building program is *not* an appropriate committee activity, although this has sometimes been tried. However, especially on larger projects, an advisory committee may be helpful.

Who Should Provide the Information?

Building programs should provide information that is broad in scope, detailed and accurate. Usually this requires input from virtually everyone associated with the library. While some staff members will contribute much more than others, all should have an opportunity to be heard. However, those most closely involved may work best if informally recognized as an advisory committee which can be assembled on a fairly regular basis. (Note here the admonition against committee authorship in the preceding paragraph.)

While staff input is needed, the librarian must guard against being swayed by over-zealous staff pursuing their personal prejudices. Buildings must *never* be programmed or designed around individuals, for during its life time the library must accommodate a wide variety of public and staff. As an example, a children's librarian who is uncomfortable with a particular age group should not be permitted to exclude areas that might be devoted to their needs. Likewise, individual offices and work stations must be programmed and designed for the tasks to be accomplished there, rather than to meet the whims of the incumbent personality.

The Process

Once the responsibility for preparing the building program has been established, a decision should be made as to how to handle the process of gathering information, evaluating it, and making decisions. (The ensuing section of this chapter discusses some of these aspects in greater detail.) The person responsible for preparing the building program usually gathers the needed information from written materials and statistical reports, supplemented by a series of informal interviews or discussions with individuals and groups sharing a common role in the library. After the information has been gathered it must be evaluated, for not all of it will be consistent or of equal value. An advisory committee may be of some help to the programmer in evaluating data and ideas.

Almost inevitably, certain questions will arise as to how a given function or procedure can best be handled when current architectural restraints are removed. It is the programmer's responsibility to weigh various alternatives that might be applicable, indicating the possible strengths and weaknesses of each. Someone must then decide which of the alternatives is to be incorporated into the building program. Unless delegated, the authority for such decisions rests with the librarian. It may be necessary for the programmer to provide background material on the alternatives under consideration before a decision is made.

Once a decision has been reached, it is important for the programmer to record the decision and the reasons for having chosen a particular option. This provides the programmer with confirmation in case the topic is reopened at a later date. Incidentally, developing a building program inevitably involves quantities of support documents, and these should be kept until the building project is completed.

Beyond the staff, important, and often overlooked, material of value may be forthcoming from various library advisory groups, faculty committees, library boards, and representatives of user groups. After all, the library belongs to more than just the staff. Sometimes significant ideas originate with those who are not directly associated with the staff. To encourage the broadest possible participation, especially among user groups, librarians have found that a conveniently located and properly identified "suggestion box for the library project" often garners excellent ideas.

Conceptual outline. Progress can be hastened and regulated somewhat by preparing a conceptual program outline fairly early in the game. The outline will provide focus for the project team's efforts and assist in identifying areas which require varying degrees of research. It will also be helpful in identifying problem areas where disagreement may exist, and that merit consideration of a number of alternatives. Another prime reason for the conceptual outline is to determine whether some items may have been forgotten. Such omissions are almost certain to haunt the project at a later date and therefore need to be eliminated as early as possible. The sample outline offered in Appendix D may be of some help in creating a conceptual outline.

Deciding on the Format

At some point, a decision should be made on the format of the program contents. As a perusal of programs from other libraries will indicate, formats range from general outlines to compilations of uniform data sheets representing each area, and to detailed narrative statements; some combine two or more of these formats. While the outline form has the advantage of being brief, it often fails to supply the details needed later on. Data sheets (Appendix E) guarantee that similar information will be gathered for all areas covered by the program. However, they lack descriptive power. Narrative programs tend to be longer, but usually provide more usable information. They have the further advantage of accommodating descriptive language which can convey concepts and relationships more adequately. Their inherent weakness is their tendency to be too long, wordy and imprecise. Part of this can be remedied by use of tables, functional relationship diagrams, and other graphic means. Perhaps the format with the greatest potential is that of a narrative presented in a strong outline style and supported with data sheets as an appendix. An early decision is needed so that proper forms can be created for gathering information which can be translated into the building program with a minimum of effort and maximum effect.

Use of Diagrams and Other Graphic Materials

Building programs should make full use of diagrams, flow charts, and other graphic forms. Functional relationship drawings, familiarly known as "bubble diagrams," tell the architect more than many, many words. Circles, ovals and other simple geometric forms, representing particular objects or portions of an area associated with a given function, show how one item is related to another. These bubble diagrams are essential in showing "what goes next to what." For this reason, architects sometimes refer to these as "adjacency diagrams."

In creating functional relationship diagrams, it is important to emphasize that the size and shape of the geometrical figure used in the bubble diagram is irrelevant to the eventual space the architect will design. The size of the geometric figure is relevant only to the extent that a larger figure usually represents something that will require more space than a smaller figure. Far more important is how these geometric forms relate to one another. The meaning of these relationships is shown in Figure 4-1. Two figures not touching each other mean that the functions they represent are distinct and separate—no functional relationship. If the figures touch, the functions are distinct but related and should be located adjacent to one another. Overlapping figures indicate that the functions are closely related and must be accessible one from the other. Two or more figures connected by arrows represent distinct functions which do not need to be adjacent to one another but which must be accessible to each other.

After gathering information about a particular function, the programmer must conceptualize the ideal relationships that should exist between all of the items that will occupy this area, such as traffic created by users and staff and the movement of library materials. This conceptualization is intended to determine what the relationships should be—not what they are at present. The capacity for imagining how spaces and things might best relate is the programmer's most important tool.

It is usually easier to develop bubble diagrams first for the more general and larger spaces. Begin, for instance, with a diagram that shows how the building and its entrances are to relate to public access, as in Figure 4-2. The next diagram might indicate the major functions to be housed in the library and how these relate, as shown in Figure 4-3. This diagram, incidentally, becomes a sort of master plan and index to all of the bubble diagrams that may follow. From this point, the relationships of each of these functions are developed in separate diagrams, such as those shown in Figures 4-4 and 4-5.

Diagramming functional relationships means answering questions. When a person enters the Reference Department, for instance, what should be most visible or convenient? Having established the answer, the programmer then asks what must go next to that item to make it work best? This line of questions and answers continues until everything to be housed in the Reference Department is accounted for and represented inside the Reference Room bubble by a symbol. Each department, area and function then follows. Complex functions may require more than one diagram to explain the internal relationships clearly.

Flow charts can also provide precise supplementary information which is easier to interpret architecturally than a verbal description of a series of events, although such a description is usually helpful as an explanation. The diagrams and charts can be kept quite simple. The chief requirement is that they be an accurate representation of the concept being illustrated. In fact, the functional relationship drawings and flow charts should be produced very early in the programming process, to provide opportunity for library staff to understand the concepts being illustrated and to facilitate such changes as may be determined. Not infrequently, staff discussion of a functional relationship diagram, for instance, will prove valuable in bringing about a consensus on a given solution because everyone can visualize from the diagram what is being proposed. This avoids some of the difficulties of strictly verbal communication. With a little practice, and assisted by a collection of templates, these functional relationship drawings can be readily drawn; a staff artist, of course, may make them more presentable for the final edition of the program.

Assembling Program Information

Program information will be collected from a variety of sources. Some valuable data will have appeared in the needs assessment study and can be transferred to the building program after suitable reorganization and review. Staff involvement, as noted in the preceding section, will also provide quantities of information. Some information may be gathered on forms designed for this purpose. Usually, such forms are limited to collecting quantitative data. Whenever they are used, it is important that the forms be accompanied by ample directions to assure accurate interpretation and uniform response.

During this period, staff may also be encouraged to visit other library buildings. Such visits may stimulate new ideas and concepts that can be included in the building program. Visits need not be limited to new buildings; sometimes fresh ideas can come from seeing how functions are handled in an older building.

Other material will come from reading professional literature and discussions with others who have had major responsibilities in building projects. The person responsible for the building program must evaluate all of this information and make use of that which is pertinent. Frequent reference to the conceptual outline, which will gradually evolve into a more detailed outline for the building program itself, will give guidance and help avoid over-emphasis of some subjects and the slighting of others.

Space Measurement Guidelines

Not long after the programming effort gets underway, staff will need to follow a common guideline in

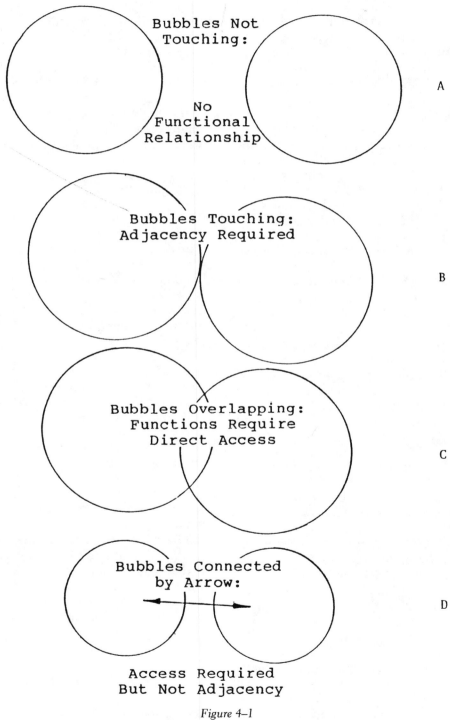

Figure 4–1
Indicating Relationships Through Bubble Diagrams

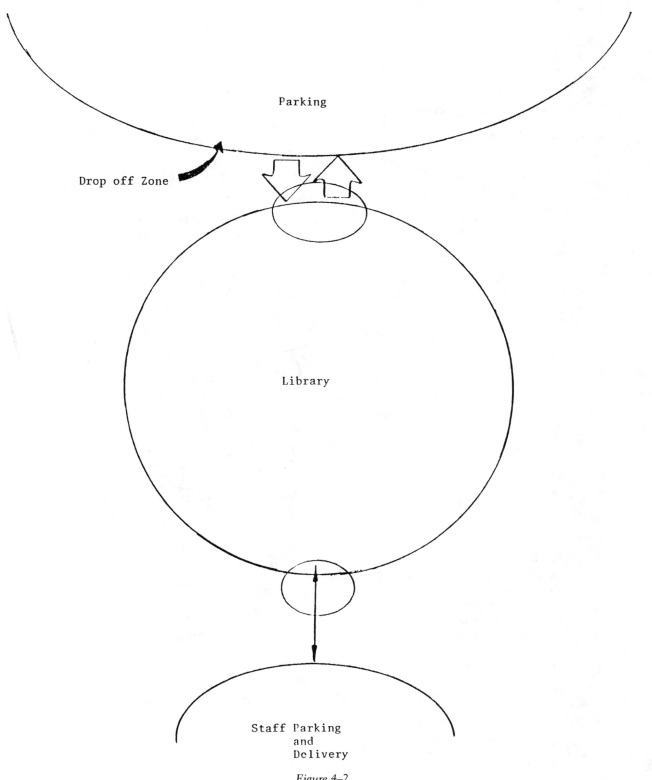

Figure 4–2
Relationships of Building Functions to Site

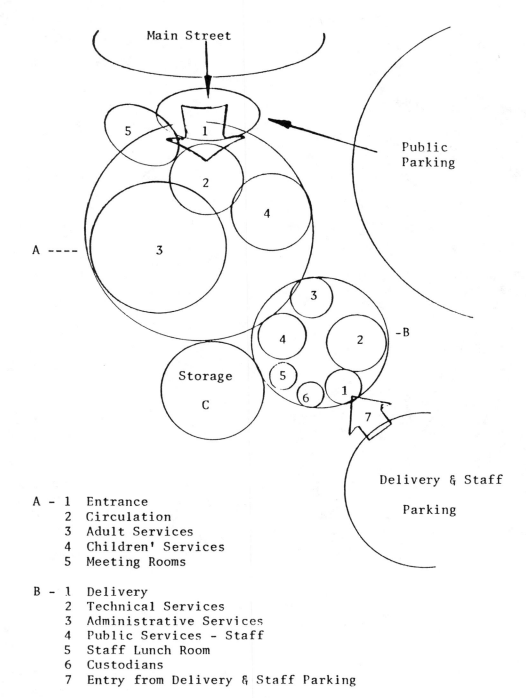

A - 1 Entrance
    2 Circulation
    3 Adult Services
    4 Children' Services
    5 Meeting Rooms

B - 1 Delivery
    2 Technical Services
    3 Administrative Services
    4 Public Services - Staff
    5 Staff Lunch Room
    6 Custodians
    7 Entry from Delivery & Staff Parking

Figure 4–3
Overview of Major Library Elements

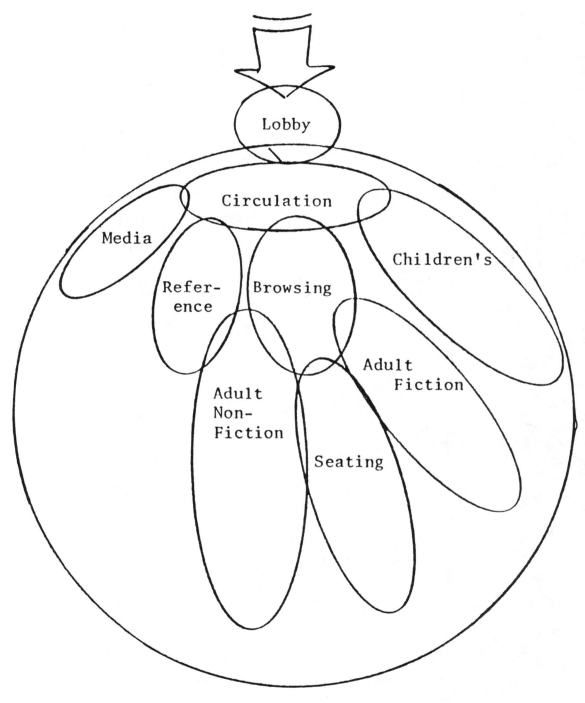

Figure 4–4
Relationships of the Circulation Desk to Other Areas

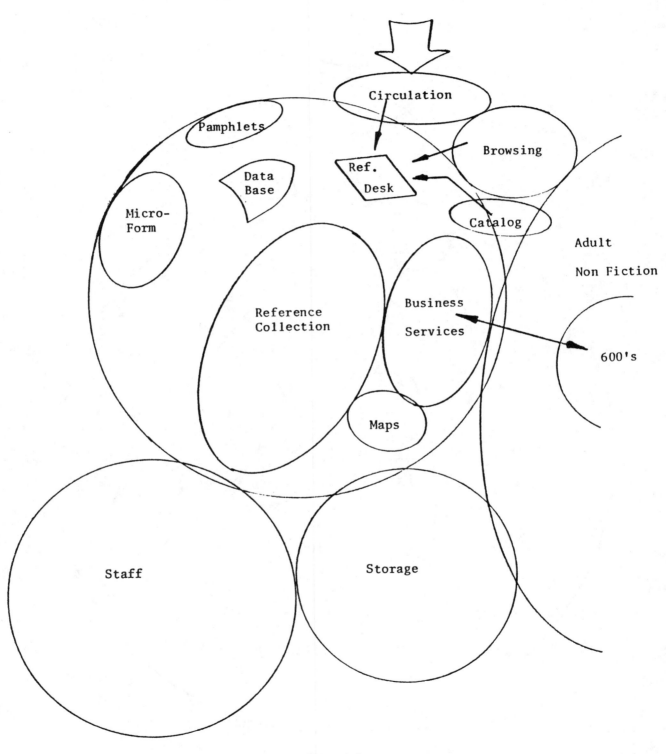

Figure 4–5
Functional Relationships in the Reference Area

estimating space requirements for collections and various pieces of furniture and equipment. This can be handled by compiling and distributing a basic source list such as that shown in Appendix A. The amount of space required by various items of shelving, files, seating, etc. usually includes the space immediately surrounding the object. For instance, space requirements for filing cabinets and card catalogs must include room for the item of equipment, the extended drawer and the person using it. While somewhat arbitrary, many of the more common space requirements will be found in the aforementioned Appendix A; others should be added as may be needed.

Of equal importance is the capacity of shelving. While one might count the contents of a number of shelves and then take an average, this is not necessary since guidelines have already been established which are generally accepted. These are provided in Appendix A (note also the discussion of this topic in Chapter 2).

Projecting Space Requirements

The general concept of projecting space requirements has been covered in Chapter 2. Obviously, the preparation of the building program requires that these tentative figures be reviewed and revised as necessary. They may appear in different categories or otherwise be manipulated to better express future space needs as they relate to a given part of the library. The formulas used for determining projections should be inserted into the building program for easy reference. Further, work sheets should be cataloged in some manner and kept as additional back-up. All mathematical computations and their results should be carefully checked by another person or persons to avoid what might be an embarrassing, if not costly, conceptual or mathematical error later on.

Selecting one or more target dates is essential to the projection of data. Usually, as noted in Chapter 2, the target is set for ten, fifteen or twenty years hence. Advancing the target year by more than two decades is often difficult because of the lack of projections for enrollment, population or other essential data. A year too far away may also introduce an element of speculation on the future of the institution or community that is usually beyond the range of most crystal balls. However, since the life of a library building is apt to exceed 50 years on most campuses and in most communities, it is acceptable for the program to indicate the general space needs which can be anticipated for that time, using such qualifiers as may be necessary. These long-range projections are most useful in determining what provisions should be made in the design for future expansion. This, in turn, has implications for the site.

Here are some further steps which are often helpful in producing reasonable projections for the target year, ten, fifteen or twenty years hence.

1/ Construct an organization chart to identify the positions and number of staff which may be required by the target date.
2/ Determine how the library's expanded services and collections should be organized for effective delivery.
3/ Estimate the growth in collections necessary to meet the anticipated needs of the user community by the target date.
4/ Identify the relationships which should exist within and between all library functions, and establish priorities where necessary.
5/ Approximate the amount of seating that will be required and separate into such categories as chairs at tables, carrels, and lounge seating.
6/ Identify special items of furniture and equipment and estimate quantities of such things as microform cabinets, microform reader-printers, vertical files, computer terminals, index tables, card catalogs, display cases, media carrels, etc.
7/ Describe the nature and estimate the number of offices and workrooms, indicating their purpose and any special relationships and/or requirements. Emphasize the number of staff to be housed in offices and at work stations; describe typical work station characteristics in terms of tasks and equipment needs.
8/ Determine and describe all special spaces which must be provided, such as conference rooms, lecture halls, study rooms, seminar rooms, spaces for special collections, etc.

As these steps are taken, data should be quantified and all calculations kept for future reference. It is especially important to retain all notes relating to the methodology used in reaching a given estimate. These notes will be an invaluable source throughout the project and will enable you to reconstruct program requirements in the future. This will save hours of time otherwise required for making new calculations and projections. Wherever possible, the projected figures should be converted into simple tables with meaningful headings which can be used in the actual building program.

Projected space requirements do not always seem realistic, especially when viewed from the cramped vantage point of the existing library. It is often helpful, therefore, to test projections in some manner. This may entail simple layouts; for example, of a workroom or office space. One does not have to be an architect or draftsman to accomplish this. Use of graph paper divided into ⅛″ or ¼″ squares is very helpful. Assistance can also be found, sometimes by referring to appropriate scale drawings in such volumes as *Architectural Graphic Standards*, or *Time Saver Standards for Building Types*. These, and similar handbooks, provide a variety of details helpful to the programmer. Estimates of space requirements for circulation desks and other service desks usually benefit if a simple sketch is prepared to include all the desired stations and other paraphernalia which must be located there. However, such sketches must not preclude the architect from using his or her own best design capabilities in providing for these functions. The layout sketch may prove that too much or too little space has been projected, or it may lead to consideration of some alternative. Also, it will provide a visual check on what may inadvertently have been left out of the projected space requirements—for instance, room for book trucks.

Assembling the Space Requirement Estimates

Space requirement estimates are among the most frequently used features of a building program. Because they will be referred to repeatedly during the architectural development phase, considerable care must be exercised in summarizing and presenting the data. This is best done by preparing a number of separate tables representing various requirements, followed by summary tables for each basic service area or other identified portion of the building, such as for staff offices and workrooms, shared spaces, group use, etc. Toward the end of the program, the totals from these summaries may themselves be compiled into a final table which presents the complete space requirement for the entire facility. Considerable caution is needed in this task and all calculations should be double-checked by another person.

Conversion of Net to Gross Square Footage

As indicated in Chapter 2 (p. 22), space requirements for shelving, items of furniture, staff, etc. are "net" figures; i.e., they do not account for such things as walls, elevator shafts, stairwells, restrooms, mechanical equipment rooms, etc., all of which occupy space. To avoid confusion, every table must carry a clear indication of whether the spaces shown are "net" or "gross." A factor of conversion, such as 25–35% must then be added to convert the total space requirements from net to gross. (Lacking any other instruction, use 30% for new construction.) The gross square footage is easily calculated by dividing the total net square footage space requirement by the amount representing the percentage of assignable space, say 70%. (The total space of 100% less the non-assignable space of 30%.) For example, a program for a building to contain 35,000 net square feet should indicate that the gross square footage will be 50,000.

The importance of clearly distinguishing between net and gross square footage cannot be over-estimated. Failure to make such a distinction can result in serious trouble. For instance, more than one project has found its total area limited to the *net* figure shown in the building space requirement estimate—officials having assumed this to be the *total* amount of space required. Once approval has been received for the project, or funding has been set, it is too late to correct such an interpretation. While the percentage allowed for non-assignable needs to create the gross square footage may not prove entirely accurate, at least such a calculation demonstrates that the librarian has not overlooked this reality.

Writing the Building Program

After the information has been gathered and the tables, figures, etc. have been worked out, the building program can be written. Before beginning this task, it is well to recall: 1/ the primary audience for which the program is being prepared, and 2/ the fact that the program's basic function is to serve as the project's *major* source book of information. In most cases, the audience consists primarily of project team members, including the design professionals and library and agency representatives. Do not assume a familiarity with libraries among team members. Omit nothing that is pertinent or illustrative of library needs. Language must be clear, concise, descriptive and unequivocal. Where it is necessary to use library terminology, definitions should be included in the text or added as a glossary with adequate referral notes. Because it must contain so much information, the building program is likely to be both a lengthy and a fairly complex document.

The Outline

Because of the scope and complexity of the material to be presented in the building program, most writers find a fairly detailed outline helpful. In addition to indicating the logical order in which the various topics will be discussed, the outline can indicate where tables and figures are apt to be most appropriate. The outline also helps assure some uniformity in presentation of summaries, etc.; it can also resolve the bothersome question of where certain information can be consolidated so that it does not have to be repeated unnecessarily.

The Narrative Form

Building programs appear in various forms, as has been indicated before. However, those which use a narrative form as the basic means of presentation seem to have definite advantages, providing judicious and appropriate use is made of other elements such as bubble diagrams, as described in this chapter. For one thing, the narrative form provides a more suitable way of presenting the descriptive information so essential to conveying concepts to the architects. For instance, the atmosphere you wish to achieve in a particular area or room can be more accurately detailed by a descriptive phrase or sentence than by filling out a grid chart or making up a list from selective terms. The narrative form also allows for the introduction of reasons supporting a particular requirement, where such arguments may be important.

Headings

As a resource document, the building program should be organized as a handbook for easy reference. This means frequent use of headings and sub-headings to indicate location of pertinent information about the subject matter under discussion. Usually, the outline for the building program will suggest where such headings should occur, as well as their possible wording. These heads and sub-heads are best identified by appropriate letters and numbers, further accentuating the outline style.

Functional Relationship Drawings

Functional relationship drawings represent one of the most significant tools available for conveying important program information. In essence, they illustrate what essential relationships are required—what is to go next to what. A single relationship drawing replaces many, many words—and often describes a situation which almost defies being put into words. These drawings should be inserted into the program where the area or function shown is being discussed. In large programs, it is helpful to duplicate the bubble diagrams and place them in an appendix to the program as well.

Before placing the diagrams into the program, a final review is needed to insure consistency in the drawings. For instance, the entrance to the building and its relationship to exterior elements such as parking and/or other major neighboring structures or site features should be the same on each drawing. Major functions shown on one side or the other of the entrance should remain in the same relative position; i.e., if reference is shown to the right of the entry and the conference room to the left, then these relative locations should be maintained wherever the same elements appear in other diagrams. Further, there should be a clear relationship between the smaller drawings of an area and the general diagram. Think of these diagrams as a system of maps, beginning with a general overall view. Succeeding maps should then show details for component areas. Each of these diagrams, then, should have a positive and recognizable relationship to others in the group.

Flow Charts

The use of flow charts provides a special opportunity in the building program to clarify procedures and processes which might otherwise be awkward to explain in words alone. For instance, a simple flow chart devised to show how materials should move through a technical services workroom can take the place of many sentences. These flow charts should be inserted in the building program where they can best illustrate the work flow for a particular function. A final review of each chart should assure that it is uncomplicated and free of ambiguity.

Diagrammatic Layouts

Earlier in this chapter, there was a warning against use of layout drawings in the building program. This warning referred to oft-seen attempts of library administrators to recommend a particular design solution for a given area—sometimes one found in another library. This inhibits the architect from using his or her own creative skills in solving what may be a deceptively similar problem in quite a different architectural context.

However, there is sometimes good reason to use diagrammatic layouts to convey certain types of information or to describe a situation more fluently than might be done in words alone. A diagrammatic layout might be used, as an example, to present a particular workstation concept or perhaps a circulation control desk. Such diagrams should be clearly labeled as such and referred to in the text as "concepts" to avoid the impression that they must be reproduced by the architect exactly as shown. Diagrammatic layouts should be drawn at a particular scale, such as ⅛" or ¼" = 1 foot. The scale should be noted on the drawing, and the diagram inserted adjacent to the relevant text in the building program.

Other Devices

The building program should use any and all devices which will help the librarian present concepts, ideas, requirements and desires. Occasionally this may include photographs, drawings, or other graphic materials. However, such material must appear for the sole purpose of reinforcing the stated requirements, amplifying a description, or otherwise adding a significant dimension to the information provided by the building program.

Special Requirements for Remodeling, Expansion, and Conversion Programs

Building programs which are developed to aid in the remodeling and/or expansion of a library or for the conversion of a structure originally used for another purpose may require some additional materials. Since the architect in such cases will be dealing with a particular building, it is possible that there will be a need to include copies of segments from earlier architectural drawings to indicate the location, etc. of certain desired changes and how they are expected to relate to the existing structure. While the same information could be presented, perhaps, in a diagrammatic layout, the existence of actual architectural drawings, floor plans, etc. make this unnecessary. When making copies, be careful to include the original scale of the drawing since reproductions made on many copy machines may change the scale.

Data Sheets

Data sheets prepared for each area of the library can be a helpful addition. These describe specific requirements for each area, using a consistent format for easy reference. If data sheets are used, they should be accumulated as a separate part or appendix rather than scattered through the building program. Each area should be given a distinct number so that exact reference can be made. These numbers may later be used by the architect to designate corresponding areas and rooms on the drawings. If systematically conceived, the numbering system can be used to indicate relationships. For instance, all spaces devoted to reference might be the only ones given numbers from 500–525. Great care must be taken to make certain that requirements shown on these sheets are the same as those described in the text.

Topics Meriting Special Consideration

Certain topics merit special consideration in the building program. These may be treated in a separate chapter where they can be given full attention. This sort of placement avoids the need to repeat information throughout the building program, and the risk of losing the impact in text devoted to other topics.

History of the Library

A brief history of the library and the library building will provide the design professionals with important background information. It should include a description of the institution or community served by the library.

General Concepts

Program requirements and concepts that are to prevail throughout the building program and be incorporated in the design can be handled in a preliminary chapter. This might include such topics as the need for flexibility, future expansion, well-defined functional relationships, effective space utilization, floor loading, communications systems, automation, and a host of such general items. Each of these should be described in a few sentences under its own heading. Placing this information at the beginning of the building program rather than scattering it through the chapters will make it easier to find and give it prominence.

Definitions of Library Terminology

It is difficult to write a building program without using some library terminology. If the same terms are used frequently, a brief glossary can be inserted near the beginning of the program, or in an appendix, for ready reference. Terms should also be defined in the narrative text when they are first used.

Site Factors

The site, whether of the existing structure or for a new building, should be carefully described. Special note should be made of topographic features, trees that may need to be saved, or traffic conditions on adjacent streets. The size, scale or architectural style of neighboring structures will be of interest since the library must fit within this context. If there is a view potential to be preserved, it should be described. Known or suspected site problems such as those related to drainage need to be indicated. While the architect will conduct a thorough investigation of the site before design work begins, the librarian's perception of the site and its various qualities will be helpful.

Security Aspects

Security for the library's users, staff, contents and structure is a pervasive factor in design. Therefore, the library building program should clearly describe the nature and level of security desired in various portions of the building. This will include such things as adequate exterior lighting along walks and in parking areas, concealed panic-alarm buttons at public desks, collection security systems, general alarm systems for evacuating the building, and any special needs such as alarms for vaults or to detect flooding in basement levels. All of these security systems are over and above the fire detection and suppression systems which are required by codes.

Concluding the Building Program

The building program should be concluded with a summary chapter which includes one or more tables

summarizing space requirements by major areas. This chapter may also reiterate the overriding requirements as a means of emphasizing their importance. In most programs, this chapter will be quite short but will be referred to often because of the summary tables. Care should be taken that the summary tables are faithful to the earlier numbers and are correctly computed.

Building Program Appendices

The building program may include a number of appendices. Some of these have been mentioned in this chapter. For instance, the tables for space requirements and the functional relationship diagrams may be duplicated and placed at the end of the building program for convenient reference. If area data sheets are used, they should appear as a second part of the program or as an appendix. Any support-document frequently referred to would be a good candidate for similar treatment, as well.

Indexing

Because the building program will be used as a handbook throughout the project by all members of the project team, easy access to the contents is important. This is best provided by a detailed index prepared after the program has gone through its final draft and the pages have been numbered. Another approach, though not as helpful, is to provide an expanded table of contents which includes all headings and sub-headings. Perusal of this description of contents will provide clues, at least, to where desired information may be found.

Summary

The purpose of this chapter has been to indicate the importance of the building program and to describe its preparation. Emphasis has been placed on the contents of the building program and devices such as the bubble diagrams needed to illustrate functional relationships. This chapter is intended to provide guidance in gathering and presenting program information so that it can be used as the project guidebook.

V SELECTING THE LIBRARY CONSULTANT AND THE DESIGN PROFESSIONALS

BUILDING projects, of whatever kind or size, involve the selection of certain professionals. The purpose of this chapter is to describe the roles these professionals play and the processes commonly used in their selection. Given the enormous effect the individuals chosen will have on the project, it is imperative that every effort be made to select people who display through training and experience the talents and traits most compatible with the project in question. It is embarrassing, sometimes, to see how little effort is put into this process when so much is at stake. Clients have been known to take more time and trouble in the selection of a single clerical or professional for an entry-level position on their staff than they spend in determining who will be responsible for the designing of a multi-million dollar facility.

There are no shortcuts to this selection process. Neither is there any truth to the assumption that one architect is about as good as another or that library consultants are more or less all alike. The librarian and client representatives will be working very closely with the people they choose for a period of two to four years, or even longer. This is cause enough to take whatever steps are necessary in selecting those with whom so much time is to be spent and in whom so much of the future is to be entrusted.

Selection of the Library Consultant

Although use of a library consultant is not universal, most projects benefit from the services one can provide. Library consultants are, in most instances, professional librarians with years of experience in the library field.[1] For whatever reason, they develop an interest in library buildings, often from having been involved in one or more projects as the client or client's representative. Through reading, attendance at workshops, observation and other means, these individuals gain knowledge that can be shared with others. By helping other institutions or communities with their facility prob-

lems, their depth of experience and knowledge grows. Some library consultants relinquish their former positions for full-time work in the field; others act as consultants on a part-time basis, using weekends or vacation time for their work.

When to Select a Library Consultant

The library consultant may enter the scene as early as the needs assessment study or as late as the development of architectural drawings and specifications. Whether a library consultant is needed depends upon the local situation, including the amount of experience of the librarian and staff and the time they have available for the various aspects of the work.

Library consultants are often retained to help with the preparation of the building program because of their experience and the amount of time it takes to prepare this document. Because of the divisive nature and importance of site selection, especially in the public library field, library consultants are often sought to help with this decision, and then continue on through the project. Sometimes the decision to hire a library consultant does not occur until the architects are selected. Not infrequently, the library consultant is brought on board at some later date when it is realized that the design is in trouble.

Ideally, the library consultant should be involved at the outset of the project. This enables the consultant to share expertise throughout the process while accumulating an intimate knowledge of the local situation and needs of the library. When selected to begin at the beginning, the library consultant is in the best position to serve the client.

How to Select the Library Consultant

Although library consultants have been active for many years, there is no certification or other program for recognizing qualifications. The only available guide to practicing library consultants is prepared by the Buildings and Equipment Section of the Library Administration and Management Association of the American Library Association. It is revised and published every two or three years as the *Library Buildings Consultant List*. As noted in the introduction to the publication, "Inclusion does not constitute or imply endorsement or certification by the American Library Association (ALA), the Library Administration and Management Association (LAMA), or the Buildings and Equipment Section of LAMA." This listing includes those who meet certain minimum qualifications, such as current experience (participation in a project in the past three years), participation in five or more library building projects within the preceding ten years, and completion of an application form listing experience, representative jobs, and other information. For each consultant, the entry highlights these responses. Many libraries now turn to this list as they initiate a search for a library building consultant, although the listing is voluntary and does not pretend to be complete.

Selection usually begins with the creation of a list of possible consultants derived from the *Library Buildings Consultant List* or other sources. The initial candidates are likely to be chosen because they appear to have had experience in working on projects of comparable size and scope. A brief description of the project is sent to each candidate with a request that a response be sent by a certain date supplying:

1/ A resume including personal background, and experience
2/ A description of library projects worked on in recent years that are similar in size and complexity
3/ A description of the role and responsibilities the consultant assumed in each project
4/ A list of references
5/ An indication of availability for the type of services desired
6/ Information on fee structure.

After reviewing these submittals, a "short list" of several consultants, usually two to seven, is formed. To these may be sent a more detailed description of the project, a statement explaining how and when the consultant will be chosen, how the consultant is to supply information on the cost of his or her services, and specific questions about the consultant's proposed methodology, list of tasks to be performed, tentative work schedule to meet project deadlines, and costs. If inter-

views are to be conducted, the number of people to be interviewed and the dates for such interviews should be indicated. A deadline for response must be included.

This information can be formalized into a Request For Proposal (RFP). The RFP process converts the selection methodology into a bidding situation. If the RFP route is chosen, greater care must be taken to obtain the maximum pertinent information on which to base the choice, such as a detailed description and schedule of tasks to be performed, and an indication of what is and is not included in the cost figure quoted for the consultant's services. (If a budget for fees and reimbursable expenses has already been established, it is only fair to so indicate. Chances are that the competitive bidding aspect of the RFP process will keep the quotations within bounds.) When the RFP does not elicit sufficient information, the client's decision is often determined by the amount of consultant's "bid" rather than by qualifications and experience.

Whether using the RFP method or a less formal approach, the resulting submittals must be reviewed and evaluated on the basis of responsiveness to the local situation. The proposed methodology as well as the description of tasks to be performed and the schedule to be followed deserve careful attention. Thoroughness and perception are important. Give particular attention to details that explain how the consultant expects to relate to client representatives in gathering information, evaluating options and reaching decisions.

A careful check of references should be made for all candidates whose RFP responses appear to merit further consideration. Reference checks should be made by telephone and should include questions concerning the consultant's observed ability to work with library staff and with design professionals. Once this screening is completed, one or more of the leading candidates should be invited for an interview. If possible, travel expenses should be volunteered by the interviewing library. Those who will be working most closely with the consultant should constitute the interview committee, though there may also be other representatives of the owner, such as one or more members from the faculty advisory committee, administration, library board, city manager's office, etc.

To be productive, an interview will probably require an hour or more. In some cases, especially if the list of candidates is very small, the interview may be preceded by a tour of the library and a briefing on project details. If this is done, care must be taken that all candidates are given similar tours and project information to avoid any possible accusation of preference or misinformation.

The first fifteen or twenty minutes of each interview period should be allocated to a presentation by the consultant covering his or her qualifications, experience and approach to the project. Client questions and general discussion should follow, leaving five to ten minutes for final questions that the consultant may wish to ask. Questions to be asked the consultant usually concern clarification of experience, qualifications and proposal details. Emphasis should be placed on questions which provide an opportunity to evaluate the consultant's compatibility with those who will be most involved. If possible, several questions worded identically should be asked of each consultant to provide a further basis of comparison. Interviews are usually successful in producing a winning candidate.

The Reference Check

Before reaching a decision on which candidate to choose, the responses from the consultant's references should be reviewed. This process is most satisfactory when telephone reference interviews have been conducted by one or two perceptive people who ask each reference the same questions. Reference interviews usually are more productive if they have been established by appointment so that there is sufficient uninterrupted time. In addition, the interviewer must be prepared to follow up with further questions and to pursue any points that need clarification or that may aduce special insights. Other questions may explore the candidate's overall performance, ability to adhere to schedules and meet deadlines, capacity for the particular tasks to be performed in this project, ability to work with both library staff and design professionals, reliability and accuracy of data supplied, capacity for creative solutions, proficiency in preparing clearly worded and persuasive written materials (ask for excerpts from building programs, plan review comments, etc.), and record for staying within sums agreed to for fees and reimbursable expenses.

Note: Do not be surprised if some previous client's comments are negative. Other librarians may not have been as careful in screening candidates or may have chosen one on price alone. Explore the reasons for such comments. Ask the consultant for his or her reaction and whether there were mitigating circumstances. While criticism may be justified, personality conflicts and misunderstandings are often at the root of dissatisfaction. These perceived shortcomings may not be applicable in another situation. On the other hand, demonstrated weaknesses indicated by more than one source would merit very serious consideration.

Besides the list of references provided by the library consultant, it may be worthwhile calling others known to have worked with the consultant in question. Sometimes this is difficult because subsequent changes in personnel have eliminated those who worked most closely with the consultant on a project several years before. Where this is not the case, responses can sometimes be illuminating, since sufficient time may have passed to affect the assessment of the consultant's participation and counsel.

Consultant Fees

The selection of the library building consultant should never be based on fees. Consultant fees vary widely due to many factors, almost none of which relate to qualifications or experience. In addition, consultant fees differ considerably in what they do or do not include. For instance, some consultants routinely provide a given number of copies of all written reports, programs, etc. Others prefer to supply copies at cost, or will give the client camera-ready copy to be duplicated at the client's expense. Fees, and what they cover, should be discussed thoroughly before a library consultant is chosen.

Consultants may work by the hour, by the day or on a flat-rate basis for the entire job. Consultants sometimes consider the fee quoted for a project to be tentative and subject to negotiation before a contract is written. This is because projects differ so much in their requirements and expectations of the library consultant. Fees should never be used as a bargaining tool.

Those who choose to work part-time as consultants may have a lower fee rate than the full-time consultant because the earnings are over and above their salaries. Most part-time consultants have comparatively low overhead, which contributes to a lower fee. In part this may be offset by limited availability, however. Typically, the part-time consultant is available only a few days at a time, since he or she is using weekends, holidays, vacation or other compensatory time. This availability will not necessarily meet the needs of a client faced with an intensive schedule and short deadlines requiring concentrated consultant effort. The full-time consultant may have a higher fee but offers increased availability and can usually meet whatever schedule and deadlines may be called for. Older librarians who work as consultants after retirement are another group whose fees may vary. Some wish to continue an active career and are competitive in vying for projects. Others may look upon consulting as a way to supplement retirement income while still enjoying contact with the profession, and therefore work at a lesser fee. None of this has to do with credentials or quality of work. That is for the client to decide. As a rule, however, there are no bargains in library consulting; what you pay for is likely to be what you get.

Another variable is the consultant's approach to reimbursable expenses. If the project is near at hand, some consultants may absorb travel costs, while others expect reimbursement. When a greater distance is involved, and especially if the consultant must anticipate costs of lodging, meals, public transportation, etc., the associated expenses are more likely to be added to the fee as reimbursable charges. During the past decade, consultants have frequently added other items to the list of reimbursable expenses, such as long-distance phone calls, air express charges, and reproduction costs for reports, drawings, etc. It is important to know in advance what items the consultant is going to charge for as reimbursable expenses and the consultant's estimate for the total cost of reimbursables. If the consultant is to be retained on a "lump sum" contract, it will be advantageous to compare the amounts projected by the various candidates for fees and reimbursable expenses.

The client is expected to indicate how the library consultant shall quote his or her cost estimate for the project. There are two basic methods:

1/ Separately itemized fees and reimbursable charges, often divided between major segments of the project; for instance, (a) needs assessment, (b) preparation of the building program, and (c) review of drawings and specifications;

2/ A total or "lump sum" amount which includes all fees and reimbursable expenses.

Both methods will probably include a condition that work beyond the tasks specifically agreed to will be charged at a given rate per hour or per day plus reimbursement for particular costs such as travel. There is generally a requirement that the number of hours or days estimated for each major segment of the work be indicated.

One word of caution here. Requiring the consultant to supply extensive detailing of the project budget is time-consuming and self-defeating. For instance, estimating the number of hours and the cost associated with every task, broken down by professional time, clerical time, etc., requires the consultant to speculate unduly about project details, schedules, client participation, and possible snags along the route.

Crucial to both the client and the consultant is whether the figures quoted are "not to exceed" amounts. The term "not to exceed" normally means that the library consultant will complete the tasks as agreed in the contract for the amount stated, regardless of the actual time required. While estimating on a "not to exceed" basis requires the consultant to protect himself or herself by making reasonably sure that the amount will be adequate, the "not to exceed" figure gives the client firm control of the budget. If this technique is used, the contract must clearly indicate whether the consultant is to charge only for the hours or days worked, if these are less than the number estimated, or is entitled to the full amount stipulated by the agreement. Generally, a "lump sum" contract means that the library consultant will be paid that amount regardless of the time spent. Again, the lump sum provides the client with a firm budget figure.

There are some situations in which neither the client nor the consultant can reasonably estimate the amount of services that will be required. This frequently happens when a project begins with a needs assessment study that must determine the eventual solution. In such cases, the client may wish to negotiate a contract based on an hourly or daily rate for the library consultant, with a "not to exceed" maximum which may be raised or lowered depending on future events. With this kind of contract, the consultant earns only the amount paid for the time actually spent on the project, plus reimbursable expenses, of course. Such contracts may be developed in phases, with fees established as each phase is completed.

It should be apparent that there are no general guidelines for determining whether a library consultant's fees are reasonable or not. Getting estimates from several consultants in a systematic manner should provide some basis for determining whether a given consultant's fees are in line. Depending on the degree of participation, a library consultant's fee, exclusive of reimbursable charges, is apt to run from .5% to 1.5% or more of the anticipated project cost. The key is the extensiveness of the role the library consultant plays and the thoroughness with which the job is done. Whatever the amount, the library consultant is almost certain to save the client several times more than the fee by savings in staff time and in avoiding costly mistakes.

Final Evaluation

With all of the data in hand from the formal response to the interviews and recommendations of references, it is time to make the final evaluation and choice. Here are some of the criteria which should be considered in the selection of the library building consultant:

1/ The consultant should have had experience in one or more projects similar in scope or size, unless the project is quite different from most others; the more complex the client's project, the greater should be the consultant's level of experience.

2/ There should be ample evidence in the consultant's written response, interview and recommendations, that the consultant possesses the level of specialized knowledge and expertise required for the project.

3/ The consultant must be available for the period of time needed to complete the project and there should be assurance of some flexibility in meeting the schedule; seek reassurance that the consultant will not be leaving on a sabbatical or extended vacation during the course of the project.

4/ After being thoroughly checked, references for any given candidate should be reasonably uniform, enthusiastic and complimentary; reference comments that point to a pleasant and productive working relationship should be given special weight.

5/ The methodology proposed by each consultant should be proven reliable and appropriate for the project's needs.

6/ The list of tasks the consultant provides must coincide with project requirements and schedule; further, the tasks should provide assurance that the quality of consultant services desired will be achieved, with emphasis on factors such as accuracy, timeliness, degree of detail, integrity and perception.

7/ Cost estimates for the consultant's services should be responsive to the project; it should be clearly evident what services and expenses are included and which are to be covered as reimbursable expenses or extra fees.

8/ The consultant's personality and philosophy of library service should be compatible with that of library team members. Ultimately, no factor is of greater importance than this.

The Contract

Once a decision has been reached, a contract should be negotiated with the library consultant. This document can be very simple, depending upon the procedures of the particular jurisdiction. Some consultants provide a form contract which can be modified to meet individual conditions. Often the most expedient and satisfactory method is to write a simple contract which incorporates the consultant's proposal by reference. This avoids the possibility of misconceptions resulting from interpretations and language used by attorneys. In any case, be certain that all of the conditions set forth in the contract are relevant and understood by both parties. Do not expect the library consultant to begin work until the contract has been approved and signed by all concerned. If the contract is delayed and the consultant's services are required in the interim, this can sometimes be done by a letter of agreement which limits the consultant's tasks to those immediately necessary and for which the librarian has funds available.

Selection of the Design Professionals

Before architectural design work can begin, the professionals who are to be responsible for this effort must be chosen. We are using the term "design professionals" here rather than "architect" since increasing use is being made of interior designers to complement the work of the architect. Choice of both the architect and the interior designer, if one is to be used (see Chapter 6), should occur simultaneously, because the talents and experience of each must complement the other's and their personalities must enable them to work closely with other members of the project team.

Design professionals may, in some instances, be selected on an informal basis. This may be the prerogative of an individual or a committee. For instance, the choice may have been determined by the conditions of a gift or bequest subsidizing the project. Some agencies and institutions retain the same architectural firms for all of their projects, in an effort to maintain a certain style or type of design. Sometimes, such firms are primarily responsible for master planning but may select other firms for the design of individual buildings. Other institutions and government agencies maintain lists of architectural firms from which selection is made.

When to Choose an Architect

Often the first question to occur about design professionals concerns when they should be retained for the project. While this may vary with the circumstances for a specific project, the general rule is that the architect's usefulness begins when the building program is completed and approved by the sponsoring agency or institution. If engaged in advance of that time, the architect can do little other than preliminary site work—something which will be done normally at the outset of the schematic design period. Little time, if any, can be gained by engaging the design professionals prior to the completion of an approved set of programmatic requirements. If design work begins before the finished program is available, an inappropriate design may be conceived based on only partial knowledge of the actual requirements.

Occasionally it may be necessary to employ the services of an architect to conduct a feasibility analysis on an existing structure, provide a site analysis or supply other data during the needs assessment phase or prior to the completion of the building program. In such instances, the architect should be retained on a special contract covering only the specific services desired, with a provision that the agency or institution may amend the contract to cover future design services when and if this becomes desirable. This contract should also stipulate that retention of the firm for this particular task in no way commits the institution or governmental agency to employing the firm for the remainder of the project. This procedure serves to define the scope of the architectural services to be provided immediately, avoids premature design work, but still keeps the door open for future coverage of the project.

Roles of the Design Professionals

It is the responsibility of the architect to prepare the plans and specifications for a building project and, in most instances, to be one of the client's representatives during construction. Work begins with the analysis of the building program and the conceptualization of a solution to the space and design problems posed by the program. Once the concept has been approved, the architect proceeds through 1/ schematics, 2/ design development and 3/ construction documents, preparing suitable drawings and specifications for each of these stages (see Chapter 6). If an interior designer is not used for the project, the architect may be given responsibility for the building's interiors, including selection of floor and wall coverings, color schemes, and furniture and equipment.

During the course of this work, the architect assembles and manages a team of engineering specialists, such as 1/ structural engineers, 2/ mechanical engineers, and 3/ electrical engineers. Depending upon the needs of the project, other specialists may be used,

such as illuminating engineers and acoustical engineers. When the building contractor is selected, the architect makes periodic inspections of the work to make certain that the drawings and specifications are being followed and to resolve any issues that may occur during construction.

Because the interior environment is of such great importance to libraries and because of the increasingly complex nature of materials, furniture and equipment, more clients today are involving interior designers in their projects. Interior design services may be provided by a division of the architectural firm or by an independent interior designer. Working closely with the design architect, the interior designer may be responsible for a variety of things ranging from the arrangement of interior spaces to the selection of lighting fixtures, wall and floor coverings, ceiling materials, furniture and equipment and the design of casework (cabinetry), as well as graphics and signage systems. This calls for very close coordination with the architect so that the interiors evolve as an integral part of the total design. The interior designer's drawings and specifications must be produced on schedule and be consistent with those of the architects. As construction begins, the interior designer assists in reviewing vendor bids, evaluates products submitted as "or equals" and works with suppliers on delivery schedules. Usually the interior designer is responsible for uncrating furniture and equipment and seeing that damaged goods are replaced. Finally, it is the interior designer's job to oversee installation of furniture, equipment, casework, wall and floor coverings, graphics and signage.

Although the roles of the architect and interior designer will be elaborated on further in this and subsequent chapters, this brief description of responsibilities should make clear the importance of their work in bringing a project to fruition. The librarian therefore has a critical stake in how these design professionals are chosen.

Identifying Basic Qualifications

Before entering the actual selection process, it will be helpful to consider the basic qualifications to be sought in the design professionals. These may run the gamut from personalities to design styles, and from the size of the firm to whether or not the firm must be local, have a local representative, or possess other characteristics. One overriding consideration is the long-term nature of the association between client personnel and design staff. The normal project is apt to run three to four years or more, and will often evolve into an intensive architect/client relationship that is subject to all manner of stress. Some have likened this relationship to a marriage, and not without reason. Personalities must mesh and there should be mutual trust and appreciation of common goals. Adversarial relationships are almost certain to be tortuous, nightmarish and unproductive experiences for all.

Before beginning the search for design professionals, it is important to understand that they each represent in different proportions a blend of artist, engineer and businessman. As a result of their professional education, subsequent experiences and relationships, they tend to exemplify or show a preference for one or more design styles. Motivation comes from a variety of sources, not the least of which is peer recognition through the receipt of awards and publication of projects in professional literature. Previous experience in the designing of a particular type of building, such as a library, is not necessarily a guarantee that the future designs will be successful. Sometimes a design professional with little or no experience in designing libraries will produce a superior building based on general aptitude and greater attention to problem solving. These are only a few of background observations which must be kept in mind as the selection process begins.

For many institutions, and for some governmental agencies, the experience of the architect in designing structures which will fit into the overall campus or governmental complex or other setting may be a major consideration. Certainly the agency or institution's past experience will have relevancy here, as well as its methodology in dealing with architects. In some cases the choice of architect will be heavily influenced by the wishes or commitments of local officials outside of the library who will be involved in the project. These individuals must be identified early on and brought into the selection process. Occasionally, other parties may participate in the selection process, such as an architect responsible for the campus or civic center master plan, or a private developer who may be furnishing architectural expertise as a part of a "design and build" project.

The Selection Process

With increasing frequency, the selection of design professionals follows a rather systematic procedure. The purpose of this process is to permit consideration and comparison of the qualifications of a number of firms. While the process will vary with each situation, it will usually follow the steps indicated below and described in greater detail later in this chapter.

1/ A list of design professionals to receive invitations is drawn up by the client.
2/ Design professionals on the list are invited to submit their qualifications and a statement of interest in the project. (RFQ)
3/ Submittals from the design professionals are received and evaluated by the client.
4/ A list of those considered most suited is compiled for further consideration and a Request for Proposal (RFP) issued asking for additional information.
5/ Proposals are received in response to the RFPs and evaluated; references are checked.
6/ A "short-list" of 3-7 firms is selected to be interviewed.
7/ Interviews are held.
8/ Following the interviews, a further check may be made of references along with visitation of projects completed by the candidates.
9/ Final evaluation occurs.
10/ Fees proposed by the architectural firms are evaluated.
11/ After considering all available information, with emphasis on perceived compatibility, relevant experience and design capacity, the final choice is made.
12/ Notification of selection is transmitted to all firms responding to the RFP.
13/ Contract negotiations begin with the chosen architectural firm.

Most of these steps are rather self explanatory; some of them will overlap. However, each requires a certain amount of preparation and forethought.

Invitation list. The first step is to assemble a list of firms to be invited to submit their qualifications. This list may include both architects and interior designers. The list can be drawn from many sources. The local office of the American Institute of Architects, for instance, can provide a list of its members. Many state libraries maintain lists of architects who have designed libraries. Similarly, large university systems may furnish names of firms with which they have worked. Some libraries have even resorted to telephone book yellow page directories—though there is no selectivity here. The LAMA office of the American Library Association may also provide names of architects responsible for buildings which have won the AIA-ALA awards for library buildings.

Librarians should also take advantage of the knowledge and expertise of others in their agency or institution who work with design professionals or follow architecture as an avocation. A city or campus architect will obviously have names for the list. As news of the impending project spreads, the client is likely to receive requests from still other architects who wish to be considered.

The length of the list of firms is a matter of local option and is usually affected by such factors as the size of the project, distance of the project from urban centers, numbers of qualified design professionals in the area, and whether or not architects with a national reputation are to be included. The preliminary list should include at least a dozen or so names to provide a reasonable field of choice. A larger list holds promise of greater variety—but also involves more client time in evaluation.

Invitation to submit: the RFQ. Once the invitation list is completed and culled to a reasonable length by the selection committee, an invitation must be submitted to the design professionals. This invitation may be officially referred to as the Request for Qualifications (RFQ), as compared to the more formal and detailed Request for Proposal (RFP) which follows later. Its goal is to provide an opportunity for architectural and interior design firms to submit basic information and to indicate whether they are interested in being considered for the project. The responses to the RFQ will be used to determine which firms will receive the more specific RFP and be given further consideration in the selection process.

The RFQ should contain a brief description of the project, its size, location, estimated budget, and schedule. The selection process should be clearly described, indicating who will be responsible for the selection, what submittals will be required, and the schedule for each step. This should be followed by clearly worded questions intended to derive information which can be used for comparative purposes. Some of the more typical questions should cover topics such as:

1/ Size of firm in terms of the number of professionals, draftsmen, and other support personnel.

2/ General statement of qualifications and experience, especially with library projects.

3/ A list of projects considered representative of the firm's work, including any libraries or other public buildings.

4/ A list of references of clients past and present.

The RFQ should allow a response time of three to four weeks. Many firms have a standard format for their reply which will include a cover letter, brochure, and attachments answering specific questions. If the number of people on the selection committee is rela-

tively small, the firms may be asked to submit multiple copies of the RFQ so that several members of the selection team may proceed simultaneously with their evaluations.

Sometimes the receipt of the RFQ will trigger a barrage of telephone calls and letters from architects requesting further details of the project. Where possible, all telephone calls should be answered by the same person to encourage continuity in response. Calls requesting copies of the RFQ may be received from architects not on the original list. These requests are usually honored. Much time can be saved by making certain that instructions are clearly stated and that the process and schedule for selection has been presented in sufficient detail to answer most questions. As the submittal deadline nears, do not hesitate to call firms which have not responded earlier. Sometimes deadlines pass unnoticed because of many circumstances and such an omission might well deprive you of considering a preferred choice.

Handling the submittal. In most cases, the client can expect the response to be fairly substantial—somewhere between 50 and 75%. This means that adequate preparations must be made to handle the paperwork, including recording the receipt of each submittal and checking each one to make certain that all of the materials requested have been included in the packet. Every page of each copy should be carefully marked with the copy number to avoid any mix-up. This may include a simple code so that RFQ pages can be reassembled if they become separated inadvertently. One master copy of each RFQ should be kept in a separate file to guarantee that a complete set is available, should the need for it arise. This set then becomes a part of the historical file that results from the project. One staff member should be delegated full responsibility for recording and keeping track of submittals and other paperwork associated with the evaluation process.

Evaluating the RFQ submittal. The preliminary review of RFQ submittals may eliminate some firms on the basis of an incomplete response or other obvious deficiencies. Those remaining are then ready for review by the selection committee. Here the goal is to evaluate the submittals against a list of agreed-upon criteria to narrow the number of firms under consideration to a handful which will receive the RFP. Obviously, the selection committee must establish such criteria prior to the preparation of the letter of invitation so that pertinent data can be presented by the various firms. Typical criteria might include:

1/ Size of firm and number and types of personnel.

2/ Experience in handling projects of similar size and type.

3/ Engineering and special services available "in-house" as compared to those which will be arranged for outside of the firm.

4/ Compatibility of design experience with that required for the library.

5/ Previous experience in designing library buildings.

6/ Information gathered from references.

Questions such as these should give the selection committee a fair idea as to which firms are most likely to have the desired experience, staff capacity, and achievement record to meet the local project's requirements. Note that the question concerning previous experience in designing library buildings has been placed at the bottom of the list. This is because experience indicates that many architects are more apt to give greater attention to a project type they have not previously encountered than to one with which they assume a certain familiarity.

While the selection committee members may review the submittals independently, one or more extended discussion sessions are likely to be needed in order to arrive at the "short list" of those firms which are to receive the full Request for Proposal. Sometimes it is necessary to gather additional information, call other references, or ask for clarification of certain details in the RFQ response before the final decision can be made. Because of the importance of this part of the selection process, adequate time must be allowed. The amount of time will depend mostly on the number of submittals made and the amount of material presented. Two to three weeks might be considered an average time frame for this evaluation process.

Request for proposal (RFP). Architectural firms on the short list of 3-7 firms are sent a formal Request for Proposal. The RFP provides additional information about the project and requests a more detailed response from the architectural firm. A list of carefully written questions may be made a part of the RFP. These questions should be geared to assembling information which provides a better image of each firm and how it performs its services. Such questions may range from philosophy of design to very practical queries about services provided by the firm. Some of the questions may be the result of the selection committee's discussions during the RFQ review. Others may be raised to help distinguish differences in approach to the project. The responses to these questions will provide a springboard for the interviews which follow.[2]

Evaluation of RFP responses. The receipt of RFP responses should be handled in the same systematic manner as used for the RFQ responses. This includes a careful record of when each response is received, number of copies, etc. Then, copies must be distributed to the various selection committee members, or other arrangements made for thorough review of the submittals. While the selection committee members ponder the responses to the RFP, other work needs to be done.

1/ An interview schedule must be established for the firms responding to the RFP.

2/ References supplied by the design firms must be checked and the responses reviewed with the selection committee.

3/ The interview agenda and questions must be prepared.

4/ Interview arrangements must be made with each firm.

5/ Selection committee members may visit representative projects completed by the design professionals who are to be interviewed.

6/ One or more meetings of the selection committee will be needed to review submittal information and prepare for the interview sessions.

Making the reference check. A detailed check of references should be made prior to the interviews. Each reference should be asked the same basic questions to create a common basis for evaluation. These may be followed by questions relevant to a particular firm and/or queries prompted by the reference interview itself. The reference check should be conducted by a library staff member thoroughly acquainted with the project and familiar with conducting telephone interviews of this sort. (Telephone interviews are normally faster and much more satisfactory than written responses.)

Of particular interest will be testimony on the firm's ability to work well with other members of a project team, willingness to follow the requirements of a functional building program, and ability to meet project budgets and schedules. Opportunity should be given the interviewer to follow up wherever respondents appear to be willing to volunteer information beyond that sought in the formal line of questioning. Responses to the reference check should be recorded on a form for each firm and made available to the selection committee members as a part of the evaluation process.

Project visitation. Selection committee members may wish to visit projects the design professionals have indicated in their RFP responses as being examples of their work. Visitation can be extremely helpful since it allows selection committee members to see the design professional's work at first hand. Further, there is the opportunity to talk to those who occupy the building and have a unique view of the project's strengths and shortcomings. During the visitation, time should be spent with those most intimately concerned with the building, and particularly those who must maintain it. Such individuals will provide very practical information on mundane but important matters ranging from leaking roofs to inadequate custodial facilities and difficult-to-relamp light fixtures.

Wherever possible, visitation should be done by teams of two or three selection committee members. Primary data about each building should be accumulated in advance of each visit so that important data are conveniently compiled on fact sheets. This enables the visitation team members to concentrate on impressions and new information which may be provided as they move about the building. Viewing each facility should include a comprehensive tour guided by someone totally familiar with the building, followed by discussion with key staff, maintenance and other personnel who can provide special insight into the adequacy of design and any problems that may not be visible.

Because visitation is costly in time, energy and travel expenses, visits should be carefully planned with specific goals in mind. Outstanding features or areas of special concern should be identified in advance wherever possible. After each visit, a report of findings and impressions should be compiled as part of the selection process records.

Selection committee meetings. One or more meetings of the selection committee will be needed to: 1/ review the content of the RFP submittals, 2/ review reference interview responses, 3/ discuss impressions from visitations, and 4/ prepare the agenda and line of questioning for the interviews. These meetings are important because they provide a time for an exchange of views before the personalities of the architects intrude into the evaluation process.

Interview invitations. An invitation to the firms to be interviewed should be sent as soon as a schedule has been agreed upon. The letter of invitation should cover at least the following:

1/ Time and place for the interview.
2/ Length of time each firm will be allowed and a schedule showing how that time will be allocated among: a/Formal presentation by the firm; b/Response to Selection Committee questions; c/Summary comments from the firm's representatives.

3/ Representation expected from the firm; i.e., Project Architect, Design Architect, etc.
4/ Notes on availability of projection screens, slide projectors, tack board, etc., to facilitate the firm's formal presentation.
5/ An RSVP number to call to confirm appearance at the scheduled time, place and date.

Preparing for the interviews. Because the interviews are often the most crucial step in the process of selecting design professionals, it is important that sufficient time be given to preparations. Each member of the selection committee must become thoroughly familiar with the firms. A pre-interview meeting of the selection committee should be held several days in advance to determine whether additional information may be required and to decide on the line of questioning for each firm. Committee members will want to discuss possible questions deciding which shall be asked of all firms and which shall be reserved for a particular firm.[3] Sometimes this preparation will result in making a request to the firms for additional information to be supplied prior to the interviews or to be presented at that time. This is especially apt to happen following the reference check and visitation.

Setting up for the interviews. For interviews to move smoothly, preparation must include anticipation of the conditions and needs that are likely to prevail. Interviews should follow a reasonable schedule permitting one to two hours for each firm. Do not try to jam too many interviews into a single day. Two interviews in the morning and two in the afternoon are taxing enough. If more than five firms are to be interviewed, spread the interviews over a two-day period to allow more time for presentations and to avoid fatigue on the part of selection committee members.

Care should be taken in the selection of a place for holding the interviews. Interviews need not be held in the library unless an appropriate room is available. A conference room setting should be used, with a large table and comfortable chairs. It is important that the room chosen be insulated from outside noise and distraction. The room should be well lighted and ventilated. Restrooms need to be convenient. If possible, a staffed reception area should be available with reasonable access to the interview area, but out of earshot. Here, those arriving for an interview can be received and await their turn. There should be access to a public telephone in or near the reception area.

In the interview room, there should be ample space on one side of the table for the Selection Committee members, with the design firm's representatives seated on the other. Both the committee members and those to be interviewed should be placed at ease in their surroundings. The room must be capable of being easily darkened for visual presentations and a projection screen should be located where it can best be seen by the selection committee members. Electrical outlets and switches should be checked out in advance to be certain that power is available. Extra projection equipment and power cords should be available. Usually refreshments are provided for the selection committee and offered those being interviewed. When interviews are scheduled close together, it is helpful to have another door through which those completing an interview can exit without returning to the reception area. Attention to the details of environment and hospitality will result in better response from those being interviewed as well as improved performance by the selection committee members.

The interview agenda. As previously mentioned, the interview sessions should operate around a well-conceived agenda and schedule. Both of these, at least in preliminary form, should be sent in advance to those who are to be interviewed. At least one hour should be allowed for each interview; an hour-and-a-half is even better. A typical interview schedule might read as follows:

1/ Introductions.
2/ Opening statement by Selection Committee leader, including an outline of the interview schedule and any guidelines that should be observed.
3/ Presentation of qualifications and record of experience, etc. by the design team.
4/ Questions from the members of the Committee.
5/ Summary by design team leader.
6/ Closing statement & "Thank you's" by Selection Committee leader.

While this schedule should not be rigorously adhered to, it does provide a framework for the interview sessions that focuses the greatest amount of time on the questions the Selection Committee wishes to have answered.

The interview session. Every effort should be made to achieve a relaxed atmosphere even though a schedule exists and the pending decision is crucial for the participants as well as the project. The person assuming leadership of the Selection Committee for the interview meetings can do much to set the proper atmosphere and pace. Knowing the agenda in advance will assure everyone concerned that there will be time for everything.

Following the introductions, the leader of the design team will make a presentation covering the firm's history, experience and qualifications. This presentation may include a brief overview of the firm's proposal, emphasizing certain aspects. Often this presentation will feature 35mm slides, overhead projections, or a video tape. Some firms will bring large posters or flip charts to illustrate certain points. Firms which employ public relations staff are apt to have very sophisticated productions that can overwhelm the unsuspecting.

Questioning begins when the presentation is finished. Using questions formulated in its work sessions, the committee members probe areas where written responses have not been sufficiently detailed or aspects which may need further explanation. Questions often begin with fairly routine queries which will be asked of each firm as a basis for making comparisons. These may include questions clarifying information in the proposals submitted in response to the RFP. Other questions follow as the committee members explore any new ground that emerges as a result of the presentation. Some questions will result from committee member perceptions and "feelings" about the design firm's responses. If possible, the responses to the questions should be noted in writing so that accurate reference can be made to them during the subsequent period of evaluation. Selection committee members often rotate in asking questions so that everyone gets an equal opportunity. However, this should not be a slavish routine which suppresses spontaneity from either group. The best impressions and information may come from a completely unscheduled but lengthy exchange that covers subjects not foreseen. While it is necessary to curb impromptu lectures on extraneous subjects, it is often helpful to allow for more than a strict question and answer approach.

With a warning that time is nearly up, the design firm's leader is asked to summarize his or her firm's qualifications and interest in the project. This may include questions needed to clarify the decision-making process and schedule, or other details. At the close of this summary, the Selection Team leader graciously thanks the design firm's personnel, indicating how the committee will proceed in making its decision and when the design firm will be notified of the committee's action.

The between-interview interval. If possible, interviews should be separated by intervals of 15 to 30 minutes to permit some latitude in the schedule and to allow a bit of time between interviews for the selection committee members to share their impressions and discuss changes in strategy, etc. These intervals can be most productive, for they allow the committee members to exchange views and questions while the interview and the personalities are fresh in mind. Sometimes new questions are posed for follow-up. To some extent, this is the time when the reactions of committee members can begin to jell. It is a time for reflecting on the question of how well the design firm members might work with the personnel who will represent the client.

Post-interview period. Most often the interview sessions leave the selection committee with one or two prime candidates standing clearly at the head of the list. While holding the others in abeyance, further in-depth reference checks should be done on these firms, unless these have already been completed.

If specific questions remain to be answered, the selection committee must move to resolve them by whatever means necessary. This may include a visit to the design firm's office, further research on past projects, and responses from additional references. Sometimes a second interview may be necessary, directed at specific points and/or limited to certain members of the design firm.

Final evaluation. After the interviews, reference checks and visitations have occurred, the time ultimately arrives for the Selection Committee to meet for the final evaluation. Often the choice is clear-cut. When this is not the case, each member of the selection committee should state his or her preference and the reasons therefor. Discussion will no doubt ensue and it is a wise selection committee chairperson who does not attempt to limit this unduly. Voting, preferably by written ballot, can take place after discussion wanes.

If the decision is still elusive, or lacks a reasonable consensus, a second round of interviews may be in order. This can be limited to the top one or two firms, or may be re-opened to all. During the second interview, the selection committee's questions must deal with those specifics which will help them make the final decision. Sometimes, the second interview is necessary—or at least desirable—to allow committee members a further opportunity for observing the personalities of the architects and to reevaluate the possibility of creating a working relationship capable of withstanding the rigors of the project for the long haul. Occasionally, visits can be made to the offices of the architects for the same beneficial reasons. In any case, the end result of the final evaluation effort is to identify the firm considered by the selection team as the most qualified to be recommended for or given the project assignment. However, even though that choice may become apparent at this point, the selection is not usually disclosed until other formalities have been met.

Considering the fee for architectural services. So far as possible, the fees to be paid for architectural services should not be a consideration in the selection process, although the basis for the fee in each applicant's case should be known. Selection should be on the basis of talent, experience and other merits rather than on cost.

Architects for many years followed a fairly uniform practice regarding fees and considered departure from the accepted fee schedule to be a breach of professional ethics. This historical practice is gradually being replaced by a trend toward fee negotiation. While many architects continue out of habit or preference to quote their fees as a percentage of project or construction costs, there is increasing latitude in the actual amounts. Moreover, certain states and various institutions and agencies have adopted strict fee limitations for architectural services. These must be understood and correctly interpreted where they are applicable.

To understand and to compare fee proposals, it is necessary that they be itemized in terms of services that are and are not to be provided, rather than considering only a total figure. For instance, one proposal may cover all or most engineering costs as part of its basic fee; another may include only certain in-house services, with the client paying extra for structural, electrical, mechanical and other specialized services. Where fee restrictions are in force, architectural fees may reflect even fewer services and can place limits on such necessary things as the number of sets of drawings furnished the client and the number of trips made to the job site—beyond these minimal numbers, the client will be expected to pay extra.

Therefore, once the field has been narrowed to one or two potential firms, it is time to reach a clear understanding of fees and what they cover. At this point the selection team will probably need the help of professionals who are well acquainted with architectural practice and can ask the questions necessary to get comparable information. Such questions will determine the scope of architectural and engineering services to be provided for a given fee and whether or not—or to what degree—such items as interior design, landscaping and construction supervision are to be covered. These items, along with many others, will become the basis for the actual contract negotiations. After this line of questioning has been completed, a comparison of fees can be made and this information given the Selection Committee members for their consideration.

The final choice. Once the selection committee has determined its choice, the recommendation usually has to be communicated to a governing or administrative body. If at all possible, the selection committee should limit its recommendation to a single choice; submitting two or more choices muddies the water and provides opportunities for lobbying and political interference. If the committee's first choice is not acceptable to the governing body, then there is time for reconsideration and submittal of an alternative.

In submitting the name of the recommended firm, the Selection Committee will want to emphasize certain positive reasons for their choice, such as:

1/ Design capability
2/ Rapport with Project Team members
3/ Willingness and ability to follow a building program
4/ Background and experience in similar projects
5/ Recommendations of former clients
6/ Capacity of the firm's personnel to handle the project
7/ Demonstrated ability to meet project budgets and schedules.

Once the final choice has been ratified by the governing body, formal announcement may be made to the public and to the architectural community. All firms responding to the RFP should be given formal notification and an additional word of thanks for their participation. Contract negotiations should begin immediately.

A *"last word" on design professional selection.* The space devoted to the discussion of design professionals in this text should underscore its importance to the project. As a "last word" of advice to those responsible for the selection process, every precaution must be taken to avoid being forced to accept firms which do not meet your criteria and needs. The selection committee must reserve the right from the beginning of the process to reject all candidates if none fill the bill; this fact should be included in the RFQ and RFP materials. Even though this means starting all over and incurring an unfortunate project delay, better this penalty than choosing a firm which does not have the selection committee's enthusiastic support and confidence. It is a much more affordable price to pay than that which would result from compromising on a choice that was incompatible with team members and/or less qualified than the project merits. In the long run, settling for second-best is almost certain to produce an inferior product with higher long-term costs.

Architectural Competitions

Although it is less frequently used, there is at least one other way to choose design professionals, known as the "design competition." The ostensible purpose of the design competition is to enable the client to choose an architect on the basis of an actual design for the proposed project. While experience and qualifications may also be taken into consideration, the design is the primary criterion. As desirable as this may appear to be, the design competition methodology involves a sophisticated process which can be time-consuming and difficult. A library wishing to consider a design competition should consult the local chapter of the American Institute of Architects on the recommended methodology.

Open architectural competitions may involve submittals from a broad spectrum of architects who respond to a general invitation. Other competitions, known as "invitational competitions," are confined to a smaller group of architects. Sometimes competitions are limited to a geographical area such as a state or defined region.

Design competitions are often proposed on the basis that submittals provide the client with tangible evidence of how an architect will actually design the project in question. Presumably, this eliminates conjecture about what the building will look like. On the other hand, since most competitions result in an emphasis on exterior design rather than internal functional relationships, the client's selection may force many compromises on function and internal environment which do not show up until it is too late, or too expensive, to change.

What is equally serious, once the client selects a particular design and the architect responsible for it, the client is limited in the modifications which can be accommodated without severely compromising design, increasing budget, and/or requiring major redesign with corresponding increases in professional fees and loss of time. Usually such obstacles can be more easily avoided when the normal progression of design has been followed, allowing possible shortcomings to be anticipated and resolved as the project evolves. All too often, design competitions result in projects being placed into a kind of design strait jacket, forcing internal solutions which require undesirable functional concessions.

In summary, while competitions may sometimes be appropriate, their value for library buildings is questionable. If seriously considered, a full evaluation should be made both of the process and the experience of those who have participated in design competitions. Such an investigation should include discussion with the appropriate office of the American Institute of Architects, which can provide valuable information and assistance including a recommended procedure. Because engaging in architectural competitions can be costly, many architectural firms will not enter them, or will limit participation to one or two projects each year.

Although still fraught with shortcomings, the invitational competition, rather than the open competition, seems to offer more advantages to the client determined on using the architectural competition as a means of selecting the design professionals.

Design competitions, despite their shortcomings, are almost certain to generate a great deal of publicity and public interest. They may be used to call attention to the local institution or community by attracting a firm of national reputation. However, publicity itself is insufficient reason for conducting an architectural competition when other, more advantageous methodologies exist.

Preparing the Architectural Agreement

The American Institute of Architects, working on behalf of its membership over the years, has evolved certain standard forms of agreement which have been thoroughly tested in court decisions. These are available through the regional offices of the American Institute of Architects as well as from the architect retained for the project. Unless there is some great, overriding reason to write an original contract, most clients will find it advantageous to adapt the appropriate standard form to their particular project needs. Because architectural services are so specialized, many of the provisions of the standard contract have been inserted because experience dictates their need to protect either the client or the architect—or both—from needless litigation in the event of adversities. This is particularly important in the present litigious atmosphere where suits over liability and other issues have become bitter and divisive products of many building projects.

If the client wishes to prepare an original contract, it should be done by an attorney experienced in this field. Sufficient time must be given these contract negotiations to satisfy all parties that the details have been resolved in the best possible manner.

Choosing the Interior Designer

While many architectural firms include interior design, in part at least, as one of the services they offer their clients, increasing numbers of libraries are turning to independent interior designers to supplement the talents of the architects. Some architects object to this for a variety of reasons, some good and some not so valid. The most important reason given for not separating the two design services is the need for coordinating architectural design with interior design: "the two should speak with a single voice," as someone has said.

Perhaps the most cogent reason for separating the two disciplines is that the interiors, more than the architectural design, influence space utilization and the functional operation of libraries. Because of the tremendous changes taking place in materials, furnishings, casework, signage, lighting, acoustics and other elements affecting interiors, it is imperative that these have the attention of a competent design professional who can devote full time to these important considerations. Moreover, by separating the interior budget from the architectural budget, the client can exercise more control over the selection of interior finishes, furnishings and equipment.

This must be carefully spelled out in the architectural contract. Bitter experience indicates that some architects may be willing to sacrifice quality interiors to achieve certain architectural effects. The quality of casework and carpeting may be downgraded, wall coverings reduced to paint, gypsum board walls substituted for ceramic tile in restrooms, and a hundred and one other compromises reached as a means of funding architectural embellishments that do nothing to enhance library functions and operations. Furniture and equipment budgets are sometimes reduced by a variety of means to perpetuate architectural clichés of the day that do little or nothing to provide efficient library service. For these reasons, it is important that the interiors be the provenance of a design professional, either architect or interior designer, who is devoted to the goal of completing a library building which will function effectively with minimum maintenance and replacement costs.

Interior Designers vs. Interior Decorators

Unlike architecture, interior design is a relatively new and evolving part of the design profession. There is no long-established professional organization such as the American Institute of Architects to monitor the emerging practitioners or to encourage comparable training, licensing, and procedures. At the moment, the group is self-divided into "interior decorators" and "interior designers." While the distinctions are somewhat unclear, the interior decorators tend toward residential and small-office work while interior designers are more often involved in large commercial, professional, industrial and public projects. Many interior designers are licensed architects; others have been schooled in architecture with supplementary coursework in interior design. A third group—again not well defined—consists of those engaged in contract furnishings. Their services to the client may be free or at a minimum cost since the bulk of their income is from the industries and vendors that supply the furnishings and other interior elements that they specify.

Interior Design Services

The role of the interior designer is not as well defined in the minds of most clients as is that of the architect. Too many equate interior design with decorations or embellishments. To some, it is merely a matter of selecting colors and bits and pieces of furniture. In actuality, interior design is much more than decoration; successful interior design involves the creation of exciting interior spaces which embody the functional requirements of the program and, at the same time, express the nature of the architectural design for the building. To accomplish this goal, the interior designer must understand and correctly interpret both the programmatic requirements for every area in the library and the subtleties of architectural design. Color, textures, lighting, graphics, and other elements are the integral tools used to achieve this objective.[4]

Whether supplied by an independent interior designer, the interior design department of an architectural firm, or by the architect, certain interior design services should be available to the client. As a minimum these include:

1/ Coordination of all interior design elements with architectural design.
2/ Layout of all furniture and equipment.
3/ Selection of all floor and wall coverings.
4/ Selection of all colors, textures, fabrics, paints, and similar items.
5/ Selection of all hardware for doors and windows.
6/ Selection of all general, task and special lighting.
7/ Selection of all graphics and signage for both interior and exterior.
8/ Ability to modify furniture and equipment designs as required for library operations.
9/ Design of all casework (cabinetry).
10/ Preparation of all drawings and specifications and bid packages related to interiors.
11/ Assistance in making decisions where vendors submit products they deem "equal" to those specified.
12/ Ability to provide accurate interior budget information, from the period of schematic drawings to the conclusion of bid documents.
13/ Familiarity with the purchasing procedures followed by public agencies or institutions as may be applicable in the case of the individual client.
14/ Supervision of the total interior installation.
15/ Follow-up service to rectify any problems.

The scope of the interior designer's role can be judged from the foregoing list of responsibilities. These, and some of their implications are discussed further in a later chapter.

Selecting the Interior Designer

The interior designer should be selected in the same manner and within the same time frame as the architect. Obviously, the questioning and investigation will run along slightly different lines. However, the preparation of the selection committee must be equally thorough and the process accomplished in the same orderly fashion. Stress must be placed on the compatibility of the interior designer and the architect. Both are professionals and both are artists with egos that are necessary to their work. They must work in harmony as a team. Some architectural firms covet interior design work because they have a real understanding of this field; others are concerned that an interior designer may plan interiors that might appear incompatible with the building's design theme. Still others have more selfish motives, knowing that control of the interior's budget can act as a contingency fund if money runs short. All of these factors, and more, will be considerations in the decision to select and retain an independent interior designer.

As with the architect, insist that those who appear for the interview are the same individuals you will work with during the project. Moreover, make certain that the work that is presented as representing the interior designer's efforts is the work of the interior designer being interviewed. Check to see if past assignments have been completed within budget and on time; lapses here may indicate inexperience or lack of staff as well as questionable competence. You should feel confident that the interior designer will develop an effective line of communications and will listen to you and your staff as the project proceeds. From other clients, learn how they were treated by the interior designer and whether staff suggestions, recommendations and directives were considered and used.[5]

Interior Design Fees

Fee practices of interior designers range from percentages of the interiors budget to a fixed fee based on an estimate of time and materials. Fees may be quoted on a cost per square foot basis, as well. These presently range from less than $1.50 per square foot to more than $3.00 per square foot depending upon the responsibilities delegated to the interior designer and the complexity of the project. Never to be considered is a fee in which payment is made in part or in whole by the future vendors of furniture, equipment and other interior items. Neither should fees be based on the value of furniture and equipment to be specified. While some manufacturers offer limited interior design services, these are not comparable to the services provided by a qualified interior design firm or interior design department of an architectural office. Contract negotiations may be based on the applicable AIA Standard Form.

Summary

This chapter has provided information on the roles played by the professionals who will bring the programming and planning of the building project to fruition: the library building consultant, the architect and the interior designer. Attention has been given to desirable qualifications and to the methodology for selection. These individuals and their cohorts, along with the client's representatives, comprise the project team which is discussed in the following chapter. The actual phases of architectural and interior design are set forth in Chapter 7.

Notes

1. Further information about the library building consultant and his or her selection can be found in the literature.

2. See Appendix F: "Questions for Architect's RFQ."
3. See Appendix G: "Typical Interview Questions."
4. Marshall Brown, an interior designer who has participated in various library conferences, offers this definition: "A successful interior is *far* more than decoration. It is the careful development of functional relationships and space planning to create responsive and visually exciting interiors that incorporate an expression of architectural design into all the construction details. Any successful building begins with the *understanding* and development of the workplace to be housed. . . . Successful buildings, which meet the test of time, are those which support and respond to the needs of their users, both during initial occupancy and subsequently as needs change! Designing from the *inside out* is an idea whose time has arrived. Interiors are now accepted as just as complex as architecture and must therefore encapsulate the same formal concerns."—In: Raymond M. Holt, ed. *Talking Buildings: A Practical Dialogue on Programming and Planning Library Buildings.* Proceedings of Building Workshops sponsored by the California State Library. (Sacramento: California State Library, 1986), p. 35.
5. Marshall Brown adds these criteria: "Verify that the interior designer worked enthusiastically as a member of the design team, contributing to a common goal. Isolationists are a handicap in the development of any project. Be certain that the interior designer responded quickly with clear solutions to any problems arising during the design, construction and installation, or even after occupancy. Look for a designer that sought new, innovative and cost-effective solutions to problems, and did not just accept the past experience with similar facilities. Look for a personality that you feel you will enjoy; the design and construction period will take several years of close association. . . . The interior designer should be a skilled professional having developed an independent understanding of the work environment and the psychological impact of the interior relationships of the built environment on users. Design is *never* applied, but results from the juxtaposition of architectural basics such as materials, light, and form."—*Ibid.*, p. 36.

VI THE PROJECT TEAM AND ITS MANAGEMENT

THE CONCEPT of the "project team" has emerged as buildings, including libraries, have become increasingly complex. Architects, on the one hand, often feel the need for more continuous contact with the client's representatives, while clients want the opportunity to participate in the design process. Membership on the project team will be determined by the local jurisdiction. Like any working group, it should be limited to those most intimately involved and willing to give substantial time to the project. Convincing arguments concerning the need for and validity of the project team approach, replete with examples, can be found in library literature. Particular help is available in the proceedings, published by the American Library Association, of various institutes and workshops sponsored by the Library Administration and Management Division of ALA (LAMA) which was formerly the Library Administration Division (LAD).[1]

Project Team Members and Their Roles

The composition of the project team will be determined by each jurisdiction in keeping with its needs and practices. The team members discussed in this section are typical. It is important that the project team include all of those required to develop the project—but none who might hinder this process.

It is likely that the Project Team will include most or all of the following:

1/ Client (Owner) representative
2/ Library representative
3/ Library Board or Committee representative
4/ Library Building Consultant
5/ Architect
6/ Interior Designer
7/ Project or Construction Manager (if used).

The first section of this chapter provides an overview of the team members and their relationship to the project. How the design professionals and the library con-

sultant may be selected is covered in the preceding chapter.

The Client (Owner) Representative

The client or owner of the project, which may be represented by the board of regents, board of trustees, city council, board of supervisors or other legal entity, holds the legal authority to authorize and finance the project and to hire project personnel. Since the client is apt to be a college, university, municipality, county or other jurisdiction, it is usually necessary to delegate responsibility to an individual who serves on the project team as the client's representative. In some instances this may be the librarian, but more often it is some other person from the jurisdiction's administrative office, public works department, facilities or physical plant office. The client representative is the official member of the team and the client. This person is often referred to as the "owner's representative" and is the official liaison for all project approvals and changes.

Librarian

As the future tenant of the project building, the librarian, by whatever title, should play a crucial and complex role as a member of the project team. Occasionally, the librarian will choose to delegate this responsibility to another staff member, perhaps one with greater experience in buildings. This may also occur if more than one library building is in progress or if the librarian does not think it wise to take the necessary time from other administrative duties.

While the exact responsibilities will vary from project to project, the librarian will generally be held responsible for information included in the building program statement and its interpretation. As the design develops, the librarian will determine how well it satisfies program requirements. In some instances, the librarian will also serve as the client's official representative. In this role, he or she will often be accountable for arranging for project team meetings, coordination with the agency personnel and departments interested in the project, and similar duties.

Library Board or Committee

Often the project team will include a member of the library board or library committee. While such a person can be very valuable, multiple representation from such groups can lead to a variety of complications, including loss of valuable time. Most difficult is finding a qualified person who will donate the large amount of time required for meetings, review and study. Project team meetings, for instance, are apt to run for one or more days at a time, in addition to meetings for presentation to officials, etc. Representatives should be able to attend project team meetings regularly and without too much personal sacrifice. While previous experience with building projects is desirable, qualifications should also include the ability to communicate ideas easily and to maintain a good working rapport with both the project team and the board or committee represented. If the client is officially represented by a board, committee or other group, this individual may also serve as the client's representative.

Library Building Consultant

As library projects have grown more complex, increasing use has been made of library building consultants. Since the library building consultant possesses a wealth of information and insight, he or she should be a key member of the project team. Of course the role will vary depending upon client need. Those experienced in working with library building consultants seem agreed, however, that the earlier the person is brought into the project, the better. Often this means that the library building consultant will be selected and at work for some time before other members of the project team are named. For instance, the library building consultant may be involved in such initial phases as needs assessment, site selection, and program preparation. Involvement may range from providing limited expertise to full responsibility for the preparation of the major documents. In many cases, the library building consultant may also be involved as an advisor during the process of selecting other project members, particularly the design professionals.

Working as a regular member of the project team, the library building consultant will offer a wide range of knowledge gleaned from previous experience and study. Usually the library building consultant will provide an effective communications bridge between library staff and the design professionals. In this role the library building consultant will attempt to translate complex or intricate library requirements into language familiar to the design professionals. By the same token, he or she can often help library staff understand architectural design concepts and building details.

The library building consultant's role as a member of the project team places a premium on communications skills and diplomacy. During the course of the project team meetings, the library consultant acts as a special information resource as well as an interpreter. As the exponent of the long-range viewpoint, the library building consultant must speak with integrity.

Such a role obviously demands the services of a person who can contribute the time and effort the project will require. This means that the scope of services agreed to by the library building consultant should be reasonably explicit. For instance, the consultant's contract should spell out responsibilities for participating in team meetings, preparing plan reviews, submitting comments on drawings and specifications, along with any other duties. If the cost of traveling to all team meetings seems prohibitive, then the contract should specify the number of such team meetings the consultant shall attend, the number of plan reviews to be submitted in writing and other details. A detailed review of drawings and specifications near the end of each major design phase will usually be included among these requirements.

The Architect

The formation of the project team usually follows immediately upon the selection of the architect. From this point forward the architect is the driving force of the design process. Usually the architect will supply the project schedule, setting the calendar deadlines for each phase of work. The frequency and length of project team meetings is customarily controlled by the architect. While the client representative or librarian may be the nominal chairperson for project team meetings, the architect will normally establish the agenda, lead the plan review process and subsequent discussion. During each project team meeting, the architect will be responsible for taking detailed notes which record all the matters covered by the group and indicate points of discussion, agreement and disagreement. These meeting notes will also record the steps to be taken for resolving particular issues, show who is responsible for pending items and when such matters are to be presented again. At the end of each session, the architect will be responsible for editing, duplicating and distributing copies of these meeting notes to all project team participants in a timely manner—often within two to three days. All project team members are expected to read and respond immediately to the meeting notes to avoid undue delay.

Except for very large projects, the architect is likely to represent the various engineering skills at most project team meetings. However, engineers from the architect's staff (structural, mechanical, electrical, etc.) or the consulting engineers on the project may meet with the project team when certain crucial issues must be solved or certain stages of plan development are reached. It is unlikely that any of these people will be regular members of the project team, per se.

Interior Designer

Like the architect, the interior designer should be an integral part of the project team. He or she should begin attending meetings as early as possible. If the interiors are to be provided by the architect rather than by an independent interior designer, then the office specialist for interiors should be present. As the work progresses, the interior designer will have the responsibility for testing the design by laying out the furniture and equipment indicated in the building program. Such layouts will be explained by the interior designer during the project team meetings. The interior designer will, like the architect, make detailed notes and supply these to project team members for their study and comment.

After the schematic design has been approved, it is likely that more time will be spent by the project team on review of the interiors than on the architecture itself. Nonetheless, it is important that the architect be present for all such sessions to interpret the intent of the architectural design and to help solve any conflicts which may arise between architecture and interiors.

Other Project Team Participants

While the foregoing roster lists the essential project team members, other individuals may be involved. For instance, a member of the library faculty committee and/or a facilities management person may be members in an academic situation. Public libraries, on the other hand, may elect to add other team members rep-

resenting the library board, the library staff and/or the community. (Sometimes a representative may be from the Friends of the Library or a similar organization.) These individuals provide input from their particular vantage points as library workers or library users.

In making these additional appointments it is important to stress that this is a working relationship—not an honorary post. Those selected should meet the same requirements as others for attendance and response to project notes, etc. Particular care should be taken in appointing someone to represent the staff. Selection should be done as democratically as possible. Time for attending team meetings and responding to meeting notes, etc. should be provided. In larger libraries, a library building staff committee may be appointed to serve as an advisory body, especially for those elements which have broad interest and involvement. The chairperson of such a committee may then be named to the project team or may be invited to attend on those occasions when matters of particular importance, such as staff facilities, are to be discussed.

Project or Construction Management

In recent years a new group of professionals has entered the project scene. They are often referred to as construction or project management. Construction management originated in the need for overall supervision of very large and complex projects. The goal of construction management is to see that projects adhere to schedules and budgets, especially during actual construction. Unless a library building is extremely complicated, or a part of a much larger project, it is unlikely that construction management will be necessary or cost effective under normal circumstances. However, if the client chooses to involve construction management during the design phase, it is quite likely that its representative will be given the authority to manage the project team.

Project Team Management

As pointed out earlier, the role of the librarian may range from serving as the owner's representative to a narrower responsibility limited to providing expertise on library functions and needs. Whatever the degree of involvement, the librarian needs to understand some of the facets of project team management.

Contract Administration

Each of the firms retained by the client for the project will require a contract. These documents are apt to be fairly involved, but it is important that the librarian be familiar with the terms of each contract so as to understand the placement of responsibilities. Architects and interior designers frequently prefer to use contracts formulated by the American Institute of Architects (AIA). This is often beneficial to the client, as well, since the provisions of these contracts have been tested in court and, through frequent revision, tend to anticipate and thereby prevent possible difficulties during the project.

The client will need to authorize someone to serve as the contract administrator. This designation is usually routine and a normal part of the duties of a particular office maintained by the institution or agency. Among other responsibilities, the contract administrator must make certain that all team members under contract perform in accordance with the terms of their agreements. Where necessary, the contract administrator will propose contract amendments to fill in voids, correct overlapping responsibilities and address other changes. The contract administrator usually, among other duties, reviews work as it progresses and certifies that work billed for has been satisfactorily completed. If questions arise as to the authorized scope of work, the contract administrator is often the interpreter. While the librarian is not likely to serve as contract administrator, it is well to understand the scope of responsibility and authority carried by this person.

Understanding the exact provisions of the contracts can prove very helpful and can prevent misunderstandings as work proceeds. Remember that those under contract take the provisions of their respective agreements very seriously. Although they may interpret certain provisions rather liberally, they cannot afford to provide every possible service or end product that the client may conceive of during the course of the project. For this reason, most contracts can be amended to cover special services on a reimbursement basis. The librarian should know what services are and are not covered by the basic fee and what money the client might need to make available for additional service. Among the contract limitations or exclusions, the following are apt to appear:

1/ The number of copies of drawings, specifications, etc. the architect and/or interior designer is to provide.
2/ The number of trips to be made to the client's office and site.

3/ Cost of preparing renderings, mock-ups, models, photographs, etc.
4/ Special studies or engineering work which exceed normal requirements such as life-cycle cost analysis, acoustical engineering, etc.
5/ Hiring consultants from special disciplines such as acoustics, lighting, materials handling, life safety, unless specifically provided for.
6/ Systems and materials testing.

By fully understanding contract restrictions such as these, the librarian can better cooperate with the design professionals and work within the terms of their agreements.

The Librarian's Role

As noted above, the role of the librarian will be defined by the client. It is imperative that the responsibilities be carefully delineated; the librarian must know what the boundaries of his or her responsibility and authority are in order to play the project team role properly. Too often it is the case that the librarian has not been fully informed of his or her responsibilities nor made aware of the amount of time and energy that will be required. Facility planning requires the dedication of large blocks of time and cannot be successfully accomplished as an add-on to an already full schedule.

The librarian on the project team must be prepared for an endless number of meetings proceeding on a relentless schedule. Across the desk will flow a torrent of meeting notes, drawings, correspondence, budgets, schedules, specifications, check lists and other items which must be read, responded to and filed for possible reference in the future. In dealing with design professionals and other consultants, remember that their time is money. Among other things, they expect that meeting participants will be fully prepared to participate in discussions with all necessary resources in hand. Any decisions which were to be made in the period following the previous work session should have been made as per schedule. If other staff are to be involved in special areas, they need to be available on a few moments' notice and come briefed and ready to participate.

On larger projects, team meetings and other project affairs may require so much of the librarian's time that he or she will find it necessary to delegate to other staff a portion of the otherwise normal administrative workload. While the project team and the general process are exciting opportunities, they consume enormous amounts of time and energy. Nonetheless, full participation by the library's representative is imperative if the project is not to be adversely affected.

It is especially important for the librarian to understand scheduling requirements that relate to decision making. Many a project has been delayed because there was a misunderstanding about when a particular decision had to be made in order to maintain the design schedule. Team members who do not understand, or ignore, the realities of the design process are most apt to be offenders.

Changes become increasingly time-consuming and expensive as work proceeds. During schematics, for instance, only a few sheets of drawings are involved when a change is made. Even far-reaching modifications in design can be accomplished by redrawing parts of one or two sheets. Later in the process, even a simple change may affect dozens of drawings including those of the consulting engineers as well as the architectural sheets. Failure to make timely decisions is exacerbated by team members who make only tentative decisions and insist on these being subject to reconsideration at a more advanced stage of work. Unless clearly agreed to by all concerned, the design professionals have no logical alternative to assuming that each team decision can be taken as final. Similarly, team members have a right to assume that changes that are agreed to by the design professionals will be adhered to in future drawings. Close readings of team meeting notes and careful review of plans are the means for confirming these results.

The librarian should insist that the project team be provided at the outset with clear guidelines concerning deadlines for decisions affecting design. What changes are permissible during each of the major design phases should be delineated by the architect, along with a description of the consequences of decisions and changes that occur after these deadlines pass. This is apt to include added design fees. In this regard, it will be helpful for the librarian to read Chapter 14: "Techniques of Plan Analysis."

Using Project Team Time Effectively

As the future tenant of the library facility, the librarian has much at stake. Therefore, he or she should do everything possible to make project team meetings productive. This means effectively discharging certain responsibilities:

1/ Faithful and punctual attendance at all project team meetings.

2/ Prompt reading of all meeting memoranda, notes, minutes, etc., with timely response as required.

3/ Arrange commitments to avoid interrupting team meetings with telephone calls.

4/ Prompt decision making when called for.

5/ Expedient response to all requests for clarification of program data or for additional information.

6/ Careful review of drawings and specifications against the approved building program requirements, calling attention to deviations.

7/ Urge prompt reconciliation of deviations of drawings and specifications from program requirements.

8/ Return telephone calls promptly.

9/ Limit involvement of other library staff—project team meetings are not to be used for staff training purposes.

10/ When other staff are to be involved in meetings because of their special viewpoint or expertise, make certain they are fully aware of their responsibilities and have been briefed on team protocol and on the latest version of the drawings.

11/ Do not send staff to project team meetings as observers; extra people in the room may hamper the progress of the meetings.

12/ Ask questions! If you do not understand a drawing, presentation, recommendation, technical term, team member's comment or other item, say so immediately and ask for clarification; otherwise your silence may be mistaken for understanding and approval.

13/ If you can not attend a team meeting, alert team members as far in advance as possible so that the meeting may be rescheduled.

14/ If you choose to have another staff member attend meetings with you, be certain that he or she is aware of the limits of their participation and that the team members, likewise, understand; without such understanding, the design professionals may get confused signals and directions.

A few more words about library staff participation in team meetings may be in order. On the one hand, staff members often know their own areas, procedures and needs better than anyone else. For this reason, they can sometimes provide valuable assistance to the project team. However, staff participation can also result in confusion and even embarrassment when a person uses the project team meeting as a forum for his or her own convictions or ideas. Staff members may appear to have convincing arguments supporting their recommendations. Their personalities coupled with determination may impress project team members whether their arguments are right or wrong in the view of the librarian. At such times it is likely to be difficult for the librarian to argue a different course of action. Project team meetings are not the place to reprimand staff or to counter their views with debate. Nor is it always possible to correct the situation by indicating that the staff member does not fully understand the situation or plan, or may be making erroneous assumptions about how the library will operate in a remodeled, expanded or new facility. To avoid the possibility of confusing other team members and loss of valuable time, it is best to keep staff participation to a minimum and directed to very specific ends.

Team Meeting Locations

Team meetings should be held amid appropriate surroundings, preferably in the library. Be certain that the meeting room is available for the scheduled time—moving from one room to another during a team session is disconcerting and a waste of time. The architect will require a large table on which to unroll drawings. It should be at least three feet wide and six feet long, and an even larger table is preferable. Lighting above the table should be satisfactory for reading drawings. The room should be reasonably quiet and free of obtrusive traffic. Arrange for one staff member to be responsible for taking calls and relaying messages in a competent and orderly manner. Anticipate that team members are likely to need access to a phone during team meetings. While there should be a phone in an adjacent room, none should be in the meeting room. Tackable wall surfaces and a blackboard will be helpful. If the meeting is to go through the noon hour, make arrangements early in the day for food and beverages to be brought in. If you act as host or hostess, it is your responsibility to see that arrangements for team meetings are complete and that normal hospitality is provided.

Responding to Requests for Information and Review

Participation as a member of the Project Team requires acceptance of many new responsibilities. Not the least of these is timely response to requests for information, prompt decision making and expeditious review of drawings and specifications. This ultimately involves schedule deadlines that the librarian must in-

corporate into his or her daily routine. Librarians who have not had prior building project experience are often unpleasantly surprised if not overwhelmed, by the amount of material submitted for review as well as the time required for researching and making decisions, and for preparing responses to specific questions. If a suggested deadline seems impractical, notify team members immediately and offer an alternative date. Otherwise, design professionals have the same right to expect the librarian to meet their schedules as you do to have them comply with the detailed project calendar.

Delays in providing added program information, clarifying a particular situation, answering a specific question or making a pertinent decision can be critical to a project schedule. If the librarian fails to meet these requirements, the project schedule is likely to be jeopardized and work postponed, or worse, design work continued without the librarian's valuable input. Special attention should be given to the time required to react to drawings and specifications. The "window of availability" for making changes is always limited, and grows more so as design proceeds.

In many cases the librarian will want to have key staff members review certain portions of the plans, which will take added time. Your intended review process with staff should be discussed with the team so that sufficient time is allowed for this critical part of the work. (See Chapter 14 for more details on plan analysis.)

Money for "Extra Services"

During the course of planning, special needs or opportunities are likely to arise which will be lost unless funds are available for them. Librarians need to identify in advance possible sources for such funds. These may be used in many ways. For instance:

1/ Most architectural contracts provide for only one or two renderings; you may wish to have additional renderings, perhaps of a special entry or interior area.

2/ If the architect's contract provides only for study models, you may want a finished or presentation model of the entire building or a portion thereof.

3/ A full scale "mock-up" of one or more critical areas may be needed for thorough study, such as a circulation desk, a reference desk, or a prototype work station for technical services.

4/ Additional engineering services may be warranted in such fields as acoustics, lighting, automation, media or security.

5/ Promotional items such as additional renderings or special drawings of interior spaces may be needed as adjuncts to a fund-raising campaign.

Knowing that funds are available for such services, should the need arise, can avoid delay and, possibly, the loss of a rare opportunity.

Communications

Library staff and others vitally concerned with the project must be kept fully informed about the progress of the project. This is an important responsibility and one that is not always easy to accomplish. At the outset, everyone anxiously awaits news of progress and can understand the initial steps with little difficulty. However, as the work proceeds, project development tends to become more complicated. Events, including delays, may not always be easily explained. The lines of communication may fray as the librarian has less and less time to relate what is happening. (A library that includes a public relations specialist who can take on this responsibility is most fortunate.)

A part of the difficulty can be avoided by anticipating the need for a vehicle for communicating information about the project in a timely fashion. For the small library this may be as simple as tacking notes on the bulletin board as events occur. For larger libraries, there may be a regular feature in the weekly staff newsletter or a special bulletin devoted entirely to the project and issued as needed. Whatever the vehicle, it is up to the librarian to see that the staff is kept informed. Otherwise, be prepared for speculation and misinformation as the staff attempts to invent answers for questions raised by the users of the library.

One of the more pervasive difficulties is in determining what news should be conveyed, and when it should be released. Many items discussed during the typical planning session may be speculative or inconclusive. Exciting ideas come and go as they are tested against budget and design realities. Premature release of such information can prove unfortunate and must be guarded against. Nonetheless, a continuous stream of accurate and timely project information is due the staff and the librarian must strive toward this goal.

Summary

The librarian has a vital role to play as a member of the project team. While the responsibilities may vary from serving as the owner's representative to a more limited part, the success of the librarian's participation will depend upon knowledge of the project team concept and processes. If the librarian serves as the leader of the project team, this understanding becomes crucial. There are many things which the librarian can do to help smooth the way of project team meetings. These range from prompt decision making to providing a good meeting place and normal hospitality. The librarian is further charged with the responsibility for staff participation and for keeping the staff informed about progress of the project. All of these responsibilities are important and must be added to other duties, making for a very full schedule.

Notes

1. For further views on the Project Team, see "Putting the Planning Team Together" by Nancy R. McAdams, in *Talking Buildings. . .* , edited by Raymond M. Holt (Sacramento: California State Library, 1986), pp. 11–17, and "Planning Team for Library Buildings" by Gloria Novak, in *Planning Library Buildings*, edited by Lester K. Smith (Chicago: American Library Association, 1986), pp. 43–55.

VII ARCHITECTURAL AND INTERIOR DESIGN PHASES

ENTERING the architectural design phase of a library building project marks a milestone of some proportions. Many important steps have been completed by this time, including programming, site studies and the selection of the design professionals. Funding may also have been established. Receiving the "go-ahead" for architectural development manifests the institution or agency's commitment to the project. The project team, described in the preceding chapter, is now assembled and ready to go to work. What is to be accomplished during this period and how the librarian may interface with the design development period is the subject of this chapter.

Overview of the Architectural and Interior Design Phase

Because the development of architectural and interior design concepts, drawings and specifications are interrelated, they are dealt with together in this chapter. The first section of the chapter will describe the course of architectural design, the second will be devoted to interior design, though work in actuality should be virtually concurrent. The need for close coordination of architectural and interior planning should emerge as the chapter progresses.

The Architectural Design Phase

The architectural design phase begins with the assimilation of the building program and site studies. From this foundation, the architect establishes a design concept which may be shown in a simple single-line drawing indicating the outline of the building and the proposed location of its major internal functions. One or more elevations will be drawn to show the general appearance of the exterior. When the concept has been approved, work proceeds through the following phases:

1/ Schematics
2/ Design development (Preliminaries)
3/ Construction documents (sometimes referred to as contract documents or working drawings).

The final stage, construction documents, provides the detailed drawings and specifications required by the building contractor to finalize the cost of the project and to construct the building. Incidentally, interior design work follows the same sequence with similar schedules and deadlines.

In most instances, moving from one phase to the next requires review and approval of the work completed to that point. The librarian, as well as other members of the project team, should view this transition seriously. Giving approval to proceed to the next phase means acceptance of the previous phase. To gain that approval, the librarian must insist that *all* of the problems have been worked out satisfactorily. If there are acceptable reasons why this cannot be done, then it is imperative that an agreement be reached *in writing* with the architect, indicating to the client how these problems will be resolved to the library's satisfaction as the first order of business in the new phase.

Failure to reach such an understanding may result in one of several unfortunate situations: 1/ the problems are never adequately resolved; 2/ solutions are postponed until the most desirable options are precluded by various factors; 3/ the librarian is forced to accept solutions which compromise the requirements established in the building program; or 4/ the design professionals invoke contract provisions that permit them to make extra charges for the services required to solve the problems. Incidentally, such charges can be quite significant and raise havoc with the project budget.

No matter what constraints the design schedule may impose, the librarian should seek to defer approval for moving to the next stage until program requirements have been met or alternatives agreed upon. Warnings of dire consequences should the schedule be revised are probably much less a threat to the project than accepting unwanted compromises in library capacity or function. Many factors motivate design professionals, some of which may not always be in the best interests of the client. Standing firm on issues of substance is important. Do not accept excuses at this point. The conclusion of each phase must be viewed as a "go - no go" situation which provides the client with an opportunity to force compliance to program requirements. One hopes, of course, that this will not be necessary.

Initial Steps

Once the design professionals have been added to the project team, a meeting is usually held for the purposes of project organization and review of the building program. If the building program has not been distributed previously, it should be given to each member at this meeting. Then, the person responsible for the preparation of the building program should provide a detailed oral review of the document. This should begin with a description of how the building program has been prepared, what it covers, and how it is intended to be used. Attention should be focused on the various areas where special requirements pertain. An informal atmosphere will be helpful in encouraging questions and a free-wheeling discussion. If a project budget has already been established, the project team will want to discuss its relevancy to the building program in terms of how much space and what quality of construction and interiors can be reasonably supported by available funds.

Project scheduling will also be a topic for this first meeting. If they have not already done so, the architects should be encouraged to produce a detailed project schedule using a Critical Path Method (CPM), or similar means to establish benchmarks of project progress and key dates including those for project team meetings. This schedule will provide target dates for the completion of the three major phases of architectural development and for placing the project out to bid. More sophisticated CPM schedules will integrate schedules for the various engineering and other specialists. While it may be revised from time to time, an official schedule is an essential document for the project.

The first Project Team meeting offers an ideal opportunity for the exchange of important information about key individuals who will be concerned with various stages of the project, as well as review procedures by official bodies. Some of the personnel to be identified include members of the design professional's staff; others will be agency or institution officials, employees in special capacities or other persons important to the project. For the client, these might include such people as the Fire Marshal, Building Code Official, Facilities Officer, members and staff of boards and commissions which may have some plan review responsibility, and administrative staff whom the design professionals may have reason to contact. Much time can be saved in the future if the librarian has prepared a roster of these names with telephone numbers, commission and board meeting dates, office hours, etc. This should include the roster of design professionals, engineers, and other consultants or specialists likely to be involved in the project.

Site Information

In most instances the client has the responsibility for making available to the architect all relevant site information. This is likely to include a current site survey map, a map showing utilities, a topographic map of the site and, possibly, soil test results. If the project includes a building which is to be remodeled and/or expanded, the client must provide all available architectural, mechanical, structural and electrical drawings and other data such as specifications. If possible, the set of drawings should represent "as built" drawings, corrected and annotated to show both changes which occurred during the construction process and subsequent changes. The architects will indicate any other information requirements vital to the beginning of their work. If a site survey has not been completed by the client, or if such drawings are not available, creating them will become a first order of business. Unless otherwise stipulated in the contract, the architect will receive an additional fee if he or she provides services of this kind.

Schematic Phase

The first phase of architectural development is generally referred to as "Schematics." At the outset of this period, the design professionals absorb the building program and gradually convert the program information into a variety of diagrams and studies. Simultaneously, the architects are reviewing site data and determining the relationship of the building to the site, considering the mass and styles of neighboring structures, landscaping and other elements.

Conceptual drawings showing the mass and location

of the building on the site are created as the process continues. These initial studies in massing and siting are crucial to the eventual design and should be fully understood by project team members. Sometimes it is necessary for the client to choose between two or more possible solutions at this stage.

Single line schematic drawings follow. These delineate the outline of the proposed structure and divide the space into major functions roughly correlated with programmed space requirements. Again, choices may have to be made as various solutions are applied to determine the optimal way library space can be organized.

Architectural practice varies considerably in the amount of time and attention devoted to the schematic phase. Some firms devote a substantial part of their total effort to this initial work, attempting to solve as many problems here as possible and to gain complete acceptance of the design solution by the client. Other firms place less emphasis on schematics and are willing to assume that their solution is sufficiently flexible to allow fairly extensive changes at a later stage. Of the two approaches, the first appears to give the client more control over the process and is more likely to produce a building representative of the program requirements. While the second methodology seems to move the project forward at a faster pace, once the schematic phase has been accepted the client must work within it, regardless of how badly flawed it may later prove to be. No matter what promises may be made, there is a reluctance to make any more changes than are necessary, once the basic design has been agreed to.

As schematic planning proceeds, the architects will produce a variety of drawings ranging from site plans and floor plans to exterior elevations and sections. The elevations show what the building will look like from each side, while the sections, like slices through a jelly roll, show some of the more critical interior dimensions and concepts. (See Chapter 14 for a further description of the various types of drawings.)

The initial layout of furniture and equipment should also occur as part of the schematic phase. This will be provided either by the design architect or by the interior designer, depending upon contractual responsibilities. Since the interior layout of furniture and shelving begins to give the project familiar dimensions, it is especially important to the project team. The plan's capacities for shelving, seating, and other furniture and equipment can now be tested against programmatic requirements. Traffic flow and functional relationships can also be traced. (See Chapter 14 for details of plan analysis techniques.)

Of all the parts the librarian can play in the unfold-

ing drama, the most crucial is this initial comparison of program requirements with capacities illustrated by the early layouts of furniture and equipment. Call it "proof of the pudding," perhaps, or "time to fish or cut bait." With the assistance of the library consultant, the librarian should very carefully account for every book stack and every piece of furniture, using the building program as a checklist. Dimensions must be measured closely to determine aisle widths, table sizes, length of shelving ranges, etc. This will be complicated because chances are the drawing will be at $\frac{1}{16}''$-scale, making accuracy difficult. While the arrangement of furniture and equipment, including shelving, will probably change in future layouts, the overall capacity is not apt to increase. What you have in the way of capacity shown in the schematics is what you are likely to be lucky to achieve in the actual building. Subsequent stages are more apt to reduce than to increase space.

Once this comparison of program requirements to the schematics has been completed, it should be incorporated into an informal report. Any shortcomings should be brought to the attention of the design professionals at the very first opportunity. Referring back to an earlier discussion in this chapter, the librarian must stand fast at this point until satisfied that each deficiency has been dealt with. Note, however, that this does not necessarily mean that it is always realistic to assume that every program requirement will be realized. Sometimes program requirements exceed the boundaries of reality as established by site, budget and other constraints. When this occurs, the librarian's job is to induce the best compromise possible under the circumstances. This may range from giving up something with a lower priority to postponing a certain feature to a future time. Virtually every building contains innumerable compromises; the best buildings are those in which the compromises have been chosen most wisely.

Toward the end of the schematic phase the architect will submit a set of outline specifications. These are rather general descriptions of building materials, mechanical, electrical and structural systems and other details. While they are subject to change, much can be learned even from these early specifications.

The schematic phase often includes a rendering and one or more models of the project. Renderings are like official portraits and are usually done in watercolors to show the building in its most pleasing perspective. Models, on the other hand, are more often created at this stage for the purpose of studying the relation of the building's mass to the site and possibly to other adjacent structures. Other models of larger scale may be prepared later on to assist in understanding the functional relationships of internal spaces in three dimensions.

Such models are often helpful in studying access, traffic flow and space allocation to various functions.

When the architect has completed the schematic phase a full set of plans, outline specifications and a cost estimate will be submitted for review. There will be several sheets of drawings including a site plan, layout of each floor, exterior elevations from each side of the building, and two or more sections, or slices, through the building, taken at right angles to one another. The cost estimate may have been prepared "in house" or by a cost-estimating firm. While it is essential that a cost estimate be produced at this juncture, the reliability of the figures is sometimes questionable because so many cost factors remain to be determined. Design professionals are fully aware of this and do their best to include a variety of estimates and contingencies to balance these unknowns. On large projects, especially, the librarian should consider having the cost estimate reviewed by a qualified third party. Cost estimating is an involved process which requires quantities of current construction data, including labor and materials. Having assurance that the cost estimate is essentially correct and that the project is within budget is well worth the extra expense for the estimator's service. If this process raises serious questions or doubts, they should be addressed immediately, well before the project proceeds any further.

For all intents and purposes, work on the project ceases until the client authorizes the architect to proceed with the next phase. Such authorization should be in writing and should include a list of all items about which there are questions and/or requirements for change. It is the project team's responsibility to produce this review document. If the schematic drawings and specifications are found substantially deficient, the architect should be required to make necessary revisions and re-submit the documents for another round of review. Where woeful inadequacies exist, the wisest choice may be to insist upon the architect abandoning the plans and beginning over with a new concept. Sometimes, no matter how promising it may seem at the outset, a given design will fail to bring one to the desired destination!

Once in a very long while, it may become evident at this juncture that the design professionals are unlikely to produce a satisfactory solution. Although this is a bitter pill, it is better to terminate the contract and start afresh with another firm than to continue on a path that seems almost certain to lead to disappointment and the expenditure of irreplaceable funds on a building that cannot meet basic programmatic requirements. Allowing the architect to proceed with faulty or inadequate schematic drawings as the basis for further design is a serious mistake and is almost certain to lead to expensive revisions, costly delays, worrisome frustration, and a potentially deficient building.

Design Development

When the schematic drawings and specifications have been approved, the design professionals are instructed in writing to proceed to the next phase of work: Design Development. (This is sometimes known as the Preliminary Phase.) As the term "design development" implies, this stage of work is devoted to expanding the work represented by the schematic drawings. Walls, which may be represented in the schematics by a single line, become double lines as dimensions are tightened. All interior partitioning is drawn and fenestration (windows) and doors are inserted in their proper places. Work is coordinated with structural, mechanical and electrical engineering consultants. Each of these determine which systems offer the most effective solutions for the building and what trade-offs must occur in the planning. The bay, or module, dimensions are verified for structural efficiency. (If changed much from the schematics, this can result in significant modification of the interiors, including capacities for shelving and seating.) Informal discussions with building officials, fire marshals and other officials occur to work out details which enable the building plan to conform to the governing codes. Adjustments are made to the interior package as the design evolves. Budget information is updated to reflect changes in materials and systems and to take advantage of more detailed information resulting from design development.

"Progress prints" are issued periodically during this phase to show how problems have been resolved. These may come as individual sheets if only a small area is concerned, or may be in fairly complete sets. About mid-way in this phase, the first drawings from the structural, mechanical and electrical engineers may be released for review. They will show the proposed systems in embryonic development. Both the architectural and engineering drawings should be reviewed carefully, with comments recorded and sent to the design professionals. Usually these review comments are then the subject of the next project team meeting.

When completed, the design development drawings and specifications along with a revised and more detailed cost estimate are submitted for formal review and approval. Again, it is the project team's responsibility to review these documents thoroughly and to provide a detailed list of questions, suggestions, and recommendations for further modification. If these are relatively minor and can be handled in the final stage of architectural work, the architects will be given written notice to proceed. On the other hand, if the documents are found inadequate, then the architect must revise them, resubmitting them for review before consent can be given to continue.

Delay in many cases is the result of budget estimates which place the project beyond available fund limits. Sometimes this can be resolved by having additional cost estimates prepared which provide less adjustment for inflationary factors and reduce contingencies. If this fails, it will be necessary to raise additional funds, or more likely, revise the drawings and specifications to reduce costs. This process can take several forms or combinations thereof:

1/ Reduce the total square footage to be constructed.
2/ Reduce the quality of building materials and systems.
3/ Leave a portion of the space unfinished.
4/ Delete a part of the building and indicate that it will be added at a later date.
5/ Create a series of additive and/or deductive alternatives.

Since the design development stage represents the last phase in which significant change in plans can normally be accommodated, it behooves the members of the project team to take sufficient time to study these documents in order to assure themselves that desired modifications will be made. Failure to do so may result in significant flaws which can not be corrected without expensive redesign amendments to the architect's contract and the loss of valuable time.

Construction Documents (Working Drawings)

When the design development documents are approved and written notice to proceed has been given, the architects enter the final phase of design, known variously as Working Drawings or Construction Documents, which are often referred to as "CDs." Whatever they may be called, the goal is to prepare a set of drawings and specifications sufficiently detailed to permit a building contractor to estimate accurately the cost of materials and labor and then to proceed to construct the project.

At this point, detailed drawings must be produced for architectural, structural, mechanical and electrical elements of the building. This requires close coordination by the architect. The complexity of the process can be illustrated by the fact that a project which was represented by a half-dozen or so sheets of drawings and 25–50 pages of specifications at the conclusion of schematic design will now require 75–100 sheets of drawings, while the specifications are likely to appear in several volumes of 500–600 pages each. This evolution carries with it the fact that what were once minor changes—move a partition a few inches this way or that, for instance—now becomes a complex procedure involving modifications to many sheets of drawings including alterations to the architectural, structural, mechanical and electrical sheets representing the exact area involved. What could have been accomplished with a stroke of the eraser and a simple pencil line during schematics, now involves hours of work for many people.

Depending on the project and the practice of the individual firm, there are usually two or three review points during the construction drawing phase. These occur roughly at the time the drawings represent a given percentage of completion. One of the more common schedules calls for review at approximately 50% of completion and at 90% of completion. The 50% benchmark is chosen because it represents a point at which minor changes can still be made and coordinated with all of the engineering drawings and specifications.

When approved, these construction drawings and specifications are ready for building contractors to use as a basis for submitting a bid to construct the project.

Cost Estimates and Value Engineering

Cost estimates and their importance were introduced in the paragraphs concerning the schematic phase. More refined cost estimates should be presented at the close of design development and again as part of the construction documents. They are an important tool and the librarian must become as familiar with them as with the library's own budget.

Keeping a project on track with its intended budget is one of the more difficult tasks of the project team. While the actual cost is never known until the work has been completed, nonetheless there are certain steps which should be taken to avoid unpleasant surprises. The cost estimates produced and submitted to the project team as a part of each of the architectural phases are essential to this process. Because the number of variables decreases as each phase is completed, the accuracy of the cost estimates should grow with the conclusion of each stage of architectural development.

While the cost estimates will usually carry contingency factors, the actual amount of the contingencies should be reduced in each phase.

Architects often furnish cost estimates worked out in their own offices. If the client does not have in-house access to a department or individual with equal expertise and current knowledge of construction costs, a separate estimate should be sought from an independent cost-estimating firm. While not necessarily more accurate or authoritative, such independent cost estimates provide a further benchmark for checking. Incidentally, most cost estimates are built on quantitative take-offs and unit prices: x number of bricks @ $ = $$$ for bricks. Because cost estimates are often done under severe time constraints, mathematical errors of significant proportions are not unknown; all math should be assiduously checked for possible mistakes. Similarly, calculations to determine quantities are likewise subject to error and deserve independent collaboration by a knowledgeable person in the construction field.

Before leaving the subject of costs, the concept of value engineering should be mentioned. In essence, value engineering attempts to determine whether or not the materials and systems recommended by the architect are the most cost-effective available for the job. Theoretically, value engineering considers life-cycle costs as well as first costs. Consultants versed in value engineering can help the client decide whether a particular material or system will result either in long-term savings or in special maintenance costs and end up being more expensive. For this reason, clients often choose to submit drawings and specifications to a qualified value engineering firm at periodic intervals as part of cost-estimating and control procedures.

An additional observation about the effect of alternatives seems pertinent. Alternatives are often used as a hedging device by architects, especially when the bidding climate is uncertain. They may also be used when an architect is uncertain about the effect a desired "architectural feature" such as an atrium or specially designed detail may have on the bids. Alternatives may also be used to determine the relative cost of two or more structural or lighting systems, or exterior finishes. Sometimes alternatives specifying less expensive materials may be used as a device to save money that can be spent for a cherished architectural enhancement which may or may not be justifiable in terms of library objectives. Occasionally, alternatives may provide a cushion against the results of inadequate cost-estimating procedures. Whenever cheaper materials are included, the librarian must be particularly concerned, for these are almost always subject to higher maintenance costs or earlier replacement. In every case, the librarian must carefully weigh all proposed alternatives in terms of library goals and long-term costs.

Bid Documents

The final set of approved contract documents later become the "Bid Documents" once they have received official approval. This means that all corrections and changes resulting from the final review have been included and new sets of drawings and specifications produced. To complete the bid document set, a section is added to the specifications providing bidders with the forms and other information they need for determining their bid and submitting it to the client (see Chapter 8). The bid documents form the final and most complete set of plans and specifications for the project and are the official documents.

The Interior Design Phase

The design of a library building's interior has a profound influence on its appeal to the user, its ability to operate effectively, and the overall image of the library. Buildings which are architectural monuments may have very poor interiors, while others, much more modest in their architectural design, may have exceptional interiors. While excellence in architectural design and interior design should go hand in hand, the point is that achieving this goal is not automatic. Good interiors do not just happen; they are planned with meticulous care to fit the requirements of the building program. Interior design should be thought of as an integral part of the total design process, rather than as something which can be applied at the end to cover blemishes and enhance appearance. This integrated approach requires coordination of architectural and interior design from the moment of concept through the completion of working drawings. If consideration of interiors is delayed until some later part of design, the result is almost certain to be less successful than if work progresses simultaneously from the very beginning.

Composition of the Interiors Package

Before discussing other aspects of interior design, it may be well to establish the scope of the interior design package. Unlike the fairly clean-cut areas traditionally covered by the architect in the design of a structure, the scope of interior design work is flexible and dependent upon reaching agreement with the architect about the division of labor. As buildings become more complex, the scope of work given the interior designer continues to evolve. This evolution results in part from the fact that architects have, until recently, controlled the design of both the structure and the interiors. Within the past few decades, however, interior design has begun to emerge as a related but separate discipline. At first, interior design included little more than the selection of furniture and, sometimes, the choice of colors. However, as the importance of the integrated interior has emerged, competent interior designers have sought input to, if not control over, all aspects of a building's interiors. This includes a fairly impressive list:

1/ Layout of furniture and equipment
2/ Selection of furniture and equipment
3/ Design of casework (cabinetry)
4/ Selection of floor and wall coverings
5/ Coordination of all interior colors and finishes
6/ Design and/or selection of graphics and signage for both the interior and exterior of the building
7/ Selection of general, task and specialty lighting
8/ Preparation of all specifications for interior elements
9/ Formulation of budget figures covering interiors
10/ Preparation of models, mock-ups and renderings of interior areas
11/ Development of prototypes of custom furniture
12/ Supervision of interior installation.

Given the possible scope of the interior designer's responsibilities, the importance of the person's qualifications and experience becomes increasingly evident.

Who Should Be Responsible for Interiors?

Since every one of the foregoing elements must be addressed in a library building project, the question of who should be responsible for them is relevant. Several of the possibilities are discussed here.

The Lay Person or Body

Most readers of this text are probably familiar with buildings for which the interiors have been planned by a lay person or a group such as a committee, board or commission. The opportunity of making all of those choices somehow appeals to some people, whether they have the necessary credentials or not. In most such cases, the architect retains control over such vital elements as lighting and casework, leaving only selection of colors and movable furniture to the whims of self-appointed interior designers. With few exceptions, this alternative is almost certain to come off second best to the well coordinated efforts of competent professionals.

The Interior Decorator

Sometimes the search for interiors expertise results in the use of a person known as an "interior decorator." Such individuals admittedly have far more experience than most lay people. However, their practice is normally associated with residential and small-office work. In general, they take a given architectural space and embellish it. Unlike the interior designer, the interior decorator spends little time on relating functions, traffic, work routines and other space requirements to the choice of furniture and the layout of functions. Moreover, the interior decorator is likely to be less familiar with the requirements and problems associated with larger-scale projects represented by most libraries. While they may have impeccable tastes in colors and furnishings, their experience in the selection of furniture and equipment typical of library installations is apt to be limited. Their knowledge of manufacturers, vendors and products required by libraries is not likely to be extensive. Further, their qualifications may not include experience in handling the magnitude of specification preparation and control required by library projects.

The Architect

Historically, architects have included interior design as a part of their role in building projects. Only in recent years as buildings became more complex and interior design evolved into a more sophisticated element have architects begun to recognize the need for specialization in this field. Whether the architect should control the interiors of a project will depend to some degree on his or her experience and aptitude in this field. Previous work should bear ample testimony to qualifications.

Many larger architectural firms maintain special divisions or branches of their organization to supply interior design services. Usually these units include personnel with advanced training in interior design and, because they are free to devote their full attention to the interiors package, they can provide competent services. Among the advantages of such an arrangement are simplified contractual administration and project coordination.

Some clients object, however, to the architect's control over interiors, fearing that the scheduling and budgeting for interiors may be prejudiced by the requirements of architectural design. For instance, preference may be given in the selection and layout of furniture and equipment to items which enhance the architectural design of the building rather than serve the programmatic functions of the library. Likewise, monies saved by lowering the quality of carpets, casework and furnishings (a fact that may go unnoticed by the client until too late) may result in more dollars for the architect's use in embellishing the architectural design.

The Interior Designer

Independent interior designers are beginning to emerge as a separate professional group offering still another alternative for interior design services. Unlike many interior decorators, interior designers often have degrees in architecture with a strong emphasis in interior design coursework. Their experience is in commercial, industrial and public buildings rather than in residential and small-office projects. Usually they work as team members from the outset of the project and share responsibilities with the architect for all design elements pertaining to the interiors. This may include assistance in space planning, fenestration, artificial illumination, choice of building materials for the interiors, and many other elements.

If an independent interior designer is retained for the project, it is essential that coordination with the architect begin immediately and continue as a close relationship for the duration. Early discussions should revolve around the concept of the building and the overall effect the interiors are to achieve. Then the quality of interior elements to be purchased must be agreed upon. After this, the interior designer will organize an interiors budget based upon the approved levels of quality and quantities of furnishings and equipment established by the program. This will be carefully modified and monitored as the work proceeds.

Steps in Interior Design

Interior design follows the same general steps observed for architectural work in the preceding chapter. Just as the architectural design goes from concept to working drawings, so do interiors. In the well-administered project, both will observe similar deadlines and the interiors package will be ready for bidding at the same time as the rest of the project goes out to bid. This means that every color, finish, wall and floor covering, casework and piece of furniture and equipment must be selected prior to the conclusion of working drawings. Meeting this demanding schedule requires the interior designer and architect to work together very closely and very harmoniously. In fact, the greatest risk in retaining an independent interior designer is the possibility that the relationship between the architect and interior designer may be less than cordial. In most cases, however, the architect and interior designer form a compatible team, respecting one another's views and professional competence.

Working with interiors requires an understanding of the differences in the size of the basic modules that will be encountered. For instance, architects are used to building materials and systems which are based on a four- or eight-foot module. Standard office furniture and equipment, however, are designed on a five-foot module. Library interiors, on the other hand, have traditionally been governed by the three-foot module basic to the design of most shelving. (Of course this is not the case when four-foot-wide shelving units are used.) Getting these different modules to work harmoniously is not always an easy task. Failure to do so is almost certain to result in spacing problems.

Schematic Phase

During the schematic phase the general concept of the interiors will be worked out and the initial decisions made regarding furniture, fixtures and equipment (FF&E) layout will be made. The layouts will be presented as floor plans with the furniture drawn in. Proposed colors will be shown on presentation "boards" which introduce a family of colors and how they will appear on various finishes: tile, paint, textiles, vinyl wall coverings, etc. A few illustrations may be used of possible furniture styles. These pictures are also known as "catalog cuts," having been taken from the catalogs of various furniture manufacturers. Basic requirements for casework (cabinetry), already set forth in the building program, will be identified and expanded. Finally, the first preliminary interiors budget will appear near the end of this phase. It will itemize the costs of major groupings of furniture and equipment, floor and wall coverings and lighting, and carry contingency amounts for works of art and other items not yet chosen.

Design Development

During design development, work will move forward on refining the decisions made in the schematic phase and making such adjustments as may be required by changes in architectural design. In addition to the furniture layout plans, each interior wall will be "elevated," i.e., shown as if being seen by the viewer. Usually casework, such as built-in desks and counters, appears in these drawings, as do wall graphics. Coordination of the wall elevations with the floor plans is a major task; every change, no matter how small, that is made to the interior of the building must be reflected in the interior drawings.

Presentations will become more refined and layout drawings more precise as work continues. At the end of the design development period, the layout of furniture and equipment will have been established and the many items of furniture and equipment chosen. Works of art and other specialties covered in the schematic cost estimate as contingency items will now be clearly defined. A revised and much-expanded budget will be provided at the end of the design development phase. This budget may be expected to define every piece of furniture and equipment as well as give fairly exact details for materials such as floor and wall coverings.

During the design development phase, the interior designer will be much involved with lighting. Working closely with the architect and the electrical engineer, the interior designer must help choose among a variety of lighting systems and types of fixtures to be used. If task lighting is extensively used, it will influence the number and location of duplex receptacles. Use of daylight monitors which provide ambient light by reflecting off the ceiling will affect the choice of colors and materials for use in the ceilings and walls. These systems, in turn, will affect the ceiling layout which the architect must prepare as the reflected ceiling plan showing location of light fixtures. Since ceiling materials have an impact on acoustics, the interior designer will be vitally concerned about acoustical requirements of the various spaces and how these requirements can be met.

The color board will be expanded. Larger swatches of carpet and other fabrics will be provided as the evaluation of samples leads to a narrowing of choices for the interior palette. Wall elevations will be revised and amplified to show casework in greater detail. Casework

will also be shown in large-scale drawings that permit greater specificity in dimensioning.

The design development period for interiors is the prime opportunity for testing proposed designs for public stations and for work stations. This can be done through careful study of the drawings and by use of models and mock-ups provided by the interior designer. Circulation desks, reference and other public desks, and work stations are prime candidates for modeling. Full-scale mock-ups will provide further help in determining strengths and weaknesses in design. Is the desk or counter the right height? the correct width? Are there a sufficient number of drawers and are their dimensions compatible with the materials and objects they are to hold? When subjected to motion studies associated with a given task, is there sufficient room on the desk or counter top for all necessary equipment and for the handling of materials? Money invested on mock-ups and models will be well spent and more than repaid by the results.

The budget for the interiors will also be amplified with the addition of many details. Unit prices will be stipulated for the individual items of furniture and equipment chosen. The interiors budget will then be adjusted accordingly. At the close of the design development phase, the library's interior spaces and their appearance will be firmly established. Individual items of furniture and equipment along with colors and materials for the interiors will have been tentatively chosen. The lighting system will be known and many of the component fixtures designated. Graphics will be drawn and the signage system designed, with the wording for many signs tentatively decided.

Construction Documents Phase

While some changes may occur in the interiors package during the construction drawings phase, most of the effort will go into the refinement of choices, the preparation of detailed drawings for casework and specifications for items of furniture and equipment. For instance, one or more products will be chosen from manufacturers for each item to be purchased; others wishing to bid will have to prove that their product is equivalent in style, construction, durability, etc. Samples of some items of furniture may be provided by the manufacturer to enable close examination by the librarian and other project team people. On occasion, a sample may be placed in the library for a period of time to test its characteristics and to determine user reaction.

The final interiors package, as it is sometimes referred to, will include detailed furniture and equipment layouts showing the precise location of every item. Floor plans and wall elevations will indicate the choice of materials, graphics and other requirements. Casework drawings will be fully detailed, giving all the dimensions and directions necessary for a vendor to supply shop drawings. A carpet seaming plan will be drawn to direct the laying of the carpets. The color palette will be delineated. Final specifications for every item of furniture and equipment will be extremely detailed and carefully written to meet the requirements of the purchasing office which is to order these items. If special pieces of art work are to be included, these will be described and a price set for them. The budget at this stage will be fully detailed.

Existing Furniture and Equipment

If existing furniture and equipment, or a portion thereof, is to be re-used in a project, certain additional steps must be taken. First, there must be a thorough inventory which identifies each item and describes its condition. The second step is to determine which items of furniture can be re-used and what work, if any, will be required to prepare them. This can be done with a simple checklist keyed to the item numbers followed in the inventory. Some of the choices include: 1/ not re-usable, 2/ re-usable as is, 3/ needs minor refinishing or repair, 4/ requires major restoration, repair or refurbishing. Once this list has been completed, a knowledgeable person must analyze the cost of the work described.

Items to be re-used will then be located on the furniture and equipment layout drawings, usually identified by a separate symbol or code to avoid confusing them with new FF&E items. A budget and schedule will have to be prepared for repair and refurbishment work and the whole coordinated with the rest of the FF&E planning. Obviously, the successful re-use of existing items of furniture and equipment can mean large dollar savings if properly administered. However, such a program requires the services of someone knowledgeable in this area and one who can advise on marginal items which may better be replaced by something new, given life-cycle costs, quality and/or cost of refurbishment.

Areas of Special Interest

Space permits little more than mere mention of some of the areas of interior design which are of special interest to library projects.

Lighting

Lighting is one of the most critical factors in successful library design. It has a major impact on the library user as well as on architectural and interior design. Few elements will affect public reception of the library more than lighting.

Daylighting. With energy conservation a focal point of architectural design, increasing emphasis is often placed on daylighting, including windows, skylights, clerestory and other methods. Daylighting has many advantages providing it is designed to eliminate glare and "hot spots" of intense light and/or heat. Artificial illumination, however, must always be available to provide light when daylighting is inadequate or unavailable. Particular attention must be given windows or other daylighting sources which may produce glare on staff at public desks and on CRT screens, or make reading areas uncomfortable.

General lighting. General lighting, sometimes referred to as ambient lighting, is used to illuminate a building's interior. It may be designed in sufficient intensity to satisfy the need for all requirements of users—reading, for instance—or be sufficient only for moving about the building. Usually, general lighting requires ceiling-mounted fixtures of some sort; with task lighting, floor-mounted or other types of light monitors may be used in place of or in addition to ceiling fixtures. Fixture styles constantly change as new products are introduced and new trends become fashionable. Before energy conservation was a desirable goal, luminous ceilings which, in effect, converted nearly the entire ceiling into a plane of light were popular. Now, individual fixtures with parabolic reflector lens have moved into vogue to reduce total wattage consumption and increase the ability to direct light at a given spot.

Task lighting. Energy conservation measures have placed new emphasis on "task lighting," which is the separate lighting of a given task, activity or work station. By combining a relatively low level of general lighting with more comfortable levels of lighting on the specific task, energy levels can be reduced while satisfying vision requirements. Libraries are especially susceptible to good task lighting applications for carrels, work stations, desks and groupings of lounge furniture. Desirable, but more difficult to achieve, is the task lighting of stack ranges, sometimes called integrated lighting. Given the increased use that libraries of all types are making of audio visual media and CRTs, task lighting with individual rheostat controls is of increasing relevance, permitting local adjustment to user need.

Specialty lighting. In addition to general and task lighting, certain areas of the library require special lighting. Wall display areas, for instance, may have general illumination supplemented by track lighting which can be adjusted to meet a variety of needs. Recessed wall-washing lamps, on the other hand, can be used for permanent display walls. Special lighting may be used to define or highlight areas of particular interest such as a distinctive part of the collection or a service desk. The creative use of specialty lighting will do much to add interest and excitement to a library.

Light switches. Few shortcomings are more obvious or vexing than the light switch located in the wrong place. Often this is due to the failure of the team members, and especially the librarian, to take special note of the location of every light switch and what it controls. Look for switches which may be located behind door swings or large pieces of equipment. Be sure that the location of switches is reviewed on all drawings after changes have been made in the placement of furniture and equipment or modifications occur in walls and partitions. Review with staff where switches need to be for lights used when entering and exiting the building. Correcting these errors after the building is completed can be costly.

Casework

The generic word "casework" (also referred to as "millwork") is generally employed to cover all types of cabinetry and built-ins. Some architects favor using components from casework manufacturers; others prefer designing their own so that units exactly fit their functions and spaces. Casework forms an important part of most interior budgets and deserves careful attention in design. Materials should be chosen which will be attractive and yet wear well. Even more important, casework must be designed to meet functional requirements. This includes the location, size and numbers of drawers, and the height, width and depth of counters and desks. During the review of interior documents, casework must be given special attention, with every detail carefully assessed by those who will use a particular work station or piece of furniture.

Partitioning

Partitions form an important part of most interiors. Designed and used properly, they add much to staff productivity and user satisfaction; designed or used poorly, they become the source of aggravation, inhibit productivity and frustrate occupants. Several kinds of partitioning are presently available and each has its application when properly selected for the job to be done. Recognize here that this discussion is about par-

titions—not about load bearing walls, which are a different matter. By definition a partition is movable and to some extent, temporary; walls, on the other hand, are expected to be permanent so long as the building exists or does not undergo radical reconstruction.

Fixed partitions. The least movable partitions are referred to as "fixed partitions." They are attached at both the floor and the ceiling, or the slab above, and separate well-defined functions for an extended period of time. Fixed partitions are used sparingly in most contemporary libraries and can most often be seen dividing major functions and spaces such as different departments or unrelated staff work areas. They may also be used to enclose conference rooms and private offices. A fixed partition may be constructed of wood or metal and firmly attached to the structure of the building. Walls may be created by lath and plaster, dry-wall, or some other material such as plywood. These can be finished in many ways ranging from paint to wood paneling or a veneer of brick or stone.

Movable partitions. One of the distinctions between movable partitions and fixed partitions is that the movable partition may be re-used entirely or in part. Movable partitions often consist of a channel base attached to the floor and a similar channel attached to the ceiling into which panels of wall board or other material are inserted. Because they attach at floor and ceiling they offer greater visual and acoustical privacy than landscape partitioning. This type of partitioning, sometimes referred to as demountable, can be assembled or disassembled with a minimum of tools by building maintenance staff. In most systems a few of the panels may be damaged in this process, so total re-use is not always possible. Since they are often placed over floor covering and beneath ceiling materials, there is immediate use of the space they occupied. The finished surfaces of movable partitions are usually painted or covered with vinyl wall coverings. However, it is possible to use paneling and other sheathing materials. Because the movable partition is basically hollow, space between the inner and outer walls can be filled with acoustical materials to limit the transfer of sound.

Landscape partitioning. The need for a more flexible way to divide office space has led to the introduction and widespread use of "open office" or "landscape partitioning systems." Comprised of various modules or units, these systems can be reconfigured like an Erector set. The partitions come in various heights ranging from about 36″ to more than 60″, depending upon the manufacturer. Each partition consists of panels, often fabric covered, with brackets and/or other means of attaching furniture components such as shelves, desk tops, drawers, etc. They are particularly adaptable to large office areas where work flow, variety of tasks, and numbers of staff tend to vary widely over relatively short periods of time. Some of the work stations are especially attractive and feature the latest in ergonomic design. Companies are competing to provide the most flexible units possible, with considerable emphasis on the nearly universal use of automated office equipment. Special attention has been given to designing components which provide for wire management and computer technology. Ergonomics is another key design word.

However, landscape partitioning is expensive. Component parts often cost more than standard office furniture of similar quality. Landscape furniture systems are more often justified in commercial and industrial applications where the tax advantages can be realized. Use of these systems requires stockpiling a variety of components against possible future need, which may never occur. Unless special precautions are taken, acoustical privacy is hard to achieve. They have been used in libraries as a substitute for traditional casework, with varying degrees of success. Landscape partitioning systems should not be used unless competent studies indicate that they provide the most cost-effective means for meeting library requirements.

Floor coverings. Carpet has become the floor covering of choice for most libraries and is used in both public and staff areas. The acoustical qualities of carpet are particularly suited to libraries, and the relatively low maintenance costs when compared to hard-surfaced materials add a further dimension to this choice. While it is impossible to prevent the soiling of carpet, certain steps can be taken to minimize this hazard. For instance, the entry area (both staff and public) is most likely to bear the burden of persistent soiling. This can be minimized by using recessed treads or other systems at the entries to control dirt, mud, slush, and water which would otherwise be tracked onto the carpet. The effects of excessive wear and soiling can be further controlled by using different pieces and colors or patterns of carpet for heavily trafficked areas. When badly worn, these can be replaced without having to match them with adjacent carpet. Because carpet fibers and weaves are constantly changing, the advice of an interior designer familiar with carpeting is of special value. The carpet seaming diagram provided by the interior designer as part of the construction documents for the interior, shows how the carpet is to be cut and laid. This diagram will keep the installers from placing seams where traffic will be heaviest and will keep the nap running in the same direction.

Very recently, traditional broadloom carpet began to be challenged by carpet tiles or squares. These offer the advantage of easy access to underfloor power and communication grid systems as well as ease of replacement when damaged or soiled. Carpet tiles are secured to the floor by being glued at their corners or along the edges. However, selection of carpet tile for library purposes must cope with the problem created by rolling heavy book trucks which tend to cause the tiles to shift, eventually breaking their bond with the floor. Experience to date has indicated that many carpet tiles will not function as well as roll carpet under this kind of traffic. New developments in carpet tile and adhesives are overcoming these problems and may become competitive.

Resilient floor coverings. Resilient floor coverings come in a variety of materials and styles. The most prevalent, probably, is vinyl tile. It has a fairly long life and is relatively impervious to soil providing it is mopped frequently. However, under comparable traffic, it often requires more maintenance time than carpet. Other resilient floor coverings have similar characteristics and applications in the library. While the initial installation may be somewhat less expensive than carpet, the long-term cost of maintenance and the poorer acoustical qualities usually relegate use of resilient floor coverings to storage areas and to rooms where spillage is apt to occur.

Ceramic tile, terrazzo and stone. Each of these flooring materials has unique properties and applications in libraries. Ceramic tile is most frequently used on restroom floors and walls because of the ease of maintenance and its sanitary appearance. Some pavement tiles are also used in entries, though they can be very dangerous when wet. Terrazzo, a polished conglomerate of stone chips, is another long-lasting material, suitable for lobbies and other high traffic areas where acoustics can be controlled by other means. However, like tile it can be very hazardous when wet. Stone, especially polished marble and granite, are often thought to be too expensive to be used as floor materials in library buildings. If selected, however, they are enduring in nature but should not be highly polished. The cost of maintaining floors of these materials will vary somewhat depending upon the traffic they bear and the standards of maintenance required.

Colors and Finishes

Preferences in colors and finishes are highly personal. Selection must be based on more than personal preference. Avoid colors and finishes which may become quickly outdated. Libraries, like other types of buildings, continue to go through successive periods of interior finishes: light vs. dark, oak vs. walnut, pastels vs. primary colors, and so on. Like every other choice for the interiors, the selection of the color palette should be based upon sound reasons and good judgment of the community's taste, and life-cycle costs. In the library environment, particular attention needs to be given to the psychology of color on both users and staff: Kelly green or lemon yellow may be an inviting stimulant to the user exposed to it for only a short time now and then, but strong colors can be a constant irritant to the staff member facing a broad expanse of them day after day.

In projects where furnishings are to be re-used and mixed with new items, their colors and finishes are apt to have a strong influence on the choice of new items of furniture and equipment to be added. However, this is less likely to occur if furniture is to be refinished or if it is to be located in a separate part of the library and not mixed with new furnishings.

There is a natural tendency to both follow the current style or fad in color selection and to choose colors and finishes which are in contrast to those the library has had in years past. Thus, light oak may be chosen instead of walnut or primary colors instead of pastels. Such selection assures the furnishings a refreshing quality providing the colors and finishes suit their uses and the tastes of those who will frequent the building.

While it would seem obvious, too little attention is given to choosing colors and finishes which promise to be durable and easily maintained. For instance, upholstered pieces should have fabrics that are soil-resistant and easily cleaned. In addition, quality furniture frequently features upholstery which can be removed for cleaning, repair or replacement. Colors and finishes must be selected with the sure knowledge that library furniture must survive very heavy and, sometimes, abusive use. A finish or color that might appear to be perfect in a residential or office setting may not be at all suitable for a library reading room.

Wall Coverings

Care in the selection of wall coverings will result in years of added wear and minimum upkeep. So-called vinyl wall coverings offer a wide range of colors and textures suitable for areas of heavy use, including hallways and staircases. Some are self-healing and can be used for occasional tackable surfaces. Others have special acoustical properties desired for offices, workrooms and conference rooms. Care must be exercised in selection and installation to provide the best possible application.

Paint is still the most common wall covering. Here,

again, the tremendous variety of paint available today requires the experience and knowledge of an expert to assist in selection. Areas subject to soiling should be covered with a washable paint, often with a glossy finish. On the other hand, matte or dull finish should be used where reflectivity is a concern. The palette of available colors is virtually endless and great discretion must be used in choosing those colors which create the best possible atmosphere for users and staff. Good maintenance practice dictates the choice of standard colors—not mixed—supplied by a manufacturer of good reputation.

Where special wall treatment is desired, walls may be clad in a textured material such as a woven fabric or paneled in wood. Solid wood paneling is, of course, expensive. However, a similar effect can be obtained by careful use of plywood paneling. Perhaps less successful are the imitation panels composed of composition or particle board. A favorite device of some interior designers is to panel one of four walls, giving the effect of richness without the expense and sometimes claustrophobic feeling of a fully paneled room, especially if it is not too large and/or has a fairly low ceiling. Wainscoting is another kind of wall treatment that has special applications, especially in hallways and offices.

Brick, tile, and stone. Other materials may, of course, be used for wall coverings. In rehabilitated structures, brick walls are often cleaned and left exposed because their texture and color are generally enjoyed. Stone walls are much less common and are usually confined to special areas such as entries and lobbies. Polished stone needs little attention beyond an occasional cleaning. Rough stone, or quarry stone, is another matter. Beautiful on installation, the stone gradually accrues a patina of dust and grime that is difficult to dislodge and is likely to remain for many years. As noted in the discussion on floor coverings, ceramic tile is most frequently used for walls and floors in restrooms, where ease of maintenance is a major factor. Occasionally ceramic tile may be used elsewhere as a wall covering. Because of the variety of shapes, textures and colors available, ceramic tile is sometimes used to create decorative wall murals. However, any hard surface on walls, floors or ceilings may create additional acoustic problems and should be used with care where noise must be controlled.

Graphics and Signage

Graphics and signage are an integral part of the interiors package and should be developed simultaneously with the layout of furniture and equipment. Graphics, as used here, pertains to any visual presentation regardless of the medium in which it is presented: painting, photograph, mural, or other form of illustration. Graphics may be informational and/or directional. They must be planned, located and designed with great care. Unless well conceived and executed, they can be an eyesore or a source of distaste for those who must look at them for long hours on end. Partly for this reason, graphics are offered in less permanent forms. Notable among these are wall- or ceiling-hung fabric banners which have gained immense popularity because they can be colorful and playful without becoming permanent fixtures. When such banners double as information/direction graphics, the ability to move and to change them is an important factor. However, in spite of their popularity, banners do tend to fade and to collect dust. They must be cleaned periodically and replaced from time to time. Because of their widespread use in the past decade or so, some people consider them to be an interior design cliché. Whether true or not, this does not diminish their effectiveness when they are well designed, properly made, and tastefully displayed.

Interest in library signage has been gaining over the last several decades. Still, library buildings are often poorly signed, as attested to by the number of homemade and hand-lettered signs found in all too many libraries. Part of the problem stems from the fact that signage has often been left to the end of the project when funds have run out and time is too short to explore alternatives. Therefore, the first step in an adequate signage program is be certain that it is considered as an integral part of the interiors package. Work should begin on signage as soon as the furniture and equipment layouts begin to jell. By this time, project members should take mental walks through the building to discover what directions the public will probably need most and where these should be located. Then the wording must be carefully worked out so that it will be as unambiguous as possible. This work should continue through the entire project, with revisions occurring as plans change. One helpful technique is to keep a set of drawings solely for recording the location and wording of signs. As work progresses, help may be needed in selecting the most legible fonts for sign lettering and establishing the format of the signs themselves. Don't forget to decide how each sign will be attached or hung from something so that it is clearly visible yet not subject to damage. Exterior signs, of course, should be large, easily read by passing traffic and fully illuminated.

Working With Design Professionals: A Personal Word

The preceding text for this chapter has been written in as objective a manner as I can muster. However, I can not leave this subject without some personal notes that are admittedly subjective. These views may or may not be shared by others—I do not know.

Without doubt, the opportunity to work with design professionals on a library building project is one that I hold dear. The creative processes involved never cease to amaze me. No matter what visions may enter my mind as I prepare or review a building program, I am always surprised by the image of the same building as conceived by the design professionals. The form and substance of the design is much different from what I might have expected. When I ask why this design rather than some other, I am often surprised by the logic of their answers, for they offer reasons I would not think of. As we work together as project team members, I can see the wheels of imagination turning and feel the creative juices flowing as problem after problem is resolved. That is why working with design professionals is an exciting and rewarding experience that I treasure for every librarian anxious for an unforgettable experience.

But there are negative factors as well which the librarian must understand and be prepared for, just in case. Architects and interior designers are artists and craftsmen; but they must also keep a business going and turn a profit. Like some other businesses, they are usually somewhere between feast or famine. In dealing with them, never forget that "time is money." To win your project, they make tight estimates on the amount of time each phase would require; going beyond that limit means cutting into profits, or worse. This is one of the reasons that resistance to making changes in drawings and specifications grows as the project moves from one stage to the next. You and I see a change as requiring a few erasures and some new pencil marks; from their point of view, it is so many hours of time for the project architect, the design architect, and maybe extra hours of drafting. Besides, there will be calls, and possibly conferences, with the structural, mechanical and electrical engineers, each with their own schedules and balance sheets to reconcile.

Summary

The architectural and interior design phase of a library building project is often the most rewarding aspect. By understanding the various stages of development and what they are supposed to achieve, the librarian can follow the progress of the project and contribute to it. Architectural and interior design evolves through several distinct phases: schematics, design development, and construction documents. Close coordination of architectural and interior design is required. Because of its effect on the users and the staff, the interiors package must be carefully conceived and therefore deserves the full participation of a trained and experienced person. Library staff, especially, must give exceptional attention to a myriad of details as they assist in the selection of furniture, fixtures and equipment. With this participation, the library is more apt to fit both the community and its function as a library.

VIII THE CONSTRUCTION PHASE

WHEN the architectural work is completed, library facility projects shift gears to enter a new phase. During this period the drawings and specifications become a physical reality. While the librarian may not appear to be directly involved, interest in the project obviously does not lapse. An awareness of what occurs during the construction of a library building will provide a better understanding of the course of events and may help the librarian anticipate various events.

The Bidding Process

Before work can begin a building contractor must be selected. Usually this is the result of competitive bidding, following the exact requirements and procedures established by the library's jurisdiction in compliance with local and state regulations. The process described in the following paragraphs is fairly typical.

Definition of "The Owner"

Until the point of bidding has been reached, it is likely that the librarian has borne the real, if not the legal, responsibility for the project. While assistance and some guidance may have come from a building department, an academic facilities division or some other similar source, much of the work has devolved upon the librarian and staff. In public library situations the responsibilities may have been shared with a Library Board, while in academic situations a building committee may have been formed with library, faculty and administration representatives. Now, however, responsibility shifts to the entity which is legally responsible for property and funding and which will hold title to the completed facility. This entity is most often referred to as the "owner."

Invitation to Bid

Following the formal approval by the library's owner of the construction documents, consisting of the final drawings and specifications, a call or invitation for bid is issued. This is a legal announcement stating the nature of the project and the regulations covering the bidding. The bid invitation will be published as a legal notice in the local newspapers. In addition, an announcement of the project bidding will appear in various trade papers circulated among building contractors. Often, the project's architects will contact particular building contractors whom, from their experience, they perceive to have special qualifications.

Assembling the Bid

Upon receiving the announcement, interested contractors obtain sets of the drawings and specifications from the jurisdiction. Then each contractor begins the laborious job of preparing a bid. This includes a careful analysis of all the building materials and work that the project will require. Specialists from various trades, including mechanical, electrical and structural contractors, usually referred to as subcontractors, or "subs" for short, will be consulted. In addition to the contractor's own experience, pricing guidelines from various services serving building contractors will also be used. Taking the best of the bids from the subcontractors and adding them together, the contractor emerges with a total construction bid sum which includes profit and, usually, a contingency factor.

The actual bid is usually presented on a form provided by the jurisdiction. Appended to this form will be such other documents as may be required, such as a performance bond and affirmative action declarations. These must be presented at the time and place specified in the call for bid.

The Architects and the Bidding Process

Policies and customs of the owner will govern much of the architect's role during the bidding process. Usually the architect will be expected by the owner to help answer technical questions posed by contractors. If such questions have serious implications for bidding, the owner will probably ask the architect to prepare a clarification covering the matter, which the owner will issue as an addendum to all bidders. The aim is to see that all potential bidders are supplied the same information.

The Bid Opening and Analysis

Depending upon the size of the project and the owner's policies, the bid period will usually last three to six weeks. At the place named and on the day and hour set in the call for bid, the opening of bids will take place. Legally, all bids submitted after the stated hour are automatically disqualified and are returned to the bidder unopened. After gathering the bids, the owner's representative opens each bid and announces the amount. Often a running tabulation is kept for the benefit of all in attendance.

In the majority of cases, all bids are "taken under advisement" by the owner for a period of one to two weeks. During this time the bids are carefully analyzed by the owner—usually with the help of the architect—and any questions about them are answered by the bidder. Bids which are incomplete or fail to meet all requirements are eliminated during this process. Finally, a winning bidder is selected—normally the lowest responsible bidder—and referred by recommendation to the jurisdiction's governing body for action. The winning bid represents the actual cost of the project, plus the cost of any change orders that may be authorized during construction.

Award of Bid

The award of bid by the jurisdiction is followed by a period of contract negotiation between the owner's representatives and the contractor. The form of agreement is sometimes a part of the bid documents, which may reduce the time required for these negotiations. Once the contract has been executed, the bidding process is complete.

Alternates

Before leaving the subject of bidding, it may be helpful to consider the role of alternates as they relate to bidding. Alternates often emerge as a result of design and cost options. They may run the gamut from extra space to a difference in materials, mechanical systems, lighting, etc. An "additive alternate" supplements the base bid while a "deductive alternate" is meant to reduce the basic bid cost. The call for bid must clearly separate the alternates from the basic bid package and require separate pricing.

The librarian should be particularly interested in any proposed alternates. Once a part of the building becomes an alternate, it may be viewed by some as nonessential. Alternates that have the potential affect of increasing long-term maintenance and replacement costs should be of particular concern for the librarian. The difference between "first costs" and long-term values make some alternates appear deceptively attractive. Alternates should also be reviewed for their possible effect on future library development and expansion. If a proposed alternate is likely to increase operational costs or inhibit future achievement of library objectives, the librarian must call attention to this possibility before the alternates are approved to appear in the bid package.

Construction Supervision

Projects of almost any size require some kind of supervision. Such supervision may be provided from one or more sources. The librarian must understand the importance of adequate supervision and the ways in which it may be supplied.

Local Building Official/Inspector

Most jurisdictions maintain some type of building department which provides a certain amount of construction supervision. The amount and quality of such supervision varies immensely. Typically, one or more inspectors tour the job at particular times to certify compliance with building codes. They are not responsible for seeing that the building is being constructed in conformance with the drawings and specifications.

The Architect's Role

The authority of the architect and the degree of responsibility for supervision to be exercised should be established in the contract between the owner and the building contractor. Under certain contractual agreements the architect may even have the authority to stop work on the project until certain changes are made or conditions are met. The architect's experience in project supervision is one of the criteria which should be weighed carefully during the process of selection.

During construction, the architect will normally make periodic site visits to determine whether the contractor is following the drawings and specifications. Time will also be devoted to working out any special details or responding to contractor's questions concerning the intent of the design. The architect will prepare change orders when it becomes obvious that construction requires a major deviation from the original design or specifications. Progress payments for the contractor will also be approved by the architect, who will certify that the work to be paid for has, indeed, been completed. When the construction is concluded, the architect will certify to the owner that the building is ready for occupancy.

While the architect will remain in close contact with the project throughout construction, he or she does not usually act as an inspector in the sense of approving the quality of materials or compliance with code requirements. Because the architect is not on the site much of the time, construction necessarily proceeds without his or her direct knowledge. For this reason, other types of supervision may be desired, especially for larger or more complex projects.

The Clerk of the Works

Since the local building officials will be responsible only for code compliance of certain building elements and the architect will have limited contact, projects of any size may merit a full-time supervisor. Such a person will act as the owner's representative on the site and will assist in the coordination of all the players. The construction supervisor, sometimes referred to as the Clerk of the Works, must have a strong background in construction and is often a former building contractor familiar with every facet of the work. He or she will review the contractor's work schedules and make certain that the contractor has the necessary material and work force on hand for each day's tasks. Cognizant of building code requirements, the clerk of the works will

continually evaluate the on-going construction and call the building inspector's attention to any suspected shortcoming. Similarly, the clerk of the works will monitor the building to make certain that the architect is aware of any deviation from the intent of the drawings and specifications. Through continuous presence on the job site and a thorough knowledge of project requirements as well as materials, construction methods and the contracting business, the clerk of the works can provide close supervision that may well result in a better building product as well as cost savings.

Construction Management

In recent years a new profession known as construction management has gained popularity in some quarters. Construction management had its genesis in extremely large and complex projects where the work and schedules of many contractors have to be coordinated. This experience is most useful when the project involves a variety of structures and other facilities costing many millions of dollars.

Construction management is apt to be more sophisticated and expensive than is warranted for most library projects. If the owner shows interest in construction management, the librarian should become familiar with this fast-changing field of supervision and prepare to understand their techniques.

The Construction Process

The construction process will vary somewhat from one project to the next. However, in general most will follow the sequence described in this section.

The Construction Schedule

One of the first steps taken by the contractor will be the preparation of a detailed construction schedule. This may follow the form of a PERT, GANTT, CPM/CPS, or other time-line charting device that anticipates the interrelationships and schedules for completing various work elements. (PERT: program planning, scheduling, and controlling techniques; GANTT: a planning and scheduling format introduced by Henry L. Gantt during World War I for controlling munitions production; CPM/CPS: critical path method, critical path scheduling, similar to PERT in form.) From this a schedule evolves, establishing when the various trades will be involved and when particular materials and equipment must arrive on the site. This schedule, in turn, determines when the contractor and the subcontractors must order their supplies, building materials, fabricated equipment, etc. Progress is regularly measured against this schedule.

Organizing the Construction Team

In preparing the bid for the construction work, the contractor has established a team of subcontractors committed to providing certain services, materials and equipment. The contractor must notify each of these subcontractors that the project has been awarded, and subsequently work out a contract with each in keeping with their earlier bids. Occasionally the contractor may not be able to negotiate a contract with one or more of the original subcontractors. If this occurs, the owner should be notified and approval given to the firm that takes the place of the original subcontractor.

Initial Job Meeting

After the construction team has been formed, the initial job meeting is held. At this time the owner's representative and the architect meet with the contractor and subcontractors to review the work to be done. The contractor often uses this opportunity to acquaint the subcontractors with the construction schedule and with any special circumstances or conditions. For instance, trucks may have to use a particular route or deliver shipments to a specific place. Workmen may have to observe certain restrictions for parking or site access.

Ground Breaking

A formal ground-breaking ceremony often heralds the commencement of a new project. The librarian is likely to be very much involved with this time-honored custom. Prior to ground breaking, a large easily read sign should be erected at a prominent location on the site announcing the name of the project and giving the names of design professionals, contractor, and officials. The date of the ground-breaking ceremonies may be included. This sign is in addition to the standard project sign which is usually the responsibility of the contractor.

Local dignitaries, the architect and contractor as well as donors, prominent citizens and respected colleagues may attend and share in the festivities. Originally, the turning of a spadeful of earth marked the climax of the ceremony. In recent years, much more imaginative and attention-getting devices are being used. Bulldozers, steam shovels, trenching machines and other heavy equipment have been substituted for the shovel. Whatever the instrument, the ground breaking remains a formality that marks the beginning of the project just as the grand opening marks the completion.

Site Work

Construction actually begins with site work. If there are structures on or in the ground, they will have to be moved or removed through demolition. Underground utilities, including storm drains, water mains and sewer lines, may have to be re-routed. A new drainage system may be necessary to protect the site from storm run-off during the period of construction. If the proper utilities are not available, they will have to be brought to the site. The construction site will usually be fenced off at this time and a yard established for the stockpiling of construction materials to be used on the project. As soon as a suitable location is established, the contractor will move a trailer or other temporary office onto the grounds.

Foundations and Slabs

When site work has proceeded to the point where it is possible, surveyors will stake out the lines for any excavating that must be done for basements, foundations and footings for columns. As work proceeds, forms are constructed and reinforcing steel—rebar—is wired and welded into place to strengthen the concrete that will support the building. After plumbing and electrical conduits have been placed in their proper locations, floor slabs are poured. If masonry columns are called for, they are framed above their footings with rebar in place and then poured—one story at a time. When steel columns are required, the heavy members are brought to the site, hoisted into position by a crane and then bolted securely to their footings.

General Construction

Once the foundations and floor slab have been put in place, general construction begins. The exact process will be determined by the structural system designed for the building. A steel structure with a curtain wall will require materials and a construction sequence somewhat different from those for a masonry structure. If more than one floor is to be built, extensive forming may be required at each level. Roof trusses will eventually be put into place and the new building will reach its ultimate height. Contractors and builders often mark this milestone with the placing of an evergreen tree at the highest point of the structure.

With the roof structure completed, the building can be enclosed on all sides. Again, the materials and building technology will depend upon the structure's design. Once the building is enclosed, interior work can begin. Plumbing and electrical work previously stubbed into floors, columns and load-bearing walls will be extended into the partitions that begin to delineate interior areas. Sheet metal duct work snakes through walls and along the underside of slab floors in a maze all its own. Chalk marks on the floor are covered as partitions rise.

When the rough construction work has been completed, finish work begins. Ceilings are installed along with light fixtures, and duct grilles. Door frames, plumbing fixtures and casework are installed. Painting is finished and wall coverings applied where called for. Vinyl tile and carpet installations are completed. When carpeting is done, it should be protected from premature soiling during the final stages of work by heavy plastic runners. Mechanical systems are tested and preliminary balancing of air flow achieved. There is a last-minute flurry of activity as cleaning, minor repairs, touch-up painting, and adjustments are made to equipment. As a final step, bookshelving and library furnishings and equipment are installed. The building is ready for acceptance and occupancy.

Interior Design Work

If an interior designer has been used on the project, he or she will arrive on the scene as the building nears completion. Having worked as a member of the project team during the design phase, the interior designer will have total familiarity with the building. The installation of wall and floor coverings, graphics, signage, specialty lighting, casework and furniture and equipment will be supervised by the interior designer. As furniture and equipment arrive on the site, the interior designer will supervise their uncrating. Each item will be checked for compliance with order specifications and examined for possible damage or other defect, then

checked off the purchase list. When all is ready, each piece of furniture and equipment will be installed in accordance with the approved plan for the layout of furniture and equipment.

The librarian should be aware that the work of the interior designer during this phase of construction requires the careful coordination of various trades, especially electrical, plumbing and painting. This coordination, in turn, depends upon the full cooperation of the contractor and subcontractor, whose contracts must clearly anticipate and allow for this work. If not provided for, jurisdictional problems can arise.

Change Orders during Construction

Various circumstances may occur during construction that require modifications in the original plans and specifications. When the necessity for such modifications are agreed too, the architect will draw plans for the necessary changes in the form of a change order. These change orders should be carefully reviewed by the librarian to determine whether or not they may have adverse affect on the capacity of the building to function as a library. For instance, a change order as simple as the relocation of a door or the repositioning of a partition to accommodate a larger duct shaft may have serious implications for the intended use of the adjoining spaces. Whenever possible, the contractor will be urged to accept the change orders without additional compensation. Sometimes several changes will offset one another in their effect on cost. An effective clerk of the works or job superintendent often finds ways to negotiate changes without incurring radical cost overruns. If payment becomes necessary, it will probably be charged to the project's contingency fund. Because excessive change orders often relate to inadequate architectural drawings and specifications, the architect's record on change orders in previous work is a valuable criterion for review during the selection process.

Creating Punch Lists

At periodic intervals, and especially as the building nears completion, various inspectors, the clerk of the works and the architect create "punch lists" which enumerate items requiring the contractor's attention. The librarian and the library building consultant should seek an opportunity to submit a punch list of their own through the clerk of the works or the architect. In this orderly fashion, attention can be called to defects and problems which might otherwise be overlooked. The fact that some of these items turn up on the lists of others merely reinforces the need for remedial action. As the future occupant of the building, the librarian has a special interest in seeing that every possible problem is resolved before the contractor leaves the job.

A Note on Fast-Track Construction

This chapter has described the sequence of events characteristic of the normal construction schedule. In recent years, a different methodology, commonly referred to as "Fast Tracking," has evolved in an effort to minimize the time required to complete a project. The presumption is that by truncating the schedule, construction costs are reduced and occupancy occurs at an earlier date. Fast tracking is particularly popular with developers and design/build teams concerned with receiving a return on their capital outlay as quickly as possible.

Because design and construction are integrated in a different manner, and because the design schedule is foreshortened, fast tracking reduces the amount of time the librarian and other team members have to review plans, spot deviations from the building program's requirements, and get changes made in the drawings and specifications. Fast tracking is also apt to limit the number of different design solutions offered at the outset. Above all, fast tracking is almost certain to put more pressure on the librarian to evaluate and accept solutions quickly so that the deadlines of the accelerated schedule can be met.

Fast tracking is a concept more than a rigid system. The term is often applied to any effort used to reduce project time by beginning construction at the earliest possible moment and well before the traditional construction documents are completed. In the typical fast-track project, site work, for instance, may be undertaken before the architect even begins design. Then, as soon as the building's "footprint" and general structural system has been established in the early schematics, excavation and construction of foundations and footings begin and the fabrication of structural members ordered. From then on, the construction schedule drives the design calendar, with the design professionals attempting to keep one step ahead of the building contractor. Obviously, design changes of any consequence are extremely hard to make and very costly.

So far as the librarian is concerned, the effect of fast tracking should be obvious. While construction time may be significantly reduced and some cost savings realized, these potential benefits may be offset by major shortcomings. For instance, decisions must be made quickly, often without the time or opportunity to explore alternatives or fully evaluate consequences. For better or for worse, the ultimate design is tied to the configuration (footprint) of the building established early in the schematic period. Because the foundations are run, the floor slabs are poured and the columns are in place, flexibility in planning during later schematics and design development is reduced to whatever compromises may be left.

Fast tracking can result in serious and costly difficulties in construction as well as in design. For instance, construction may be divided into several packages, such as site work, foundations and footings, structural and enclosure, and finish work. Each of these phases represents a progressive refinement of the initial design and specifications. However, fast tracking may employ a different contractor for each of these stages, with coordination provided by a construction management firm. When several contractors are involved, it is often difficult to fix the responsibility for any problems that may be discovered. Each tends to hold prior contractors responsible for whatever deficiencies or cost overruns that may evolve. This can lead to costly delays, expensive and time-consuming litigation, and unsolved building problems. Further, multiple contracts can complicate the coordination of schedules and the work of the various trades. Taken as a whole, fast-track construction appears better suited for commercial and industrial buildings than for libraries.

The Librarian's Role during Construction

While not directly concerned with construction, the librarian has a role to play. At a minimum this should include the review of all change orders and the checking of casework shop drawings produced by the company furnishing cabinetry and other built-ins. Dimensions of drawers, shelving and other components should be checked with care—a drawer meant to be used for a particular sized form will not work if it is undersized, for instance. The creation of a punch list by the librarian has been covered in a previous section. If possible, the librarian should be among those receiving progress reports on construction so that he or she may, in turn, keep staff and others intelligently informed.

The Library Consultant's Role during Construction

If possible, the library building consultant should continue to be involved throughout construction. Work will include review of change orders and shop drawings as well as of interior design elements. Items of furniture and equipment chosen for the building will also be reviewed. The library consultant can be especially helpful in projects where unexpected conditions may arise, as during remodeling or additions. Accompanied by the librarian, the consultant may make one or more site visits during construction, especially as the building nears completion. During such visits the consultant may call attention to construction details observed from experience to be possible sources of future difficulty. Preparation of a punch list by the library building consultant and the librarian has been discussed in a previous section of this chapter. The consultant's ability to understand and interpret the languages of architecture, construction and library science can be helpful. The experienced library building consultant can bring additional insight to problem solving and add weight to the owner's position during crucial periods of the construction phase.

Visitation during Construction

In many jurisdictions, while under construction the building is technically owned by the contractor. Therefore, the contractor has the right to restrict accesses to the premises. Even though the librarian will be the eventual occupant and therefore more interested in the progress of construction than most, he or she may not walk onto the site without the building contractor's express permission. To this end it is essential that the librarian maintain a good working relationship with the building contractor, the site superintendent, the clerk of the works (if there is one) and other project personnel. This will involve exhibiting more than idle curiosity; there must be evidence of interest, an appreciation of the contractor's responsibilities, and a demonstrated willingness to follow the contractor's instructions regarding site visits.

When you wish to visit the site, set up an appointment in advance. Arrive on time. Don't bring extra people along. Have patience with the contractor, knowing that there are many demands on his or her time and interruptions are apt to be the rule of the day. Determine whether or not there are special hazards on the site or areas which you should not visit because of on-going work procedures. Restrict your questions to important matters. Observe all safety provisions, including wearing a hard hat at all times while on the site. Do not ask questions of workmen or engage them in conversation, no matter how willing they may seem to be. Channel all of your questions and comments

through the owner's representative to the building contractor. Consider site visitation a special privilege that is not to be abused.

Acceptance of the Building

As noted, during the period of construction, often the contractor in effect owns the library building—or in the case of an addition, that portion being added. When work is completed, and the corrections called for by the punch lists have been made, a final inspection tour should be completed by the architect and owner's representative. Particular attention must be given to the operation of mechanical equipment, electrical systems, plumbing fixtures and special systems such as public address and security systems. Special care should be given areas affected by remedial work, in order to be certain that no damage has occurred during repairs to ceilings, wall and floor finishes, doors and door jams, windows and window frames, mirrors, porcelain fixtures, etc. All light fixtures and receptacles should be tested. Plumbing fixtures should be tried for proper flow and possible leakage. Graphics, signage and art work should be in place, unless otherwise provided.

A full set of warranties, guarantees and instructional literature covering the installed equipment should be turned over to the owner's representative, with provision made for training of the owner's staff responsible for the maintenance and operation of equipment. Literature should include instructions for cleaning and maintaining surfaces of furnishings. A complete list of product manufacturers and their local representatives should be provided the owner for use if problems arise during and after the warranty period.

After all remedial work has been completed, a notice of completion is filed with the jurisdiction. In effect, this notice certifies that the contractor, to the best of his knowledge and belief, has completed construction and that the construction has been in substantial conformance with the approved plans and specifications. Approval of the notice of completion results in the transference of responsibility for the project from the contractor to the owner, subject to any special conditions, warranties, etc. that may be in effect. At this time the keys to the building are turned over to the owner. (Except for the smallest building, the librarian should insist upon the contractor installing a key box in a secure location, providing a labeled hook for every key; each key should be properly identified by the contractor before being relinquished to the owner.) Incidentally, it is often a good practice for the owner to have all of the locks changed at this point to avoid misuse of any keys that may have been in circulation during construction. Issuance of keys should then be carefully controlled, especially the allocation of master keys.

Beneficial Occupancy

For some projects there may be a period of a few weeks or months between nominal completion and the actual acceptance of the building. Whether or not the library should move in during this period, sometimes called "beneficial occupancy," depends upon many factors. Sometimes there is an urgency about moving from the old quarters that makes this desirable even though the contractor may impose restrictions on the areas to be occupied and how they are to be used. For instance, approval might be given for the movement of collections but not for staff or for public use.

In the case of an addition to an existing library, occupation may occur progressively so as to vacate other areas for remodeling. In any case, the owner must understand that occupying the building prior to its full acceptance may complicate the placement of responsibility for any damage done during this interim period: broken glass, scraped walls, scratched counter surfaces may all be attributed by the contractor to the moving of the library rather than to construction activities. Before taking advantage of beneficial occupancy, the owner should have a written agreement with the contractor covering such eventualities, including liability and risk insurance.

"As Built" Drawings

One of the final requirements for the contractor to fulfill is the preparation and delivery to the owner of one or more sets of "as built" drawings. As the term implies, "as built" drawings show how the building was actually constructed. Such drawings are necessary because construction details may change during the building process due to unforeseen circumstances or slight errors and deviations from the working drawings. Electrical conduit and plumbing pipes, covered in a slab or wall, may run several inches away from the location shown on the working drawings. A ventilating duct may have been rerouted to provide greater clearance for other equipment or structural element. Last-minute changes may occur to provide electrical outlets or light fixtures to conform to the furniture layout. Unless these changes are noted on the drawings, it is not possible to determine the exact location of wiring, piping, ductwork, etc. This becomes important when changes are required or remodeling is planned. Therefore, the contract with the building contractor should include a requirement for a detailed set of as-built drawings fully annotated with all changes and correction—usually marked in red ink. For further protection, these should be checked by the project architect before being accepted.

Summary

This chapter has traced the construction process from the time contract documents are ready for bidding. Construction is a complex process and involves a variety of subcontractors following a detailed project schedule. Construction supervision is important and should be the responsibility of a qualified person, perhaps a clerk of the works. During construction, each of the project team members has a role to play that remains vital even though activity centers on the building contractor. For the librarian it is important to be in a position to receive up-dates on construction progress, to review change orders before they are approved, and to assist in preparation of a punch list at the end of construction. The building contractor has numerous responsibilities to discharge in preparation for filing the notice of completion. Acceptance of the building transfers legal responsibility for the project from the contractor to the owner.

IX OCCUPYING THE BUILDING

PLANNING for the move into the new building and the orientation of staff and public that must follow deserves attention long before the building project is completed. In the case of a remodeled facility, with or without an addition, the move-in may occur in stages and at various intervals. The schedule will be determined by the needs of the building contractor. For these reasons, this chapter concentrates on the occupation of an entirely new building or a very major addition which significantly increases the original space.

Moving a library might not be much more complicated than moving an office if it were not for the collections. The ramifications of moving collections and other items peculiar to libraries have given rise to a number of articles in professional literature and at least one book, *Moving a Library* by William H. Kurth and Ray W. Grim. Valuable suggestions emanating from experience are contained in this literature and should be read by librarians preparing to move a library.

Addressing Basic Questions about the Move

A great deal of time and effort—to say nothing of expense—may be saved by anticipating some of the questions which moving a library is likely to raise. The areas explored in this chapter are meant to be indicative rather than comprehensive. Indeed, local conditions and circumstances will play a major role in both the questions to be answered and in their resolution.

When Is the Right Time to Move?

In the previous chapter the possibility of moving in before the building project is officially accepted was discussed under the topic "beneficial occupancy." The librarian should be aware of this possibility and discuss the ramifications with responsible officials of his or her agency. In any case, the move-in schedule must be carefully coordinated with the closing out of construction. Here the cooperation of the building contractor

will be needed. Scheduling the move too close to the project's completion date may result in having to postpone the move due to unforeseen delays in the contractor's work. On the other hand, allowing too much leeway may result in leaving the building completed but unoccupied—much to the embarrassment of all.

Besides waiting for the completion of construction, other factors may be involved, such as the availability of moving crews. If a commercial moving company is to be involved, when can they be available for the length of time necessary? If students, volunteers or other labor are to be used, when will the best work force be available? Obviously, a move involving students on a college campus should not occur during final exams! Setting a tentative date early, with provision for some deviation, is often helpful for planning purposes; it allows the planning process to proceed while the construction schedule is being monitored.

What Is to Be Moved?

At first glance, it would seem that this is a ridiculous question. However, more than one library has approached moving day without clearly determining beforehand every item to be moved, left behind or otherwise disposed of. Some items of furniture and equipment may seem to be of marginal value and not worth the cost of moving. Other items may not fit the new spaces or surroundings. To make these determinations in a logical manner, the library should prepare a careful inventory, naming every item of furniture and equipment. Then each item should be examined to determine whether it is to be replaced, or re-used in the new building. Furniture and equipment to be re-used should be placed on a separate list, noting the items which must be sent out for cleaning, refurbishment and/or repair prior to the move. A schedule for this work will then need to be prepared and followed so that all is in readiness.

If an interior designer has been involved with the

project, he or she will be extremely valuable in this effort. Besides creating the inventory and evaluating each item, he or she may take charge of the cleaning and repair work, and may recommend that various items be refinished to fit into the new color schemes and decor of the project building. The expertise of the interior designer will be especially helpful in deciding which items should be replaced.

While the inventory applies mainly to furniture and equipment, collections are not totally immune from consideration. If weeding has not kept pace, this is the time for extra effort. Why pay to move materials which are candidates for withdrawal from the collections? Because weeding is a long and involved process, evaluation in preparation for the move should begin as far in advance as possible.

Will Collections Be Reorganized?

Moving into a new building offers a unique opportunity for deciding whether or not the collections should be reorganized. Because organization determines the order in which materials appear on the shelves, any plan for reorganizing collections has direct implications for moving. Planning for the reorganization of collections is, in itself, an involved process and its execution even more tedious. For these reasons it is imperative that any reorganization be completed prior to moving day, whether it involves interfiling previously separated materials, creating new collections, or changing the way in which the collections are to be arranged. During the preparation for the move classification numbers and location symbols must be added, changed or deleted from book spines as well as corrected in the catalog or data base. If the work is not completed prior to the move, the resulting confusion is certain to lead to frustration among staff and users alike. The goal should be to present a logical arrangement of materials with call numbers matching those in the catalog or data base.

Special problems arise if the location and sequencing of collections is to be affected by the configuration of the building and/or the number of floors. While the general arrangement of the collections should have been a part of the work completed during architectural design, the exact implications for shelving may not be considered until it is time to plan for moving.

Precise shelf and volume counts must be made and projected for growth to avoid large shifts in the near future. Then detailed calculations should be made,

with accurate notations written on furniture drawings showing where each classification is expected to begin and end. Anomalies and awkward breaks in the sequencing of classifications will soon become apparent, making it possible to consider alternative arrangements. Staff involvement in this process is helpful, if not imperative.

Who Will Do the Packing and Moving?

The question of who will pack and move the library contents has been mentioned in previous paragraphs of this chapter. Numerous articles in library literature will help explain the pros and cons of the various alternatives. The choice may hinge on the size of the collections to be moved, the distance between the existing and new facilities, the availability of workers, and budget. A quotation from one or more commercial moving companies can provide valuable information on both costs and schedules. Such quotations should be sought well before it is necessary to budget or schedule the move.

Where the collections are large and/or the distance more than a very short walk, commercial movers are most often employed—at least to transport the materials and furnishings. Staff, students, volunteers or a few chosen workers may be given the task of packing and unpacking library materials. Again, the experience of numerous libraries is documented in the literature and should be considered before a decision is made. While there have been many instances where crowds of students or citizen volunteers have gathered to move a library, there are also some sad experiences where such cooperation did not materialize. Each librarian must decide this issue on the basis of local interest.

Not the least of the concerns in using staff, students and/or volunteers is the library's liability for any injuries that such workers might sustain. Lifting of cartons of library books or moving of furniture by those not accustomed to such exertion can lead to injuries and accidents. If steps or stairways must be negotiated in the process, the hazards and possible incidence of injury increase. For these reasons, the librarian should discuss the liability aspect with his or her risk management officer before making a decision. The potential savings in labor cost may be small compared to the possible liability costs. While commercial movers cost money, they are equipped to do the work and good business practices dictate that they complete the job satisfactorily.

Moving Special Items

Many libraries accumulate materials, works of art or other items which require special treatment during a move. These should be inventoried separately with appropriate descriptive notations. Statuary, paintings, collections of rare or fragile materials, and antique furniture are among the candidates for this list. The moving plan should provide detailed instructions on how each of these items is to be handled. The dimensions and weight of oversized objects should be recorded. Those responsible for the actual move should view these items at first hand and respond with a detailed plan for handling them. Most moving companies have recourse to specialists in these fields.

Insurance

When the contents of a library are moved, a special risk is incurred. Coverage of this risk will depend on who does the moving. Commercial moving companies offer insurance plans for this purpose. However, if the library elects to use students, volunteers or others, it will be necessary for the librarian to determine whether or not the library's current policies cover this situation. This matter can be referred to the jurisdiction's risk management office if such an office exists. If not, the librarian should review the need for insurance with the library's insurance broker. Special insurance may be called for if the contents of the library include significant special collections, art objects or other items that may be subject to unusual risk during the move.

How Long Will It Take to Move?

Obviously, many variables play a role in determining how long it will take to complete the moving of a library. These include the amount of materials, as well as furniture and equipment, to be moved, the distance between the old and new facilities, any structural barriers that may have to be overcome, the number of people involved in moving and the equipment to be used. Weather conditions are also a factor in some cases. Commercial moving companies, many of which have access to specialists in moving libraries, can usually provide a fairly accurate estimate. Otherwise, the librarian must make an educated guess, based perhaps on some experimentation. Generally speaking, a longer time will be required if the move is not handled by commercial movers, unless the distance is short and

there is a massive response of students or volunteers. Although the actual move may take a matter of a few days, a year or more of planning time is not unrealistic.

Should the Library Attempt to Remain Open During the Move?

Once again, this question must be answered on the basis of local conditions and resources. The experience of others may be helpful here, as well. Public goodwill may be worth the additional effort. However, maintaining even a small portion of the library's collections and services in working order during a move can be frustrating and difficult. Whether or not the move will impose unusual hazards for the public must also be a consideration. If the library does remain open, the area available for public use must be closed off from the rest of the building. User traffic must be carefully separated from traffic generated by the movement of library materials, furniture and equipment—not always an easy job. Since moving plans often call for the direct and heavy involvement of library staff, particular attention must be given staffing requirements for remaining open.

Where it is necessary to close a library for a period of time to expedite the move, consideration should be given to some temporary arrangement to provide at least minimal access to library services and resources. This may be done by transferring critical materials and services to branches or, in extreme cases, by opening a small collection in temporary quarters. In any case, sympathetic attention to public need should be given a prominent place in planning for the move.

The Librarian's Responsibilities for the Move

The preparation of the over-all plan for moving and the negotiations for the services of those who will move the library often fall on the shoulders of the librarian. It is usually the librarian's responsibility to see that planning begins on time, involves the appropriate individuals and moves according to a schedule that permits opportunity for evaluation and consideration of alternatives. Coordination with any agency office that might be involved in the move is a part of this responsibility.

If a commercial moving company is to be used, the librarian must see that the necessary routines are followed; these may include bidding and the issuance of contracts and purchase orders. Obtaining adequate insurance may be another part of the librarian's task.

Unless it has been clearly delegated to another person, the librarian must assume full command of the actual moving operation to see that all items are properly boxed, labeled, transported and placed in the correct location in the new building. Finally, it is incumbent upon the librarian to make the move a part of the overall public relations effort for the project. This includes frequently repeated announcements of the dates when library service will be restricted by the move and any instructions about alternate sources of library materials and services during this period.

Making the Move

After much planning, moving day finally arrives. Assuming adequate planning has been done, a detailed schedule is available which directs each person to the particular tasks he or she is to perform. Instruction in moving techniques and boxing collections, for instance, should have preceded moving day. Now is the time for action!

Handling Collections

There are many ways to prepare collections for moving. These are covered in numerous articles in the literature. If the move is over a relatively short distance, materials may be taken from the shelves and transported directly on book trucks. Mechanical conveyors have been used with some success in certain instances. Where large numbers of people are available, a bucket brigade arrangement for passing books hand to hand may be used. All of these methods, of course, assume dependable supervision at both ends of the line.

Because of distance or other factors, many libraries end up having to box collections for the move-in. There seems to be no way to avoid this labor-intensive task in some situations. There are two keys to success: 1/ a carefully considered notation system indicating the contents of every box and its location in the new facility, and 2/ workers trained to transfer materials to and from the boxes in proper sequence. Again, the literature has many examples of how this may be accomplished.

In the new facility, temporary signs and shelf labels may be used to guide workers in finding the proper location for reshelving materials. Color coding on the boxes and shelves is extremely helpful and multiplies

the versatility and accuracy of the notation system. However, nothing substitutes for the alert supervision of staff on the scene. In spite of the best laid plans, questions are inevitably going to arise which require immediate response if delay or possible mistakes are to be avoided.

Transporting Collections

As noted above, collections are sometimes moved by booktruck, conveyor, or hand to hand. Enterprising folk have also derived various bits of equipment such as shelf-length troughs to accomplish this task. When boxes are used, they must be stacked in order and then transported to and from trucks using two-wheel dollies. Several boxes of books comprise a heavy load and precautions must be taken in handling them. If ramps are necessary along the way, extreme caution must be used to avoid accidents. Before packing begins, attention should be given to creating staging areas where empty cartons can be assembled. Other spaces will be needed for the orderly arrangement of boxes filled with materials and awaiting transport to the new building. In the new facility, similar staging areas will be necessary to provide space for the arrival and distribution of the boxes to their respective destinations. Once emptied, cartons must be broken down and stacked for return to the moving company.

Moving Furniture and Equipment

The handling and moving of library furniture and equipment usually merits the use of a commercial moving company. Again, each piece must be coded with notations indicating where it is to be placed in the new building. Special attention should be given automation equipment, office machines and other sensitive items. As previously noted, particular care will be required for art objects, antique furnishings and oversized pieces. The interior designer, if one is used, will often be involved with the placement of furnishings and equipment as they arrive in the new building. If not, one or more staff members familiar with the disposition of furnishings should be delegated the task of supervising the placement of items.

Settling In

Once everything has been relocated into the new facility a period of settling in follows. Inevitably some adjustments to the original arrangements will occur. The librarian should be prepared to handle these changes. No matter how thorough the final punch lists have been, it is probable that a few days occupancy of the building will reveal several undiscovered—or un-corrected—problems. These may range from electrical outlets that don't work to seams opening in carpets, unwelcome drafts in offices, or locks that fail to function properly. Correction of most such problems will involve the building contractor.

Settling in also involves the collections. A thorough job of shelf reading is usually a desirable place to begin. This is particularly important where the move involves the consolidation of previously separated materials, or, vice-versa, the segmentation of a larger block of the collection. Once shelf reading is completed, any necessary adjustments can be made to the arrangement of the collections. Sometimes awkward breaks in sequential arrangement can be remedied by shifting a few shelves or sections of materials.

Staff Orientation

Like most things connected with a new facility, staff orientation requires advance planning. Staff should have an opportunity during the period of architectural planning and construction to become familiar with the general plan of the library and the specifics of their own locations. Staff tours just prior to occupation are most helpful. Additional familiarity will occur as the staff assists in planning for the move. However, staff orientation should go beyond this, with a goal to increase productivity and to encourage an understanding and appreciation of their new surroundings. How disappointing it is to visit a new library and find the staff only vaguely familiar with their new home! Or, more eager to reveal its faults than its strengths.

Moving into a new facility—or even into a remodeled and expanded one—requires library staff to adjust to new surroundings and working conditions. While some preparation for this can be done before the move, most staff orientation will occur afterward. This training should begin with tours that take every staff member, including part-time personnel, through every nook and cranny including mechanical equipment rooms, storage areas, custodial spaces, etc. Sufficient time should be allowed for answering questions. If possible, the tours should be followed by frequent staff meetings where questions can be raised, minor problems resolved and attention given to other building-related matters such as new operating procedures.

Training drills can be very helpful in encouraging prompt and accurate responses to the inevitable array of directional questions the public is sure to pose. This should include directions to restrooms, drinking fountains, public telephones, offices, meeting rooms, special services, and popular collection areas. Staff members may divide into groups, some giving directions and others attempting to follow them. This will help to establish the most effective landmarks needed in order to refer a person to a particular place.

Other exercises may involve particular portions of the staff. For instance, the reference staff may profit from drills which help familiarize them with the new locations of more frequently used materials. Circulation staff will benefit from drills that help them understand the handling of questions they are sure to be asked. Among the most important are custodial staff members, who should have training in the proper care of the new furnishings, floor and wall coverings, etc. Cleaning schedules must be established as well.

New Equipment

Almost inevitably a new building will involve new equipment and systems. If possible, the staff should be trained in their use before encountering the public. Such training may begin with demonstrations, followed by hands-on experience. This should include, but not be limited to, the use of the telephone, intercom and public address systems, which tend to increase in complexity and are quite likely to be more sophisticated than systems the staff has been using previously. Similarly, staff members who are expected to use entirely new pieces of equipment such as automation and office machines should receive adequate training at this time. Time spent in training should be amply repaid in higher productivity and fewer problems.

Public Orientation

Like the staff, those who are going to use the new facility must become acquainted with it. Planning for orienting users to the new library should be made well in advance of the opening day. The purpose of public orientation, of course, is to encourage maximum use and appreciation of the new facility and to minimize the need for involving staff in answering obvious directional questions.

Aids to Assist Public Orientation

The number of ways in which the public can be assisted in its orientation to the new facility is limited only by imagination, energy and budget. Much of this effort will continue to be needed as new students, faculty or public users enter the building for the first time in the years ahead. Only a few of the more prevalent orientation tools can be described here. Useful samples of materials produced by others are available through most state library agencies and from the American Library Association.

Brochures and Directories

Perhaps the most obvious and popular tool is the brochure which describes the features of the new library and provides a directory of the most frequently requested services, collections, and offices. Some brochures err in being too brief and/or too general to be very helpful. Others get bogged down in detail. Illustrations and floor plans should be incorporated to provide visual reference points. Brochure language should repeat the wording of prominent signs as a means of reinforcing identification of particular routes or areas. It should go without saying that the brochure should be attractive, readable and practical. Additional brochures should be prepared to cover special departments, services or features of the building.

Tours

Tours conducted by staff or volunteers are among the most frequently used orientation techniques. On opening day, and for the first several days thereafter, tours are likely to be extremely popular. To maximize the value of this experience, tour leaders should be given appropriate instruction, complete with pertinent facts and figures. After the tour route or routes have been determined, trial runs should be made to determine what questions are likely to arise and whether or not there are any potential difficulties. For instance, if an elevator is to be used along the way, tour groups should not be greater in number than an elevator can accommodate, or the group will become fragmented. The route should avoid devious winding through stack areas where people may linger to browse. After dedication day, tours must be modified to avoid disrupting staff in offices and workrooms. Tour leaders should make practice runs prior to leading groups.

Fact Sheets

A lot of staff and tour-leader time can be saved and many questions answered by the preparation of a detailed fact sheet. Again, samples will be helpful in deciding what should be included. Information should be provided on a wide range of details, beginning with the names of the firms associated with the project, including architects, engineers, and contractors, then continuing through the building's vital statistics, data on collections, and manufacturers of major furniture and equipment items. Fact sheets prepared in simple fashion will suffice; it's the information and not the format that counts. These sheets of information will aid tour leaders in providing accurate and consistent answers to questions. They can also be included as part of the kits supplied to the media prior to the opening of the library. Fact sheets remain useful for years to come as a source for answering questions posed by other libraries. The time they require in preparation is saved many times over.

Floor Plans

While general floor plans should be a part of the orientation brochure, additional floor plans presenting the layout of particular areas may be useful, especially in larger or more complex buildings. Floor plans are most helpful when they show the layout of furniture and equipment. Plans for stack areas should indicate the location of materials by broad classification numbers. This will save hours of time for the user as well as the staff. Particular note should be made of frequently requested subjects or items such as unabridged dictionaries, atlases, and copy machines.

Floor plans should be in scale with all legends and notations easily found and read. The base floor plans will often be those produced by the architect or interior designer as part of the design process. Just be certain that they accurately portray the actual location of stacks and furnishings as the user will find them. Before floor plans are reproduced they should be tested for accuracy and readability. This can best be done by someone who is unfamiliar with the building.

A-V Materials

Audio-visual materials are also useful for orientation purposes. Cassette tapes can provide self-guided tours, especially of larger buildings. These are particularly valuable for student orientation. Instructions and descriptions must be clear. The voice of the narrator must be pleasing and easily understood. Although tapes usually follow a written script, the accuracy, coherence and logic of the narrative must be tested by listening to the tape while walking through the building. Needless to say, the narrative must be up-dated whenever changes occur in the layout.

Visual orientation materials include slide shows, films and videotape—the latter replacing film because of its flexibility and lower cost. Visual presentations have the advantage of greater ease in identifying library landmarks. They are equally effective used in or outside the library building. However, the preparation of an adequate visual presentation may be more expensive than an audio cassette and requires equipment and a place for viewing. Production of video materials should follow a well-written narrative script and take full advantage of the many techniques available to the photographer or video producer, such as panning and close-ups. While theatrical shots from unusual angles will enhance the viewing pleasure, the viewer must always be able to relate to the scene in terms of recognizing the area and how to reach it.

Interactive video presentations using optical disc technology are likely to become a useful orientation tool. Public familiarity with interactive video is increasing as theme parks, hotels, convention centers, shopping malls and others use it to provide information and guidance. Because of the almost limitless capacity of the optical disc, this medium may offer the best means for orienting library newcomers in the future. Video screens in nicely designed cabinets can be stationed at strategic points to provide convenient access to directional information, which could include detailed directions to specific portions of the collections as well as more general guidance. At this time the cost of creating an optical disc is its greatest drawback. However, technological and marketing developments are expected to reduce this hurdle in the near future.

Holograms

While not yet a practical methodology, in the future orientation materials may include a series of holograms to provide a three-dimensional presentation of the new facility. It is still difficult to predict exactly how this technology might best be used for orientation materials. However, the potential is there for the clever and enterprising librarian to work with not too many years hence. In their simplest forms, holograms might supplant floor plans, for instance.

The Dedication Day

Dedication day offers a special opportunity to give recognition to all who have contributed to the project as well as to introduce the new facility to the user. Planning for this event should begin months in advance, especially if a formal ceremony is to be held. Ideas for dedication programs can be gleaned from sample programs available through the collections maintained by various state library agencies and the American Library Association. The planning for dedication programs is often the responsibility of a special committee appointed for that purpose, with broad representation from the user public, the administration, the library and other interested groups.

A decision that must be made fairly early is whether the dedication ceremony should occur at the time the building is opened or at some later date. While the decision depends upon many local factors, it is generally felt that public interest reaches its peak at the time the building opens its doors for the first time. Whether the dedication occurs then or later, media coverage is apt to focus on the library when the building first opens. This is particularly true if the library has mounted a sustained public relations program focusing on each key event in the construction and move-in process. The opportunity to capitalize on this wave of publicity and rising awareness often outweighs other factors in favor of dedication coinciding with the actual opening.

The dedication of a new library building is usually a sufficiently momentous occasion in the life of an institution or community that it merits more than a single day's celebration. Because of this, many libraries plan events which extend over a period of several days, with the focus changing from day to day. Attention can then be drawn to special areas or features of the library buildings. Tours of these special interest areas can be more detailed than time allows on a general visit.

So much can be gained from the well-planned dedication that it is worth all the effort that must go into it. It is an unparalleled opportunity for expressing thanks to those engaged in the project and to achieve campus or community-wide involvement.

Period of Adjustment

Once the new facility is open, a "shake-down" period follows. During this time staff become familiar with their new work environment and the user begins to learn where collections and services are located and what new delights the library may offer. Meanwhile, the librarian must be prepared in many situations to cope with a variety of special problems. Fortunately, most buildings carry at least a one-year warranty from the contractor, with specific items of equipment and materials guaranteed for somewhat longer.

During this period Parkinson's Law, "if anything can go wrong, it will," is apt to prevail. Some of the modifications are predictable. For instance, fine tuning the building's HVAC system can not be completed until the structure has been fully occupied and has passed through the entire cycle of seasons, establishing its response to the heat of summer and the cold of winter. Therefore, adjustments to the system can be expected, with a few of them involving some discomfort when the HVAC system is shut down for a period of time. Roofing and weather stripping will likewise be tested during this period. Some changes in lighting may occur since it is not always possible to predict where glare or unwanted shadows will occur.

Most of the adjustments required during this period will involve the contractor and one or more of his sub-contractors. Now and then the architect will need to be brought in, especially if there is a question as to whether poor performance is due to design or to construction or installation. These questions of liability, especially if they involve a major installation such as a roof or a large system such as the electrical or HVAC, can lead to prolonged arbitration. Recognizing this, the librarian must press for remedial action with costs adjudicated at a later date by the proper court.

Unless building problems are handled by someone else on the campus or in the government agency, the librarian will need to establish and maintain a favorable working relationship with these individuals. Whenever questions or problems arise, they should be communicated in writing so that a paper path can be created and retraced as necessary. Unfortunately, it is sometimes more difficult to get attention from architects and contractors once the building has been completed.

Prior to the end of the first year of occupation, the librarian should make a detailed punch list including every item requiring attention. The architect and/or interior designer should be involved also, since they may find items that the librarian is not aware of. Before the warranty period has expired, the contractor should be requested in writing to remedy all of the conditions noted. Agreement should be reached on all controversial items. Promises of later repairs should be given in writing. Once out of warranty, the cost of building repairs are not likely to be borne by the contractor.

Summary

Occupying a new library facility involves moving, orientation of staff and public, and a period of adjustment to new surroundings. Planning is the key to successful moving and to the dedication of the new facility. The library should prepare itself to capitalize on the public relations opportunities that moving and dedication provide. A variety of techniques and materials can be used to assist in the orientation of staff and public. Planning and preparation are, again, necessary. After the move-in, the librarian can anticipate the normal routine being interrupted by a variety of unexpected situations. Handling these successfully requires an understanding of the building as well as maintaining a working relationship with the building contractor and the architect. A final punch list should be created before the library has occupied the building for one year; all necessary remedial work should then be completed in keeping with the general warranty conditions.

X SITE SELECTION

THE LOCATION of the library facility plays an important role in the success of an academic library and has even greater consequences for public libraries. Unfortunately, site selection is not always within the control of the librarian. Site selection sometimes bogs down in an emotional conflict among the proponents of various locations, leaving the library to continue its sufferings in an inadequate building. This chapter is intended to explore some of the criteria and methods that may be useful to the librarian and others who may be involved in site selection.

The Site Selection Process

How a site is chosen for a library building is one of the major project variables. Unless predetermined by gift or master plan, the choice is unlikely to be made in a logical fashion. Indeed, few elements of the library building project are apt to be less systematically approached or more fraught with emotion than the selection of the site. In part this is due to the widely divergent perceptions of library objectives and the circumstances which contribute to their success. Some continue to see the library as a warehouse, others as a monument, while a growing number recognize it as a service agency.

The librarian faced with a project in which the site has not been predetermined should devote time to understanding the primary criteria and developing a workable process. Unfortunately, criteria have yet to be reinforced by more than experience and the testimony of individuals. Conclusive evidence is difficult to cite. Nevertheless, those who have had broad experience with libraries testify that location is a major determinant in encouraging library usage on the campus as well as in the community.

The Academic Library

Site selection for academic library buildings is more often than not determined either by history or by the campus master plan. This plan may have been created

years in advance of the need for a new library building. The librarian should be thoroughly familiar with the master plan and determine whether or not the site selected is appropriate. If the location is faulty, then the librarian should voice concern and ask for review by the administration. As part of this process, the librarian should draw attention to the primary site criteria which contribute to the success of an academic library and indicate how the proposed location falls short. Alternative sites which better meet the criteria can be analyzed by way of comparison.

When the librarian is directly involved in the site selection process, whether for the master plan or an actual building, emphasis should be placed on educating others concerning the criteria. This usually works better than choosing a particular location and then defending it, at least in the early stages. Where possible, the experience of other academic libraries faced with similar choices can be useful. Some of the techniques discussed below for the public library can also be applied. To this end, and because of the paucity of the literature on academic library locations, the librarian should be familiar with site selection criteria for public libraries as a way of developing an awareness of the process.

The Public Library

While the location for a public library may be foreordained in some communities, more often than not this is not the case. Therefore, the librarian is more apt to play an active role in site selection than his or her academic counterpart. If selection is not obvious, then it is all too likely to become a divisive issue. Again, the librarian should try to defuse this potentially explosive issue by beginning early to educate and to offer a process by which reason and logic may hopefully prevail.

Overview of the Site Selection Process

Assuming that a location has not been predetermined by a master plan or other device, the librarian should

115

anticipate the need for an orderly site selection process to reduce, if not eliminate, the potential for dissension. This requires lead time to prepare officials who will participate in selecting the site and in initiating the selection process well in advance of architectural planning. Needless to say, it is imperative that the site be agreed upon before the architect begins so that site implications for design can be studied and incorporated.

Establish Criteria and Priorities

The first vital step in a logical selection process is to establish selection criteria based upon priorities of library requirements. Usually the first of these is convenience for the user. Others may be proximity on the campus, for instance, to major classroom buildings. The public library will include ease of access and high visibility along with other criteria. As the list of criteria develops it should be arranged in priority order.

Criteria and priorities may be established by the librarian and then presented to officials, or may be the end product of joint effort with the project committee, library board or other group ultimately responsible for selecting or recommending the site to other officials. The librarian must have a clear vision of library objectives and how location may affect their achievement, and back this with relevant positive arguments. Gathering experience from other libraries and from the professional literature is the most useful resource for this purpose.

Analyze Potential Sites

After the list of criteria has been agreed upon and put in priority order, it is time to analyze potential sites. The list may be long or short. However, it should be reasonably comprehensive, including any sites that may have received previous attention or are apt to be supported by special groups or interests. Each of these sites, carefully delineated, can then be evaluated in accordance with the established criteria.

Weigh and Evaluate Sites

The process of site analysis should weigh the characteristics of each site against the approved selection criteria in an objective manner. This is particularly important when the library site threatens to become a controversial issue. A methodology which results in a clear-cut numerical score has many advantages. Another tactic is to retain a qualified consultant to prepare an independent evaluation. This latter strategy has its own advantages and pitfalls which will be discussed later in this chapter.

Site Selection Criteria

Discussion of site criteria in this chapter must be limited to some fairly general concepts. In many cases, local circumstances will add other criteria which compel or merit consideration. Before beginning the task of establishing criteria, it is important that the librarian becomes familiar with the more important discussions of site selection in the literature.

Criteria Accepted by the Profession

There has long been a realization in the library profession that the location of a library affects library service. However, this belief has not received the kind of research that many other elements of library service have enjoyed. Literature searches, therefore, are apt to be fairly short. It might be argued that the very fact that so little has been produced indicates a passive consensus among librarians. Certainly, such literature as does exist seem to indicate that librarians generally agree on how locations influence library usage.

Academic Libraries

Much less has been written about the locating of academic libraries than public libraries. Perhaps this is because the location question is often moot due to a pre-existing campus master plan. In many cases, the sheer size of the academic library building may eliminate all but one or two available sites. Occasionally the terms of a major donor's gift will be the determinant.

Nonetheless, whenever a new site must be selected, site selection criteria will be needed. They will probably be few in number and will likely reflect local considerations. Among the general criteria most likely to be included are:

1/ Size of the site
2/ Relationship to adjacent facilities—present and future
3/ Relationship to vehicular and pedestrian access

4/ Geographic orientation
5/ Soil conditions.

Size of the site. While it might seem too obvious to be included, the size of the site must be given a prominent place on the list of criteria. All too often a site selected without this in mind results in an architectural solution involving extra service and stack levels which add cost to initial construction and to long-term library operation. The site must be large enough to accommodate future expansion as well as the original structure.

Applying this criterion requires some understanding of how large the building will be, both in terms of site coverage initially and in its ultimate development. Even a very preliminary needs assessment analysis of space requirements based on library objectives, present and projected enrollment, and related factors should result in an estimated building size. If it is necessary to resolve the site problem before the architect is available, the librarian will need to estimate the ground floor coverage (footprint) of the building. This may be approached by determining which elements are to be situated on the ground floor and then estimating the related square footage required.

Keyes Metcalf provided a table for this purpose.[1] For the purposes of this table, he assumed that the ground floor should contain library service elements such as circulation control, reference services, reference and bibliographical collections, the public catalog, and the acquisitions and cataloging departments. The applicability of Metcalf's assumptions must, of course, be tested against the realities of the individual library situation and adjusted accordingly. For instance, the automated catalog has reduced, if not eliminated, the need to place the acquisitions and cataloging departments adjacent to the public catalog on the ground floor.

The results of these calculations can be tested by applying the experience of other libraries of comparable size. Generally speaking, experience indicates that optimum coverage will range between 20,000 and 50,000 net square feet. When the floor area exceeds this size, additional staffing is apt to be required and vertical connections are more economical than horizontal access between functions. Converting this figure into the number of floors the building will require is a problem the architect will eventually have to solve.

Relationship to adjacent campus facilities. How the site relates to other campus facilities is another useful criterion. There is some consensus that academic libraries are used more frequently if they are situated in proximity to classroom buildings rather than to dormitories or other facilities. Motivation and convenience are both factors. Students are more apt to use a library if

it is within easy walking distance of their classes. This seems particularly true of institutions where a substantial portion of the student body commutes daily.

Vehicular and pedestrian access. Locating the academic library where it is easily accessible to vehicular traffic is particularly important for non-residential colleges and universities. Unless parking is reasonably close, student use will be adversely affected. Likewise, pedestrian access from major classrooms, dormitories and other campus facilities should be by convenient and clearly defined routes. Students are likely to be less concerned about the time required or the distance between the library and dormitories or student unions than they are about proximity to classrooms.

Geographic orientation. Architectural design can overcome many site deficiencies. However, when all other things are equal, preference should go to the site which permits orientation of the library building to take advantage of north light. This is particularly true with the renewed emphasis on use of natural light and energy conservation. If a view potential exists, this should be considered as an extra dividend.

Soil conditions. While often assumed to be a factor that should not be considered in site selection, soil conditions, nonetheless, can be a determinant. Presumably the librarian can obtain information about soil conditions from work done on adjacent buildings. Where indicated, soil tests may be made on the location or locations of primary interest. Soil conditions determine whether or not construction of basements may encounter ground water which would make them expensive or impossible. Footings may also be affected by poor soil conditions, resulting in expensive site work and foundation construction. It would be discouraging, indeed, to complete the arduous site selection process only to have the architect discover at a later date that substantial problems either preclude construction at the location or require expensive solutions. Soil conditions, therefore, have a legitimate place in the list of criteria.

Public Libraries

By comparison, somewhat more attention has been given the effect of location on the use of public library buildings. Much of this stems from the work of Joseph Wheeler. Again, accepted criteria have been the result of observations and experience rather than any form of scientific research. This does not necessarily detract from the validity of the criteria since there is near unanimity on the subjects.

Whether a main library or a branch, whether located in a large city or in a village, the major criteria remain constant. These criteria are based on the assumption that the primary objective of most public libraries is to provide library materials and services to the greatest number of people of all ages at the lowest operating cost. In this respect the public library is often likened to a large-volume retail store where the volume of sales is a major determinant in the cost of doing business. Unit costs of operation are reduced as usage increases. Higher circulation, greater reference use, more attendance at library programs, for instance, mean that the jurisdiction's investment in the library's facility, collections, staff and operating costs is bearing a greater return.

Applying this concept in most communities will place the public library building with corresponding retail and commercial facilities at, or very near, the downtown crossroads. While urban blight and sprawl have caused some to question whether this tenet is applicable in some instances, it is generally conceded to remain relevant. Joseph Wheeler's landmark work on the locating of public library buildings[2] contains many convincing examples selected from years of observation and discussion with public librarians. Perhaps the only deviation from Wheeler's concepts is a greater emphasis on vehicular access and the availability of off-street parking. In most situations, access by pedestrians is given lesser emphasis, an acknowledgment of increased dependence on the automobile.

Although other criteria may be considered, especially those derived from the local situation, the following seem to be basic:

1/ Convenience and accessibility to the maximum number of potential users.
2/ Sufficient land for the building (including future expansion) landscaping and parking.
3/ High visibility from major vehicular and pedestrian access routes.
4/ Proximity to compatible traffic-generating land uses, usually as a part of a significant retail commercial center.
5/ Topography and soil conditions.
6/ Possibility of hidden obstacles.
7/ Availability.
8/ Cost.

While other criteria may be added, these should probably be considered essential for almost every situation. They are discussed in the following paragraphs. It is only fair to indicate that while most librarians adhere to these tenets, a few do not. Some librarians tend to downgrade the importance of location, claiming that the size of the collection, rather than accessibility, is the primary determinant in usage—the larger the collection, the greater the number of users.

Convenience and accessibility to the maximum number of potential users. If public library site selection criteria were to be reduced to a single tenet, this would probably be the most universal. Use patterns for many types of facilities, public libraries included, are highly sensitive to the ease in which potential users can reach them. Convenience has become a watchword among most people and accessibility is the primary attribute—if not a synonym. Of course convenience is more than mere proximity. Along with accessibility it is a perceived quality that has many overtones which may include safety of access and hospitable surroundings.

In many situations, following this axiom will place the public library building at or near the crossroads of the community. Incidentally, the crossroads has no necessary correlation with the geographic center of the jurisdiction—a fact that sometimes is not understood. Perhaps the best test of the convenience criterion is to ask whether the same location would be chosen for a bank or retail store that must depend in part on the magnetism of surrounding facilities to draw trade to its doors.

Sufficient land. As with the academic library, the site for a public library building must be of sufficient size to meet the building's requirements. However, the requirements must be expanded to include off-street parking and landscaping as well as required setbacks from adjacent streets and property lines—elements not necessarily considered by the academic library. Space for future expansion must also be considered along with room for any additional parking such an increase in the structure's size may dictate.

High Visibility from Adjacent Vehicular and Pedestrian Access Routes

Facilities which have high visibility are more likely to be considered convenient and accessible. This is particularly true of libraries, which must depend upon easy identification as part of the access requirement. A library building located where a large volume of traffic passes by each day is much more likely to be used than one that is a block or so off the beaten path and obscured by intervening structures. Obviously, attaining high visibility is a product of architectural design as well as of location. But the best possible design is apt to be lost on a poorly situated site.

Compatibility with adjacent land use. The public library should be located amid compatible surroundings. It should be an integral part of a "magnet" site drawing people from throughout the service area. This includes types of facilities which are apt to attract people who are also potential users of the library. Community libraries, including branch buildings, have proven much more successful when located in shopping centers, for instance, than elsewhere. Parks make poor sites as do locations close to other recreational facilities such as theaters, bowling alleys and skating rinks. Sites within residential areas are not acceptable candidates, either. Obviously, factories and industrial parks do not make good library neighbors.

Finally, a further word of warning: in an era when the redevelopment of blighted areas is so popular, great care must be taken to see that the public library does not become a pawn in this campaign and end up at a location which compromises its objectives. Civic officials are sometimes prone to use funding for municipal projects such as library buildings to further other goals, including downtown redevelopment projects. The promise that the new library building will be a valuable anchor encouraging rehabilitation of a depressed area has not been fulfilled very often. Instead, the general public retains its perception of the blighted area and looks elsewhere for library services.

While present conditions of adjacent land uses can be observed, site investigation must include study of the zoning regulations which will determine the future of the area. The local planning office can supply information on zoning plans as well as possible restrictions. More than one librarian has found it necessary to change site recommendations after discovering zoning restrictions on a given site. These may include such things as the percentage of land the building can cover, setbacks, landscaping and parking requirements, as well as the type of enterprises expected in the area.

Topography and soil conditions. Investigation of soil conditions is as important for public libraries as for academic libraries. Investigation should include actual soil tests where experience on neighboring properties shows that problems may exist. Soil tests are relatively inexpensive and will eventually be required for the designated site, in any case, before architectural planning can begin. Unstable land formations, poor drainage and high water tables are further deterrents.

Hidden obstacles. Even a smooth, level site sometimes proves deceptive when thoroughly examined. During the site investigation, it is important to determine whether or not hidden obstacles to construction lie below the surface. These obstacles may vary from the buried foundations of previous and long-forgotten structures to toxic wastes. A former basement may have been filled in with broken concrete or other rubble.

Tanks containing solvents, fuel or other noxious materials may have been allowed to remain in the ground when earlier buildings were razed.

While the existence of such debris does not necessarily preclude use of the site for a library building, the presence of hidden obstacles signals the possibility of additional site costs and possible construction delays. Obviously, a price must be paid for digging up and hauling away any foreign materials. Then, after the buried material has been removed, the excavation must be filled with new soil and compacted to an acceptable density. There will also be an added cost for handling and disposing any toxic waste materials unearthed on the site.

Availability. Whereas most colleges and universities already include the proposed library site as part of the existing campus, public library site selection must frequently deal with land not owned by the governing jurisdiction. Availability then becomes a necessary criterion.

Upon investigation the librarian may find that the site under consideration is owned by another government agency which is reluctant to forgo its own plans. It may be that the land has been purchased for private development and architectural planning may be well under way. Or, the site may be part of an estate where ownership is divided among numerous heirs, which vastly complicates acquisition, especially if the estate happens to be in litigation. While most jurisdictions have the power of eminent domain, there is often an unwillingness on the part of public officials to exercise the right of condemnation. This reluctance may spring from lack of precedence or from previous experience; sometimes this kind of action raises public ire and sympathy for the property owner. The potential for loss of time and higher acquisition costs may be further deterrents to condemnation.

Cost. Every effort should be made to make cost only one of the several selection criteria—all too often it is allowed to become the dominant factor. Methods for estimating the probable value of land are covered in the next section. At this point, the librarian should be extremely cautious; handling cost information requires great care. Land values are highly speculative and premature release of cost information can damage the prospects of acquiring the property. This is particularly true if the jurisdiction resorts to condemnation proceedings.

How much should a library cost? This question will undoubtedly be asked during the site selection process. This question, along with suggestions for presenting evaluating cost information, is included in the next section of this chapter.

Analysis of Potential Sites

Once the site candidates are determined, analysis should proceed systematically. It is important that the same kind of information be gathered for each site and that objectivity be maintained. As poor as some locations may appear, they may have their supporters in the community and rational, sufficiently documented arguments will be needed to show why other sites are superior for the library's purposes.

Plat maps and ownership records. One of the first steps in analysis is to secure plat maps and ownership records of all sites under consideration. Usually these are obtainable through a tax office, a Hall of Records or similar source. The plat map will provide an accurate description of the site and the corresponding dimensions and include existing structures and major topographic features. The record of ownership will show the legal owners of the property. Both of these records may provide surprises. It is not unusual, for instance, to find that a parcel is of a different size and shape than popularly assumed and that ownership may be divided between a number of people.

Relate sites to library space requirements. Once the plat maps are available, the amount of land in each parcel can be accurately determined. This space can then be related to the library's building requirements. As previously noted, this involves an estimate of the ground floor size based on the space needs of library elements to be located there. Allowance must be made for setbacks, landscaping and parking. It may be necessary to check with the local zoning department to determine these requirements, which may vary depending upon location.

Site visitation. After the plat maps and records of ownership have been studied, and the amount of land available has been verified, some sites may be eliminated on the basis of the findings. The remaining sites should then be visited. To provide comparable data a checklist will be helpful and should note such things as topography, drainage, neighboring land uses, potential views, traffic, type and condition of existing structures and any unusual features including large trees. Be sure to walk the entire site; sometimes important items are not visible from the adjoining streets or sidewalks. If the site is fenced or otherwise restricted or signed for trespassing, seek permission to enter the grounds before proceeding. Vacant land that has been previously occupied by structures may contain hazardous areas not always visible to the eye.

Ascertain availability of sites. During the site analysis process, some candidates may appear unavailable for various reasons. These usually include complex ownerships, property with clouded title, or land that is in litigation. Land that is undergoing development may also be difficult to acquire. Existing structures sometimes pose a problem, particularly if they have any local historical value or are architecturally noteworthy. Such sites should be placed in a separate category, to be considered only if other locations fail to qualify.

Determine approximate cost. Arriving at the value of a particular parcel of land can be difficult. In some states a formula may be applied to assessed valuation of the property, assuming that the land is on the tax rolls and appraisals are current. If nearby parcels of similar size and location have changed hands recently, their selling price can be used as a gauge. When other means are not available, it may be necessary to employ the services of an appraiser, who will provide an estimated price along with a detailed account of the basis for his or her conclusion. Again, the librarian should be aware of the very sensitive nature of this kind of information.

Site Comparison

Once the analysis has been completed, it is time to evaluate and compare the findings to arrive at a recommendation. Various methods can be used for this process. To begin with, a simple table may be used to compare the basic findings for each site, such as the example in Table 10-1. The length of the table and the number of factors compared will vary with each situation. Presenting this information in the form of a table of facts provides a convenient index to relevant details and helps avoid sheer emotional decisions.

After this table is completed, a second technique can be employed to determine how well the sites meet the previously adopted site criteria. This involves assigning weights to the various criteria, as shown in Table 10-2. The assignment of weights should provide reasonable leeway in expressing differences. A scale of 1–9, for instance, allows 5 to be the mid-point, with 1 standing for very poor or unacceptable while 9 would be excellent or exceptional, perhaps. One of the important goals is to recognize that some criteria are more relevant than others to the successful location of a library building. Table 10-3 shows in a very simplified way how the application of weighted criteria can be used to compare sites. This fictitious example is for a main library building in a city with a population of 30,000. The building program indicates that an acre and a half of land will be needed for the building and off-street parking.

Table 10-1
Summary of Site Findings

Criteria	Site Findings		
	Site 1 Main St.	Site 2 Forest Park	Site 3 Homewood
Brief site description of location	½ block site was formerly that of Main St. furniture store	On SE edge of city's Forest Park	4 lots in the old Homewood subdivision
Convenience & accessibility to maximum number of people	In core of central city business district	Borders freeway on north side of city; Glade St. is primary feeder street	In old residential part of city; no nearby arterials
Sufficient land: acre and a half needed	Tight: about 62,000 ft²	Up to 3 acres available but site is narrow	Acre and a half in site consisting of 4 lots
High visibility from major access routes	Good exposure from Main St.; some visibility from Center Ave.	Some exposure from Glade St.	Very limited view from corner
Proximity to compatible traffic-generating land uses; part of magnet site	Near retail center of city; focal point for local traffic	Parks & rec. facilities attract devotees	Surrounded by single- & multi-family homes
Topographic and soil conditions	Flat site	Hillside; follows Glade Creek	Swampy depression runs through center of lots
Hidden obstacles	Fill dirt contains demolition debris	Rock outcroppings	High water table
Availability	Possible competition from a new merchant seeking a downtown business location	Subject to purchase by city of additional adjacent land for park	1 lot: for sale; 1 lot: in estate; 1 lot: owner plans to build; 1 lot: abandoned house
Cost (estimated)	Negotiable: asking price is $475,000	Up to $75,000 for land the city wants	A realtor estimates cost at $130,000 if litigation is avoided
Special considerations	Accessibility and visibility should increase library use and cost-effective delivery of library services	Panoramic views possible; location would require most users to travel further than other sites	Hard to find for those unfamiliar with this residential area; loss of use expected

While the evaluation of sites inevitably involves personal judgment, use of the preceding techniques tends to minimize this element. If site selection has involved several people, as it often does, then each person can rank the sites using the suggested criteria and weights. The composite results would form a basis for selection and recommendation. In spite of all the variables, more often than not, one site will emerge a clear favor-

Table 10-2
Table of Assignable Weights for Site Selection Criteria

Value	Weight
Outstanding	9
Superior	7
Acceptable (average)	5
Substantial limitations	3
Virtually unacceptable	1

ite if the process of analysis has been systematically carried out.

Cost comparisons. Making objective cost comparison is often the most troublesome part of site evaluation. This is particularly true where the most desirable site turns out to be the one with the largest price tag! Cost comparison often involves answering the question of how much the library should spend for a building site. Obviously, there is no pat answer. From time to time formulas have been suggested relating site cost to construction as a percentage of total project cost. However, such rationalization has not generally been accepted.

A better solution is to approach the site cost from the vantage point of the businessperson who is more concerned with the effect of the location on long-term sales and cost of operations. This involves a degree of speculation, of course, although the experience of other libraries can sometimes be drawn upon. Begin with the premise that a building of a given size will require the same staff and general overhead and operating costs no matter where it is located.

Construct a comparison model for each site by adding the site and construction costs to the annual operating costs for a specific number of years. For purposes of this example you will need to factor in a conservative inflation factor, perhaps 5% per year. In most instances, the total for the various sites will be quite similar given this long-range view.

Example A

Site 1:

Land	$150,000
Construction	2,000,000
Operating costs for 25 years	12,500,000

Total cost, 25 years = $14,650,000; ave./yr = $586,000

Table 10-3
Application of Weights to Site Criteria

Criteria	Main St.	Forest Park	Homewood
Convenience and accessibility	9	3	3
Sufficient land	5	9	9
High visibility	9	3	1
Compatibility with adjacent land uses; magnet site	9	3	1
Topography and soil conditions	7	3	3
Hidden obstacles	5	3	3
Availability	9	5	3
Cost	5	7	7
Special considerations	9	3	1
Totals	67	39	31

Site 2:

Land	$375,000
Constuction	2,000,000
Operating costs for 25 yrs.	12,500,000

Total cost, 25 years = $14,875,000; ave/yr = $595,000

From this example, it is clear that a site costing more than twice as much as the lower-priced location makes a difference of only $9,000 per year in the long run. Assuming that site 2 will increase library usage, the additional cost seems minimal.

As a further means of evaluation, calculate annual unit costs for familiar items such as circulation and response to reference questions, based on the anticipated usage of the library as dictated by each site. A frequently used analogy is drawn with the retail shoe store, where location is vital to sales. A site which will yield greater sales lowers unit costs and increases profit. While public libraries are not in the business of making a profit, they do share the need for a high turnover on their collection inventory and heavy utilization of staff. Using the figures from the earlier example, note what effect site might have on unit costs. In this example, it is assumed that Site 1 lacks the accessibility and visibility possessed by Site 2, and therefore will receive less use.

Example B

Site 1:

Annual cost	$586,000	
Circulation	145,000	
Cost per circulation		$4.04

Site 2:

Annual cost	$595,000	
Circulation	220,000	
Cost per circulation		$2.70

If we assume that this hypothetical library maintains a collection of 60,000 volumes, the turnover rate would amount to 2.41 circulations per volume for Site 1 as compared to 3.67 for Site 2—a commanding difference purchased at an annual cost of about $9,000! These examples may appear extreme at first glance, but they are actually well within the range of experience. Certainly they provide a better basis for site evaluation than emotional appeal.

Summary

Site selection is almost certain to precipitate considerable community interest, especially for public library buildings. Locations for academic libraries are often predetermined by campus master plans. Academic sites can be evaluated on the basis of certain desirable qualifications such as proximity to classrooms and accessibility to students. Selection of a site for a public library building may be more involved. To provide a rational evaluation, a process is suggested which includes detailed investigation and comparison of site characteristics followed by testing against weighted criteria. Accessibility and visibility are particularly important to public library locations. Cost information requires careful handling. Both academic and public library sites should be evaluated in terms of size, soil conditions, suitability of adjacent land use, topography and orientation. The site selection process should be objective, with the ultimate goal of identifying the site most in keeping with the library's objectives.

Notes

1. Keyes D. Metcalf, *Planning Academic and Research Library Buildings* (New York: McGraw-Hill, 1965), p. 390.

2. Joseph Wheeler researched and wrote two major publications on public library site selection. Though written more than two decades ago, both have application today: Joseph L. Wheeler, *The Effective Location of Public Library Buildings*. University of Illinois, Graduate School of Library Science, "Occasional Papers" No. 12, July 1958. Joseph L. Wheeler, *A Reconsideration of the Strategic Location for Public Library Buildings*. University of Illinois, Graduate School of Library Science, "Occasional Papers" No. 85, July 1967.

XI FUNDING LIBRARY BUILDING PROJECTS

BUILDING projects usually involve substantial sums of money and may well represent the largest single outlay the librarian must cope with in an entire career. Therefore, it is important that the librarian understand: 1/ the cost factors a building project involves, 2/ the major sources of funds, 3/ project cash flow, and 4/ implications a building project exerts on the annual operating budget.

While securing project funds is not usually the librarian's personal responsibility, it will be to his or her advantage to thoroughly understand the sources and the processes involved. Such information should be gathered well before it is needed. The librarian should know who will be involved in the process and be prepared to supply information as needed. Providing advanced notice of pending needs and keeping appropriate offices informed can be advantageous. In part this may be an outgrowth of participating in long-range planning and preparing the annual update to the capital improvements plan (CIP).

Cost Factors

How much is a building project going to cost? Sometimes this is one of the first questions a librarian must answer. While there are some variables, most building projects will involve expenditures for similar elements. To avoid unpleasant surprises, a knowledge of these and how to estimate their probable amounts is important.

Land Acquisition

If a site has to be acquired, land acquisition is one of the first cost factors to be met. This is less often a concern of the academic library since facilities are likely to be constructed on property within the confines of the campus. Public libraries, on the other hand, more often have to purchase land for expanded headquarter facilities and for branch library buildings. In addition to the information on this subject in the preceding chapter, it should be noted that negotiations for property may involve an exchange of land as well as a cash settlement. Land acquisition may also require fees for appraisals, litigation, and other consultants. The cost of demolition of any existing structures on the site may be considered a part of land costs in some instances. Because of the many variables, the cost of land acquisition will vary project by project; it bears no relationship to the total project cost.

Fees

The services of a variety of professionals will be required on most projects. Usually these begin with the selection of a library building consultant. Fees related to specialists concerned with land acquisition have been noted in the previous paragraph. It is possible that an architect, soils engineer or other professionals may also be needed at a very early stage. Usually the fees for these professionals are negotiated on a lump sum or per diem basis after agreement has been reached on the scope of services. Since the fees will vary with the nature of the assignment and the fee structure common to a given area, it is not possible to generalize here.

Fees for architectural services were once considered non-negotiable. This is no longer the case. Some architects continue to base fees on a percentage of project cost ranging from 6% to 8% (less on very large projects, perhaps more on smaller ones). Some states and some institutions have invoked regulations setting maximum fees—a factor that the librarian needs to be aware of. Using these percentages will provide at least a rough estimate of cost, to be honed, possibly, by negotiation.

In comparing fees for architectural services it is imperative that the range of services to be covered be clearly stated. For instance, it is customary for architects to include the fees for certain engineering services, such as mechanical, electrical and structural, as part of their basic fee. However, when competitive bidding or negotiations occur, architects may choose to reduce or eliminate certain engineering services. Since the building can not be designed without such assistance, the client will end up paying for them whether they are in the architect's fees or are separate from them. Many other services may also become variables of which the vulnerable client may not be aware until too late. For instance, the architect may shift costs for the reproduction of architectural and engineering drawings to the client, and this can amount to a considerable figure on a large project. It is important, therefore, to establish what is included in the fee and what will be considered as extra services or services for which the client will need to contract separately.

Fees for library building consultants are also difficult to predict. Such fees are generally negotiated on the basis of the scope of work. To be on the safe side, one to one-and-a-half per cent of the project costs should be set aside for this purpose.

Most projects deserve the services of a qualified interior designer. Such services may be provided by the architect or by an independent interior design firm. In either case, the cost will be over and above the architectural fees. Interior design fees will vary depending, again, upon the scope of services. For instance, graphics and signage may or may not be a part of the job. For budget purposes, assume that the fee will be between $1.50 and $3.00 per square foot, depending upon the complexity of the project.

Site Preparation Costs

Building contractors normally assume in their bidding that the site is clear of structures and is ready for grading. For this reason, site preparation is done in advance so that the building contractor can proceed without delay on construction. Site preparation often includes surveying and soils analysis—both nominal costs—but these too need to be anticipated in the project budget.

Where sites include existing structures and/or require re-routing of utilities, storm drains, water mains or sewer lines, site preparation will have to occur either as a preliminary step or be added as part of the building contractor's job. This is often the case when demolition or extensive excavation or land fill must be completed before construction can begin. Demolition work is usually done by a specialist under separate contract based on a negotiated price. The cost will depend to some degree on the estimated value of salvageable materials as well as the size, structural characteristics and the amount of dirt and compaction required for filling

basements, holes left by foundations, etc. Other site development costs may be incurred if trees must be removed, and especially if they must be boxed and saved for replanting on the site.

Once a site has been approved, an architect or civil engineer can usually determine the approximate amount of work that must be done and can then provide a rough estimate of site preparation cost. Site preparation costs may be included as part of the construction cost or may be a separate expense: whether paid separately or as part of construction, they are a necessary consideration in putting together the total project cost.

Construction Cost

While the actual cost of construction can not be determined until the contract is awarded to a building contractor, it will probably be necessary for the librarian to arrive at an estimated construction cost long before. This necessity may arise even before architectural plans and specifications are available. A general estimate can be made once the square footage has been determined by the building program. Such estimates use square footage costs for recent buildings of similar construction in the area. Other methods include use of figures published in standard cost indexes and by the construction industry. The application of these unit cost indexes is best left in the hands of the architect. In some cases, the services of a cost estimator may be used. The estimated construction cost, by whatever method arrived at, must include an allowance for anticipated escalation in building costs. Again, it is best to seek advice from an architect or professional cost estimator since the escalation factor may be affected by local labor contracts as well as by general inflation.

In arriving at an estimated construction cost one of the most frequent and serious errors results from failure to base estimates on gross rather than net square footage. Building programs, which are often the basis for square footage estimates, frequently employ net or usable square footage. However, this represents only a fraction of the building, probably 65–75% at most. If funding is based on the estimated cost of the net square footage, it is obvious that the construction budget will be under-financed and that the size of the project and the quality of construction will be substantially reduced. The librarian must be certain that the cost estimate is based on the gross or total square footage. A method for converting net to gross square footage is covered in Chapter 4.

Interiors, Furniture and Equipment

Construction costs normally include the structural, mechanical and electrical systems and the exterior and interior finishes. In effect, these represent the shell of the library building. Additional money is usually required to finish the building and purchase necessary furniture and equipment, including library shelving, seating, office furniture, graphics and signage. Special wall and floor coverings, art work and casework may also be a part of the interiors package.

Estimating the cost of this part of the work should involve an interior designer or architect familiar with library interiors and the requirements for furniture and equipment. Until these are fully delineated, the interior designer or architect will probably base the estimate on a cost per square foot. One of the variables the librarian must pin down in such an estimate is the quality of the furniture, equipment and other items covered and the anticipated discount from the manufacturer's or vendor's list price. Currently the cost of library interiors will range from $15 to $25 or more per square foot.

Moving and Occupancy Costs

The amount of furniture and equipment to be moved, the distance involved in the move, and any special handling requirements will determine the cost of moving. Even if student or volunteer help is expected to be used, it is often helpful to obtain an estimate from a moving company as a basis for covering this expense in the project budget. If moving costs are relatively small and work is to be done entirely by the library's employees with the assistance of a few volunteers or casual labor, the cost may be omitted from the project budget and absorbed by the library in some manner. However, moving costs should be recognized as a legitimate and necessary part of library building projects.

Most costs associated with occupancy, such as the balancing of the HVAC system, installation of furniture and equipment and signage, should be covered in contracts with the various professionals and trades involved in the project. However, the librarian will need to monitor all contracts to make sure that this is the case. For instance, receipt of furniture and equipment prior to installation may require the library to provide interim storage. This can be an added cost. While balancing the HVAC system is often covered for a year under the installation contract, sometimes only the initial balancing is included. Most systems require periodic adjustment throughout the first year, at least, and the cost for this service should be a part of the project budget.

A small amount of money will also be needed to defray costs associated with the orientation of public and staff to the new or remodeled facility. This may be limited to a few hundred dollars for printing brochures, fact sheets and other materials for distribution. Or it may be a larger sum including payment for dedicatory events.

Major Sources of Project Funding

One of the first questions raised about a proposed library facility project is, "How will it be paid for?" Fortunate, indeed, is the librarian who can respond that funds are already available through philanthropy or a capital improvement fund! Such a response is likely to be the exception rather than the rule, however. Therefore, it may be helpful to review some of the major sources for project funding.

Academic Libraries

The major source of funding for private academic library projects is through various philanthropic devices such as bequests and gifts. As the cost of construction steadily increases, many library projects must be funded by a combination of several such legacies or gifts, which may be added to other sources such as foundation grants. Some projects will be funded by capital campaigns, others may be supported by institutional building funds accrued for this purpose over a period of years. Other methods of financing include commercial bank mortgages and the issuance of construction bonds.

Tax funds. Libraries in academic institutions supported by tax funds may use similar sources but are more likely to be funded through legislative appropriation. In most states this is apt to be a long process requiring the college or university to submit detailed needs assessment analysis and other supportive documentation. When accepted, the project is then added to the capital improvement project queue, to be funded as part of a future fiscal year's expenditure. Under such a system, project funds may be allocated over a period of several years to coincide with the costs of planning, site development, construction and occupation. Such a system requires adherence to a strict process that may entail considerable effort and paperwork. Often one of the first hurdles is to gain priority on the local campus in competition with other capital improvement needs. Depending upon the state, similar competition from other state academic institutions may determine the library project's ultimate place in the long queue. Obviously, political clout is an added factor.

Design/build alternative. Used by both academic and public libraries, the design/build alternative is a means of designing and constructing a library building under a single contract.[1] Rather than bidding the plans and specifications for a building, a contractor forms a partnership with an architect and bids on designing and constructing a library in accordance with program requirements to meet a budget established by the institution or government agency. Because of the partnership arrangement, it is often possible to save both time and money. The close cooperation of the architect and contractor is supposed to reduce construction costs by using a design, materials, and engineering systems the builder considers most economical. The design/build methodology is also conducive to "fast tracking," which permits construction to begin before architectural and engineering drawings and specifications are complete (see discussion in Chapter 8). This savings in time can translate into a substantial savings in money, especially when building costs are rapidly escalating.

With these acknowledged advantages, there are also potential disadvantages. For instance, the abbreviated schedule forces rapid decision making with less than the usual time to weigh alternatives and to consider possible consequences. Unless the institution or agency has access to a facilities office or building department which can keep abreast of the design and construction activity, serious shortcomings, which might otherwise have been corrected, may go undetected and unremedied. How the design/build stratagem affects funding will depend upon the contract negotiated with the contractor/architect partnership. Usually, however, the cost of the project, including all fees, must be paid for whenever the building is completed.

Public Libraries

Although there are those who think that public library buildings are still funded by Andrew Carnegie, financing library construction is not that simple! Occasionally a public library building may be funded by bequests or gifts, but these are rare exceptions. Foundation funding also occurs now and then. More often though, other methods are required. Methods of funding differ from state to state and from jurisdiction to jurisdiction. The librarian should cultivate a familiarity with the various funding methodologies available through appropriate local and state channels. A variety of possible funding devices are briefly described below.[2] While some of these may not be available in a particular situation, an awareness of the different funding sources and methodologies should provide incentive in these days of creative financing.

Referenda/general obligation bonds. Securing funds through public referenda or general obligation bonds secured by property taxes was, at one time, one of the more common means of financing public library construction. With the advent of legislation such as California's Proposition 13, this is no longer possible in a number of states. Where this option is still available, general obligation bonds must be approved by a majority, or in some cases a 2/3 majority, of those voting on the referendum. Passage of the measure authorizes the local jurisdiction to issue bonds for the approved amount. Use of this means of financing construction is almost certain to involve the librarian in the campaign promoting passage of the ballot measure.

Participation in such campaigns calls for special skills and circumspect political action. Considerable assistance can be derived from the experience of other librarians and from the files of campaign literature that may be available through state libraries and the ALA.

Lease-purchase. Called by many names, lease-purchasing provides another approach to financing public library construction in some states. Essentially the jurisdiction enters into an agreement to lease (with option to purchase) a library building constructed by a private developer, or a quasi-public corporation formed for this sole purpose. The lessor finances the project through bank loans, bonds or other means secured by the value of the building and/or the lease agreement. Exempt from property taxes, the building can be leased at favorable rates to the local jurisdiction, with interest payments exempt, usually, from federal and state income taxes. This arrangement is most frequently used for smaller buildings where the purchase option is more likely to be exercised in the early years of the lease. However, some very large, multi-million dollar projects have been financed in this manner. The fact that the lease-purchase method circumvents the necessity for voter approval has resulted in it being used with caution in many jurisdictions and prohibited in some states.

Lease-purchase financing is apt to affect the library's participation in the project. Unless otherwise provided in the lease agreement, the lessors have only a general obligation for providing a building designed to meet the exacting requirements and conditions of the library.

The lessor is often bound by terms in the financing of the project to construct a building that can be competitive in the market place with other commercial structures if the jurisdiction fails to meet the terms of the lease agreement. Other possible shortcomings, from the librarian's standpoint, have occurred. For instance, the selection and services of a library consultant are problematic since they represent an added expense. The choice of architect may also be left to the lessor rather than to the jurisdiction. Participation in the programming and planning effort is apt to be reduced. If this method of financing is considered, the librarian may wish, therefore, to have his or her role, and that of the library consultant, specified in the lease agreement. The building program supplied by the library should be referenced in the agreement as the guidelines the architect is to follow.

Certificates of participation. In some states, lease-purchasing has been expanded to include Certificates of Participation, in effect establishing a tax-exempt real estate investment trust. This is particularly useful for larger projects. A non-profit corporation established for this purpose is selected by the jurisdiction and becomes the lessor. The lessor, in turn, appoints a bank, insurance agency or other approved agency to serve as the trustee empowered to receive payments. As the trustee, the bank or other agency, issues Certificates of Participation, which may be in the amount of a few thousand dollars. These are marketed by an approved underwriter. Certificates of Participation are normally secured by the jurisdiction's annual appropriation rather than by the property or improvement thereon.

Sale-leaseback. Multi-million-dollar projects may be funded in some states by sales-leaseback arrangements. These require the jurisdiction to sell buildings or other property to a non-profit agency and then lease them back from the agency. The funds obtained from this transfer can then be used for new projects. For instance, the jurisdiction could negotiate the sale to a qualified non-profit agency of the city hall, police building and fire station, then lease the same buildings for an annual sum. The remaining funds from the transaction could be used for the construction of a new public library building. Such arrangements usually provide a way for the jurisdiction to buy back the buildings sold to the non-profit agency under specified terms and conditions. Like all such funding methodologies, sale-leaseback is complex and should be undertaken only with the assistance of an experienced underwriter or financial counselor.

Local revenue sources. In many states, local jurisdictions can elect to raise construction funds by allocating funds from specific tax levies for that purpose. These may include a sales tax, utility taxes, license taxes, property transfer taxes, or other special forms of taxation. Dedication of this revenue may be used to defray lease costs or to create a capital improvement fund which eventually can be used for construction. Public hearings are required in most instances prior to jurisdictional approval. However, voter approval, as such, is not necessary.

Developer fees. In some states local jurisdictions may require developers to pay fees for the privilege of developing subdivided property. These fees may be accumulated and used to construct capital projects. Use of developer fees are sometimes restricted to certain types of projects such as schools, which are directly impacted by residential development. While developer fees increase the cost of housing, the developers pass these fees on to the ultimate buyer. This fee for developers is justified on the grounds that fast-growing residential areas should have direct responsibility for the construction of facilities which would otherwise not be necessary.

Air rights or setback easements. In heavily built-up urban areas, it may be possible for the jurisdiction to sell air rights or setback easements as an incentive for encouraging participation of private developers. By purchasing such rights, the buyer secures the privilege of building a commercial structure which would otherwise be excluded. In essence, this is a sharing of public property or multiple use thereof. This has been demonstrated in several instances, perhaps most notable of which is the planned expansion of the Los Angeles Central Library building. To be a salable commodity, the jurisdiction's property must be located in a highly desirable area where available land is scarce.

Commercial space. Under certain circumstances it is possible to obtain at least partial financing by including commercial space within the library building which can be leased. This is especially true where the library site is located along a busy business thoroughfare where there is strong competition for available shops. An alternative is to include leasable office space as part of the library building. Both of these have the possible advantage of conversion of commercial space to library use sometime in the future. Obviously, jurisdictions considering either of these options must have their potential revenue capacity carefully researched and documented.

Community development block grants. Sometimes called HUD grants because they are offered by the federal office of Housing and Urban Development, Community Development Block Grants can be used under certain circumstances, especially for branch libraries. Since regulations and their interpretation change from time to time, the librarian will need a current opinion on the use of these funds before encouraging jurisdictional interest. The Small Cities Program, which is a part of the Community Development Block Grant program, specifically excludes central libraries. The regional office of HUD can provide technical assistance and interpretation of the regulations and the amount of funding that might be available.

Historic preservation. Library building projects that involve remodeling, restoration or expansion of a structure of intrinsic historic interest may qualify for a portion of their funding through the federal Historic Preservation Grants-In-Aid program. Most of these grants are devoted to financing plans and specifications rather than construction. In addition, some states may have special funding programs that relate to historic buildings, and these merit investigation. The possible availability of such funds should not override the judgment of the librarian as to the suitability of the structure to meet contemporary library service requirements.

Library services and construction act (LSCA), title II. After the lapse of a number of years, the federal LSCA Title II for library construction has been revived—at least temporarily. Besides new buildings, Title II includes additions to existing buildings, conversion to library use of buildings constructed for another purpose, and remodeling to 1/ meet the needs of the physically handicapped, 2/ provide for use of modern technologies, and 3/ energy conservation. Note: general repairs and renovation are excluded.

General administration of LSCA Title II funds is delegated to the state libraries, which are responsible for determining requirements and establishing regulations. Not surprisingly, these vary from state to state. In most cases, Title II funds must be matched by local funds, which may include expenditures for site acquisition, architectural planning services, furniture and equipment, and related project costs. The regulations and the distribution formulas tend to be changed from year to year. In a number of states, application for LSCA Title II funds requires considerable lead time, which may be a factor to consider in evaluating this funding source. A certain amount of extra accounting and paperwork will also be necessary in most cases.

The amount of money available will vary depending upon the federal appropriation for the year and the formulas established by the individual state. Generally speaking, funding is limited to a percentage of the project cost, and there is usually a ceiling. The maximum payment is invoked to insure the spreading of funds among several projects rather than having the appropriation absorbed in a single building—although the latter has been approved in a few cases. Information and applications are available from state libraries.

State construction funds. A slowly increasing number of states are making construction funds available to public libraries within their boundaries. These programs vary considerably in the amounts of money available and in the regulations for their application and use. Librarians should be aware of such a program if it exists in their state and should acquire current information on the details for applying.

Bequests & gifts. Public libraries, like academic libraries, occasionally benefit from bequests and/or gifts. Some libraries have mounted successful campaigns to establish building funds from such sources. Because of the tax-free status of gifts to public libraries, corporations may be encouraged to make significant contributions. More and more public libraries are establishing foundations to receive and manage such funds. Bequests and gifts in themselves may not be sufficient to fund a major construction program, but they can serve as matching funds, trigger other resources, or pay for designated portions of the project—often furniture and equipment. Campaigns to secure gifts and bequests often appeal to those seeking memorials. An active public information campaign aimed in part at such individuals is sometimes very productive. Friends of the Library or other public library support groups can be effective participants in such efforts. Advanced planning and sufficient lead time, along with attractive incentives, are important requisites. Items of furniture and equipment, special rooms and pieces of art are likely candidates for giving. Bequests and gifts provide a means for greatly enriching the building project, even if they do not totally meet the construction budget.

Fund-raising professionals. Public libraries occasionally use the services of a professional fund raiser. For either a stated fee or a percentage of the amount raised, the fund raiser mounts a campaign in accordance with the objectives and scope of his or her contract. Sometimes the fund raising involves a general campaign soliciting contributions from the general public. More often the goal is to reach specified individuals, businesses, institutions and foundations. Professional fund raisers have the advantage of experience in this field and may have developed entrée to some of the prospective sources. Great care must be taken in selecting a fund raiser, however. The public library's image in the community as well as public goodwill must not be sullied by the campaign, which some people may resent.

Cash Flow

While the responsibility for payment of building project bills seldom falls on the librarian, it is still helpful to know when certain sums are likely to be needed. No matter what funding sources are involved, money is apt to come in increments. Matching these with the need for paying bills is the real trick.[3]

Planning Money

Usually, the first call is for planning money. This includes sums to pay for the library building consultant and any other specialists required early in the process. For instance, an architect or engineer may be involved in site analysis or evaluating an existing structure for possible remodeling or expansion. The fees for these services will be fairly nominal and can often be covered by transfers from operating funds or other current revenues. If necessary these early funds can be repaid at a later date from the general project funds if such a provision is made.

Site Acquisition

If a new site must be acquired, the cost of acquisition including any fees for appraisers, litigation, realtors, etc. will often occur before the project is fully funded. Again this may be handled through special allocation of local funds which, if necessary, can be reimbursed from the total project budget when that becomes available.

Site Preparation

If site preparation is undertaken outside the general building contract, payment may precede the availability of capital project funds. Site preparation may include fees for surveying and other civil engineering services, soil tests, grading, demolition, removal of trees, rerouting of utilities, sewers, storm drains, and water mains, among other things. The amount of money involved varies with each project but it is usually a small part of the total project cost. Sometimes the jurisdiction accepts these costs, or a portion thereof, to be a legitimate part of its on-going operations. More often, money may be advanced from the current budget and must be refunded when the project budget becomes available.

Architectural and Other Consultant Services

Fees for architectural and other consultant services may begin a year or more in advance of construction

and continue until the building is completed and occupied. The total will again vary with the project but is apt to range between 10 and 15% of the construction budget. Fees for the initial work may be covered by the project budget or may be paid from a special appropriation designated by the jurisdiction for this purpose. Eventually, most if not all of the fees for architects, engineers and other special consultants are likely to be taken from the project fund. Most such fees are paid on an incremental basis depending upon the stage or percentage of work completed. This has the advantage of spreading payment over a period of time. Each contract should provide a schedule of fees as well as a work schedule with target dates that will help identify the time when each payment will be due.

Construction

Construction will obviously require the lion's share of the project funds. Because of the large amount of capital required for construction, payments are usually made monthly and some provision may be included for advancing funds for procurement of materials and major equipment items. These payments constitute "progress payments" and usually require authorization by the architect, clerk of the works or project manager, verifying that work being billed for has been completed. A final payment is usually withheld until all punch lists have been complied with and other details covered by the contract, such as as-built drawings, have been provided the client. This follows completion of the building and occupancy by as much as a year. Since much of the contractor's profit is represented by the final payment, it becomes a potent instrument.

Furniture and Equipment

Furniture and equipment, in part or entirely, may be financed from the project funds or from other sources including annual operating funds. Payment for furniture and equipment is usually channeled through the jurisdiction's normal purchasing office and procedures. Invoices are paid after furniture and equipment have been received and, in most instances, installed. Contracts for furniture and equipment should be checked in advance to determine whether such items as taxes and shipping costs are included in the bid price or will be added to the invoice as an extra expense to the client.

Moving Expenses

The cost of moving may be borne by the project budget but is much more likely to come from other revenue such as the current operating budget or a special appropriation for this purpose. If a commercial moving company is responsible for the move, payment will be in accordance with the contract. Usually the moving company invoice will be payable upon receipt, or within not more than 30 days. Care should be exercised to see that any necessary insurance claims or other adjustments are taken care of before the bill is paid in its entirety. When moving is done by workers hired by the jurisdiction, the usual personnel procedures for casual labor will probably be invoked.

Opening and Orientation Costs

The librarian should anticipate that a small amoun of money will be necessary for costs associated with the opening of the library. Various printed materials and other orientation items will need to be produced. In some instances honoraria will be given to one or more people appearing at the dedication ceremonies. Unless donated, refreshments and special decorations may have to be paid for. Sometimes such costs are underwritten by a library support group such as the Friends of the Library. Donations may be received for this purpose, also, or the jurisdiction may choose to use current operating funds.

Start-Up Costs

While it may be difficult to predict start-up costs with any degree of accuracy, they are almost certain to occur. They are likely to include utility deposits, payments for new rental equipment, special custodial services, re-keying of locks, and small items of furniture and equipment and miscellaneous supplies that were overlooked (wastebaskets are a frequent omission, for example). If payment is made from current operating funds, spending adjustments will need to be made to avoid exceeding budgetary limitations before year's end.

Building Project Implications for Operating Budgets

Building projects are likely to have a major impact on the library's on-going operating budget. For this rea-

son, the librarian should be especially alert to the possible implications as planning and construction proceed. It is not possible to cover all the areas in which change is apt to occur, but some of the more important are indicated in this section.

Consideration of these implications will help the librarian to distinguish between what are known as "first costs" and "operating costs." First costs have to do with the original cost of the building, its furnishings and equipment; operating costs are the continuing costs of providing services within this building. Understanding this concept helps in the evaluation of alternatives throughout the building project. In fact, a question the librarian must ask continuously is, "What effect will this decision have on long-term operating costs?" Will material "A" be cheaper or more expensive to maintain than material "B", for instance? Will this building configuration require more staff than another? How will staffing be affected by this layout of furniture and equipment as compared to another plan? When seen in the light of first costs vs. operating costs, decision making takes on new importance as planning proceeds.

As all of these decisions are being made, the librarian should be projecting them into operating costs. A tentative budget for the first year's operation should be drafted and updated as the implications of the new building become apparent. The importance of projecting operating expenses is reinforced in many instances by a jurisdiction's management, which may require the librarian to provide such an estimate as a part of the project's justification. Whether done at that time or not, it is an exercise which should be completed as early as possible, and then updated as new and more detailed information about the building becomes available.

Communicating this information to the responsible jurisdiction officials will decrease the possibility of a most unpleasant surprise when reality sets in after the building project is completed. Some of the typical areas that will be impacted are discussed below.

Personnel

In spite of efforts to minimize the effect of a new building on personnel, the impact is usually significant. To a large degree this is because collections, users and services—and consequently staff—are spread over a much larger area. Supervision and service require more personnel if the library is divided into several floors. New buildings are likely to provide additional collections and services not heretofore available. New departments and special collections such as local history, audio-visual services, personal computers, and services to special age and interest groups also have staff implications.

When programming space in the form of public meeting and conference rooms become available for the first time, or are expanded, new demands are also made on staffing for scheduling, program preparation and participation. Support services may also expand in keeping with new services and enlarged collections. Often, the new building provides the library for the first time with space for special services and functions such as an adequate graphics and duplication department.

Needless to say, new libraries, including those that have been remodeled and/or expanded, will experience increased use, especially in circulation. This increase may range from 25 to 100%. Adequate response to such an increase may require additional staffing at circulation and reference desks. All of these staffing implications should be converted to personnel costs and entered into the projected first-year budget.

Utilities

New buildings often have a profound effect on utility budgets. On the one hand, new opportunities for energy conservation will promise savings. However, it is likely that such savings will be somewhat less than the cost of heating, lighting and cooling a larger facility. The contractor or his subcontractors can, with the help of the architect, estimate probable utility costs for the completed building. These should be reviewed with appropriate officials in the jurisdiction and, possibly, with utility company personnel. Figures from such calculations can then be inserted in the projected first-year budget.

Operating Costs

Many aspects of the operating budget will be affected by the new building and, especially, by the increased level of usage it receives. These include everything from office and library supplies to rental equipment such as copy machines. The projected first-year budget should include the results of a systematic evaluation for each budget item. Incidentally, this item-by-item analysis may also result in identifying certain line items that are no longer applicable to the new situation and/or document a requirement for a new budget item.

Collections

Anticipating increased library usage, many libraries prepare for a new building by adding extra materials to their existing collections as well as establishing new collections to support new and/or expanded services. Planning for collection development and the costs thereof may precede the new building. However, funding for public library projects frequently includes substantial sums for collection development. This is almost unavoidable when the building in question is a new branch.

Costs projected for the number of items to be added should include the costs for selection, acquisition, cataloging, processing and temporary storage if the latter is necessary. Whether funded as a part of the project budget or absorbed as part of the annual operating budget, these costs need to be isolated. If collection development is to continue at an increased rate beyond the opening of the facility, its effect on the operating budget must be estimated as well.

Custodial Services and Supplies

New, expanded or remodeled library buildings are almost certain to have an impact on custodial services and supplies. Larger floor area, perhaps more windows, and special features require more cleaning help. New standards are apt to be set for the maintenance of floor and wall coverings, furniture and equipment. Custodians must use more equipment and cleaning products to clean and maintain all of this effectively. Increased user traffic will affect everything from the number of times waste-paper baskets must be emptied to the vacuuming of heavily traveled carpeted areas and the frequency with which restrooms require attention.

If custodial services and supplies are to be provided under contract, qualified firms should provide estimated cost figures for the projected first annual budget. Otherwise, assistance may be sought from the jurisdiction's maintenance head in estimating the amount of additional labor and supplies that may be needed. These estimates can be made on the basis of the detailed architectural and interior layout drawings, augmented by furniture and equipment lists.

Mechanical Equipment and Other Maintenance Requirements

During the first year the new library building is open, much of the mechanical equipment will be covered under warranties of one kind or another. The librarian should be familiar with this coverage. Where such coverage is not provided, the cost of maintenance contracts will need to be included as part of the projected first-year budget. Likewise, the cost of extending the original warranties or replacing them with new ones should be investigated so that these costs can be incorporated into future budgets.

Incidentally, increasing numbers of new HVAC and lighting systems are coordinated through the magic of an automated system. If this is relevant, what will it cost to maintain the automated system? Who will service it and how expensive are maintenance contracts? More questions for which answers should be found.

One of the expenses that is sometimes forgotten is that of light bulb and tube replacement. While lamps no doubt have been routinely replaced in the existing building, there are apt to be many more of them in the new building and a greater variety—some quite expensive if HID lighting (High Intensity Discharge) is used. Again, warranties are likely to cover a period of several months—or even a year, but the librarian must verify this by consulting contract warranties. In any event, the cost of replacement will eventually become an operating expense which should be a part of the projected budget.

Valuable advice on lamp replacement can be given by the building's electrical engineer and/or the architect. For instance, it is important to know the life expectancy of the various types of lamps and ballasts as well as to learn which ones should be replaced as they burn out and which should be routinely replaced en masse. Incidentally, this exercise will provide an opportunity to find out what energy conservation steps can be taken to reduce utility bills. Do not forget to include labor costs, which may be affected by ceiling heights, the type of fixture and lamp, and hard-to-reach places which require scaffolding or other special access. Will lamp replacement be a regular part of the maintenance crew's duties or will it be done under contract? The answer will further impact the budget.

Landscaping and Parking

In making cost estimates for the projected first-year operating budget, do not omit the care of landscaping and the parking lot. New building projects often involve specially landscaped areas and new plantings which require more than the usual care, including water. Many new buildings include extensive interior landscaping with a variety of plants. Who will water

and care for these? If they perish, who will pay for their replacement? Should a landscape maintenance contract be negotiated with a service company that will tend the plants and replace them when necessary? Similar questions must be answered about the landscaping outside the building. Who will perform this service and how much will it cost?

Similarly, the parking lot will require periodic attention. Will the jurisdiction's street crews provide necessary cleaning and maintenance or will this be done through outside contracts charged to the library? The cost of snow removal will be another item for those libraries situated where accumulations of snow and ice must be cleared. Again, who will do this and how much will it cost? Has provision been made for stockpiling snow on the premises, with adequate drainage to carry off melt? Or must snow be removed by truck?

Revenue Balance

After the future operating budget has been estimated, it is important to compare it with projected revenues. The usual sources for such projections can be used. If a significant difference appears between operating costs and revenues, then the librarian must take the steps necessary to inform appropriate officials that this is the case. Steps can then be taken to review both revenue and expenditure projections to bring them into line well in advance of need. This process should result in a smoother transition from the old library to the new facility.

Summary

This chapter has discussed a new building project's implications for funding. The process begins with a detailed estimate of project costs. Funding sources are next discussed. Academic and public libraries share some possible sources such as bequests and gifts but otherwise generally differ at this point. Finally, some of the implications of new buildings on future operating budgets are described. To determine how operating budgets may be affected, estimates need to be made of the major categories which will feel the impact of a new facility. Ultimately these cost implications must be compared with projected revenues and a balance achieved.

Notes

1. For a more extensive discussion of the design/build methodology, see: "The Design/Build Alternative" by Gloria J. Novak, in *Planning Library Buildings: From Decision to Design*, ed. by Lester K. Smith (Chicago: American Library Association, 1986), pp. 175–188.

2. A more detailed description of funding sources is provided in *Facilities Funding Finesse: Funding and Promotion of Public Library Facilities*, edited by Richard B. Hall (Chicago: Library Administration and Management Association, American Library Association, 1982).

3. An architect provides additional information on cost estimating and cash flow in "Construction Cost Estimating and Project Cash Flow" by Bud Oringdulph, in *Talking Buildings* . . . , ed. by Raymond M. Holt (Sacramento: California State Library, 1986), pp. 117–127.

XII SPACE PLANNING FOR SEGMENTS OF THE LIBRARY

CHANGING conditions and requirements are common to library practice. Many result in operational changes that require space modifications short of major remodeling or the addition of more space. When this occurs, there is a need to re-plan the use of existing space. The purpose of this chapter is to discuss general space planning methodology for these situations.

The Need for Space Planning in Existing Facilities

The need for space planning within an existing facility can be triggered by many things, most of which are quite apparent. For instance, in a public area, overcrowded shelving is easily observed and with the inexorable acquisitions programs of most libraries, become more apparent day-by-day. Similarly, when people complain about the lack of seating and sometimes find themselves sitting on the floor, it is evident that additional seating is needed. Adding a new format to the collections, such as videotapes or compact discs, will precipitate the need for space planning in many libraries. Long queues at circulation desks may be symptomatic of an insufficient number of check-out stations due to an undersized circulation counter. Overworked reference desks may mean that a larger desk or an auxiliary desk in another location should be considered. The inauguration of services such as computerized database searching, for example, is almost certain to create a new competitor for available space.

The signal that office and workroom facilities need attention is usually equally obvious. For instance, one sign of inadequate workroom space is when there is no room to add another desk and staff members are forced to share work stations. Less obvious is the loss of productivity which gradually increases as workers try to perform their tasks under poor environmental conditions. Another clear sign of workroom inadequacy occurs when it becomes necessary to divide functions and place workers in relatively obscure or isolated portions of the building simply because a small niche can be

found there. Determining whether there is a lack of office space for supervising personnel requires little more than comparing available office space with the number of staff requiring acoustical and visual privacy. The absence of conference rooms where staff can meet as part of their routine work becomes painfully clear when available rooms are overbooked and groups are forced into cramped offices or corners of the building. While staff members tend to be long-suffering, their eventual protests over the lack of adequate work space can become a highly motivating factor in prompting space planning efforts.

The increasing use of automated systems is also forcing many libraries to become involved in extensive space planning. The ubiquitous terminal is rapidly supplementing, if not replacing, typewriters in many offices and workrooms. Use of some terminals is shared by several staff members, while other machines are dedicated to a single work station or office. Terminals require a different environment, type of office furniture and space allocation than are usually planned for traditional offices and work stations. Effective use of automated equipment depends upon space planning as well as the choice of systems and software.

Still another driving force for space planning is the changing pattern of library tasks, especially where automation is involved. Circulation and cataloging routines, for instance, are quite different from those associated with the pre-automation systems around which most library offices and workrooms were planned. Catalog cards and overdue notices are produced by automation, rather than by clerks sitting at typewriters, for example. What happens to the work stations where these tasks were formerly done?

Space planning is sometimes triggered by forces outside the area of normal growth and change. For instance, upgrading buildings to comply with building code requirements can result in structural modifications that impinge on adjacent areas. This has frequently been the case in recent years as library buildings have been remodeled to meet the standards for handicapped access. Inserting elevators where none existed or enlarging restrooms, for instance, can alter the space available for library functions. While access may be improved by such renovation, many library buildings lose usable square footage in the process. In severe instances, these changes reduce space to the point where it becomes necessary to relocate entire functions. This often creates a domino effect.

Methodology

The methodology for space planning is the same whether the end result is rearrangement of an existing space, a fully remodeled building, an addition or a new structure. However, most such efforts do not involve design professionals and may be handled almost entirely by library staff and/or craftsmen such as carpenters, electricians and plumbers available through the library's governing agency. Implementation may require the help of certain trades, such as electricians, but probably will not necessitate the use of a building contractor. However, if a significant amount of space or function is involved, it may be helpful to acquire the services of a library consultant who can offer an independent and fresh point of view as well as other assistance.

Identify Scope and Time Frame

Before beginning the actual space planning study it is important that the scope of the service area to be modified is carefully defined. Many service areas can not be considered as islands—they have intrinsic ties to other services and activities. Changes in one may result in changes elsewhere. For instance, to give an overcrowded workroom more space, it may be necessary to intrude on a public service area. Providing more office space may result in taking over a conference room, faculty studies, or spaces dedicated originally to other uses. It is important that the ultimate impact of this domino effect be understood early in the planning effort. Further, preliminary study must include the functional relationships that are involved so that cost-effective work patterns are not jeopardized.

Identifying the time frame for which space planning is to be effective is another factor to be considered at the outset. Is the space-planning effort geared to temporarily relieving a situation, or is it to be a long-term solution? Is permanent relief certain to come soon as the result of a plan for major remodeling, an addition or a new structure? It is easier, obviously, to justify more

costly solutions, the longer they are expected to be effective. Even seemingly simple short-term solutions can become costly if, for instance, they involve relocating a large number of computer terminals, structural walls, or plumbing. Cost-effective space planning, then, must seriously consider the length of time a rearrangement or relocation of functions will prevail. Moreover, the time line must establish a date against which space needs can be projected. Obviously, the consequences of satisfying space needs may be viewed quite differently if space planning is geared to a very few years rather than a much longer span of time.

Gathering Information

The first step in the space-planning effort is to gather valid information about the department or area under study. This process uses the same techniques discussed in Chapters 2, 3, & 4. Supervisors and employees in the area involved should be a major source of information. Observation of how space is currently used will lead to insights on traffic and work flow. An inventory of furniture and equipment used in the department or area, with the dimensions of each piece noted, will prove helpful if not indispensable. Particular attention will need to be given to environmental concerns such as lighting and ventilation.

Sometimes important facts can be derived by analyzing the reasons why the current space shortage came about. The solution may rest in a change in operation rather than a change in space. Has every reasonable effort been made to increase shelving capacity by shifting to equalize collection load? Is there an active and on-going weeding program in effect to rid the stacks of unused material? Have the possibilities of storing less frequently used titles (on-site or off-site) been fully explored? Could compact storage shelving be used in a non-public area to relieve collection space in the public area?

If the lack of public seating is a problem, you will want to address related questions, because adding more seats may be only one answer, and not necessarily the best. Is seating at a premium most of the time or only briefly at certain peak periods? When are the greatest number of potential readers inconvenienced by the shortfall in seating, and how many seats does this group represent? What type of seating seems most popular (first to be occupied)? Which areas of seating are the last to fill up with users? Why? What caused the seating shortage: an increase in the number of users? Replacement of seating areas by shelving, microform readers, catalogs, computers, index tables or other furniture and equipment? Some other factor? Is/are the cause(s) temporary or permanent?

If the circulation desk and/or other service points seem to need expansion, other questions should be answered. How frequently do lines actually form at the circulation desk or other service points? At what times does this traffic occur and how long does the crowding last? Is the crowding intolerable? Or merely a nuisance? Who's complaining, staff or users? If one and not both, why the difference in perception of the situation? Why do lines form at those particular times? Have changes been made in desk routines which require the user to spend more time there? For instance, what services may have been delegated to the circulation or other public desk besides those originally planned for? In some cases, relief may be as close as a change in procedures or the reallocation of tasks, including where they occur.

In thinking through the possible cause of space shortages for staff areas, it may be helpful to ask questions such as these: Is the shortage of space because there are more staff in the work area than it was originally designed to house? How have changes in organization of the department or its operations affected work flow? What has happened to the volume of work handled in the area? Are more materials passing through the work area? Has the amount of shelving or the number of booktrucks significantly increased? How has the installation of new equipment affected spacing of aisles, work stations, etc.? Has the placement of windows and doors, columns, light fixtures and electrical outlets limited the adaptability of the present space? What effect has the shape of the room had on making effective use of the space?

Responses to questions such as these are likely to be helpful in determining an approach to meeting current space needs. In addition, knowing why a space shortage has occurred may result in solutions which avoid the shortcomings of past space-planning efforts.

Consideration of the Future

Solving the space problem must include consideration of the needs of the immediate future. Therefore, concurrent with the gathering of information about the present use of space, it is important to project future needs and other developments which have space implications. What changes are apt to occur in levels of staffing? Is a reorganization of staff likely that might modify staffing levels? Will the area be impacted by changes in funding for acquisitions? What effect will the diversification of media have on space require-

ments? How will implementation of automated systems affect the area? Are there other developments in the offing which will effect the number of staff and/or their work routines?

The answers to questions such as these should help clarify space organization and needs. In fact, just posing these questions may be enough to prompt solutions, some of which may be revisions in policies and procedures rather than in the reorganization of space.

Arriving at Space Requirements

Assuming that a given service area or staff work area is proven to have insufficient space, the next step is to determine how much space is needed. This involves use of the space-estimation techniques employed for needs assessment and discussed in a previous chapter. The current space requirements must then be modified by projection to the date established for the time line, as discussed earlier.

With this information in hand, it is time for the librarian to consider all of the factors which may influence the use of space for a given function. Further, the opportunity is ripe for placing a particular space need into a broader perspective that involves related parts of the library. For instance, how will the space in question be affected by the continued development of the library's collections and diversification of formats? Are there demographic forces at work in the community, or curriculum changes pending in the school or academic institution, which may change the pattern and volume of library users? Is public usage apt to be affected by other library facilities such as new branches or departmental libraries that are not yet a reality? How much of the current space shortage will be alleviated when fully automated systems are in place? Is any of the present space shortage due to having dual systems in operation while installing automated systems? What effect will long-term budget projections have? Is there a likelihood that library services and operations might be reorganized so that certain functions may change locations?

Functional Relationships

Space planning provides an excellent opportunity for studying functional relationships in affected areas. Sometimes space shortages are aggravated because desirable functional relationships have not been achieved. The technique for describing functional relationships through the use of bubble diagrams was discussed in Chapter 4. This methodology is just as vital to space planning when only a portion of a building is involved. As the bubble diagrams are drawn, it may become apparent that lack of space is not the only problem. Functions which may belong together have somehow become separated. Similarly, disparate functions may be sharing space. Sometimes these anomalies arise because a particular service or operation began as a very small thing and may have been the responsibility of someone particularly interested in it. As time goes along, the "baby" has grown, exceeding all expectations and, perhaps, changing somewhat from its original form and requirements. Staff, too, may have changed and the person originally interested and responsible may no longer hold the position. As a result, a foreign or obsolete operation or function is imbedded in a service area or work area where its space needs adversely affect the amount of room available for other more congenial functions and operations.

For instance, microform materials may originally have consisted of a few newspaper titles and one or two readers. Because the initial interest came from the then current newspaper and periodical librarian, and because the reference librarian thought other priorities should be addressed instead, the single microform file and the one microform reader were placed in the Newspaper and Periodical Reading Room. However, the ensuing years have resulted in a major expansion of the microform collections, which now occupy numerous file cabinets and are supported by a score or more of readers. Not unexpectedly, shelf room for newspapers and periodicals is at a premium and there is little space for users. Concurrently, users of Reference Services have found that the sources cited in periodical indexes are located in the Newspaper and Periodical Reading Room, some distance away on another floor. Not a problem when the number of microform titles were few and the runs brief, the situation has now become burdensome for staff and user alike. The necessity for adding another microform file and reader result in a space crisis which presents the librarian with the opportunity to address a distortion of functional relationships while finding a solution to the space needed for microforms.

As a device for critically examining how space is used, the functional relationship diagram is invaluable. It should be a basic part of the space-planning analysis and contribute significantly to the design of alternative solutions.

Preparing Alternatives

Once all of the relevant facts have been fathered, it is time to prepare alternative solutions. In some cases there may be but one obvious means of improving the existing condition. However, most situations are subject to several alternatives, and each of these should be carefully described. Diagrams drawn to scale are essential to prove that the space allocated will be sufficient. These diagrams should also test how well functional relationships will be achieved. Since all of the alternatives may not provide for exactly the same quantities, i.e., number of volumes, seats, work stations, etc., the differences should be noted. These disparities may have a considerable effect on the final decision.

In bringing these facts together, the librarian should estimate the amount of relief the area in question will gain from each alternative. This estimate will require some quantification of the goal to be achieved: number of volumes to be housed, number of staff to be provided work stations, number of seats to be added for the public etc. Solutions may well vary in their benefits. Therefore, it is important to estimate whether a given solution will achieve 100% of the goal, or only 50%, for instance. Those alternatives that have the higher scores are obviously the most promising, all other things being equal.

As a final part of preparing the alternatives, a price tag will need to be applied. This can be a complex task. Some of the items involved will be easy to price; others will not. However, all contribute to the cost. Here are some of the more frequently encountered cost items:

1/ Furniture and equipment to be purchased;
2/ Systems, including automation, which are to be installed or modified;
3/ Payroll to be affected by changes in personnel;
4/ Modification to lighting, power supply, HVAC and plumbing;
5/ Additions or modifications to existing casework;
6/ New walls, partitions, doors, windows or other structural changes to be made;
7/ New carpet or other replacement floor covering;
8/ Remodeling/redecoration required to make the space habitable;
9/ Loss of productivity during the period of change;
10/ Cost of moving furniture, equipment, shelv-

ing, etc., including reshelving all materials affected by the move;

11/ Fees for any professional services that may be incurred.

Evaluation of Alternatives

After the alternatives have been prepared and the pros and cons including cost have been described, it is time for evaluation. Consideration should be given to the practicality of each alternative in terms of the time and money required for implementation. Work disruption during the period of change is another factor of importance. Given two alternatives of about the same merit, the decision often goes to the more simple solution, perhaps the one requiring the least outside assistance. Those which impinge less on adjacent spaces and functions are frequently preferred. However, the likely degree of improvement must be one of the deciding factors. Though less costly, an alternative that promises a 25% improvement is not as attractive as one which anticipates a 75% gain even though it is more expensive. Costs must be weighed not only in the dollars required to implement the change, but also in the effect on staff productivity. The saving of a part-time or full-time staff member's salary and benefits over a period of several years can justify substantial capital expenditures, for instance.

Alternative plans should also receive technical review before a decision is made. This action may be taken as a matter of course by libraries serving agencies and institutions which have professional design staff and/or facility management departments which approve changes before they are funded. Where such a resource does not exist, the librarian should seek help from a design professional and a building official who will provide a tentative code review. For instance, building—or removing—a simple partition may seem a straightforward and benign solution to a space-planning problem. However, that partition may violate the compliance of adjacent areas with code requirements for emergency exiting. Better to know this before planning goes too far.

Dividing larger spaces into partitioned offices and workrooms—or creating a large space by removing partitions—is likely to affect HVAC in some rather profound, and sometimes costly, ways. Moving functions from one area to another, and especially from one floor to another, may have structural implications. Not all library buildings were designed at every point to accept the floor loads exerted by bookstacks, map cases and

microform files, to say nothing of compact shelving. Review of the plans by a design professional should pinpoint such possible difficulties and perhaps suggest some solutions.

Implementing Space Planning Decisions

The implementation of space-planning decisions will involve careful planning and scheduling. Advanced planning will result in dividends, including the prospect of keeping within the budget and time schedule. Such planning often involves key staff members who can provide additional insight into likely hazards as well as specific information.

Anticipating Hurdles

As part of the planning process, it is well to anticipate hurdles that may need to be overcome during the implementation period. Some of these are quite obvious; others, like well-hidden traps, lie in wait for the unwary.

Some space planning changes require only the shifting of existing furniture and equipment or the substitution of shelving for seating in a public area. In other cases, new partitions may be necessary and/or casework for public desks remodeled or replaced. The plan for implementation should detail every single item involved and make it a part of both the time-line and the cost estimate. Here are some other items.

Work area modifications are apt to be more involved, since moving a desk is likely to require relocation of electrical power outlets, telephone lines and cabling for computers and other electronic communications devices. Exactly how will these outlets be brought to each location? Through the floor? ceiling? walls? Do the library's current electrical panels and conduit have sufficient capacity for these additions? Similarly, partitioning for private offices is likely to involve changes in ceiling lights and air conditioning ducts. How will these changes be made and what are the consequences?

Use of the popular office landscape furniture systems may solve some problems in creating additional offices and workrooms. However, power and communications linkage must still be brought to them. Landscape office furniture systems, despite their many advantages, may not suffice for those who need visual and acoustical privacy. Unless there is an expectation that offices and workrooms will be subjected to frequent reconfiguration, other solutions for partitioning may be more cost effective.

Implementation of space-planning changes may result in a variety of environmental modifications that need to be foreseen. As an example, windows may be covered, which will reduce or eliminate daylight for certain interior areas and create a windowless area that is oppressive to many people. Eliminating a door or creating a new door often results in unexpected changes in traffic that may affect those located nearby; the introduction of annoying drafts is another possible consequence.

Older buildings often have less capacity and flexibility for change. For instance, the requirement for additional electrical outlets may be difficult, if not impossible, to fill unless the total power supply is increased and new switch panels are installed to provide distribution capability. Changes in lighting may have the same effect. Similarly, air conditioning capacities and duct work may be unable to meet new requirements without extensive modification, augmentation or replacement. Presumably, such eventualities will have been fully explored in the establishment of costs and the evaluation of the alternatives.

Funding Implementation

One of the major steps required for implementation is the securing of sufficient funding based on a review of the estimated costs. If the building trades or other outside agencies are required by the plan, firm cost estimates will be needed. Some jurisdictions will require these amounts to be established by formal bidding or quotation procedures. In many cases, funding will have to be established in a subsequent budget request, or as an amendment to the current budget. Like any other part of the library's budget, funding for implementing space planning decisions must be defended during budget hearings.

Some jurisdictions will combine the library's work with similar work proposed for other departments and fund it as part of an overall capital improvements budget. This may involve establishing a priority based on need or may require the library project to take its place in a long queue of projects making up a Capital Improvement Project (CIP) list. When the amount of money is very small and the project requires a minimum purchase of outside assistance, furniture and equipment, etc., it may be that the library can fund the work by transfer from within the library budget. Few

libraries, however, have the prerogative of taking such action without the consent of their governing body.

Initiating Space-Planning Decisions

Once funding is assured, implementation can begin. Depending on the size and nature of the work to be done, certain preliminary steps need to be considered. For instance, all of the staff to be affected must understand what kind of construction, moving or other work is to be involved and how it will affect the performance of their tasks. The public, too, should be informed if implementation is going to affect their use of the library. If temporary quarters are needed for services or staff, these must be found and outfitted with desks, counters, power, telephones and cabling for computer terminals where applicable. When portions of the collections are affected, they may need to be boxed and stored in a safe place. Temporary storage may be necessary for some items of furniture and equipment, as well.

Don't forget to provide suitable storage for any fragile items and works of art that might be affected. Framed art, for instance, should be carefully covered and removed to a safe location; statuary should be removed or, if too large, protected by a covering of sufficient strength to withstand any potential mishap. And don't forget to protect commemorative plaques and signage that are considered permanent. If one or more public service points are affected, interim locations must be found and properly wired for power, telephone and computers, if appropriate. The purchase of new furniture and equipment, including replacement floor coverings, should follow the usual procurement procedures, with sufficient lead time to be sure that items will be on hand when needed.

Unless the project is very simple, a detailed schedule should be constructed which provides a time-line marking the beginning and ending of all major events as well as their order. If building trades are involved to any extent, a building contractor may be needed to provide supervision and coordination. Such expertise may or may not be available within the jurisdiction's own staff. The schedule may have to be revised one or more times if delays occur.

The responsibility for recruiting and organizing the necessary labor force is another task the librarian must assume. For simple moves, ample labor may be supplied by library pages and/or custodians. Other members of the library staff may also assist, of course. However, the librarian must exercise great care and make certain that standards of health and safety are strictly adhered to. Many an employee has been injured by engaging in unusual tasks, including lifting heavy boxes of books or assisting in moving furniture and equipment. Consultation with the agency's risk management officer or insurance carrier is advised before using library personnel. Filling out accident reports and workmen's compensation forms is not a desirable by-product of space planning! If at all in doubt about the use of library employees, the librarian should seek help from other sources.

With a clear-cut plan of action and a time schedule in hand, the librarian should carefully follow the course of the work. Librarians who absent themselves at these times, on the mistaken notion that it is a good time for a vacation, usually return to find complications which might otherwise have been avoided. The presence of the librarian is also needed as a psychological support for the plan, as well as for answering questions as they arise. There is often a need for reassurance that changes are going according to plan or that an unforeseen problem has been noted and will receive attention.

If the space-planning effort results in a major change in functions some re-training of staff may be necessary. New functional relationships may create different adjacencies for staff, resulting in further personal adjustments. These changes may affect productivity as staff members get used to their new surroundings and neighbors. Where changes have been made in public areas, staff may be temporarily disconcerted by the relocation of collections, which can reduce their ability to locate given items. The public, too, may require more assistance until they become acquainted with the new layout. However, with adequate planning, none of these transient situations should prove insurmountable, and should certainly not deter implementing an option that holds promise for improved use of space.

Space Planning for Public Use Areas

While the objectives for every space-planning effort will be different, some general observations may be helpful. The first of these concerns public areas.

Collections and Shelving Capacities

Space planning for collections usually requires attention to: 1/ the amount of space a given number of volumes will require, 2/ convenience of user access, 3/ relationships to the content and purpose of adjacent spaces, and 4/ maintaining sequential integrity by author (fiction) and call number (non-fiction). Earlier chapters have discussed methods for determining the space requirements for collections. However, when planning for changes within a very specific part of the collection, it is likely that the number of volumes to be dealt with may need to be even more precisely defined. (See the discussion under "Collections" in Chapter 2.) Basing collection space needs on an actual volume count of the materials affected is almost mandatory when space planning involves the movement of collections. Great care must be taken in the making of calculations, and worksheets should be retained for future reference.

Seating and Personal Space

Among the more common averages used by design professionals for seating space are 25 square feet for a person sitting at a table and 30 to 35 square feet for a person using a lounge chair. These figures allow for the chair, table and circulation space. A four-place table, therefore, would require approximately 100 square feet. Carrels should be figured at a minimum of 25 square feet each—more if a carrel wider than three feet is used. This is not to say that a greater number of people cannot be crowded into lesser-sized spaces. They can, but tighter spacing almost inevitably creates unpleasant crowding; many people resist such crowding and will leave the library rather than submit to it. Estimating the number of people who can be seated in a particular area must also take into account impediments which may impinge on seating arrangements, such as columns, walls, aisles, doors, service desks, etc. In the long run, the only accurate way to estimate seating capacity for a given area is to lay it out on a floorplan that is drawn to scale and allows you to take into account the realities of the actual space and its adjacencies.

When arranging seating, it is imperative that full consideration be given the psychological realities of people seated in a library. Studies point to the fact that many people seek a certain amount of isolation. Therefore, in public places, a four-place table is apt to be occupied by no more than one or two people until no tables remain with less than this number. Filling the fourth seat is usually resisted except as a last ditch choice. Similarly, couches meant to seat several people are apt to be monopolized by one or two—sitting together if they are acquainted or at opposite ends if they are not—no matter how large the sofa or how many it was designed to seat. For this reason, libraries are usually better off choosing individual lounge chairs which can be arranged in small groupings rather than couches which take up significantly more room.

Lighting, colors, fenestration and ceiling heights are among other factors which affect the psychology of personal space. Low ceilings, dark colors and poor lighting, for instance, tend to increase the feeling of being crowded. Windows provide some relief. Breaking up large areas of seating into smaller groupings with low shelving or other devices is usually helpful in avoiding the impersonal massing of tables and chairs that intimidate some people. Inserting a few lounge chairs here and there will also make seating areas more inviting. Reading a good text on behavioral psychology as it relates to public spaces will help the librarian become more aware of the specific conditions to be avoided. In spite of its age, not the least of such references is the book *Personal Space: The Behavioral Basis of Design* by Robert Sommer (Prentice Hall, 1969). A pioneer in this field, Sommer drew many of his examples from observations of library users.

Traffic Aisles and Queuing Space

Planning of public use areas must include consideration of adequate aisle space and room for lines which form adjacent to public service desks, copy machines, water fountains, and other points of service. Usually a three-foot-wide aisle is considered an absolute minimum. Fire marshals often require maintenance of a 44″–48″-wide aisle for access to required emergency exit doors. A check with local code officials is important to avoid having carefully drawn furniture layouts rendered useless by the failure to provide an aisle of adequate width or in the proper location. Incidentally, spacing between reading tables (from the face of one table to the face of an adjacent table) should be at least five feet to allow easy chair access. Some layouts whittle this to four feet; while possible, this will frequently result in chair backs clashing as people rise from their seats or try to pull a chair out to be seated. Where possible, even more liberal spacing is desirable.

Insufficient queuing space adjacent to public service points such as circulation and reference desks, copy machines and drinking fountains is almost certain to create traffic problems under peak-load conditions. It is all too easy, unfortunately, to underestimate this requirement when trying to rearrange an area for optimum capacity. There are no guidelines or rules to

follow here. Observation of peak-period traffic is the best guide. Excellent information on the human dimensions which must be considered in creating adequate space is provided in such guides as *Architectural Graphic Standards* and *Time Saver Standards for Building Types*.

Noise and Light

Avoiding or overcoming deficiencies in light and acoustical control is another important goal for librarians preparing space plans for individual areas. Care must be taken that the moving of book stacks, for instance, does not create dark areas where seating is to be located. Additional lighting provisions may be required in areas converted to public space from some other use.

Space planning must also consider the impact of a new layout on acoustics in public areas. Noise is usually associated with public and staff traffic patterns. Layouts should avoid functional relationships which require large numbers of users to pass through quiet areas. For instance, access to browsing and popular collections should be separated from reference collections and services. In public libraries, children must be able to reach their area without intruding into adult areas. Copy machines, typing rooms and other equipment that produce noise and attract many users should be visually and acoustically screened from reading areas.

Public Desks

Space plans often include or may be focused on the rearrangement of public desks for circulation, reference or other services. Often this is triggered by the need to effectively house and use computer terminals tied to the various systems employed by the library. Sometimes public desks must be changed because of increases in usage or changing patterns of use. Whatever the reason, space planning for public desks requires careful attention because of lasting implications for staff productivity and user satisfaction.

Circulation desks (most often designed as counters) are a particular source of concern for space planners, especially in existing buildings where the size and shape of the space they are to occupy are predetermined. Librarians, for good reason, tend to resist the monumental circulation counters that architects sometimes design to embellish the entry space. Efficient design depends upon a careful analysis of work flow and traffic, as well as a sympathetic understanding of space esthetics. The primary objectives should be user convenience and maximizing staff productivity. Space limitations usually require that the functions to be housed at the circulation counter be restricted to those absolutely necessary for the control of materials. Tasks which can be performed elsewhere should be removed to an appropriate workroom.

Circulation desks may be designed in many ways, each geometric form having its own requirements, strengths and weaknesses. An "island" desk, for instance, permits service points around the entire perimeter and is a popular solution where a large lobby space is available. The divided circulation desk separates certain functions, usually placing those associated with the return of materials near the entrance, and the checking-out processes close to the building's main exit. For the small library, or the library with limited circulation, the divided desk is almost certain to prove labor-intensive since this configuration eliminates the opportunity for circulation staff to both receive and discharge books during lulls in the check-out process. However, for the library with a large circulation, this separation may have many advantages for both user and staff, especially when an automated circulation system is in use.

It has been common practice in many libraries to locate the circulation staff workroom adjacent to the circulation desk so that circulation staff can accommodate sudden bursts of activity with a minimum of time lost to travel between the two points. This relationship continues to be important for the small library but may be less so for larger libraries, especially those using automated circulation systems. Maintaining such a relationship requires use of valuable space near the library's entrance for a workroom. This often results in use of prime public space for a non-public function, and may distort other basic relationships.

Designing an effective circulation desk requires study of traffic patterns of users, staff and materials—all flowing by, around and through the circulation area like a stream. Undue turbulence occurs when objects and opposing traffic get in the way, especially during peak periods. When functions are not in an orderly array as perceived by the user, traffic becomes confused and generates additional noise. Where possible, the public should enter through one door and exit through another, creating a clear pattern without disruptive crossover. Traffic control is sometimes complicated further by security system sensing devices, which have special requirements for their location. Creating an effective circulation control desk requires an awareness

of all of these factors and a solution of the problems they represent.

Circulation desk design is further complicated by the equipment which must be installed to handle the circulation control system. With increasing frequency this equipment consists of computer terminals, usually with keyboards and sometimes with printers. These must be located according to their function and in a suitable environment which enables library staff to use them with maximum efficiency. This means that screens must be free of glare and keyboards located at the proper height, which is usually 27″ rather than the standard desk-top height of 29″. In some situations, the screen must be mounted on a turntable which can be turned toward the user when necessary. There must be sufficient space on either side of the terminal to handle library materials being checked out. A counter width of four to five feet and a depth of thirty to thirty-two inches appear nominal.

The internal configuration of the receiving desk must provide adequate space for book trucks to move about, especially where books are returned and discharged. To this end, the entire book return process deserves to be thoroughly analyzed before a new circulation desk is designed, in order to avoid perpetuating expensive and unnecessary operational steps. The surface of the circulation counter should be designed with specific types of equipment in mind. For instance, a well should be created for a cash register, if one is used in the collection of fines or other payments. Terminals may require pull-out shelves or "breadboards" for their keyboards. Whatever the proposed design, library staff should have the opportunity of testing it in a full scale mock-up before it is approved.

Reference desks and other public service desks deserve the same kind of research. The question of whether these service points should be at desk or counter height must be resolved. Counters should be scaled for average heights, not for the tallest or shortest members of the current staff! Consideration must also be given to the physically handicapped, both staff and public. A counter that is too high will cause discomfort for staff and users alike. Toe space and knee space must be incorporated into counters to make them comfortable. Usually a counter serves best where user contact is frequent and brief, as in the case of information, ready reference, and media services. Desk height configurations, with provision for side chairs to seat users, are apt to be more suitable as service points where prolonged contact between user and librarian occurs. Where computer search strategies and searches take place, desk-type accommodations are also more desirable.

The location of staff desks should take into consideration the convenience of staff access to frequently used materials such as ready reference collections, indexes, catalogs and equipment. The ability to supervise a given area visually is of great importance and may be tested by drawing sight lines from the desk across the area to be supervised. Columns, shelving and other potential blocks to visual supervision will be easily detected by this simple device. Sometimes shifting the desk only a few feet will make a great difference. Service desks should be easy for the user to find and identify—user friendly should be the goal. Because necessary conversation between staff and users at these service points may otherwise be disturbing, reader seating should be some distance away or shielded in some manner.

Space Planning for Offices & Workrooms

The changing nature of library services and operations, along with the introduction of automated systems, places new demands on library offices and work spaces. Not surprisingly, many libraries face the need to rearrange available office and workroom space to accommodate these changes. The same general guidelines for space planning apply, with emphasis on creating effective work-flow patterns and logical routing of traffic. Particular attention must be given to the design of efficient work stations, each tailored to its own function. The work environment should be conducive to staff productivity.

Whenever space planning for offices and workrooms occurs, the possibility of using the partitionless "open office plan" is likely to be raised. The primary virtue of the open office plan, using landscape partitioning, is its ability to respond to frequent reorganization of tasks and personnel. Individual work stations can be reconfigured and entire areas changed without removing or creating walls. This has given rise to a genre of office furniture commonly referred to as "landscape systems." Fixed partitions have been replaced by panels which support counters, shelves, files, storage cabinets and other units. As the number of systems increase, so do the choices in components, which now permit virtually any configuration. Panels are of several heights and are offered in various colors and textures, some of these materials providing a certain amount of acoustical control. Many systems now include internal wire management systems which support task lighting, electrical outlets, telephones, computers and other hardware. However, power, telephone and data transmis-

sion lines must still be brought through the building and connected to the partitions.

Although open office systems are being used in some libraries, they may not be the answer to all situations. For one thing, they tend to be more expensive than conventional office furniture. Moreover, experience indicates that continuing flexibility requires the purchase and stockpiling of components which may or may not be used for some time. These systems are most widely used by offices and industries which benefit from tax credits and depreciation allowances not usually available to libraries. The added price for the flexibility inherent in landscape systems is most likely to be justified in those libraries which have large acquisitions and cataloging departments that respond in size and configuration to frequent major changes in funding and volume of work. In the case of academic libraries, such expenditures might also be justified in situations where dynamic changes in curriculum are occurring or new departments or colleges opening that require a concerted effort to develop segments of the collection over a short period of time.

While most workers seem to enjoy the environment created by landscape office equipment and the variety of components available, the lack of privacy for supervisors and managers is a major drawback. If voice-activated computers become popular, acoustical control will be of even greater importance in all work areas and especially those where libraries have traditionally placed emphasis on a quiet atmosphere.

Whether created by landscape furnishings, traditional office furniture or a combination of casework and furniture, office and work station design must be related to the responsibilities and tasks of the occupant(s). This requires study of each position in terms of work flow and tasks. Where does the work station fit into the work flow? What should it be adjacent to, and to whom? Are there any special environmental requirements such as lighting, HVAC and acoustics? What kinds of office equipment are needed to perform the tasks delegated to the position? How many electrical outlets will be needed for this equipment? Are data lines required? Will the work station have its own computer terminal or will the occupant share use with others? If so, with whom? Is this situation likely to change in the foreseeable future as automated systems become more prevalent in the library and individual stations become less costly? What sort of work surfaces are most useful (desks or counters) and what are the most desirable dimensions? Are booktrucks used? Is there a need for filing space? Shelving? If so, how much space is needed? Does the person confer often with others or supervise other staff? When these and many related questions are answered, the work station or office can then be designed and located to suit the functional relationships that will promote maximum productivity.

Perhaps it should be noted in passing that the size of work stations and offices is increasing as a result of automation. Old space standards are no longer applicable and attempting to abide by them will result in cramped and inefficient work stations and offices. Space must be provided for terminals and, in many cases, for printers. As automated systems become more prevalent and as terminals, especially personal computers (P.C.s), are used with greater frequency, there appears to be a trend away from the shared computer station. Higher personnel costs translate into higher operating costs when staff do not have access to a terminal when they need it.

Some libraries have approached this problem by rigorous scheduling, and this may maximize terminal use but result in staff inefficiencies. Other factors contributing to larger work station and office spaces include the need for typewriters in addition to terminals for many staff members. Despite the many advantages of computers, the typewriter still has a place and is not likely to be eliminated in the near future. Further, while cutting out some paperwork, automated systems seem to be creating even more paper as computers churn out reams of data and reports that were previously impossible to produce. The offices of supervisors, managers and other staff, therefore, often require expanded filing capability, either on shelves or in vertical or lateral filing cabinets.

Meeting Facilities

There appears to be a steady rise in programming activities in both academic and public libraries. As a result, there is often additional pressure for the improvement of space or the addition of facilities for this purpose. In part this is due to the fact that programming is often less successful if library programs must be presented in spaces located in other buildings. This imposes limits on library programming since schedules must be coordinated with those of other users of the same spaces. Further, off-site meeting places may be less convenient to many would-be attendees and thereby affect participation. If the meeting place is not in the library building, the library loses the advantage of visible sponsorship and the proximity of collections that may be related to program content.

Library meeting rooms can be divided into two general groups: 1/ those required for small groups, usually

with 25 or fewer participants, and 2/ those geared to larger groups, often in the range of 100–300 people. The first category may be referred to as conference rooms, the second as meeting rooms. Both types share the requirement of being accessible outside of library business hours. This usually means locating them close to the main entrance in an area which can be closed off from the remainder of the library while providing access to restrooms and the entry. In any case, the location of these facilities must not require users to travel through public reading or stack areas or to penetrate staff offices and workrooms.

In order to create greater flexibility in programming, some libraries have created larger conference and meeting room facilities equipped with folding doors which can be used as dividers splitting rooms into two or more parts. Unfortunately, these folding or accordian partitions, which come in many forms, are not totally sound-proof and their use often results in very mediocre acoustic conditions. Before making this choice, librarians should decide how often use will be made of the folding partitions and whether or not they are worth the cost and the possibility of dissatisfaction on the part of users. If folding partitions are used, planning must include traffic studies to determine how users will get to and from each meeting room without disturbing those in adjacent rooms.

Conference Rooms

Academic and public libraries of any size often provide one or more public conference rooms in addition to those required for staff. Space planning for conference rooms usually begins with determining the uses to be made of the room, the number of people to be accommodated and the basic seating arrangement to be used. In an academic library, the conference room may be used for library instruction, small seminars or classes, and informal meetings. Given the frequent use of the conference room for such purposes, the idea of using it also as a group study room is often resisted, and with good reason. These elements largely determine space requirements and the shape of the space. If refreshments are to be served, a small kitchenette may be desired for the preparation of hot beverages and for serving. Most conference rooms must be capable of using a wide variety of media ranging from overhead projectors and 35mm projectors to video cassettes and television programs. A ceiling-mounted movie screen is often desirable, along with tack board and marker boards.

If people are to be seated around a conference table,

as is most commonly the case, space planning must allow for a table of sufficient size and shape. Larger tables are often made up of several components, permitting a certain amount of flexibility. Special lighting fixtures on dimmer switches should be located in the ceiling above the table to provide excellent glare-free light. Space planning should allow for 20–25 square feet per person—some configurations require slightly more or less. This does not include space that may be required for storage of furniture and equipment such as lecterns, projection stands, portable screens, video monitors, and stack chairs.

Space planning for conference rooms should include consideration of environmental factors such as lighting and acoustics. While windows are attractive, provision must then be made for heavy drapery to darken the room when media are in use. Windows may also cause distraction as well as conduct heat or cold into the room from the outside. Conference rooms should be acoustically treated to eliminate the transfer of sound to and from adjacent areas.

Meeting Rooms

Larger meeting rooms are frequently provided, especially in public libraries. Space planning for a large meeting room must give primary consideration to access and traffic. In most libraries, this includes locating the meeting room where people can enter and leave when the library is otherwise closed. Those entering and leaving the meeting room must not be required to pass through library services areas or complicate traffic around the circulation desk. The next step is to determine the type of programming to be presented and the number of people to be seated. The types of programming offered will do much to determine other requirements and decisions. If most programs are expected to be presentations such as lectures, panel discussions and films, fixed seating on a sloped floor offers many advantages. However, if programs will require physical activity on the part of the participants or a variety of seating configurations, a flat floor facility with stack chairs may be the best answer.

Space planning for larger meeting rooms must, like that for conference rooms, include provision for use of various media formats. A properly sized motorized ceiling-mounted movie screen should be located where it can be seen by the most people. In the larger meeting rooms, a projection room may be justified, with space for two 16mm projectors or several 35mm slide projectors to sit side by side for continuous film projection of feature-length films. The number and location of video monitors for the meeting room is another factor to be determined in space planning.

A small kitchenette will be required for the preparation of beverages and the serving of light refreshments. If properly designed, this may be shared with one or more of the conference rooms. Storage space will be needed for lecterns, stack chairs, tables, projection carts and other paraphernalia.

General Staff Facilities

Space planning often includes general staff facilities such as lockers, lunch rooms, mail boxes, restrooms and first aid or quiet rooms. In larger libraries, these facilities are usually located near the staff entrance. Lockers may line the staff entry corridor or form a small alcove with a bench to accommodate staff who wish to seat themselves while changing footwear. Full-length lockers should be used wherever climatic conditions require staff to wear heavy outer garments. Half- or third-size lockers might be used where weather is less rigorous and staff are less likely to wear overcoats and boots. The number of lockers will depend both on the number of staff and on the provisions made in offices for individual coat racks or closets. Where lockers are used for storage of lunches, doors should have heavy wire mesh rather than solid panels. Staff mail boxes may also be centralized if this is desired.

Staff lounges and lunch rooms are often planned as a single space visually divided by the arrangement of furniture. The number of seats in the lunch area will depend upon the number of staff who routinely dine there rather than going elsewhere for their meals. Kitchen facilities should include a microwave oven, range, oven, refrigerator with freezer, trash compactor, and dishwasher. In very warm climates a separate ice-making machine may be added to the list. There needs to be enough counter space so that several staff members can do limited food preparation simultaneously. Tables should have seating for a maximum of four people—a mixture of two- and four-place tables may be preferred.

The size of the kitchen area must be determined by estimating the number of staff who will use it at any one time. Where libraries permit departments to have their own beverage equipment and refrigerators, this number will be smaller than in libraries that discourage this practice.

A pleasant staff lounge is a great asset and deserves careful planning. Again, the amount of space needed will depend upon the practices of the individual library.

The number who will use an attractive lounge will obviously be greater than the number who will use a less desirable room. There should be space for a variety of lounge furniture ranging from individual lounge chairs (rockers are loved by many) to small sofas. Provision should also be made for two or more vending machines, at least one of which will contain soft drinks.

The staff lunch room and lounge should be adjoining spaces providing the HVAC is designed to eliminate strong food odors. Every effort should be made to create an atmosphere that is restful and as much a contrast as possible to the remainder of the library. Windows are a very important feature, especially if they look out on a quiet and pleasant scene. Acoustical treatment of walls and ceiling is necessary to eliminate transfer of sound to adjacent public and staff areas.

If smoking is to be allowed at all in the staff area, a separate room must be set aside for this purpose. The HVAC for this room must be adequate, with the air-handling system exhausting the air to the outside rather than recirculating it through filters into the general system.

First Aid or Quiet Rooms

Most libraries will benefit by adding one or more first aid or quiet rooms. These should be small rooms equipped with a cot, a bed stand and coat rack. They will be used by staff who are not feeling well and by members of the public overtaken by illness while in the library. These facilities should be located near the staff restrooms.

Staff Restrooms

When space planning for staff areas, special attention should be given to the provision of adequate staff restrooms. Fixtures should be sufficient in number to avoid people forming lines at break time and when noon and evening shifts occur. The women's restroom should have a separate but adjacent powder room. Both men's and women's restrooms should be equipped with favorable lighting and full-length mirrors.

Storage Rooms

The amount of space available for storage in most library buildings amounts to whatever is left over when everything else is taken care of. This is not the way it

should be; storage is a vital library function and deserves the same attention in space planning as is given other areas of the library. There are no guidelines to the amount of space that should be devoted to storage. However, experience indicates that libraries which have devoted less than 5–10% of their net square footage to storage are usually handicapped. Storage facilities should be located reasonably close to the delivery entrance. If on another level, elevator access is necessary.

Library storage can be divided into several types of space, each with its own purpose and requirements. Supply storage may be provided in a central storage center or divided departmentally. The amount of office and library supplies to be stored will depend upon many factors including the availability of central stores operated by the library's governing agency and by purchasing policies. Space for supply storage should also consider inventory control practices.

General library storage usually requires several kinds of space. Open floor storage space is needed for items other than collections. Such items may range from furniture and bulk supplies to equipment awaiting repair. Experience is the best guide in determining the amount of space that should be given this function. Another area of storage will be equipped with standard steel book shelving with aisles narrowed to thirty inches; this will be used for certain library materials ranging from gift books awaiting evaluation, assimilation or disposal to periodical back-files and volumes that are used infrequently. A portion of the storage area should have industrial steel shelving that is deep enough to house large cartons.

Larger libraries, especially, should consider using a portion of their storage space for compact storage shelving. Such shelving has the ability to double the capacity per square foot. Normally such shelving requires a floor load strength or capacity of 300 pounds per square foot—twice that required for other stack areas. This means that space planners should locate compact storage on the ground floor in most instances.

Summary

The purpose of this chapter has been to provide guidelines for those who may need to plan for changes in library spaces when remodeling, expansion or a new building are not involved. The first part of the chapter was devoted to general considerations, while the second half discussed selected areas of the library beginning with the entry and ending with storage.

XIII SPECIAL PROBLEMS ASSOCIATED WITH REMODELING, ADDITIONS, AND CONVERSIONS

WHILE the content of the preceding chapters is generally applicable to projects other than new buildings, certain problems arise frequently with remodeling, additions and the conversion to library use of buildings that were originally designed for another purpose. The intent of this chapter is to alert the reader to areas which may require special attention during the planning stage.

Remodeling

Remodeling the existing library structure is one of the options that may be considered as a result of the needs assessment study discussed in an earlier chapter. Although treated separately here, remodeling is frequently combined with an addition to the building. Whether primarily for cosmetic purposes or for improving space utilization, remodeling is a serious and complex task that involves the librarian in territory that may be largely unknown and somewhat feared. Because it involves the structure a librarian is most familiar with, a remodeling project tends to be a more intensive personal experience than an entirely new building constructed at another location. In part this may be because with remodeling, as with a toothache, there is no way to avoid the discomfort that may result from the process.

Anyone who has had the experience of remodeling a home or apartment can appreciate that the process is full of unexpected consequences and requires careful planning in order to avoid unpleasant surprises. Unfortunately, sufficient time is not always given to planning, perhaps because remodeling deals with a known space and may seem less involved than the creation of an entirely new building. While one pleasantly anticipates the desirable changes remodeling can bring, nonetheless there is usually a certain amount of dread. Knowing that the building, or parts of it, will be in disarray for a period of time is not a pleasant prospect.

Neither is the certainty of construction workers invading the library and disrupting normal routines and displacing collections, users and staff. Nor can one contemplate with serenity the clutter and debris that is sure to litter the building and premises. Although good planning can not eliminate these aspects, careful organization and a complete understanding of the process can help to make remodeling tolerable.

Conceptualizing the Remodeling Project

One of the greatest obstacles to successful remodeling is the difficulty of realizing all of the possibilities offered by the building. Working under restrictive conditions and within well-defined spaces for a prolonged period, it is often difficult to see what changes might be brought about through remodeling. Perhaps the most helpful technique is to use floor plans of the library which show only the exterior walls, load-bearing interior walls, stairwells, elevator and duct shafts and columns. Erase from the mind the present arrangement of services and collections and redraw the outline of the building with only the above elements in place. Now, attempt to visualize how the various pieces might be reassembled in different ways.

If this is difficult, consider brainstorming with other staff members to break the perception barriers. A germ of a usable idea may come from the most far-fetched idea. Avoid assuming that changes may be impractical or too costly. Encourage the imagination to look at the building as if anything were possible. Perhaps relocating the main entrance may remove a stumbling block. Or maybe an elevator is needed to provide access to a basement or another floor. Since most library collections and functions grow to overcrowd the spaces allocated them, it may be necessary to reorganize them to fit into different spaces. This action often makes remodeling more meaningful in terms of long-term benefits.

151

This is not an easy exercise and is sometimes handled more effectively by a library consultant or design professional who can look at the internal spaces from a fresh viewpoint. Uninhibited by the present layout, the consultant or design professional is free to consider alternatives which might not occur to someone fettered by the realities of the present arrangement. Sometimes, of course, the existing layout of services and collections proves to be the most logical solution. In other cases, remodeling opens the way for a major reorganization program. Whatever the results, the time used in conceptualizing what might be possible will be well spent.

Planning the Remodeling

Planning for remodeling requires many of the same steps as are discussed elsewhere in this text. A program should be written describing the requirements for the project. The preceding chapter on space planning should be particularly helpful in preparing the program. Design professionals will be required to assist in the planning and to evaluate and advise on code compliance of the building's various systems. Architectural drawings and specifications will be necessary wherever changes are to be made in the building. Interior design services will be very important to the remodeling effort. Once the planning is completed, a contractor familiar with remodeling and sympathetic with the library's needs must be hired to provide construction services.

Anticipating Hurdles in Remodeling

Before detailed planning can begin, the librarian must understand what effect the remodeling effort is going to have on the library building, its contents, staff and users. In describing what has happened during remodeling, the phrase "I had no idea . . ." often occurs. All too often, that is exactly the case! To avoid this, the librarian should conceptualize how the project is going to proceed and how it will impact every aspect of the library.

Once the detailed planning for the remodeling has been completed, the librarian should meet with the design professionals, having established this objective as the sole agenda item. This is the time for very frank questioning and for arriving at a preliminary detailed schedule of work, if this has not already been done. It is imperative that the design professionals understand the librarian's concern about the potential impact of remodeling on the interim delivery of library services. Although this preliminary schedule may be revised somewhat after the contractor has been chosen, there should be sufficient detail at this point to understand the scope of work and sequence of events. From this information the librarian can extrapolate the impact of construction.

Questions should relate to the nature of work to be undertaken, what areas of the library it will affect and the sequence of construction activities. Obviously, all of these details will vary enormously depending on the scope of the project and the complexities of the remodeling. Some of the discussion which follows will be applicable only to larger or more involved jobs.

Preparing for a remodeling project is somewhat analogous to the foresight one must exercise in planning for a lengthy trip to a distant and previously unvisited destination. Just as such preparations require anticipation of such things as weather, modes of travel, kinds of activities to be indulged in, and types of lodging, so planning for remodeling should be based on answers to a host of questions such as these:

- What areas of the library will be involved in the remodeling?
- Where will remodeling begin?
- In what sequence will the various areas be involved?
- How much of the library will be affected at any given time?
- Will construction involve loss of utilities for periods of time?
- If utilities are to be affected, how much advanced warning will be given?
- Will a construction fence be required? If so, where will it be located?
- How will collections and equipment be protected from dust and debris?
- Are substantial amounts of construction materials required? If so, where will they be stockpiled?
- How will construction affect the HVAC system?
- How will windows and doors be affected?
- What provisions need to be made to keep the building weather-tight to protect the contents, users and staff?
- How many construction workers are apt to be in the library at one time?
- What provisions are being made to keep the building clean and to dispose of trash?
- What areas of the building are likely to be off-limits to the public? Staff?

- Will the delivery entrance be involved?
- What kind of security will be provided during the remodeling?
- What is the schedule for completion?

The significance of raising questions such as these can be readily seen once the implications for the library are deduced. Obviously, the date remodeling begins is of great importance both for the planning preparations the library must make and for the publicity that should be given the event. Comparing the beginning date with the library's calendar of events is required to avoid or minimize conflict with the academic or community calendar. Architects and contractors have no way of knowing how proposed schedule dates may affect the library; it is the librarian's job to foresee and advise on potential trouble spots.

Remodeling often begins in one area and proceeds in some fashion to other parts of the library. Knowing this sequence and schedule is necessary in planning shifts in collections and services, as discussed in a later section of this chapter. If major portions of the library are to be affected at any one time, the librarian will have to determine what steps need to be taken to blunt potential hardships to users and library operations. For instance, if large segments of the collection area will be off-limits for a period of time, a cross-section of the most popular items might be temporarily housed in another part of the building. Other solutions might include bolstering collections in branches or moving to a temporary off-site location.

The loss of utilities at any time can play havoc with library operations, especially where electrical service is involved. If the library uses automated equipment, the unexpected loss of power can spell disaster to valuable files as well as other inconveniences. Knowing the critical nature of such losses, it should be possible to work with the architect and contractor to schedule utility down time to those hours when the library is not in operation or to place essential equipment and lighting on temporary circuitry that can remain operational— at a cost, of course. Utilities also include natural gas which may be used to heat the building. If gas is turned off during the dead of winter for a period of time, will the library continue to function? Having the water shut off means that restrooms become useless and the HVAC system may not be able to heat or cool. What then? Restrooms may also be closed if sewer lines have to be replaced or moved. This is more than mere inconvenience!

A construction fence around the site may be required only if major repairs are planned for the exterior and/or roof. Should such a fence be necessary, where will it go and how will users and staff gain access through it to the building?

Remodeling is usually a very dirty job, resulting in quantities of dust and debris. The librarian must learn what protection will be afforded collections, staff, users and equipment. Draping plastic sheets over collections, for instance, might appear to be an adequate response. But what assurance is there that these sheets will stay in place and not be poked full of holes, slit, torn or otherwise rendered ineffective during the course of remodeling? Sheets can be easily removed by staff or users anxious to retrieve a particular volume or out of idle curiosity. Once the tape seals are broken, dust seeps in insidiously.

If structural alterations are part of the remodeling project, it is likely that the contractor will require space for stockpiling building materials on the site. More than one library has found its already limited parking lot commandeered for this purpose. Curbside parking may also be involved. Under such circumstances where do users and staff park? How will the chain link fences, usually used to protect storage areas on construction sites, affect access to the building? Will there be any conflict between library traffic and construction traffic, including vehicles delivering goods to the site? Is the library expected to provide inside storage areas for building materials? How much and what kind of space will be needed and for how long?

Besides the possibility that the loss of utilities will shut down the HVAC system from time to time, construction may have some other effects on the HVAC system. For instance, the large amount of dust may overwhelm the filtering system. More filters and a greater number of HVAC maintenance hours may be needed than the library has budgeted for. If the HVAC system is maintained under contract by a private firm, will there be extra charges for its services during this period? If portions of the building are opened to the outside during repair or replacement of windows or roofing, for instance, it may be necessary to shut off HVAC ducts to those areas. This may cause the remainder of the system to be thrown out of balance and require additional service calls. Remodeling often involves major repairs, upgrading or replacement of HVAC components, placing the equipment out of service for days or even weeks at a time. Will it be necessary to close all or at least portions of the library during these periods?

It is possible that some buildings might go without windows while being remodeled. However, this could spell disaster to a library, opening it to vandalism and the weather. Provision must be made in the plans for adequate protection against such occurrences. Collections and furniture adjacent to windows may need to be covered while windows are removed and replaced. When exterior doors are being repaired or replaced, the openings should be securely closed with heavy construction materials unless temporary doors fitted with adequate locking mechanisms are installed.

Openings can also occur in the roof, especially if major roofing repairs are being made or skylights repaired. Again, measures must be taken to protect the building and its contents from weather and intrusion. Heavy plastic sheets are frequently used for this purpose and are usually adequate providing they are properly installed to withstand wind and precipitation. Additional precautions will be necessary for libraries located in areas subject to heavy snowfall if remodeling occurs during the winter months. Roof repairs may play temporary havoc with gutters and downspouts unless adequate provisions are made for drainage of rain or snow melt.

Most projects require contractors to be responsible for clearing construction debris and waste materials from the site. However, there is wide variation in the frequency and thoroughness of such clean-up. Where critical public and staff areas are involved in remodeling, the librarian will want to make certain that trash will be hauled away frequently. Such provisions should be written into the contractor's requirements. Trash disposal raises the question of where trash will be deposited on the site and how often it will be removed from the premises. If dumpsters or other large receptacles are used, they must be located where they interfere least with traffic and library operations. The fact that they can be fire hazards means that such containers should be placed at some distance from the building.

Learning the number of construction workers to be on the job at any one time will aid the librarian in determining their effect on parking. More than one librarian has found staff parking and portions of the public parking spaces usurped by construction workers and their equipment. If parking space is critical, it may be necessary for the contractor to compel workers to park in some other designated spot. The location of portable toilets should also be of concern to the librarian, for they are not an attractive sight if placed near the entrance and can be a public nuisance.

The implications of questions raised earlier should now be clear. Librarians must make up their own lists, seek the answers and understand and interpret the inferences. The course of remodeling is apt to go much more smoothly if the librarian has taken this precaution.

Impact on Ongoing Functions

Directly, or indirectly, the responses to most of the questions concerning construction during remodeling have an impact on ongoing library functions. In some cases the accumulated effect is such that the library may need to close its doors for a period of time to permit remodeling to proceed without conflicting with daily use. Work often proceeds faster and is less expensive when the building is vacated, leaving the construction workers to their duties. Whether or not this is practical depends on many factors, most important of which is the availability of an adequate temporary facility to house portions of the library's collections and some accommodations for users and staff. This decision must be made on the basis of a realistic analysis of alternatives and their costs.

Assuming the library elects to remain in the building while remodeling is occurring, the librarian must anticipate how construction activities will affect each area. Even though the library remains open, some services and collections may need to be relocated for periods of time; others may be closed altogether during certain periods of the work. Library services may also be reduced to a few essential ones such as a small circulating collection and basic reference. Even these may have to be moved one or more times during the progress of the project. Portions of the staff may be relocated to temporary quarters off-site to avoid working under very adverse conditions that might seriously reduce productivity. Technical services departments are often prime choices for such moves because of their relative independence from other library functions. This is particularly true for technical service departments with on-line capabilities that reduce their dependence on easy access to a central card catalog.

A question occurring with increasing frequency concerns the possible consequences for automated equipment. This is particularly true if the remodeling involves the room where a Central Processing Unit (CPU), or mainframe, is housed with all of its special environmental requirements. Moving the CPU to another location means finding a suitable place and time for the change. Depending upon the equipment, a specialist with experience in moving electronic equipment may be required—a further bit of scheduling and expense.

Before the librarian is finished with the task of assessing the impact of remodeling on the library's ongoing functions, every facet of the library will need to be studied. There are no pat answers to the problems raised by remodeling. Each situation must be separately considered and a pragmatic solution found.

Scheduling Interim Moves

The librarian must work closely with the contractor and the remodeling construction schedule to coordinate any necessary interim movement of collections, services and staff. Gaining sufficient lead time is usually the greatest problem. Where elements of the library may be temporarily moved to other quarters, the librarian must create a detailed description of the amount of space required and any special conditions that may pertain. Often the librarian will work directly with a department in the academic institution or government agency that is responsible for facility management. Where such an office does not exist, the librarian may be compelled to seek help from a realtor or leasing agent. Space offered to meet the library's needs sometimes requires remodeling before it can be useful. The floor loading capacity is critical—at least 125 pounds per square foot. Additional electrical outlets and telephones may be needed, floor coverings may have to be patched or replaced, lighting may need to be increased, etc. All of these can incur delays and additional costs. Finding space is often further complicated by lease or rental costs that are beyond the budget.

Whether the space to be moved into temporarily is within the existing library or elsewhere, planning must be handled carefully. Collections need to be boxed and transported, along with furniture and equipment. If a public area is involved, the public services desk will have to be relocated, as will seating and other furniture. New signage will be needed and other public relations aspects, discussed in the following section, will require attention. All of this must be done according to a realistic schedule that will clear the area occupied by the function in time for the construction crews to meet their own deadlines. Close coordination with the project contractor will be necessary.

Handling the Public Relations Aspects

Embarking on a remodeling project opens up a host of public relations opportunities as well as imperatives. Those who use the library with some frequency, as well as the general public, will be interested in the progress of the work. They also want to know how, when and in what ways their use of the library will be affected.

The public relations effort should begin with publicity about the remodeling project as soon as it is first approved. Additional releases should occur throughout the planning period. The data when work is to begin should be emphasized as soon as it is established. Posters and other signage in the library should reinforce publicity in the local media. Newsletters can be used as a further means of reaching library users. A ceremony akin to a "groundbreaking" for a new building should mark the commencement of actual construction.

The public relations effort should consciously address any potential inconveniences the users of the library may suffer. These may range from lost parking opportunities to locating any satellite facilities that are being used for the duration of construction. The user may experience a variety of other inconveniences and frustrations such as finding a not-too-visible temporary entrance, being denied certain services and access to parts of the collection, finding limitations imposed on seating, being annoyed by the noise of construction crews, and encountering sawdust or other debris.

Signs help in this regard, although many people do not read them or disregard them. Signs are in no way a panacea, but they are a handy tool that must be used. Signs and other public relations efforts indicate the library's awareness of the public's discomfort and sympathy for the user's plight during remodeling. Prominently located signs should be displayed well in advance of deadlines to indicate the future closure or relocation of any function, service or collection.

While library staff sometimes tire of these signs, it is important to remember that many library users do not enter the library every day—or every week, for that matter. Therefore, signage must be posted for extended periods if it is to be effective. One device to make signs more apparent is to create a standard format, including perhaps an unusual shape, a commanding size, and lettering and graphics in vibrant colors. And be sure that the sign's message is clearly and succinctly stated. When posted in highly visible locations, such signs are less likely to be ignored.

Bookmarks, flyers and similar materials may be used to spread the word. However, these often go unread and should be considered a reinforcement of other devices rather than the primary source of information.

Remodeling can create public relations opportunities for news stories and feature articles in the local media, and these should be fully capitalized on by the library. These opportunities include milestone events which begin or end certain phases of construction. In older buildings, remodeling is almost certain to lay bare something that has been covered over and long since forgotten—a bit of library local history to be retrieved and enjoyed. Discoveries may range from dedication plaques and cornerstones that have long been hidden to paintings or pieces of sculpture recovered from some remote closet or recess. An alert building contractor can help by calling attention to any bit of hardware, carved woodwork or other item that exemplifies craftsmanship of a bygone era. Such items may even be placed on display with suitable notes about their importance.

Because remodeling calls attention to the structure that houses the library, this is an excellent time to remind the public of the origins of the library building and the lives of those who were instrumental in its construction. Items in the collections associated with that era, including photographs, correspondence, newspaper headlines, can be used advantageously. Public relations can contribute much to the success of the remodeling process and should be planned as carefully as the remodeling itself.

Liability for Collections, Personal Safety, Etc.

Remodeling can result in greater risk to the library building, its contents, staff and users, and the librarian should work with the risk management or insurance agent responsible for the library to determine what additional protection may be needed. Provisions of insurance policies should be carefully checked to determine whether coverage is affected by remodeling; additional insurance and/or special riders may be needed. Insurance protection may also involve the contractor and his contract for the remodeling project.

Regardless of the insurance in effect, the librarian should make a concerted effort to see that proper precautions are taken to protect the library's users, collections and staff, as well as any portions of the building not involved in the remodeling. This involves keeping informed on the progress of the work and being diligent in anticipating possible risks before they occur. For instance, collections and furniture hastily draped with plastic covers just before the painters arrive are apt to be less secure than those installed well in advance. The contractor's attitude, and that of his workers, can sometimes be sensed from the way tools and materials are treated and left at the end of each day. If they are carefully arranged and put away, risks are apt to be less than from crews who leave power cords plugged in, materials scattered and tools strewn about.

Because remodeling may involve many small, as well as major, changes in the location of collections, furniture and equipment, the librarian may be tempted to rely on staff members for help in moving these items. Staff members are a convenient source for such labor. However, the risk of serious accident should preclude use of staff for this purpose. In all probability, moving is not in the job specifications for most library personnel. Strained backs, hernias, and other injuries cause suffer-

ing for the individual and may result in lengthy periods of recuperation or lasting disability. Meanwhile the library loses the services of a valuable staff member, with resulting complications. Accidents are also likely to involve the librarian in insurance claims and, possibly, in legal proceedings. It is better to avoid this eventuality by employing workers for the specific purpose of moving. Such workers engage in these tasks wittingly and can be separately insured.

Security

A library building undergoing remodeling is apt to be a greater security risk than one operating normally. The librarian should be aware of this and take appropriate steps. Remodeling may upset familiar opening and closing routines, because the hours that construction crews work may not be the same as library hours. This may mean that doors normally closed are open before library staff arrive, leaving the building vulnerable to anyone wishing to enter. Sometimes keys to the library are entrusted to a foreman or other worker who is unfamiliar with all of the windows that should be closed and doors to be locked upon leaving.

Other security risks abound. For instance, paint cans left on the premises with dabs of paint in them may entice someone to paint graffiti on freshly finished walls or dump paint on new floor coverings. Windows awaiting installations can be targets for rocks. The possibilities for increased vandalism are limited only by the ingenuity of the would-be vandal and the ease of access to the library.

The possibility of fire is certainly increased during remodeling. Spontaneous combustion is a threat when building material scraps and inflammable liquids are tossed into a heap with dirty rags and left for future clean-up. Carelessly disposed cigarette butts may smolder for hours before bursting into ruinous flame. Power tools may overload circuitry already strained to capacity and result in the tripping of breaker switches, or worse.

While increasing the risk of fire, remodeling may simultaneously reduce the ability to control the fire. For instance, the library's fire extinguishers may be removed from their wall cabinets while repairs are made to partitions. Sprinkler systems may be partially or totally inactivated while a new ceiling and light fixtures are being installed. The fire alarm system may be disconnected from time to time as work proceeds, raising the potential peril further.

Obviously, building security goes beyond protection from vandalism and fire. However, these few comments should illustrate the effect remodeling can have on security. The answers are not easy, nor are they inexpensive. A first step is to increase the awareness of library staff and seek their cooperation in promptly reporting any potential risk condition. The librarian should also make certain that the contractor is aware of this concern and will take appropriate preventative measures. While the campus police or local police or sheriff's department will undoubtedly maintain periodic patrols, it may be necessary on larger and more extensive remodeling projects to employ security guards. In any case, planning for remodeling should include provision for adequate security.

Additions

More and more libraries are remodeling and adding on to their existing buildings rather than constructing new facilities. Perhaps the two major reasons are: 1/ constructing an addition is apt to be less costly than a new building, and 2/ additions fulfill the promise of the original design which included such expansion. When space shortages occur, an addition to the existing structure may prove to be the most economical and expedient solution. Whether specifically designed for expansion, or not, a modular building is likely to be a good candidate for an addition providing site conditions are favorable. Buildings that are not modular in design may present more problems, as will older structures that have load-bearing walls which must be maintained with little or no modification.

Additions can be used to overcome serious functional difficulties as well as to increase capacities in existing libraries. For instance, a new addition may include a new on-grade entrance, thereby eliminating barriers for the physically handicapped or improving access from the parking lot. A large addition may house all public functions, leaving the original structure to be remodeled for increases in staff and collections. Limitations on access for the physically handicapped can often be eliminated by using an addition to house an elevator, new restrooms, etc. A properly designed addition can lengthen the useful life of an older structure by many years.

Choosing the Addition as a Solution to Space Needs

An addition, nevertheless, is not always the best choice nor a panacea. Sometimes there are drawbacks which may point to another alternative. Before choosing the addition as the best solution, certain factors require consideration. Adding on to the existing structure is likely to commit the library to remaining in the building for a very long time, regardless of any shortcomings. Here are a few points that should receive attention before the choice of an addition is made.

Recognizing that a greater investment in the library's physical plant is likely to anchor the library to its present location for many years, the librarian should determine whether or not the present site is the most effective one available (see Chapter 10 for site selection criteria). If the existing site places the library where it can function well on the campus or in the community for the next several decades, then the question is answered. If not, then the matter of location requires resolution. Why invest more money in a building that is no longer conveniently situated or, according to planning data, will soon be in a poor location?

Is the site large enough for the intended size of the addition? Will the expansion reduce off-street parking below the minimum? If there is insufficient land available on the library site, are contiguous parcels available for purchase at an affordable price? Does the configuration of the site or its topography pose limitations on size, orientation, or access? Will the addition place the library too close to a non-compatible neighbor? (This may include a tall building which may shadow the library or a structure with a glass facade that produces serious glare, as well as buildings that house functions which create loud noises, unpleasant odors or competing traffic.)

What are the code implications of constructing an addition? In many areas of the country, an addition representing a specific percentage of the original space or of its estimated value automatically requires upgrading structural, electrical, mechanical and plumbing systems in the existing building in order to meet current codes. As warranted as this requirement may be, such retrofitting can be extremely costly and may make other alternatives more realistic. This is especially true for libraries located in seismic zones 2, 3, and 4, where recently revised building codes are placing increasingly stringent conditions on structural reinforcement.

The useful life of the existing building is another factor to be weighed. An addition to a relatively new building is likely to be more cost effective in terms of lengthening its usefulness than an addition to a much older structure. This is particularly true when design and structural elements such as load-bearing walls limit flexibility for remodeling.

For how many years will the addition solve the library's space needs? If the solution is temporary, ten years or less, the advisability of an addition may be questioned, for hardly will the addition be completed before the library begins to feel the pangs of another space shortage. Conversely, as noted above, will the addition commit the library to its present building and site long after they are likely to be functional?

Feasibility Study

The foregoing questions and many that follow should be addressed in a feasibility study. Such a study establishes the amount of space needed and explores some of the possible ways an addition, among other possible solutions, might be created. (See Chapter 2, "Needs Assessment," for help in preparing this study.) Space requirements established in the needs assessment study, which should be refined later by the building program, can be compared with the amount of space available in the present building. The balance represents a pre-program estimate of the amount of space that is needed to meet library needs for a given period of years. If the needs assessment study has been carefully done, it should be within plus or minus 10–15% of the ultimate requirement represented by the building program.

After the data for collections, users, staff, etc. have been collected, it may be advisable to confer with an architect about the suitability of an addition as an option. At this point the drawings and specifications for the existing building, including any previous additions, should be brought out. (If copies are not in the library's archives, drawings may be found in the office of the campus architect, facility maintenance office or local building department. Depending upon the age of the building, the architectural firm responsible for its design or any subsequent remodeling or addition may also have a set of drawings.)

Careful review of the drawings may prove very beneficial. For instance, a master site plan might be found that shows the location and dimensions of a future addition as originally conceived. The structural drawings may show walls that were designed for easy removal to accommodate such an addition. HVAC drawings may indicate that major duct runs and chases have been sized in anticipation of a possible addition. Conversely, examination of the drawings may reveal structural or other obstacles that may be difficult and expensive to overcome. This is especially the case where load-bearing walls are in place or where partitions hiding important structural elements may have been added in the intervening years.

Reconfiguring the Existing Library Building

An addition automatically changes the configuration of the existing structure. Warning: if the library building appears on a list of historical structures, additions are likely to be unacceptable! In other cases, several basic factors determine where an addition may be made, how it will be configured, and how large it might be.

Perhaps the most obvious determinant is the site. Is there sufficient land available for the addition? Even though the existing structure may have been designed with an addition in mind, subsequent events such as the construction of other campus buildings or the sale of property to other owners may have resulted in the use of the land originally intended for library expansion. If this has happened, are there adjacent parcels which can be purchased, or otherwise added to the library site, that might make physical expansion of the building feasible? How does the space available on the site relate to the existing building? Is it adjacent to functions which need space the most? Does the lack of land force an undesirable design for the addition? For example, a one-story library of 30,000 square feet requires the addition of 20,000 square feet on a site that will provide a maximum footprint for the addition of 4,000 square feet. The result would be a five-story "tower" addition, totally out of scale and probably very inefficient. The question of site should be easily answered in most cases; either enough space exists for the desired addition, or it doesn't!

Typical Addition Configurations

Assuming that the site is not a limiting factor, where can the addition be made most advantageously? The answer must relate both to the internal functions of the library and the configuration of the existing structure. Figure 13-1 shows some typical building shapes and indicates how the configuration helps determine where an addition may be placed. Obviously, the end product is a building with a radically different shape. The librarian needs to consider how this shape may affect the internal organization of collections and services; some forms are more efficient than others. Additions of all types may contain the same number of floors as the original structure, or may contain fewer or more. Design considerations as well as space needs can affect the decision.

"In-fill" additions are likely candidates where the existing structure is irregular in shape. There seems to be a tendency to want to "square off" such forms.

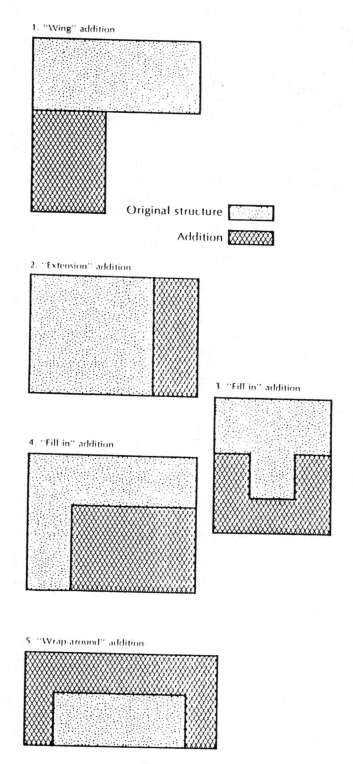

Figure 13–1
Typical Building Configurations and How They May Be Changed by an Addition

"Wings" are also popular, especially for buildings that were created originally as rectangles. This design can also be used to create a new entrance facing a direction 90 degrees away from the existing structure. Wings can also be added near the mid-point of the building to create a "T"-shaped form. While popular, wing additions often result in rather drastic reorganization of collections and services, and may strain functional relationships and increase personnel requirements. Perhaps wings are best suited to situations in which a well-defined collection or department can occupy most or all of the new space.

Additions can also be made to one or more sides of an existing structure, creating an "extension." This form is particularly useful when space requirements are restricted to one or two functions, such as expansion of the general collection or increased reader space. Since "extensions" usually occur at the extremities of the building, they usually affect internal relationships less than other forms.

The "wrap around" addition, as its name implies, tends to enlarge a building on two or more sides, keeping the original structure somewhat in the center. If the site permits, this sort of addition can provide a substantial amount of space. It has been effective in meeting space needs while preserving an older building of the Carnegie period. In such circumstances the addition may provide for a new on-grade entrance, elevator access to the upper and lower floors of the original building, restrooms to meet requirements for the physically handicapped, and proper environmental conditions for computers and other high-tech equipment.

However, the wrap around addition may be more costly than other forms because of the large amount of perimeter walls and the extensive interfacing with the original building. In some cases, the "wrap-around" addition has been used as a means of replacing an existing structure in a multi-phased operation: 1/ the wrap-around addition is constructed surrounding the original library on three sides, 2/ after moving services and collections into the addition, the old building is demolished, and 3/ finally a "fill in" addition is used to take the place of the former library building. Clearly, this is an expensive process and should be used only when justified.

Underground Additions

Although it is used infrequently, still another alternative, the underground addition, may be worthy of consideration. While constructing a basement beneath an existing building is seldom attempted, adding a be-low-ground addition under an adjacent parking lot, campus mall, or other open space is a valid choice in some instances. This is especially true when the added space is to be used for large-scale collection storage. However, by using lightwells and other architectural devices, such underground space can be made pleasant enough for public services as well.

Underground spaces sometimes have the advantage of lower construction costs and less expensive HVAC operating costs. Before making this choice, however, it is important to ascertain whether the water table and other ground water conditions are favorable. If there is insufficient evidence on this point, test-borings on the site will help provide data.

Whatever the form of the proposed addition may be, the librarian must study it carefully to determine its effect on library functions and operations. An addition which creates a long, narrow building will result in functions strung out in linear fashion. A wing in the wrong location may divide collections and services inappropriately. The in-fill addition may not necessarily create space where it is most needed or useful. Distributing the collection, services and staff over too many floors will result in higher operating costs as well as inconvenience for staff and users.

Vertical Expansion

The previous discussion has considered plans for additions that expand an existing building horizontally. Vertical expansion is another possibility. In fact, some building designs assume and specifically provide for adding one or more floors to the structure at a later date. Whether or not this remains a practical solution when the time comes for expansion is subject to study. For one thing, building codes have become much more stringent in their structural requirements over the past decade or so. The result is that the structural system of columns and/or load-bearing walls designed originally may no longer suffice. Remedial work in the form of strengthening columns, walls, floors and other structural elements is often prohibitively expensive and so disruptive that the library would have to be moved out for an extended period of time.

The floor-loading requirement of 125–150 pounds per square foot for library buildings sometimes creates a problem since it is twice that of many office and commercial buildings. The library building's original designers may or may not have considered this additional weight in their calculations for footings, foundations, columns and load-bearing walls which are involved in vertical expansion. A floor-load limitation severely restricts capacities and flexibility in organizing collections and services. Under such circumstances, a floor that should be used for public services and/or collections may be sufficient only for staff offices and workrooms with their lesser weight requirements. Such a possibility will be of obvious concern to the librarian.

An architect skilled in such analysis should be asked to review drawings and specifications of the building to determine exactly what provisions have been made for vertical expansion. Are structural elements sufficient to carry the load for vertical expansion? Can elevator shafts, stairwells, duct chases, etc. be extended without complications? Is the elevator designed for additional floors? (If not, replacement can be a considerable expense.) Must the HVAC equipment be moved? If HVAC units are roof-mounted now, it is almost certain that the library will have to be moved to other quarters for the duration of the construction. Speaking of roofs, how will the library building and its contents be protected from disastrous flooding when roofing materials are removed as an early step in adding another floor or floors? If the roof contains skylights or light wells of any kind, the problem may be even more critical.

Where structural conditions are found to be conducive to vertical expansion, consideration must then be given to the effect that constructing such an addition may have on interim library operations. The site will be impacted by its use as a storage and staging area for building materials. This may restrict access to the library's delivery entrance as well as reduce or eliminate on-site parking. One or more cranes will be in use to bring building materials to the upper level during much of the construction period and a portion of the adjacent streets may be blocked for intervals of time, further restricting access to the library.

There are also design considerations. For instance, was the eventual vertical expansion considered in designing the exterior of the original building? How will the building appear when it is taller? Will it be out of proportion? How well will it relate to adjacent structures? Can the exterior facade be redesigned to complement the structure? Again, an architect is needed, unless the original plans contain drawings indicating how the exterior is to respond to vertical expansion.

Condition of the Existing Library Building

Whether an addition is a desirable means of gaining space may be determined by the condition of the existing library building. As noted earlier in this chapter, making a substantial addition to a structure is likely to require it to be brought up to standards provided by the applicable codes. Depending on the age of the building, how well it has been maintained, and other factors, this can be either a nominal expense or, more likely, a fairly costly matter. In any case, it is important to have the building and its systems closely inspected by an architect, and, if necessary, by engineering specialists, to determine its condition and what will probably be required to bring it into conformance with the various codes. This review should result in a written report with estimated costs for repairs and modifications. Until such a report is in hand, no decision should be made on whether an addition is the most logical means of acquiring needed space.

Project Costs

The project cost for an addition will include both the expenses of the new space and those for remodeling and achieving code conformance for the existing building. If land must be acquired or extensive site work completed, these costs must be included as part of the total. Construction costs for the addition are likely to approximate those for a new stand-alone building. Depending on how complicated the procedure, there may be additional costs for demolition of walls and the linking of the two structures. These figures must be added to the estimate for remodeling. If the library, or any portion of it, must relocate during the period of construction, costs for this purpose should be added. The librarian will also want to include any change in operating costs directly or indirectly associated with the addition and remodeling. Such costs may include staff, renovations and repairs for temporary quarters, special insurance, etc. The total cost for the proposed addition can be compared to the projected cost of other alternatives under consideration.

Getting the Space Where It Is Needed

A major consideration is whether the addition will create space where it is most needed. Libraries often run out of space for one purpose but not for others. For instance, a campus library for a university with a stable student enrollment and staff may require more space for collections long before additional room is needed for users or personnel. In such an instance, it is imperative that the increase in space provided by an addition be located for optimal expansion of the collections. Unless the building was planned with such expansion priorities in mind, it is possible that the site or other considerations will dictate an addition which is not compatible with this adjacency. In such cases, the librarian must determine whether or not library services and collections can be shifted to make the addition functional. This may involve only cosmetic changes or may require wholesale remodeling and major re-organization. Under such circumstances, it must be determined whether an addition is the best option.

Operating During Construction

Planning for an addition must include planning for operations during construction. The basic decision to be made is whether the library should remain in the building during construction or whether part or all of the functions should be moved to other quarters. This subject has been covered in some greater detail in the preceding section of this chapter under the topic of Remodeling. Once an addition has been decided upon, the librarian should have a frank discussion with the architect (and building contractor if one has been chosen) to determine the conditions and possible hazards that may arise during construction. Given this information, the key decision to remain or move must be made.

The Conversion Alternative

Converting a building from one use to another is an age-old practice and one familiar to many librarians who find themselves occupying a structure originally designed for another purpose. The tremendous rise in building costs in recent years and the increasing availability of empty buildings in many communities have given conversions, or rehabilitation projects as they are often known, a new life. Public libraries, especially, now often consider the wisdom of building at a time when crowded urban areas and land costs place acceptable sites well beyond reach. In such cases, it may be wise to accept a well-located building of approximately the right size rather than consider other alternatives.

Again, the librarian should use needs assessment techniques to establish basic space and functional requirements. Knowledge of these is essential in evaluating buildings that may be available for conversion to library purposes. An architect should also be involved in analyzing buildings to determine their adaptability and the probable cost of converting them to library use.

When looking at a building that has been suggested for conversion, a number of very basic items must be considered. Failure in any one of these areas may be critical.

Size and capacity: Is the building large enough to meet the library's space needs? Square footage figures provided for commercial and industrial buildings are often deceptive. Using scaled floor plans or actual measurements taken within the building, it is necessary to determine the approximate net square footage within the structure that can be used for library purposes. Advertised figures may include satellite structures or ancillary portions of the building which may not be usable for library functions.

Location and site: Does the building location meet basic site criteria? If not, what is being compromised and what are the consequences in terms of library access and performance? Is there sufficient land for parking and any future additions? If the site is reasonably accessible, but lacks visibility, are there possible architectural remedies?

Building configuration: If the building meets other criteria, does its shape lend itself to the functional layout of the library's collections and services? A simple rectangular shape is best. Wings, "L's" and other configurations tend to break up the usable sequence of collections and may increase supervision and staffing requirements. Similarly, a multi-floor building, while it may provide enough space, is apt to splinter collections and services, resulting in the need for more staff.

Floor load: Unless the building can sustain a floor load of 125–150 pounds per square foot, it can not be used for library collections. Strengthening the floors to meet this requirement can be a costly procedure that involves not only the floors but also the support columns and walls. Where only a portion of the floor meets the floor-load requirement, the librarian must understand the difficulties involved in arranging collections and services around this limitation. Flexibility is forever constrained.

Ceiling height: An elementary fact of library building design is that standard full-height book shelving is approximately 7'6" high. Ceilings must be tall enough not only to accommodate the bookstack, but also to permit circulation of air and distribution of light above the shelving. Normally, this calls for a minimum ceiling height of 10' or more. Library ceilings are typically in the range of 10'–14'. Lower ceilings become claustrophobic as well as barriers to air and light. Lifting a ceiling, or lowering a floor, is prohibitively expensive in almost all circumstances.

Column spacing: Libraries require flexible open spaces as uninhibited by walls and columns as possible. Columns occupy valuable space. They interrupt the sequence of collections and become barriers to supervision. Modular library buildings use bays with dimensions that accommodate the basic three-foot-wide section of shelving; odd spacing further reduces the amount of space for shelving and flexibility in its arrangement. Contemporary library buildings of more than one floor are likely to have columns spaced 24 to 30 or more feet apart; a lesser spacing should be looked upon with disfavor. Changing column spacing in an existing structure is, of course, almost beyond the realm of possibility.

Load-bearing walls: For many years now, libraries have avoided structures that contain more than a minimum of load-bearing walls because of their effect on flexibility in arranging collections and services. Load-bearing walls in a structure which is being considered for library use should be limited to those required for perimeter walls and enclosures around elevator shafts and stairwells. Removal of load-bearing walls, like the moving of columns, is too complex and expensive to be seriously considered in most instances. However, they may, on occasion, be pierced for doorways or other purposes if this is absolutely necessary, though the cost may be high.

Access for the physically handicapped: If the building was constructed prior to the enactment of regulations requiring public buildings to be accessible to the physically handicapped, special attention must be given to how these requirements will be met. Restrooms in most commercial and industrial buildings, for instance, will have to be enlarged or replaced. Access from the entrance may require elaborate ramps or lift devices. Elevators may or may not exist or may be inadequate. Incorporating an elevator into a structure can be expensive.

Meeting code requirements: In converting the existing building from its former use to library use, all systems will have to be brought into compliance with applicable building codes. This has been discussed in previous parts of this chapter and is equally applicable here. However, there may be a distinct difference between upgrading a building which has always served as a library and a structure that was designed and used for an entirely different purpose. For instance, floor loading has already been discussed.

HVAC system: Another major item affected by a change in occupancy is the HVAC system. Its capacity, controls and the routing of duct work may have been geared to a particular occupancy whose needs are quite unlike the library's. Obviously, there is considerable difference between the HVAC requirements of a car dealership or grocery store, for example, and those of a library; in the case of an academic or school library, a building that was created for a gymnasium, multi-purpose assembly room, offices or classes presents similar problems. To fulfill library needs new duct work may need to be installed, a filter system provided and the capacity of the furnace and cooling equipment enlarged. All of these take space. As a result, the ceiling may have to be lowered and the mechanical equipment rooms enlarged. What effect will this have on usable space?

Electrical power and lighting: Libraries are heavy users of electricity for power and lighting; can this requirement be met by the current electrical service or must it be upgraded? If upgrading is necessary, how extensive must it be? Will there need to be new electrical panels? Will wiring have to be replaced? How will power be brought to individual work stations, public desks, and other equipment? Is there any way the library can hope to achieve the kind of flexibility and access to power receptacles that are of increasing importance? How expensive is this going to be? What compromises will the library have to accept?

Lighting is another major consideration. In many buildings the amount of light provided is insufficient and the type of light inappropriate for libraries. Fixtures may not be correctly placed for library purposes. Switches are likely to be inadequate as well. How much remedial work will be needed to provide adequate and appropriate light? Will ceilings be high enough for good distribution of light above shelving? Are the ceilings too high for effective lighting above readers?

Concrete barriers and other concerns: Some potential concerns may be literally embedded in concrete. For instance, the floor may be at more than one level, with a few steps in between—devastating for most library purposes. Stairs between floors may have been designed with risers and treads unevenly spaced or greater in dimension than is allowed under current building codes. Are stair runs of proper length and interrupted as frequently as necessary by landings which are of sufficient dimension? If stairs must be rebuilt to meet code requirements, is there sufficient space for the longer stair runs? If not, where will stairs be located?

A review of a building used for industrial or commercial purposes may result in the discovery of elements which may have to be removed before the space can be used for library purposes. An industrial building, for example, might have reinforced cement platforms emerging out of the floor to serve as bases for heavy equipment. Extensive loading docks, possibly with depressed ramps, may have to be eliminated. Some buildings will have space devoted to refrigeration equipment and storage rooms that have no place in a library. Hoists and pits, common to an automotive dealership or garage, will have to be cleared away. Depending upon its former use, each building is likely to have certain equipment for which the library will have no use. The cost of eliminating these barriers may be considered as a part of the evaluation.

Fenestration: Fenestration in an existing structure may or may not be appropriate for a library. Large expanses on the east, south and west sides of a building tend to increase the load on HVAC equipment and on utility costs. Windows that are too low affect the use of wall shelving and the collection capacity. If windows border a busy thoroughfare or active railroad, acoustical control may be a problem. Improperly constructed or installed windows tend to leak; whether they do or not should be established by inspection. Large plate-glass windows, such as exist in many showrooms, may create problems in the organization of internal functions. Besides, they are expensive to replace if broken. Similar attention must be given to skylights: how will their location relate to internal functions? Do they show signs of leaking?

Flooring: While carpeting will cover many minor blemishes, the floor should be reasonably level and in good condition. In most cases, existing floor coverings will have to be removed and new floor coverings, usually carpet, installed. If at all possible, the surface of the slab floor should be inspected. Large cracks may indicate a structural problem arising from settling, poor foundations and footings, or deficiencies in building materials or construction methods. If the floor is uneven, it will be difficult to install shelving units plumb, level and square. Carpet can not be properly installed on a floor surface that is badly chipped, cracked or pitted. Some floors may be made of materials which will not accept carpeting. Floors may also be permeated with oil or other materials that inhibit use of desirable

floor coverings. Where adverse conditions are found, it may become necessary to add a new layer of concrete to create a flat, level surface that can be carpeted. Besides being expensive, this process will reduce the space between floor and ceiling, a matter that can be crucial.

In buildings with wood floors, similar inspections should be made. Sound construction, with joists and flooring free of termites, dry rot and other destructive conditions, is necessary. Like the concrete floor, the wood floor should be flat, smooth and level. Particular attention needs to be given to deflection in wood floors. This may be a sign of weakened floor members or poor construction. Remember that book shelving is unforgiving in its weight and that certain other pieces of library furniture and equipment such as microform cabinets and map cases can be even heavier. If flooring is rough, it may be sanded to a smooth surface or covered with plywood or other sheet goods to make a smooth surface for carpeting.

Fire protection: A review of the building under consideration by the fire marshall is of great importance. That officer will determine whether present provisions for sprinklers or other suppressant devices are adequate. He or she will also examine the building's provisions of exits in terms of the library's occupancy requirements. If additional exits are to be required, their location may be critical to the arrangement of collections and services. These and related matters should be carefully considered with the fire marshall.

Plumbing: Access to restrooms by the physically handicapped has already been touched upon in a prior paragraph. However, plumbing should be looked at as a total system by the architect or a mechanical engineer. What is the condition of piping? Are hot water facilities adequate? Roof drains that penetrate the building through walls and/or columns should be inspected. If the building's prior tenant made extensive use of plumbing fixtures, water pipes, etc. that are not needed by the library, how will they be removed, capped off, or otherwise taken care of? Are there floor drains in the restrooms? If not, how can they be installed?

Roofing: An inspection of the roof and roof drains is an essential part of the evaluation process. This may begin with a search for tell-tale signs of leakage inside the building. Records of the building's owner should be requested so that you can determine when major repairs or replacements have occurred. The life expectancy of the existing roof should be ascertained by a qualified roofing specialist. The cost of any needed repairs should be included in the roofing inspector's report.

Miscellaneous items: The preceding paragraphs call attention to some of the major areas which require evaluation when you are considering a building for conversion. Other items, less critical perhaps, may also merit attention. For instance, anything that might affect the amount or shape of the space to be used for library purposes deserves consideration. Will HVAC ductwork be adequate in size, or must it be replaced by larger duct shafts, thereby decreasing usable space? Are electrical panel and telephone equipment rooms of sufficient size? Or will they have to be enlarged or relocated?

Face-Lifting

If the building available for conversion is acceptable on all other grounds, it is time to determine what may be required to make it an attractive home for the library. Both the exterior and the interior must be considered. Beginning with the exterior, will a new entrance be necessary? Is the present facade attractively designed, or will it need to be reshaped in some way? One or more architectural sketches showing conceptual designs for the exterior should be provided for esthetic evaluation and for cost analysis.

The interior "face-lift" is probably even more complex. Using the building program as a guide, the librarian should arrange all of the library functions within the building envelope. The architect will have to advise on the effect that any remedial work required to correct deficiencies and comply with building codes is likely to have on space planning.

When this task is completed it will be obvious whether the required capacities and the desired functional relationships can be achieved. What may appear at the outset to be a spacious building may prove otherwise when column spacing, load-bearing walls, shafts and other elements are allowed for in the arrangement of furniture and equipment. On the other hand, creative and judicious effort may yield ways to take advantage of the building's idiosyncrasies and enhance the eventual layout.

When the layout has been achieved, an interior designer or architect should evaluate the scheme in terms of possible decor such as well and floor coverings, casework, partitioning, etc. The end result should be a budget figure that will tell the librarian approximately how much it will cost to transform the building into an attractive and usable facility for library purposes.

Estimating Impact on the Operating Budget

Once the layout of functions has been completed and capacities determined, the librarian should estimate the impact that use of the building as a library facility will have on the annual operating budget. Here, staffing requirements are a major concern and should prompt the librarian to determine probable personnel allocation. A crucial factor will be the number of public service desks which will have to be staffed while the library is open. Depending on the number of hours the library is open each week, every public desk station (there may be two or more stations at a given location, of course, as at circulation) represents 2.5–3.0 people when off-desk duties and substitute coverage for holidays, vacations, and sick leave are considered. Calculations for personnel costs should include both direct pay and fringe benefits. A reference desk might, for instance, require three people for coverage of a 68-hour-per-week schedule. If the average salary + benefit amounts to $30,000 per year, the staff cost for operating that particular reference desk would be $30,000 × 3 = $90,000.00. Given such costs, a building which, by virtue of the number of levels or other configuration peculiarities, requires one more reference desk than another building will increase annual operating costs by more than $90,000. This can be a persuasive point in making comparisons between possible solutions.

Operating costs will also be affected by utilities and maintenance. Usually the architect can provide estimates for costs in these areas. Higher utility and maintenance costs are almost implicit in the operation of any building larger than its predecessor. However, whether the escalation is reasonable or not can best be determined by comparing figures for different options. Where projected utility and maintenance costs seem unrealistic, the architect may supply justification or be able to indicate the cause and suggest possible remedies.

Evaluation

When all of the data have been assembled, a judgment can be made as to whether the building is, or is not, a good candidate for conversion to library use. Further, a comparison can be made between the costs and advantages/disadvantages of converting such a building and those of other options available for solving the library's space needs.

The decision should not, of course, be made on the basis of cost alone. It is imperative that the librarian indicate inherent advantages and disadvantages for the potential user and for library staff. When converted, will the building meet the library's space requirements? If so, for how many years? Can it be expanded at a later date to serve for a longer period? What limitations or conditions does the building impose on the distribution of library services and collections and on staffing? Is the building likely to be well received by both the users and the staff? (If not, it is probable that the decision to convert a particular building to library use will be considered a failure, regardless of its price.) Esthetics must not be overlooked, either. How will the building compare in appearance with others on the campus or in the community?

Comparing Alternatives

Having investigated two or more alternatives, the librarian and those who make the ultimate decisions on capital projects for the academic institution or government agency must make a choice. Too often this is a dollar and cent decision: which solution costs the least? The librarian should strive to avoid action based mainly on dollar values, though costs must remain an important consideration.

A technique which works well is to compare alternatives on the basis of their merits in accordance with certain characteristics. This can be developed as a grid similar to that described in Chapter 10 for evaluating different library sites. A more elaborate methodology assigns logical but arbitrary weights to each of the factors under consideration in order to express qualitative values. The scores for the various alternatives can sometimes be more convincing even than the cost figures. Whatever the methodology employed, the ultimate decision should provide the library with a building which will permit the cost-effective delivery of library services. The adopted solution, it is to be hoped, will be for the long term.

Conclusion

In addition to constructing a new building, a variety of other solutions to a library's space needs may be available. These include: 1/ remodeling, 2/ one or more additions, and 3/ conversion of a building constructed for another purpose. Each of these alternatives has been discussed in this chapter in terms of how they can be evaluated. It is important that the librarian have professional assistance from architects and others in gathering technical information. The process of evaluation requires attention to many details. While the cost of a given solution is of vital interest to decision makers, the librarian must emphasize other aspects, including the impact on library users, staff and operations. Fair consideration of all these factors should result in an equitable decision.

XIV TECHNIQUE OF PLAN ANALYSIS

PARTICIPATING in a library building project without at least a rudimentary knowledge of plan analysis is not unlike traveling through a foreign country on foot, lacking any understanding of the people, their customs, or language. Such a person is likely to miss so much of the potential value of the trip that he or she might be better advised to stay home! In a sense, the same thing is true for the librarian who enters a building project without the ability to read, understand or interpret drawings and specifications. The limitation on the individual's capacity for evaluating and contributing in a meaningful way during the planning process should be obvious. The purpose of this chapter is to discuss various aspects of plan analysis from the viewpoint of the librarian. Although illustrations for this chapter have come from a typical building project, it is not intended that the text here substitute for other methods of learning blueprint reading.

Plan Analysis: Why and What

Plan analysis, loosely, is the process of reviewing drawings and specifications produced by design professionals. For the librarian, it must also involve comparing the requirements established in the building program with the capacities and characteristics of the building as it evolves. This process is extremely important because it is the only way the librarian can be certain that the requirements and other conditions set forth in the building program are being met.

Interpretation of plans and specifications requires an ability to mentally convert space shown in two dimensions on drawings to three dimensions. Further, it means learning and using a new language of symbols and abbreviations. Plan analysis requires time and methodical attention to detail on the part of the librarian. Most projects run on tight schedules, necessitating prompt review and response to drawings and specification submittals regardless of what other priorities the librarian may have.

Many design professionals enter library projects with limited understanding of library requirements and operations. Neither do they know what role the librarian will play in the analysis of plans. Therefore, at the first opportunity, the librarian should discuss this aspect of the work with the design professionals. This discussion should emphasize the importance the librarian attaches to participation in team meetings and in the review of plans and specifications as the project progresses. As soon as a design schedule is available, the librarian should review it with the architect to make certain that adequate time is reserved for plan analysis.

These early meetings are a good time to determine how the librarian's comments on plans and specifications should be prepared for the architect and how the architect will respond to them. Practices vary considerably. From the librarian's vantage point, it is important that all review comments be presented in written form. It is also imperative that the librarian know how the architect will respond to those comments—again a variable in architectural practice. Unless the architect replies in some obvious manner, the librarian cannot know whether the review comments have been considered or what effect they may have had on resolving program and design issues.

There is no standard way for the librarian to prepare review comments. Perhaps the most satisfactory method is to make a running list of items and to key each to a number written on the drawings. Usually it is helpful, especially as the number of sheets of drawings increase, to indicate the sheet number and, if provided, a cross-reference to room number or grid coordinate. (These terms will be explained later in this chapter.) An example of plan review comments is included as Appendix H. The architect should supply additional copies of the plans so that the librarian can mark a set for library files. If only one set is provided, the librarian should make a copy of those portions of the drawings which contain the keys to the comments. An alternate, and somewhat less satisfactory, method is to write the comments directly on the drawings. While this eliminates the need for the key numbers and the list of comments, it is often difficult to find space enough on the drawings to write everything necessary in a given situation. It is also harder to review comments made in this way and to refer back to earlier reviews.

How the architect will respond to the librarian's review comments will vary from person to person. Perhaps the most productive way is to devote a team meeting to the review of the comments. Then the architect, librarian and other team members can consider each review comment and explore alternatives in whatever depth may be necessary, checking off each item as the review is completed.

Drawings and Specifications: What They Are

Some background information on what drawings and specifications represent, how they come to be and how they are organized and presented may be helpful. Drawings, of course, illustrate in great detail how a building is to be put together and what it will look like when completed. The specifications describe the requirements for materials and workmanship. Drawings are usually issued as a set of blueprints, while specifications are bound in one or more volumes. Neither the drawings nor the specifications emerge overnight; both are the end product of the labor of a variety of contributors. Together the drawings and specifications provide all the information that an experienced contractor requires to construct the library building.

The Drawing Process

It is helpful for the librarian to understand the drawing process which produces the blueprint to be reviewed. This process is not unlike that followed by most writers in preparing a complex piece of written work. The first step is schematics, sometimes broken into two parts: 1/ concept, and 2/ schematic design. The concept drawings are likely to be on one or two sheets and illustrate the architect's perception of a solution to the problem represented by the building program and site. This is similar to a writer stating the scope and intent of an article or book in a few sentences. In the schematic design, the architect carries the solution forward in simple scale drawings that show more detail than the concept drawings. These schematic drawings indicate where major functions are to be located and the approximate amount of space they will require. The schematics are like the outline a writer would prepare to show how ideas will be related and in what sequence.

Design development drawings, the next phase, incorporate project details including architectural, struc-

tural, mechanical, and electrical. At this point the building design tends to solidify, making major changes and modifications increasingly complicated. Several revisions will probably occur during this period. These are known as progress prints. Progress prints may or may not be issued as complete sets. Often, only the sheets on which revisions have been made will be offered for review. For this reason, the librarian must keep a file of previous drawings, clearly marked with the date of issue. When completed, the full set of design development drawings will consist of many sheets, the number depending somewhat on the size and complexity of the building. Design development drawings are similar to the first full draft by the writer.

Construction documents, or working drawings as they are sometimes referred to, represent the final phase where previous drawings are revised and augmented as necessary to provide the eventual building contractor with the information required to construct the building. These drawings, like the writers final draft, are the result of much revision and fine tuning. A great deal of coordination is necessary to be certain that the information on all of the drawings is accurate and consistent. This is the same process a writer must go though to avoid errors and unwanted duplication of text.

The Drafting Process

The process of preparing drawings is dependent to some degree on the number of staff in the architect's office, the methodology adopted by the office, and a variety of other factors. In the small office, the architect is apt to do much more of the drawing than in a large office where a corps of drafting staff is available. In nearly every case, however, the architect responsible for creating the design for the building will prepare the original concept drawings. The same person is likely to do most of the work on the schematic design drawings because the plan is still evolving and requires close involvement of the mind that conceived the solution. Once schematic drawings have been approved, an increasing amount of the work is likely to be done by the drafting staff under the supervision of a job captain and the project architect. The design architect will continue reviewing changes which affect the character of the design. Because of the design architect's unique creative abilities, a larger office will assign the project at this point to a job captain or project architect whose task it is to see the drawings through to completion. The design architect remains in touch with the project as a consultant to help with any major problems that may occur.

As the design development phase begins, the floor plans are given to the engineers who will be responsible for the structural, mechanical and electrical systems. (Some preliminary engineering work may occur during schematics, especially on complex projects.) The various engineers will use these floor plans as the basis for their own specialized drawings. Larger architectural firms may have their own in-house engineering staff; smaller firms will retain independent engineering firms to do this work for them. Regardless of whether in-house staff is used or the work is delegated to an outside firm or firms, close coordination is required. Unfortunately, this does not always occur and the librarian may see evidence of this if arriving progress prints show uneven development of the plans. For instance, it is not entirely unusual to see one or more of the engineering firms using base architectural drawings that do not reflect changes, sometimes substantial ones, that have been made in the architect's office. This may signal a breakdown in communications, an overload in one or other of the offices, carelessness, or some other adverse condition. Whatever the reason, the librarian should be very aware of this possibility and promptly call any suspected deviation from current drawings to the architect's attention.

In most architectural offices the architect and his or her staff of designers and draftsmen draw their plans on "drawing sheets," sometimes referred to as "vellums" or "mylars." These materials provide a surface which readily accepts pencil and ink drawings. When revisions and corrections are made to the drawings, they are incorporated by erasing and redrawing the information on the drawing sheets. An increasing number of architectural and engineering offices are using Computer Assisted Drawing (CAD) programs. Drawings are then transferred to a reproducible stock by a graphics printer. After drawings are finished, the drawing sheets are reproduced by one of several processes as blueprints— though the print may actually be black.

Before looking at the drawings, the librarian should note other information on each sheet. Along the top, on one side or at the bottom of each sheet will appear the name of the project and the architect's name, address, etc., which is known as the "title block." A list of the engineering consultants will be shown beneath the architect's name. Other information may include notation on the revision, the date of the current revision, phase of work, scale of the drawing, sheet number and title of the sheet describing what it contains.

It is important for the librarian to understand how drawings are created so as to appreciate what changes mean to the architect in terms of office time. During the schematic stage, changes in the location, size or configuration of the circulation desk, for instance, require erasing and redrawing on only one or two sheets. As the drawings progress through the design development and construction document phases, an increasing number of drawings are affected because the circulation desk appears on several sheets. This does not mean that the librarian should ever hesitate to require that necessary changes be made; only that such requests for modification should occur as early in the process as possible.

The amount of information appearing on a drawing increases as the process passes from one stage to another. The changes in the architectural set are shown in the figures which follow that trace the Circulation area of the Redwood City Public Library from concept to working drawings (Figures 14–1 to 14–9). In this instance, the concept drawing is more advanced than may sometimes be the case when "single-line" drawings are drawn almost freehand without showing furniture. Note how the functions have evolved as various ideas were tested from schematics through construction drawings (Figure 14–7). Even the details shown in the construction drawing are but the tip of the iceberg. To gain full knowledge of the Circulation Desk, the librarian will find it necessary to review comparable drawings on the sheets for structural, mechanical, electrical power and communications, lighting, and plumbing (these are not shown here). In addition, the architectural set contains other information about this area on sheets that show interior elevations, the reflected ceiling plan, and drawings for the casework including the circulation desk (Figures 14–8 and 14–9). To reiterate, the plan analysis can not be considered complete until the reviewer has studied and correlated all of this information from these various drawings for each portion of the building.

Typical Contents for a Set of Drawings

A set of drawings, beginning in the design development phase, will consist of several parts, each representing a particular aspect of architectural design or engineering. Each sheet bears an identifying letter and number as part of the title block. There will be several sheets for each section of the drawings, generally appearing in this order:

"A" *sheets*: Architectural drawings, which may include the site plan and landscaping and sometimes other civil

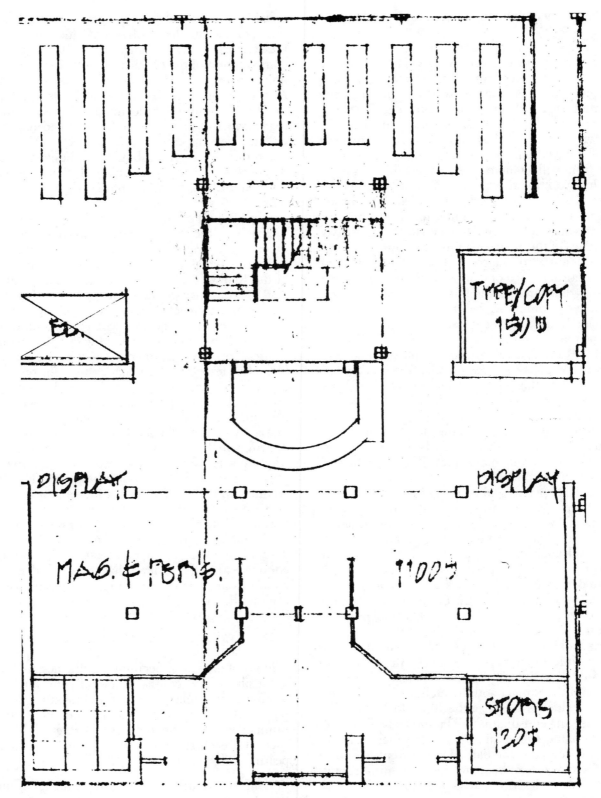

Figure 14–1
Circulation Desk at Concept Stage

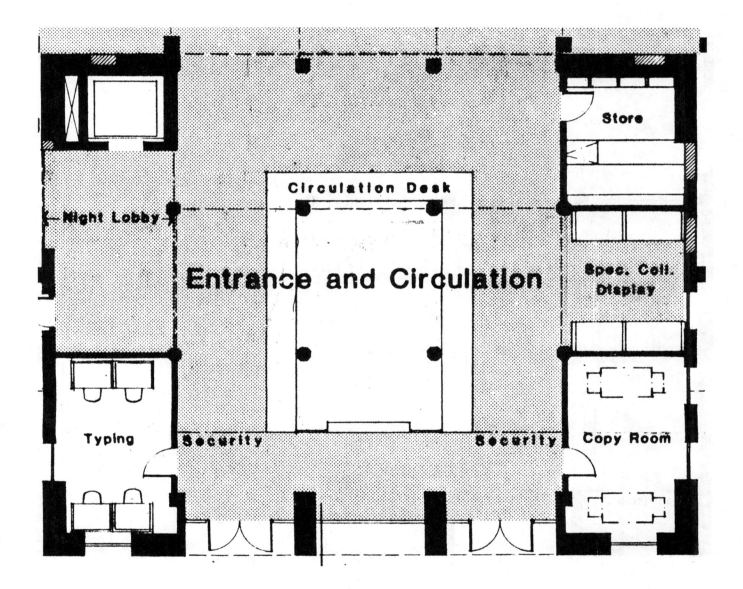

Figure 14–2
Circulation Desk at Early Schematic Design Stage

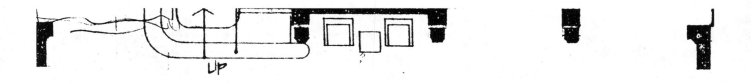

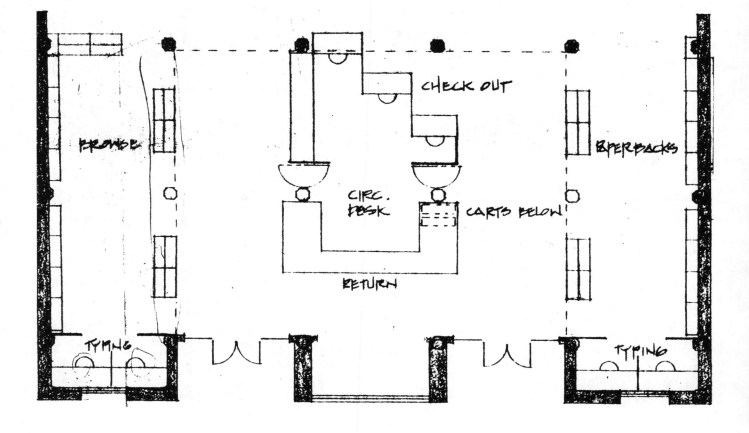

UP

CHECK OUT

BROWSE

PAPERBACKS

CIRC.
DESK

CARTS BELOW

RETURN

TYPING

TYPING

Figure 14–3
Circulation Desk at End of Schematic Design Stage

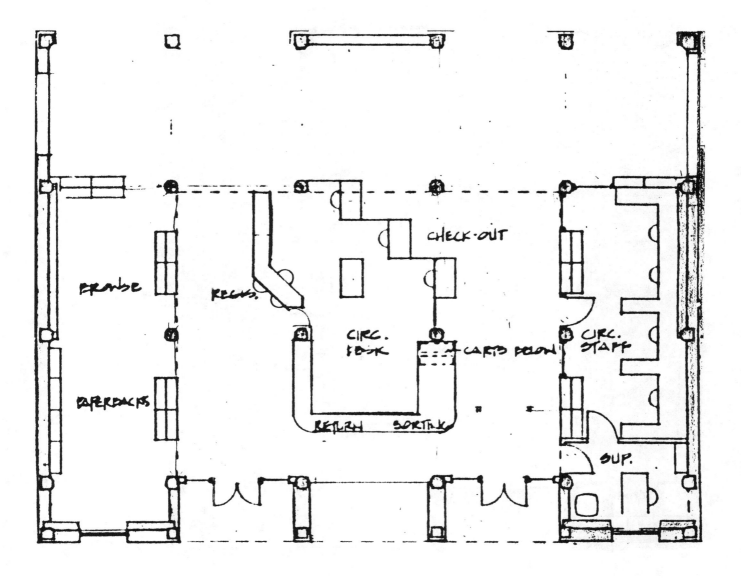

Figure 14–4
Circulation Desk at Beginning of Design Development Stage

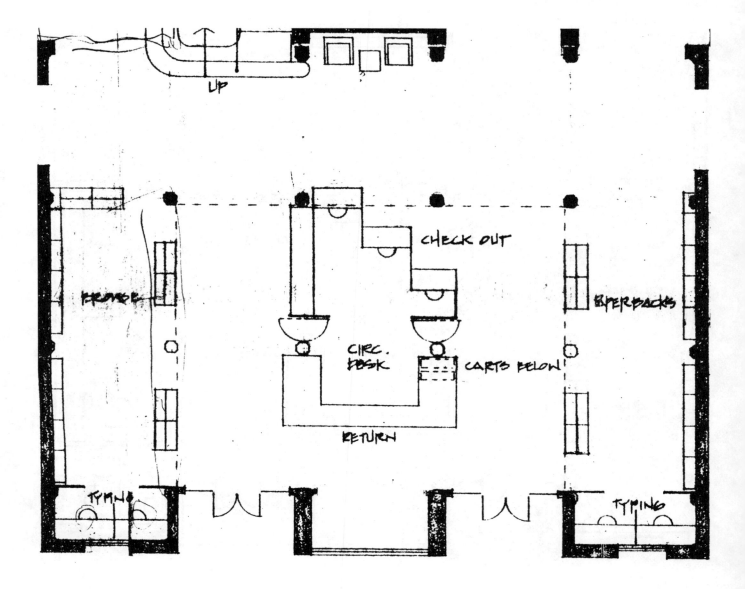

Figure 14–5
Circulation Desk at Midpoint of Design Development Stage

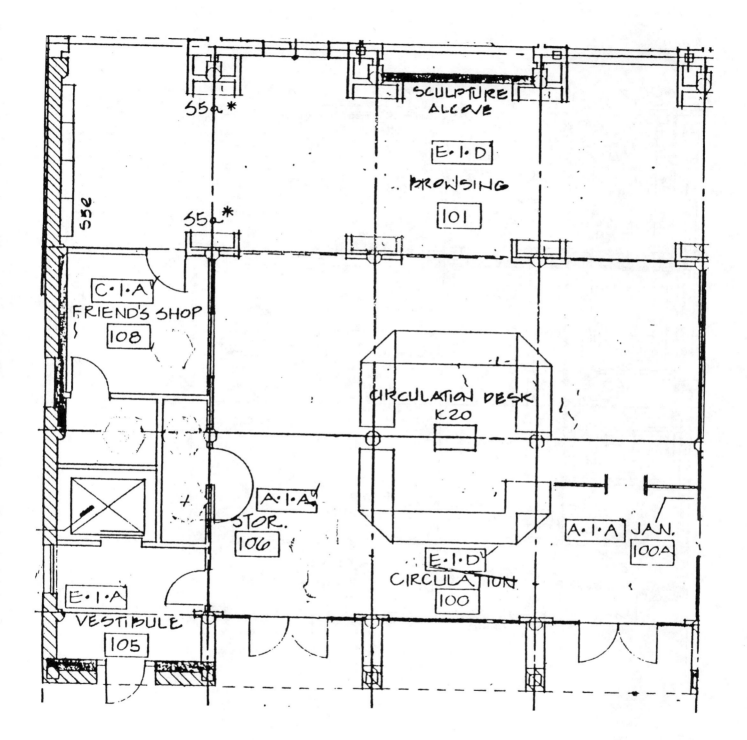

Figure 14–6
Circulation Desk at Midpoint of Construction Document Stage

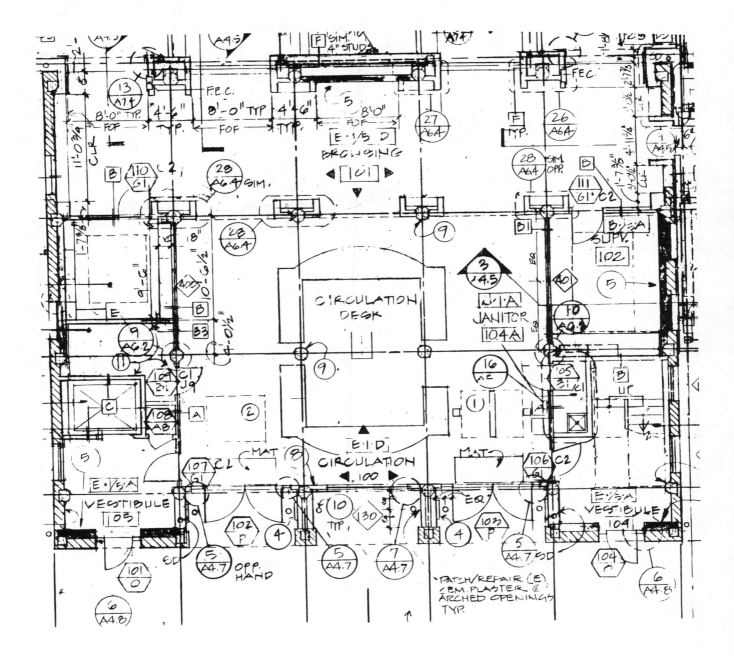

Figure 14–7
Circulation Desk as It Appeared in Final Construction Drawings

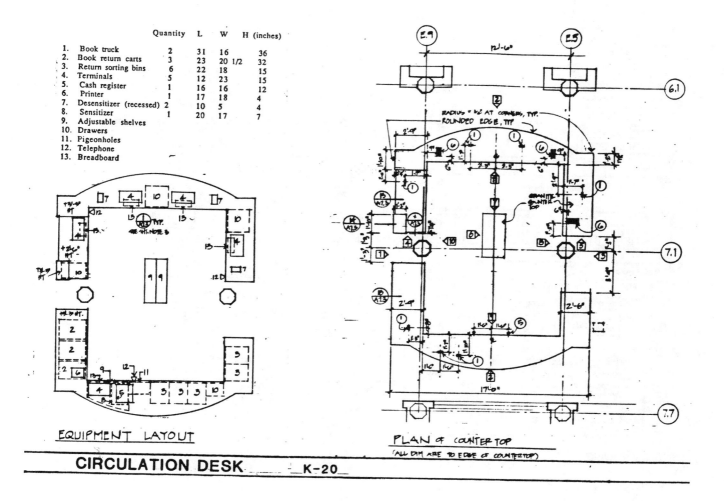

	Quantity	L	W	H (inches)
1. Book truck	2	31	16	36
2. Book return carts	3	23	20 1/2	32
3. Return sorting bins	6	22	18	15
4. Terminals	5	12	23	15
5. Cash register	1	16	16	12
6. Printer	1	17	18	4
7. Desensitizer (recessed)	2	10	5	4
8. Sensitizer	1	20	17	7
9. Adjustable shelves				
10. Drawers				
11. Pigeonholes				
12. Telephone				
13. Breadboard				

EQUIPMENT LAYOUT

PLAN OF COUNTER TOP
(ALL DIM ARE TO EDGE OF COUNTERTOP)

CIRCULATION DESK   K-20

Figure 14–8
Circulation Desk: Equipment Layout at Conclusion of the Construction Drawing Stage

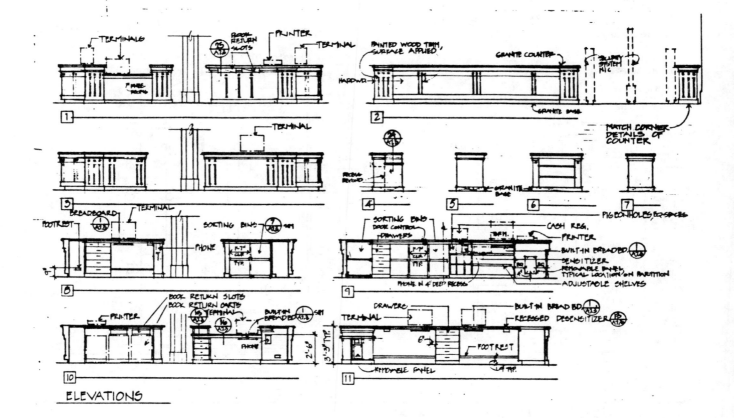

Figure 14–9
Elevations of Casework: Drawings for Circulation Desk as They Appeared in the Construction Drawings

engineering drawings. Architectural drawings are those of greatest interest to the librarian since they contain the floor plans, sections, exterior elevations and interior elevations.

"C" sheets: Civil engineering drawings, if not included as part of the "A" drawings. These contain information on plans for drainage, streets, and grading.

"L" sheets: Landscaping, unless included as part of the "A" drawings.

"S" sheets: Structural drawings which detail how the skeleton of the building is to be put together.

"M" sheets: Mechanical drawings indicating the location of the heating, ventilating, and air conditioning system (HVAC), including duct work.

"P" sheets: Plumbing drawings showing where pipes and plumbing fixtures will be located; may include piping for landscaping.

"E" sheets: Electrical drawings, divided between lighting and power; often include communications (telephone, signal wiring, etc.).

If interior design drawings are not included as part of the "A" group, they are apt to follow the "E" sheets with a designation such as "I" or "F." Although the librarian will need to review all of the sheets in each set, the greatest amount of attention will be given the "A" sheets. The organization of the "A" sheets will vary from one architect to another, but drawings will usually fall into the following groups:

- Site plan
- Landscaping
- Floor plan for each level of the building
- Exterior elevations of each side of the building
- Sections (cuts) through the building
- Interior elevations of each wall
- Details of particular areas
- Casework
- Schedules for doors, windows, finishes
- Reflected ceiling plans
- Furniture layouts

Specifications

The volume of specifications includes the requirements for materials and craftsmanship which the build-

ing contractor must provide. Any deviation from the specifications usually requires prior approval from the architect and/or other officer in charge of the project. Specifications are fairly standardized for many building components. Among other things, they may require conformance to the provisions of a particular code or standard generally accepted in the industry. The advent of the word processor has made specification writing much easier in many offices, and "boilerplate" can be modified as required for each job and printed without rewriting entire pages of repetitious material. While fewer errors are likely to occur, changes are not always made in the specifications to make them relate to the library project. In one such instance, for example, there were repeated references to a mortuary rather than to the branch library for which the specifications were intended. Suspicious incongruities, not always so obvious or blatant, must never go unquestioned.

Specifications are usually arranged under the following 16 major divisions:

Division 1: General Requirements
Division 2: Site Work
Division 3: Concrete
Division 4: Masonry
Division 5: Metals
Division 6: Wood and Plastics
Division 7: Thermal and Moisture Protection
Division 8: Doors and Windows
Division 9: Finishes
Division 10: Specialties
Division 11: Equipment
Division 12: Furnishings
Division 13: Special Construction
Division 14: Conveying Systems
Division 15: Mechanical
Division 16: Electrical

The divisions are in turn broken down into sections, each representing a particular subject or aspect. The final set of specifications will usually include the bidding requirements and contract conditions, including various forms needed by building contractors interested in bidding the project.

Specifications generally do not make for exciting reading and the librarian will not need to understand the more technical aspects. However, a general knowledge of the contents will be helpful. Some portions will be essential because they provide details not on the drawings, indicating, for instance, which manufacturer's products are considered acceptable. In addition to the librarian, the person who is in charge of the agency's plant facilities should review the specifications to be certain that products are being specified which have performed well in other buildings with which he or she has had experience.

Preparations for Plan Reviews

Before plan review can begin, the librarian needs to acquire a limited number of tools and to make other preparations. The items needed by the librarian include architect's and engineering scales. These scales permit the user to read measurements directly from the drawings. At least three scales will be needed. Except for small buildings, the architect will probably draw schematic plans at $\frac{1}{16}$" or $\frac{1}{32}$" scale ($\frac{1}{16}$" or $\frac{1}{32}$" = one foot). These are usually combined on one scale about a foot in length. The second scale, which will be used most of the time, will show measurements for $\frac{1}{8}$", $\frac{1}{4}$", $\frac{1}{2}$", $\frac{3}{4}$", 1", and perhaps other scales such as $\frac{3}{32}$" or $\frac{3}{16}$", $1\frac{1}{2}$" and 3". The majority of the drawings, once schematics have been completed, will be at $\frac{1}{8}$" = one foot, with other scales used for special drawings. The third scale is an engineer's scale, which is used primarily for measuring distances on the site and other civil engineering drawings. This scale will have readings ranging from 1" = 10 feet to 1" = 50 feet, with some scales going higher. Architect's engineering scales can be purchased from most drafting supply shops or blueprint shops. A pocket version of the architect's scale, less than 7" long, is most convenient for checking some drawings.

The librarian will also want to have a roll of tracing paper. Using a piece of this laid over a drawing enables the librarian to trace the outlines of furniture, rooms, etc., and test them in other orientations without changing the original drawings. Several templates, such as those available for office furniture and equipment, may also be convenient. While the creation of the drawings is the architect's responsibility, many librarians find that at some point it is easier to convey a concept by sketching it in scale rather than trying to describe it in words. Rolls of tracing paper in various widths are usually available in drafting supply shops. A roll 14" to 16" wide should be useful.

If the librarian is unfamiliar with the symbols used on drawings, it may be helpful to have a copy handy. While the final drawings will have symbol keys printed on the sheets, the earlier plans will not. Fortunately, a fairly comprehensive list can be located in *Architectural Graphic Standards* under the subject "Symbols for drawings."

Since plan reviews involves large sheets of drawings

generally measuring about 36" × 42", an unencumbered desk or table at least twice this long is needed. Sets of drawings, stapled together, will come to the librarian. Usually the staples should be removed so that the information on two or more sheets can be compared without laboriously leafing back and forth. Another nearby table should be available for a notebook, a calculator, the volume containing the specifications, reference books such as *Architectural Graphics Standards*, a copy of the library building program, and any other materials the librarian finds useful.

Plan review is tedious work, requiring good lighting and freedom from distraction. If office space is too cramped or interruptions too frequent, the librarian may wish to move elsewhere. While it is helpful to have staff available from time to time to discuss particular areas or concerns, the librarian should expect to devote long, mostly solitary, hours to the job.

Reading Drawings

There is no secret to reading blueprints. It is a process that most people can learn with ease. Numerous texts are available on the subject and it is not the intention of this brief description to substitute for such sources or for attending a class on blueprint reading. (Several examples of helpful texts are listed in the bibliography.)

If there is a key to reading drawings it is in understanding the meaning of the signs and symbols that are used as a kind of shorthand to guide the reader. These road signs are easily detected once drawn to the reader's attention. Since the librarian will be most concerned with floor plans, the examples are taken from such sheets. Road signs are added gradually during the design process as the drawings become increasingly more detailed. All of the signs described in this chapter are apt to be included in sets of drawings which have reached the construction drawing stage. Incidentally, the blueprints chosen for use with this part of the chapter are from the construction documents prepared by Ripley and Associates, Architects and Planners of San Francisco, for the Redwood City, California, Public Library, a 45,000 square foot project which combines the conversion of an old fire department building with new construction.

Notes

The review of drawings should begin with a careful reading of all notes written on each sheet. Notes often appear along one side or at the top or bottom of a sheet as well as being incorporated in the drawings. They are usually numbered and may either be general in nature or keyed to particulars of the drawings. In any case, they convey important information, often not found anywhere else. Sometimes called "sheet notes," these messages may range from an explanation or description of a part of the design and a listing of special requirements to legends necessary for the correct interpretation of the drawings. If such notes are not carefully read at the outset, a good deal of time may be lost and/or misinterpretations may occur.

Grid Lines

Drawings are usually laid out on a grid which makes it possible to refer to a given part of the plan in an unmistakable manner. The grid line often follows the column lines, with the rectangular space formed by the grid lines outlining each bay or module. In Figure 14–10, the grid is marked by capital letters across the top and by arabic numbers along the side. If one wanted to comment on the sink in the workroom, it could be located by following the grid lines, or coordinates C and 2.

Section Indicators

Between grid lines B and C and above grid line 1, there appears an arrow shaped sign with a long stem. Inside is a circle divided in half with the letter E above the legend A3.4. This sign indicates that a section drawing has been made through this part of the building. The letter E stands for Section E and the reference A3.4 shows that Section E will be found on drawing sheet A3.4. It is important to note which way the arrow is pointing since this shows the direction toward which you will be looking when you view this slice of the building. Having found this arrow, the reader should look on the opposite side of the drawing to find its mate. A line drawn between the two will show exactly what you can expect to see. Areas selected for section drawings are usually chosen to provide information on the more complex parts of the building. Sections deserve careful attention because they reveal the vertical organization of the building and contain information such as ceiling heights, which is not shown elsewhere.

Room Numbers

Room numbers usually appear in rectangular boxes or oval shapes and are located within the space referred

to. For instance, a supervisor's office in Figure 14–10 is numbered 130 in this drawing at grid line B-2. If review comments concern this office, reference should be made to Room 130. Architects sometimes prefer to use one number for a particular area and then follow that number with a letter to identify a particular office, workroom or other functionally related space. For instance, the entire technical services area might be given the number 187, with the office of the head cataloger numbered 187A.

Door Numbers and Schedules

Every door is identified by a number which appears in a hexagon. For instance, the door in the Supervisor's Office is no. 140. The notation G1 in the lower half of the hexagon describes the type of door chosen for this location, with the letter G standing for the type and the number 1 indicating the dimensions. To know what is meant by this code, it is necessary to turn to the door schedule shown in Figure 14–11. Although a tedious job, it is necessary for the librarian to review the door schedule very carefully to make certain that the right kind of door is at each location.

Finishes

The key to the materials that will be used for floors, walls, and ceilings is indicated for each area by letters and numbers enclosed in a rectangle somewhat larger than that required for the room number. Above room number 131, for instance (Figure 14–10), there appears a box with the code D-1-B. The D stands for the floor material and base, the number 1 indicates the materials to be used on the walls, and the letter B refers to ceiling materials. To learn what these materials are, the reader has to look at the Finish Schedule on another sheet which is shown in Figure 14–12. For this room the code would be interpreted as:

Floor (D):	Carpet
Base (D):	4″ Vinyl
Walls (1):	Gypsum Board Painted
Ceiling (B):	Suspended Acoustical Panels—Lay-in

Obviously, the finish materials to be used in the building are a matter of considerable interest to the librarian, so each room should be carefully checked.

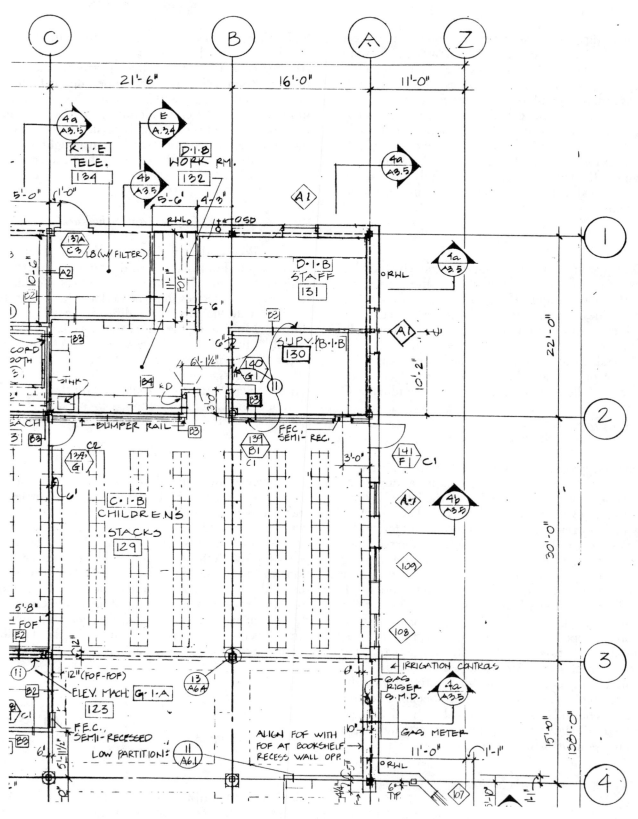

Figure 14–10
Grid Lines

DOOR SCHEDULE

TYPE

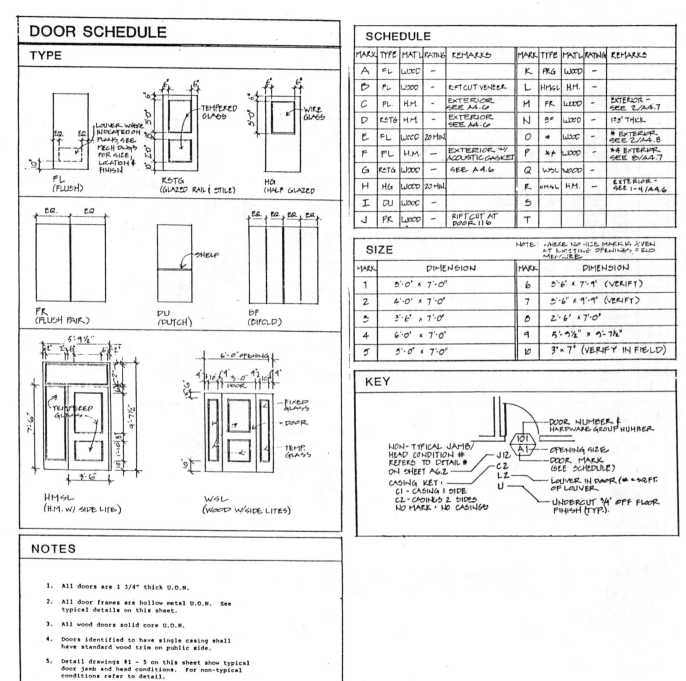

FL (FLUSH)

RSTG (GLAZED RAIL & STILE) — TEMPERED GLASS

HG (HALF GLAZED) — WIRE GLASS

LOUVER WHERE INDICATED ON PLANS, SEE MECH DWGS FOR SIZE, LOCATION & FINISH

PR (FLUSH PAIR)

DU (DUTCH) — SHELF

BF (BIFOLD)

HMSL (H.M. W/ SIDE LITE) — TEMPERED GLASS

WSL (WOOD W/SIDE LITES) — FIXED GLASS / DOOR / TEMP. GLASS

SCHEDULE

MARK	TYPE	MAT'L	RATING	REMARKS	MARK	TYPE	MAT'L	RATING	REMARKS
A	FL	WOOD	–		K	PRG	WOOD	–	
B	FL	WOOD	–	RIFT CUT VENEER	L	HMSL	H.M.	–	
C	FL	H.M.	–	EXTERIOR SEE A4.6	M	FR	WOOD	–	EXTERIOR – SEE 2/A4.7
D	RSTG	H.M.	–	EXTERIOR SEE A4.6	N	BF	WOOD	–	1⅜" THICK
E	FL	WOOD	20 MIN		O	*	WOOD	–	* EXTERIOR SEE 2/A4.8
F	FL	H.M.	–	EXTERIOR W/ ACOUSTIC GASKET	P	**	WOOD	–	** EXTERIOR SEE 8/A4.7
G	RSTG	WOOD	–	SEE A4.6	Q	WSL	WOOD	–	
H	HG	WOOD	20 MIN		R	HMSL	H.M.	–	EXTERIOR – SEE 1-4/A4.6
I	DU	WOOD	–		S				
J	PR	WOOD	–	RIFT CUT AT DOOR 116	T				

SIZE

NOTE: WHERE NO SIZE MARK IS GIVEN AT EXISTING OPENINGS, FIELD MEASURE

MARK	DIMENSION	MARK	DIMENSION
1	3'-0" x 7'-0"	6	3'-6" x 7'-9" (VERIFY)
2	4'-0" x 7'-0"	7	3'-6" x 9'-9" (VERIFY)
3	3'-6" x 7'-0"	8	2'-6" x 7'-0"
4	6'-0" x 7'-0"	9	5'-9½" x 9'-7½"
5	3'-0" x 7'-0"	10	3" x 7' (VERIFY IN FIELD)

KEY

NON-TYPICAL JAMB/HEAD CONDITION # REFERS TO DETAIL # ON SHEET A6.2

CASING KEY:
C1 - CASING 1 SIDE
C2 - CASINGS 2 SIDES
NO MARK - NO CASINGS

101 / A1 — J12, C2, L2, U

DOOR NUMBER & HARDWARE GROUP NUMBER
OPENING SIZE
DOOR MARK (SEE SCHEDULE)
LOUVER IN DOOR (# = SQ.FT. OF LOUVER)
UNDERCUT ¾" OFF FLOOR FINISH (TYP.).

NOTES

1. All doors are 1 3/4" thick U.O.N.

2. All door frames are hollow metal U.O.N. See typical details on this sheet.

3. All wood doors solid core U.O.N.

4. Doors identified to have single casing shall have standard wood trim on public side.

5. Detail drawings #1 - 5 on this sheet show typical door jamb and head conditions. For non-typical conditions refer to detail.

6. At door 126 verify clear dimension of opening. Consult with architect for providing door and frame closet to height specified while maintaining clearance from structural brace.

Figure 14-11
Door Schedule

FINISH SCHEDULE

	FLOOR / BASE		WALLS		CEILING
A	CERAMIC TILE / CERAMIC TILE	1	GYPSUM BOARD PAINTED	A	SUSPENDED GYPSUM BOARD
B	CARPET / 6" VINYL, WOOD	2	CERAMIC TILE	B	SUSPENDED ACOUSTIC PANELS - LAY-IN
C	CARPET / 6" VINYL	3	CAST PLASTER COLUMNS	C	SUSPENDED ACOUS. PANELS CONCEALED SPLINE
D	CARPET / 4" VINYL	4	ACOUSTIC SURFACE	D	ACOUSTIC TILE DIRECT APPLIED
E	TERRAZZO / CAST SYNTHETIC	5	NOT USED	E	EXPOSED PAINTED
F	CARPET / CAST SYNTHETIC	6	NOT USED	F	EXPOSED UNPAINTED
G	SEALED CONC. / 4" VINYL	7	WOOD WAINSCOT	G	NOT USED
H	NOT USED	8	NOT USED	Z	VARIOUS SEE CEILING PLAN
J	VINYL COMPOSITION TILE / 4" VINYL				
K	CONDUCTIVE VINYL COMPOS. TILE / 4" VINYL				

FINISH SYMBOL:
— FLOOR FINISH
— WALL FINISH
— CEILING FINISH

A · 1 · A

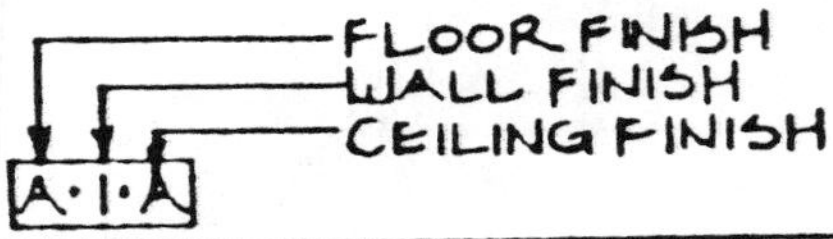

NOTES:

① FOR SPECIAL WOOD MOLDINGS, BASES AND CASINGS SEE INTERIOR ELEVATIONS & DETAILS.

Figure 14–12
Finish Schedule

Windows

Letters appearing in diamonds indicate the type of windows to be used. Again, it is necessary to use a window schedule on another sheet to interpret the code. Opposite grid line A between grid lines 1 and 2 (Figure 14–10) there is a diamond enclosing the letter A-1. Referring to the Window Schedule which is shown in Figure 14–13, the letter A-1 indicates 2 Double "acoustic" window of certain dimensions.

Partitions

The small square boxes which contain both a capital letter and an Arabic numeral denote the type of partition to be used in a given location. Since partitioning varies widely in its ability to control sound, for example, the type of partitioning must be checked along with other details. Near the juncture of grid lines A and 2 (Figure 14–10) there is a box containing the code B3 with arrows pointing to ajacent walls. By referring to the Partition Schedule on another sheet, shown in Figure 14–14, a description can be found for B3, along with a section drawing of the partition.

Interior Elevations

During design development and construction drawings, the architect will draw the interior walls. These are known as "interior elevations." Walls that have been "elevated" are indicated on the floor plans by an arrow similar to that used to identify section cuts, as described earlier. Two such symbols appear in Figure 14–15. One shows a 7 enclosed in a semi-circle above a triangle forming an arrowhead and containing the sheet number A8.3; the other shows a 9 above the same sheet number. Note that the arrows point toward the wall which will appear in the elevation drawing. Symbol 9/A8.3, for instance, is pointing toward the Periodicals Room, the elevation of which is shown in Figure 14–16. Looking at the elevation shown in Figure 14–16, note such features as the entry to the Periodicals Room, a window, the outline of certain pieces of furniture, and changes in ceiling heights. Book stack ranges and pendant lighting are represented by dashed lines.

For the reviewer of drawings, the interior elevations are of extreme importance and interest. For one thing, details appear in the interior elevations that may not be found elsewhere, or found only with difficulty. For instance, except for section drawings, this is the only place floor-to-ceiling heights along the walls can be determined. Other useful dimensions can also be taken from these elevations, such as the height of windows above the floor or height of book stacks. The librarian should carefully relate the interior elevations to the floor plans as a means of determining visual relationships. Whatever furniture, equipment, and shelving is shown can be checked against program requirements. Interior elevations are among the most useful drawings in the set of plans and deserve special attention by the reviewer. If these drawings deviate in any way from the floor plans or any other drawing, the architect must be alerted.

Column Numbers

Columns are often numbered for ease of reference and to illustrate dimensions and other details if they vary in size or character. Such numbers, enclosed in a geometric shape, will be adjacent to the respective column and make it easier to follow the design of very large and complex buildings. Since the columns have not been numbered on the plans being used for illustration here, no example is shown.

Casework

There appears to be a growing trend toward using unitized casework design. For architects using this approach, casework, sometimes referred to as cabinetry or millwork, is divided into a number of units or components, each with a distinctive number. In this instance, casework is designated on the drawings by the letter K, followed by a number to identify the particular component. In Figure 14–17, Office 223 for the Director is to have three units: K5, K2b, and K3. Going to the casework schedule, shown in Figure 14–18, it is apparent that casework for this office will include an open counter, K2b, with shelving above, K3, and flanked on one side by a closet, K5. Details for casework design are shown on other sheets.

A Set of Drawings: Probable Contents

Drawings are usually submitted as sets of sheets, each sheet having a distinctive purpose. Knowing what is supposed to appear on each of these makes it easier to find and correlate information.

Usually the first step in reviewing a set of plans is to look briefly at each sheet in succession to determine

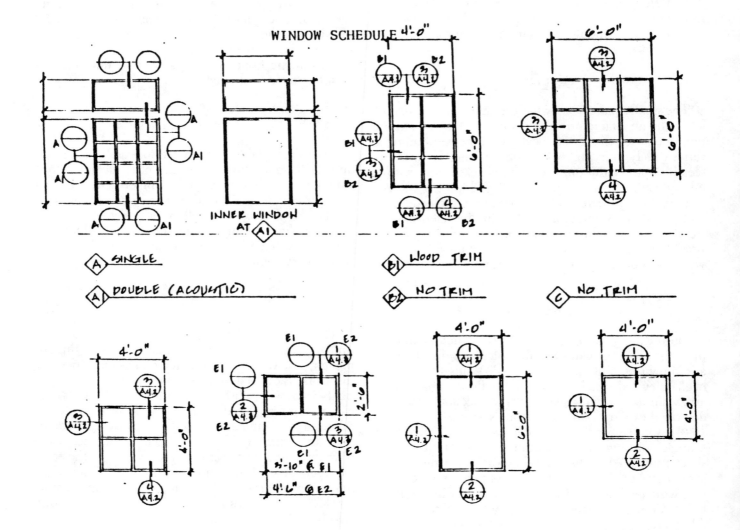

Figure 14–13
Window Schedule

TYPE	DESCRIPTION
A	**TYPICAL PARTITION** — ONE LAYER 5/8" GYPSUM BOARD EACH SIDE / 3 5/8" METAL STUD AT 16" O.C. / TILE SHOWN DOTTED WHERE OCCURRING - SEE SCHEDULE FOR LOCATIONS & SETTING METHOD.
A1	SAME AS A, 1-HR. RATED, FULL HEIGHT TO STRUCTURE ABOVE
B	**SOUND PARTITION** — DBL LAYER 5/8" GYP. BD. EACH SIDE AT TYPE B2 / ONE LAYER 5/8" GYPSUM BOARD EACH SIDE / 3 1/2" METAL STUD AT 16" O.C. / ACOUSTIC BATT INSULATION / ACOUSTIC CAULKING AT PERIMETER, BOTH SIDES
B1	SAME AS B, 1-HR. RATED, FULL HEIGHT TO STRUCTURE ABOVE
B2	SAME AS B, DBL LAYER 5/8" GYP. BD EACH SIDE, ACOUSTIC INSULATION, AND ACOUSTIC CAULKING @ PERIMETER BOTH SIDES
B3	SAME AS B, DBL. LAYER 5/8" GYP. BD ONE SIDE, SINGLE LAYER OTHER, ACOUSTIC INSUL, & ACOUST. CAULKING @ PERIMETER BOTH SIDES.
C	**SHAFT WALL, 2-HOUR RATED** — TWO LAYERS 1/2" TYPE X GYPSUM BOARD / 2 1/2" C-H METAL STUD 24" O.C. / 1" GYPSUM BOARD
D	**DOUBLE STUD PARTITION** — DBL. LAYER 5/8" GYP. BD. AT TYPE D2 / 5/8" GYPSUM BOARD BOTH SIDES / TWO ROWS 2 1/2" X 20 GA. OR 3 5/8" METAL STUDS 16" O.C. EACH SIDE (CONTRACTOR'S OPTION) / CERAMIC TILE W.O. SEE NOTE AT TYPE A / NOTE: CONTR. HAS OPTION TO USE TYPE E METHOD IN LIEU OF THAT SHOWN. / ACOUSTIC INSULATION AT TYPES D1 AND D2 WITH ACOUSTIC CAULKING @ PERIMETER.
D1	SAME AS D WITH ACOUSTIC BATT INSULATION
D2	SAME AS D WITH DOUBLE LAYER 5/8" GYP. BD. ON LIBRARY SIDE (AWAY FROM BATHROOM) OF PARTITION AND WITH ACOUSTIC INSUL.
E	**DOUBLE STUD PARTITION AT STRUCTURAL CROSS BRACING** — DBL LAYER 5/8" GYP. BD. @ TYPE E2 / ONE LAYER 5/8" GYPSUM BOARD EACH SIDE / 1 5/8" METAL STUDS 16" O.C. EACH SIDE / 8"Ø PIPE BRACING - SEE STRUCT. DWGS. / MET TRACK CROSS-BRACING, 2'-8" O.C. / ACOUSTIC INSULATION AT TYPES E1 AND E2 WITH ACOUSTIC CAULKING @ PERIMETER EA. SIDE / CERAMIC TILE, WHERE OCCURING
E1	SAME AS E WITH ACOUSTIC BATT INSULATION
E2	SAME AS E WITH DOUBLE LAYER 5/8" GYP. BD ON LIBRARY SIDE (AWAY FROM BATHROOM) OF PARTITION AND WITH ACOUSTIC BATT INSULATION.
F	**FURRING** — CERAMIC TILE, WHERE OCCURS / 5/8" GYPSUM BOARD ONE SIDE / 2 5/8" METAL STUDS @ 16" O.C.

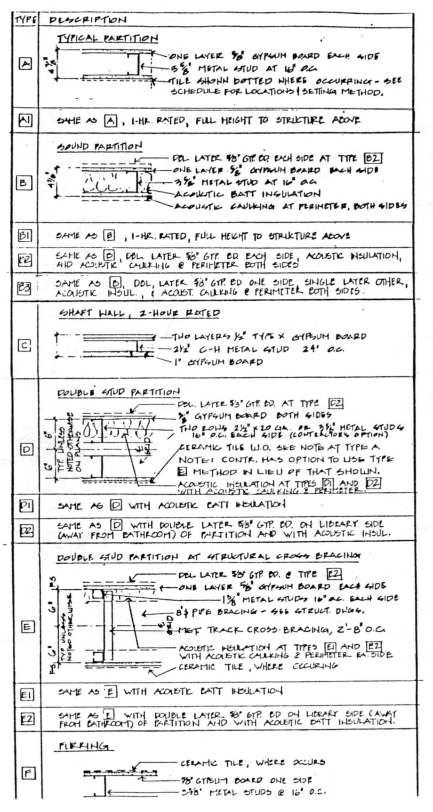

Figure 14–14
Partition Schedule

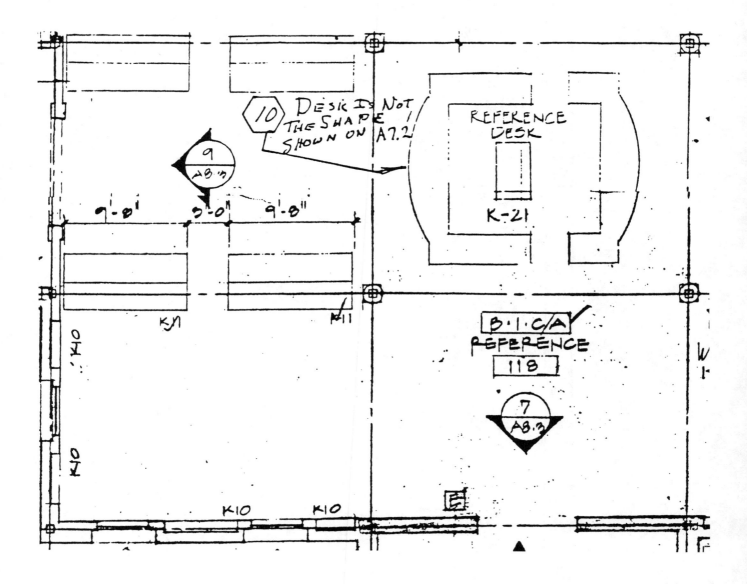

Figure 14–15
Interior Elevations: Key Symbols

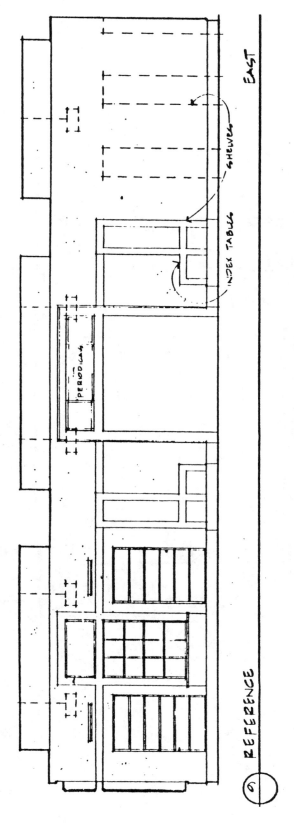

Figure 14–16
Interior Elevation of a Wall

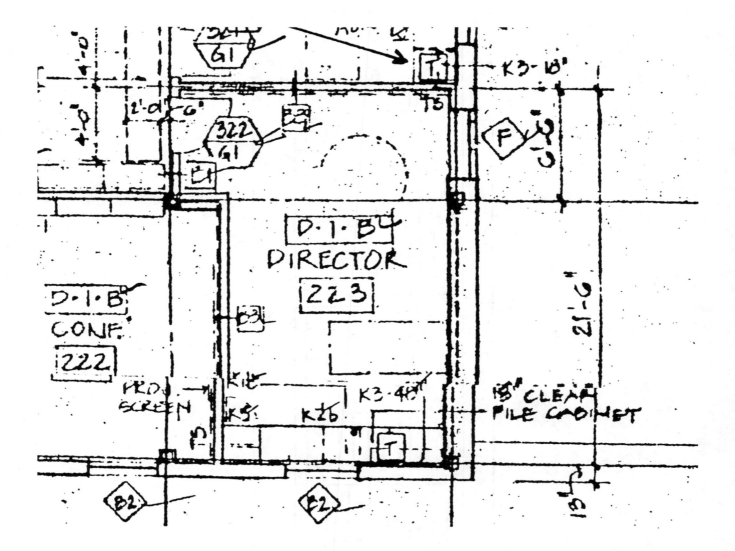

Figure 14–17
Casework Required for the Library Director's Office

PLASTIC LAMINATE CASEWORK SCHEDULE

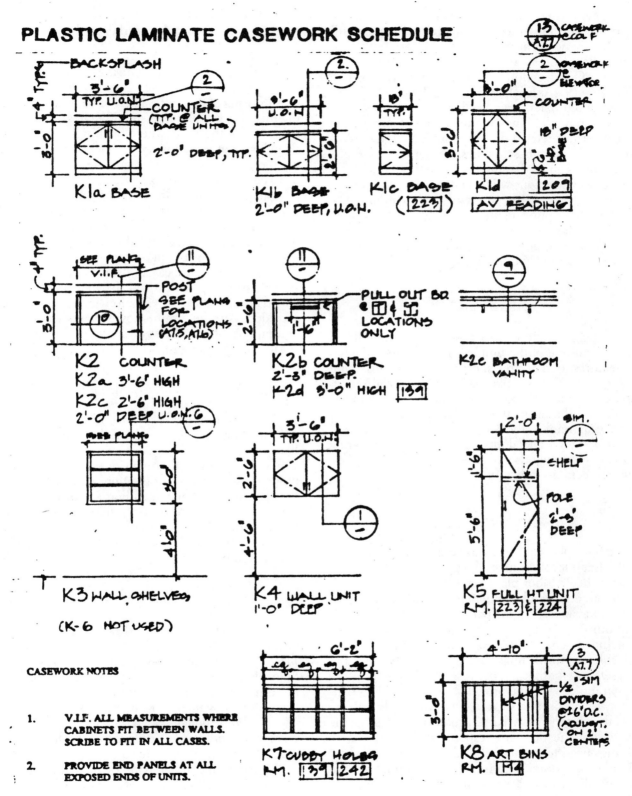

Figure 14–18
Casework Schedule for Cabinet Components

what drawings have been included and the order in which they are presented. Some architects make this easier by providing an index to the set on the first or second sheet; this is almost invariably true with sets during the Construction Document phase, as shown in Figure 14–19. As each drawing is reviewed, the librarian should systematically follow all of the road signs discussed above. This will require frequent reference to other sheets for related drawings and additional information in the form of schedules. Unstapling the sheets so that they can be handled easily will facilitate this effort. Some questions will also involve perusal of one or more sections in the book of specifications. The following description of the major types of drawings should be helpful in understanding the organization of the drawings and determining where particular information is most likely to be located.

Site Plan

A site plan usually appears as the first drawing. It will show the outline of the building on the site and adjacent features such as streets, driveways, sidewalks, and parking lots. The site plan is likely to provide topographic information and landscaping details. Compass directions will indicate the orientation of the building. This is important to the reviewer in terms of the location of windows and doors, especially where glaring sunlight, strong winds and seasonal storms are associated with certain directions.

Floor Plans

The floor plans are likely to be the second group of sheets. Each level of the building will usually be on a separate sheet. Floor plans serve as the base drawings for the project, which further emphasizes their importance. They will show the perimeter walls and interior partitioning. Furniture and casework may or may not be included depending on whether the architect is responsible for furnishings or an interior designer has been selected for this part of the work. Where furniture and equipment is to be provided by the building contractor, it will likely appear as a continuous line drawing of the object; a dashed line usually indicates that the item is not the builder's responsibility (NIC). These drawings need to be studied in depth in terms of how program requirements for functional relationships and space needs are met. As successive sets of progress prints are issued, the librarian will need to review new information supplied in the form of notations referencing

various schedules for doors, windows, finishes, partitioning, etc., as described earlier in this chapter.

Roof Drawing

A drawing of the roof is likely to be next. In examining this plan the librarian should note such features as the pitch of the roof, where openings may occur for skylights or other items, and what equipment, if any, will be located there (see Figure 14–20). If there are parapet walls around the perimeter, their height should be noted, especially if the building is located in an area where heavy snowfall and icing conditions occur. The potential for a roof to leak is reason enough for a librarian to be interested in this drawing. A thorough discussion of the roofing system with the architect is needed. If the architect has elected to place the HVAC system, or any part of it, on the roof, be certain that adequate acoustic and vibration protection has been provided. Also determine how workers will reach the equipment when the HVAC system requires service, repairs or replacement.

Exterior Elevations

Exterior elevations, as shown in Figure 14–21, are used to show what each side of the building will look like. Doorways and windows will be indicated along with other details and dimensions. Letters or numbers representing the grid for the floor plan will appear on the elevations and help the librarian correlate the exterior with locations inside the building. Numbers inside circles or other shapes will refer to plan notes or parts of the building drawn to a larger scale and presented elsewhere in the drawings.

Section Drawings

Section drawings, as noted earlier, provide a means of determining how the building is structurally organized. The location of each section is flagged on the floor plans as described earlier in this chapter. These building "slices" provide information not available from other drawings. For instance, as shown in Figure 14–22, ceiling heights can be determined as well as any changes in floor levels. Some of the structural elements can be seen in place. The thickness of load-bearing walls, floors and other parts of the building can be measured from these drawings. Most of all, though, they provide an added sense of how the functions are organized and a feeling for interior space.

DRAWINGS INDEX

GENERAL

A1.0   Index, Symbols, Abbreviations, Notes

CIVIL

C1.0   Plot & Finish Grading Plan
C2.0   Utility Plan
C3.0   Site Details

LANDSCAPE

L1.0   Landscape Layout
L2.0   Irrigation Plan
L3.0   Planting Plan
L4.0   Construction Details
L5.0   Irrigation Details
L6.0   Landscape Details

ARCHITECTURAL

A1.2   Demolition Plan
A2.1   First Floor Plan
A2.2   Second Floor Plan
A2.3   Roof Plan
A3.1   Exterior Elevations
A3.2   Exterior Elevations
A3.3   Building Section/Elevations
A3.4   Building Section/Elevations
A3.5   Wall Sections
A4.1   Wall Details
A4.2   Window Schedule/Details
A4.3   Exterior Details
A4.4   Exterior Details
A5.1   Toilets
A5.2   Stairs
A5.3   Stairs
A5.4   Elevators
A6.1 * Finish, Partition, Door Schedule/Details
A6.2   Interior Details
A6.3   Interior Details
A7.1   Shelving and Casework Schedules
A7.2   Main Desks
A7.3   Casework Details *
A8.1   Interior Elevations
A8.2   Interior Elevations
A8.3   Interior Elevations
A9.1   Reflected Ceiling Plan - First Floor
A9.2   Reflected Ceiling Plan - Second Floor

STRUCTURAL

LIBRARY

S1.0   General Notes & Typ. Conc. Details
S1.1   Typical Details
S2.1   Foundation & First Floor
S2.2   Second Floor Plan & Low Rf Framing Plan
S2.3   Roof Plan
S3.1   Foundation Schedule & Details
S4.1   Steel Column Schedule & Details
S4.2   B.F. Elevation & Details
S4.3   Steel Details
S5.1   Stairs
S9.1   Fire Station Floor & Roof Plans
S9.2   Wall Elevations
S9.3   Sections
S9.4   Sections & Details
S9.5   Sections & Details

MECHANICAL

M1.0   Symbols, Abbreviations, and Schedules
M2.1   First Floor Plan
M2.2   Second Floor Plan
M2.3   Roof Plan
M5.1   Details and Sections

PLUMBING

PFP1.0   Legend, Schedules and Details
PFP2.1   First Floor Plan
PFP2.2   Second Floor Plan

ELECTRICAL

E1.0   Legend, Abbreviations and General Notes
E2.1   First Floor Plan - Lighting
E2.2   Second Floor Plan - Lighting
E3.1   First Floor Plan - Power & Communication
E3.2   Second Floor Plan - Power & Comm
E3.3   Roof Plan - Power *
E4.1   Details *
E5.1   Single Line, Fire Alarm & Commun...
        System Diagrams

COORDINATION

ME1.0   Mechanical/Electrical Coordinati...

* Indicates future sheet

Figure 14-19
Index Sheet for a Set of Drawings

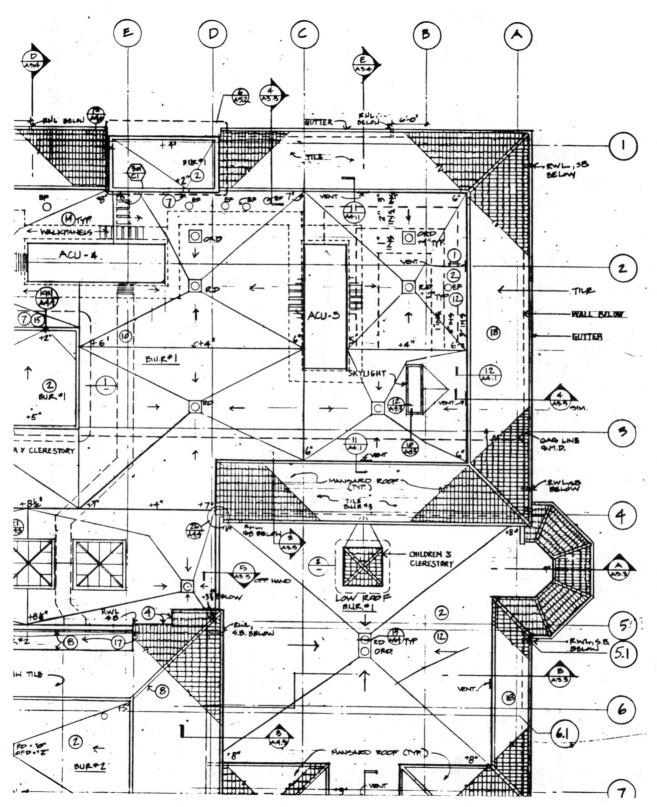

Figure 14–20
Roof Drawing

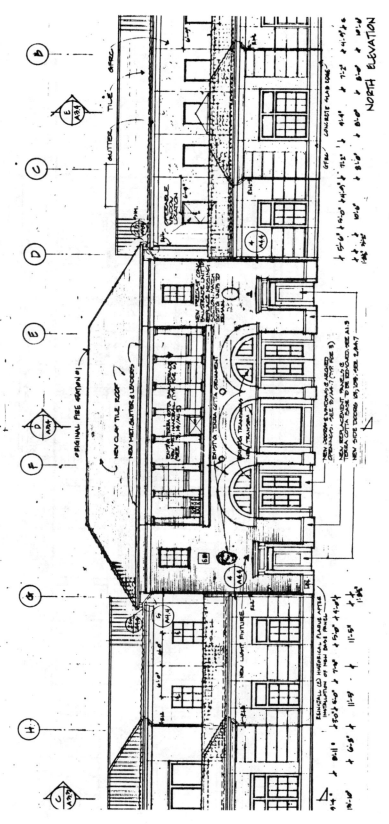

Figure 14–21
Exterior Elevation: Entrance

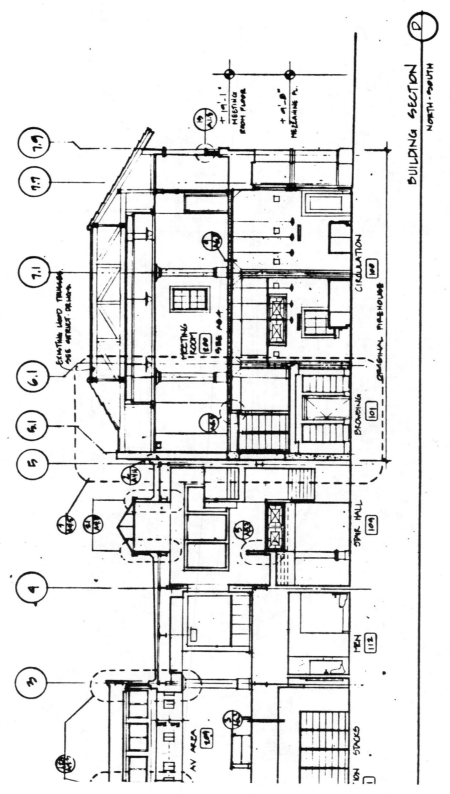

Figure 14–22
Building Section

Reflected Ceiling Plans

Few drawings are more likely to be confusing to the reader than the Reflected Ceiling plans. Such drawings, as shown in Figure 14–23, show the location of lighting fixtures, HVAC diffusers and returns, patterns of ceiling materials, public address system speakers, sprinkler heads, etc. While it would be natural to assume that the drawing is taken from the vantage point of a person looking up at the ceiling, it is not. Instead, the plan is a view of the ceiling as if seen from above. Reflected ceiling plans are often intricate and they supply valuable information to the librarian. By correlating these drawings with furniture and equipment layouts, it is possible to determine whether light sources, for instance, are correctly related to shelving, work stations, etc. The location of diffusers for the HVAC system can also be checked to determine their potential for creating drafts above desks and work stations. If a public address system is called for, these drawings will show whether speakers are properly located. Finally, the choice of ceiling materials can be evaluated area by area.

Casework Drawings

The appearance of casework in the architect's drawings depends upon whether this responsibility has been delegated to the architect or to an interior designer. In either case, the casework drawings will eventually appear for review. The librarian and staff, it is hoped, will have had significant involvement in establishing the specific casework requirements. Casework includes all of the items of furniture and shelving which are built-in rather than purchased and installed. Sometimes casework is referred to as millwork or cabinetry, though it may include items other than cabinets.

Casework drawings may include layouts and elevations, such as those shown previously in Figure 14–8 and Figure 14–9. The layout drawings establish the horizontal dimensions and show the shape of counters and other pieces. Elevations, on the other hand, provide the vertical dimensions and details. The review of casework drawings must be thorough and should, whenever possible, involve those who will use a particular desk or work station. Initially, the reviewer should establish that all of the functional requirements are satisfied: the number of drawers, equipment locations, under-counter shelves, etc. Then, the dimensions must be carefully checked. Desks, work stations and counters, for instance, must be the correct height and width. Spaces into which equipment will be fitted must

be of proper size. Any slots in a desk and the receptacles beneath them must be checked: are they properly dimensioned to receive the cards or materials to be dropped through them? If the casework is for a public desk, internal space for the movement of staff and book trucks should be given very close attention. Finally, casework drawings need to be correlated with both the floor plans and the interior elevations in order to avoid possible errors.

Structural Drawings

Beginning with the structural drawings, the librarian will become involved with plans created by engineering specialists. Each of these disciplines has its own symbols and codes which usually appear on the first or second sheet of the respective drawings. If these are inadequate or unclear, refer to the tables of symbols in *Architectural Graphic Standards*, which are more or less commonly used.

Of all the drawings, the structural drawings are apt to be of the least interest to the librarian. However, they do help the reviewer understand how the building is put together and may provide answers to particular questions. Foundation and footing details will be found here as well as cross-sections of load-bearing walls and column details.

Mechanical Drawings

Mechanical drawings for the HVAC system are superimposed on the base floor plans, Figure 14–24. These drawings show the duct runs for the HVAC system and the location of the diffusers (which deliver the air) and the returns (which vent the air to the outside or return it to the chiller or heater). The volume of air passing through the ducts is usually indicated in terms of cubic feet per minute (CFM). Duct dimensions may be given as well. The task of the librarian is to make certain that no area or room of the library is passed by. A question should also be raised if a diffuser is found in a location where it is apt to create a draft for someone at a work station or public desk.

Plumbing Drawings

Drawings for the plumbing system are likely to appear with the rest of the mechanical plans. These drawings, again superimposed on the base plan, as shown in Figure 14–25, will indicate where plumbing fixtures

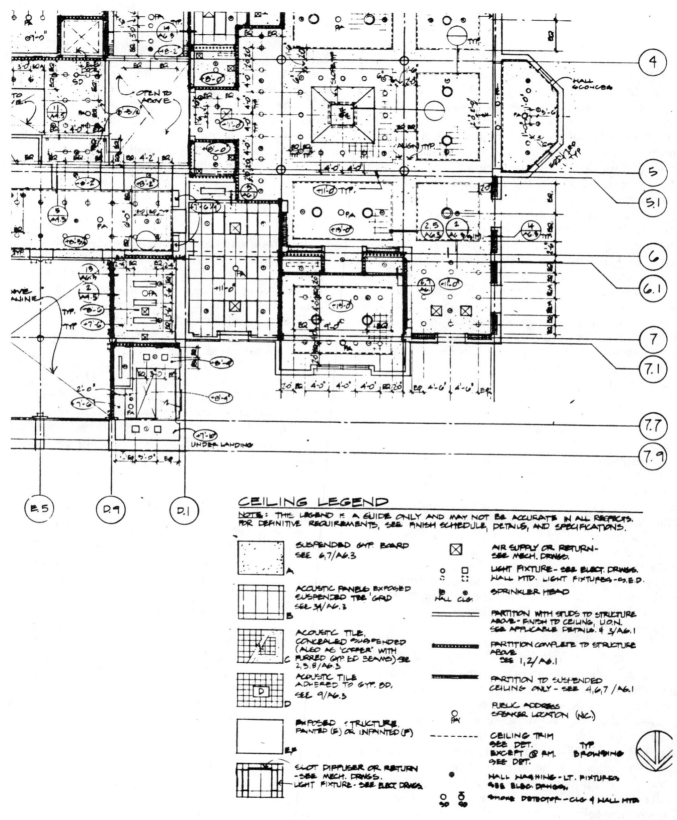

CEILING LEGEND

NOTE: THE LEGEND IS A GUIDE ONLY AND MAY NOT BE ACCURATE IN ALL RESPECTS. FOR DEFINITIVE REQUIREMENTS, SEE FINISH SCHEDULE, DETAILS, AND SPECIFICATIONS.

A SUSPENDED GYP. BOARD SEE 6,7/A6.3

B ACOUSTIC PANELS EXPOSED SUSPENDED TEE GRID SEE 3A/A6.3

C ACOUSTIC TILE, CONCEALED SUSPENDED (ALSO AS "COFFER" WITH FURRED GYP. BD BEAMS) SEE 2,3,8/A6.3

D ACOUSTIC TILE ADHERED TO GYP. BD. SEE 9/A6.3

E,F EXPOSED STRUCTURE PAINTED (E) OR UNPAINTED (F)

K SLOT DIFFUSER OR RETURN - SEE MECH. DRWGS. LIGHT FIXTURE- SEE ELECT DRWGS.

AIR SUPPLY OR RETURN- SEE MECH. DRWGS.

LIGHT FIXTURE- SEE ELECT. DRWGS. WALL MTD. LIGHT FIXTURES-O.E.D.

SPRINKLER HEAD

PARTITION WITH STUDS TO STRUCTURE ABOVE- FINISH TO CEILING, U.O.N. SEE APPLICABLE DETAILS. & 3/A6.1

PARTITION COMPLETE TO STRUCTURE ABOVE SEE 1,2/A6.1

PARTITION TO SUSPENDED CEILING ONLY - SEE 4,6,7/A6.1

PUBLIC ADDRESS SPEAKER LOCATION (NIC)

CEILING TRIM SEE DET. TYP EXCEPT @ RM. BROWSING SEE DET.

WALL WASHING - LT. FIXTURES SEE ELEC. DRWGS.

SMOKE DETECTOR - CLG & WALL MTD

Figure 14-23
Reflected Ceiling Plan

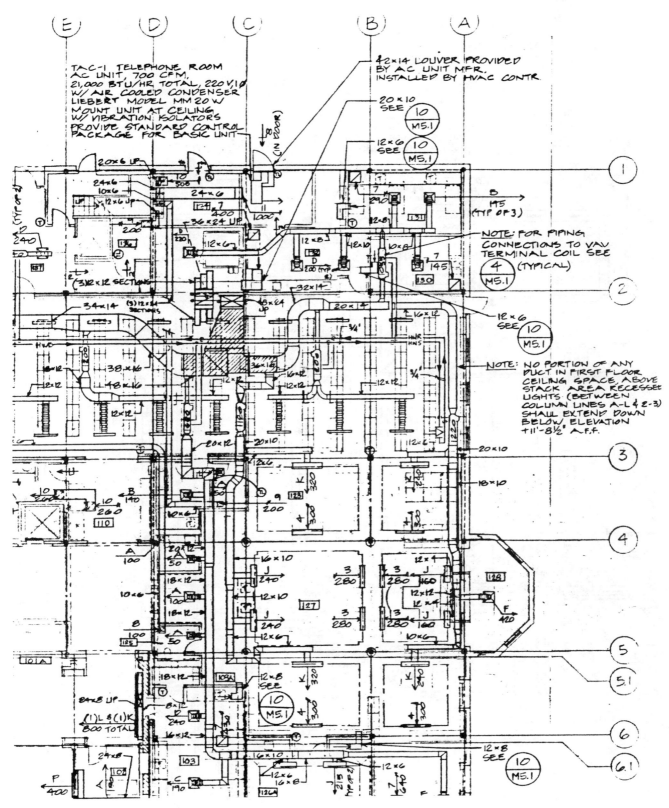

Figure 14–24
Mechanical (HVAC) Drawing

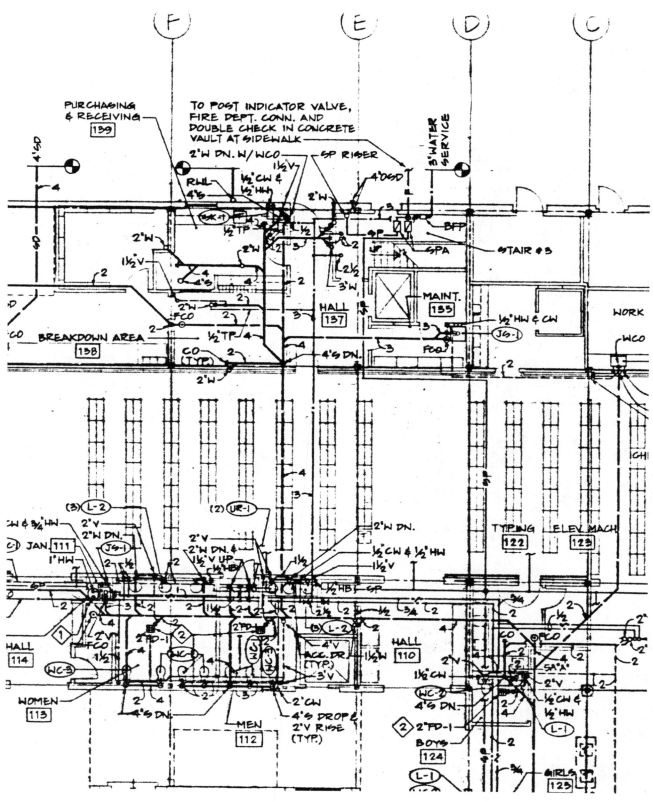

Figure 14–25
Plumbing Drawing

will be located, how they will be supplied with water and where waste water will be taken. The librarian should make certain that the sinks and other fixtures called for in the building program are included; a look at the specifications for plumbing fixtures may be quite helpful. These drawings should be carefully checked to make certain that floor drains are called for in all restrooms and wherever else running water may pose a potential threat for flooding adjacent areas.

Electrical Drawings: Lighting

Electrical drawings will be divided into two or three parts. Usually the first sheets will deal with lighting, Figure 14–26, and the second group with power and communications, Figure 14–27. The drawing for lighting will show the location of all light fixtures. A symbol key on the drawings will match the outline of the fixture with the type of luminaire it represents. Lines radiating from the fixtures trace the path of circuits. Knowing how critical lighting is to the library, the librarian will want to make certain that appropriate lighting fixtures have been provided for every space. The examination of the lighting system should include discussions with the architect and the electrical engineer to ascertain the level of illumination they expect to be maintained in each area. The drawings should also be checked to determine what provisions have been made for emergency lighting and where these lights will be located. The power source for emergency illumination, if not indicated on the drawings, should be found in the specifications.

Electrical Power and Communications Drawings

Electrical power and wiring for communications, including computer terminals, public address systems, and the like, grows more important every day. The drawings for electrical power and communications may be combined or provided separately, depending in part on whether they are created in the same office or by two different sources.

These drawings must be reviewed to determine whether adequate power distribution has occurred. Offices and work stations, with a multiplicity of items to plug in, run out of outlets quickly. A duplex receptacle with its capacity for two pieces of equipment is insufficient for many work stations. If the number of available duplex receptacles is inadequate, extension cords with their inherent dangers and inconvenience will soon be in use no matter how new the building.

If the building requires an emergency power generator to support a computer mainframe or for some other reason, be certain that it meets program requirements. Look also for acoustical isolation if the generator uses an internal combustion engine. The location of fuel tanks for such generators will also be important.

As with power, the requirement for telephones, including lines needed for data communications, continues to rise. Fortunately, the conversion of telephone systems to the new plug-in type means that outlets can be maximized without the expense of installing an instrument at every location. Again, the librarian and staff must review these drawings to ascertain whether or not sufficient telephone outlets are planned and whether they are properly located in relation to desks and computer stations.

Provisions for future power and communications needs, established in the building program and, hopefully, discussed with the architect and electrical engineer very early in the design phase, should be carefully reviewed. The system should provide flexibility, easy access, and economy. Additional conduit capacity should be provided along with electrical switch panels and telephone backboards that can be expanded to include more circuits.

Other information to be checked on these drawings includes provisions for video monitors and cameras, security systems, signal wiring for doorbells, fire alarms and other devices. The power and communications drawings are among the most critical and involved drawings the librarian must review.

Reviewing the Drawings

Preceding sections of this chapter have, among other topics, described some of the road signs the plan reviewer must recognize in order to understand the information contained in the drawings. The following section relates typical review techniques to the sets of drawings which will be received during the various phases of architectural planning. Attention is drawn to areas most likely to be critical from the librarian's point of view. Some of the typical questions are asked that a plan reviewer may pose as he or she examines a set of drawings.

When drawings are received for review, they are likely to be accompanied by a transmittal form which indicates what phase the plans represent, the date of issue, what work is expected from the reviewer, and the deadline for return. This single page form should be retained with a notation of date received.

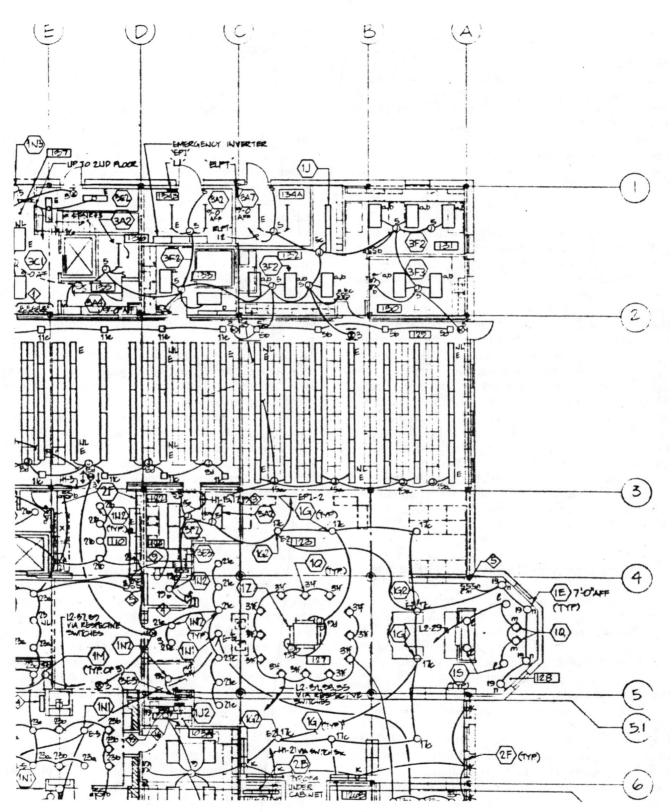

Figure 14–26
Drawing for Lighting

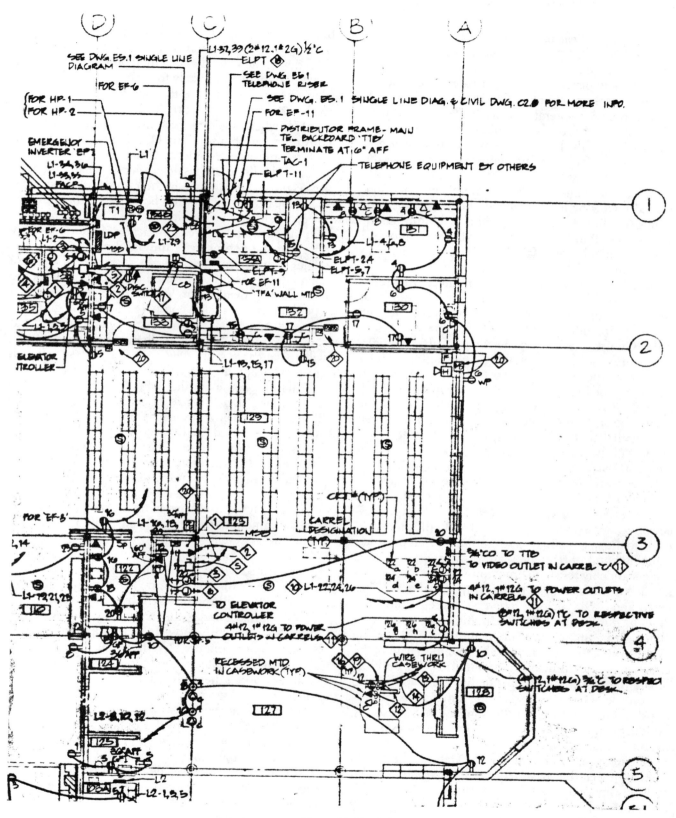

Figure 14–27
Electrical Power and Communications Drawing

Schematic Drawings

During the schematic phase, drawings are apt to be limited to: site plan; floor plan for each floor; exterior elevations; sections. For the first review, look at each drawing in a very general way to become familiar with the major features of the building. Note the general configuration of the building, its architectural style and the number of floors. Locate major features such as the public entrance, staff and delivery entrance, circulation desk, and major functions. Then begin the more detailed review by looking at one sheet at a time, but turning to others as needed for additional information. Jot down questions and comments as they occur to you. It takes time to become familiar with the drawings; do not despair.

The site plan indicates how the architect proposes to locate the building. This plan will show provisions for parking and for any street improvements that may be necessary, including driveways to the library and sidewalks. Compass points will be shown—at least an arrow pointing north. This establishes the building's relationship to the path of the sun, which is critical in evaluating the location of windows, for instance. Note the scale at which the site plan is drawn: because of the size of the site, an engineer's scale has probably been used, with 1 inch representing 10 or more feet.

Most of the librarian's review time will be spent on the floor plans. The first set or two of schematics may not show furnishings—just blocks of space labeled for the major functions, offices and workrooms described in the building program. The lack of furniture, especially bookstacks, may make it difficult at first to relate to the spaces since these familiar objects provide a valuable point of reference. However, most architects understandably resist the time-consuming task of drawing in furniture until at least a conceptual design has been approved. Before schematics are completed, though, it is essential that the architect provide a floor plan with a tentative furniture plan, because that is the only way that the librarian can be certain that all of the collections and furnishings required by the building program will fit. Until then, the librarian will have to rely on use of the scale for sensing dimensions. Knowing the dimensions of familiar spaces in the existing building can be very helpful and provides an excellent means of making comparisons.

The floor plans should be very carefully checked to be certain that the space requirements and functional relationships of the building program have been met. It is important that the architect be asked to explain any apparent deviation from the building program. If func-tions are not properly related at this stage, their relationships are not apt to improve as planning proceeds. Experience indicates that potential problems appearing in the schematics are likely to become more crucial as planning proceeds unless they are called to the architect's attention and corrected. Take nothing for granted; when in doubt, ask questions and insist on constructive responses. The librarian will have to live with the mistakes for a long while.

Once the librarian has determined that all functions are accounted for and are in their proper relationships, space measurements should be made. Depending on the geometry of the building this may be a simple task, or it may be much more complicated if there are many offsets in the perimeter of the building or circles, triangles or other geometric forms are involved. If these calculations are difficult, the librarian should ask the architect to provide them. When completed, these area calculations should be compared to the program requirements. Areas where space deficiencies occur should be noted; chances are that subsequent planning will make these spaces even smaller unless action is taken at this point.

Having become familiar with the general layout of the building and the size of the various spaces, the librarian should be ready to examine the drawings more critically. This process can be facilitated by reviewing the building from two separate vantage points: 1/ that of the user, and 2/ that of the staff. Are functions logically located? Will the user understand the organization and arrangement of functions when entering the building? How far will the user have to travel to reach key areas? Are staff functions properly related? Will supervision of public areas be effective?

Another helpful approach is to project the major traffic created by users, staff and the movement of materials. This will indicate how freely traffic will move and where possible points of conflict may occur. Examine the entrance and circulation area very carefully for the latter is a key function. Is there sufficient space for the circulation functions? Will the location and shape of the space promote a smooth flow of traffic? Will users be able to orient themselves at this point to other major collections and services? How far must books and other materials be moved and what route will they follow to be reshelved? Where are the public restrooms? How easily can they be identified by the public? Will they be within the visual supervision range of staff? Look also for the location of spaces designated for rooms where mechanical systems, electrical equipment, telephone panels and elevator machinery will be located. If they are not on the plans, ask about them. These rooms are essential to the building and tend to grow larger as planning proceeds.

In areas containing offices and workrooms, make certain that compatible functions are properly related. Has sufficient space been provided for the projected number of staff in each workroom? Do offices and workrooms relate well to one another? Where are the general staff facilities such as the staff lunch room and lounge? Has provision been made for separate staff restrooms and are they conveniently located? Where will the staff enter the building and how far must they travel to their respective desks, offices or work stations?

The exterior elevations will probably be shown on one or two sheets of the schematic drawings. Caution: these are not apt to be perspective drawings. Therefore, they are somewhat more difficult to visualize than a rendering or other perspective drawing. Nonetheless, they represent the architectural style that the designer anticipates will characterize the building. Review the exterior elevations in terms of what effect a design of this type has on internal functions. Also, determine how a building designed in this style will relate to neighboring structures. Does the style project a positive and inviting image of the library? Or is it too austere or foreboding? Based on the design of other recent buildings on the campus or in the community, does it seem to fit? While form should follow function in the creation of architecture, everyone is quite familiar with the fact that styles come and go in architecture just as in clothing or automobiles. The client should avoid a design which is faddish or contains architectural clichés which will date the building.

Usually, schematic plans include drawings which show at least two sections through the building. These drawings represent how a portion of the building would look if sliced into two parts at some specified point. Arrows or other symbols usually appear on the floor plan to indicate where the sections are taken. One of the drawings will probably be drawn at right angles to the other. Often the slice is made where the construction is most complex or where major functions adjoin one another. The sections deserve careful study. If the building contains more than one level, this is made clear in the sections. Measurements should be taken to be certain that there is sufficient floor-to-ceiling space—a minimum of 10–14 feet should be required. The sections must be mentally correlated with the information on the floor plans. Drawing a line on the floor plans between the section arrows may help. Note that the arrows point in the direction that the viewer should face when looking at the sections.

In working with the schematic drawings, the librarian will necessarily go back and forth between the various sheets. A question raised by something on one may be answered by information on another sheet. Or new questions may arise. Where comments are to be made, the librarian should mark a box of some sort that is readily distinguishable. These boxes are to be numbered systematically to correspond with the review comments. Numbering should begin with the number one on each drawing. A list of review comments and questions should then be compiled, including items offered by other staff members. When completed, the review comments and a set of drawings with the key numbers must be returned to the architect for study and response.

Specifications at the schematic stage will be limited to "Outline Specifications" which provide only general information. Nonetheless, they should be read by the librarian, if for no other reason than to become familiar with the format that the architect is going to use on the expanded specifications. Specifications are seldom paged continuously. Therefore, any review notes must reference both the section number and the page. An alternate method is to write the comments on the page and duplicate the page on a copy machine. These pages with comments are then returned to the architect as part of the plan review.

Experience indicates that a plan which does not meet program requirements during the schematic stage is almost certain to have serious deficiencies in later stages. One of the greatest dangers in planning is to accept the schematic design before there is reasonable assurance, supported by the drawings, that the building program requirements will be met. All too often, the client is motivated by a desire to meet a particular deadline or schedule at this point and is unwilling to prolong the schematic phase until a fully satisfactory scheme is provided.

Sometimes architects encourage such decisions by assuring the client that all of the problems associated with the schematics can and will be resolved in the next phase of work. Unfortunately, a plan which exhibits serious deficiencies in the beginning is likely to prove all the more defective as work proceeds. Remember that the schematic phase is the time for testing solutions. While the architect obviously hopes that the first design submitted will be acceptable, the librarian is not required to approve it if it is found to be unsatisfactory. Instead, insist on seeing other design concepts before proceeding beyond schematics. Approval of the schematic design locks it into place as the only design to be developed. No matter how poor a solution and how inadequate it may prove to be as design work continues, the architect is likely to be entitled to additional fees if a new design is required.

Design Development Drawings

Design development, still known as "Preliminaries" in some offices, begins as soon as the architect receives official approval of the schematic drawings and specifications. The design development drawings which result will be much more detailed and will include drawings prepared by mechanical and electrical engineers. From a handful of sheets in the schematic phase, the drawings will grow several fold. During the course of design development, they will be sent periodically, in partial or complete sets, as "progress prints." Each set should be reviewed carefully to determine what changes have been made and how they effect fulfillment of the building program requirements. If team meetings occur regularly, the librarian's review notes will probably be considered a part of the agenda. It is essential that the librarian warn the architect if a problem seems imminent so that it can be resolved with the least loss of time and effort.

The design development drawings are apt to introduce several new details. For instance, the drawings will be on a grid with lines in the margins labeled by letters of the alphabet in one direction and by Arabic numerals in the other direction. This makes it relatively easy to reference a particular point, just as you would do on a map. Another addition will be room numbers. Usually these are three digits long. The first floor will begin the series with 100, the second floor with 200, and so on. The drawings will probably be at ⅛" scale. If the building is unusually long or irregularly shaped the floor plan may no longer fit on a single sheet. A "match line" is then shown to indicate where the two drawings must be joined to show the entire floor.

The review of design development drawings and specifications will involve the same process as that begun with the schematic drawings. Trouble spots that appeared in the earlier drawings must be looked at with special care to see how they have been resolved. One of the hardest tasks is the correlation of information presented on various sheets for the same part of the building. After becoming thoroughly familiar with the floor plans, interior elevations should be studied. This adds a further dimension. Then the lighting and power plans need to be correlated for each area. What kind of lighting is planned: fluorescent? incandescent? HID? other? What kind of fixtures are contemplated? (See the re-

flected ceiling plans and the specifications when they become available.) Does it appear that lighting fixtures are well located with reference to the spaces they are to illuminate? Are there sufficient power receptacles and are they properly located? Sometimes these details are not entirely available until construction drawings are in the works. However, the architect should be encouraged to supply this information as early as possible so as to avoid changes later on.

After the electrical drawings have been correlated, look at those for the mechanical systems. Note where the mechanical equipment rooms are and what they are adjacent to. Will special acoustical materials be needed in walls, floors and ceilings to isolate noisy equipment? If roof-mounted units are to be used, what functions will they be above? How will those servicing the mechanical equipment reach the equipment rooms and/or the roof when repairs must be made, including replacement of major parts or components? Looking at the layout of ducts, are there any areas that seem too far from diffusers?

Plumbing drawings are usually fairly simple and direct. They indicate where pipe runs will occur and where fixtures will be located. This is a good time to check on the adequacy of the number of fixtures in the public and staff restrooms, their location in relation to supervision, and compliance with access for the handicapped. The drawings for plumbing should show the location of faucets for use around the outside perimeter of the building; all too frequently these are not supplied in sufficient numbers or they are located in awkward places. Piping for any fire extinguishing system should also show up on the plumbing drawings. Check these to see where control valves that need periodic testing are located.

Additional sheets will contain enlarged drawings of certain areas drawn at ¼" or ½" scale, or larger, to show details. Foundation plans and sheeting plans for the roof will also be drawn as work proceeds on the design development set. Some architects provide preliminary schedules of finishes, doors and windows in the form of tables or grids. By this time each door is given a number and it is important to compare this with the schedule to be certain a door of the right type and dimensions is designated. Similarly, finishes for each room or area will be shown on the drawings as a series of alphanumerical notations—a kind of shorthand that can be easily interpreted by consulting the finish schedule. This schedule tells the builder what the floor and wall coverings are to be and the nature of ceiling materials. Because it is such an exacting task to put together, mistakes do occur: the wrong designations can call for tile floors in the librarian's office and carpet in the restrooms! In some instances, the librarian may wish to question the choice of finishes specified for certain areas. Don't depend on others to question even the most obvious errors; they can go undetected.

Specifications issued near the completion of design development are likely to be much more extensive than those seen before. Again, they require careful reading and correlation with the drawings. Sometimes they are in conflict with what is shown in the drawings. While such occurrences are rare, they are exceedingly important and should be called to the architect's attention. Bear in mind that where specifications and drawings do not agree, the specifications will be followed.

Construction Documents

The final stage of work begins when the design development drawings and specifications have been approved. The construction documents are even more detailed than those drawn in the design development phase. By and large they do not represent major decisions or changes in the approved plans. This does not mean that the librarian is free of the task of plan review, however. Subtle changes do occur and sometimes have a pronounced effect on meeting program requirements. The architect is likely to ask that review coincide with certain milestones in the progress of the work, usually given in terms of the percentage of work completed to that time: 50% completion and 90% completion are common benchmarks. A thorough review of both drawings and specifications should occur on these occasions. Drawings are apt to be much more detailed than before, with many notations including dimensions.

The 50% review (or whatever is closest to this period) is especially critical since the architect expects that virtually all the corrections and adjustments necessary can be made at that time. The 90% review, while thorough, is more of a check to be certain that prior changes have been made and that no glaring errors or omissions have crept into the drawings. Normally, the final set of drawings (100%) are not reviewed outside the offices of the architect and engineer except perhaps for those sheets which required more than minor modifications. It is this set which will become a part of the bid documents and will govern construction. The librarian should have a set of these final drawings and specifications for the library archives. Prior sets should be carefully labeled and saved at least until the new building is completed.

Specifications

Specifications for the building should be read by the librarian, if for no other reason than to better understand the complexities of construction. Actually, some parts of the specifications are of particular interest to the librarian for they establish the requirements for the finishes and equipment which are inextricably involved in future building maintenance cost. Are paints specified for walls washable? What is the projected life of the carpet and can it be easily cleaned? Are sufficient overruns of carpet and wall coverings such as vinyl materials being specified for replacement use? Are the plumbing fixtures manufactured by companies that have proven satisfactory before? Will exterior wall materials require frequent upkeep? Can thermostats and other regulating devices be locked to inhibit tampering? If shelving is specified, are the recommended manufacturers acceptable based on the librarian's experience?

The group of items arranged under Division 10, Specialties, will be of particular interest since they include such equipment as chalkboards, lockers, toilet and bath accessories and flag poles. Doorlocks and keying are covered under Section 08700, while elevators are described in Section 14200. Reading the specifications will enable the librarian to raise intelligent questions about individual items that may later become very important in the operation of the facility. Knowing why particular products have been chosen can be most helpful later on.

Summary

This chapter has dealt with the details of the plan analysis process. The rationale has been provided for reviewing plans and specifications from concept drawings through the completion of construction drawings and specifications. The process of creating drawings has been briefly described as further background. General instructions for reading plans and specifications include a brief introduction to the extent of drawings associated with each phase, how sets of drawings are organized, and identification of certain key road signs which enable the reader to understand the information shown on the blueprints. Drawings from a typical library project have been used to illustrate some of the road signs the librarian will follow. Examples of other drawings from the same project indicate how the complexity of drawings increases as various stages are reached. Some of the questions or points to be kept in mind as plan review progresses are given.

Participation of the librarian in the plan and analysis process is an essential part of functioning as a project team member. Having shared in this plan analysis process, the librarian will have a heightened appreciation of the intricacies of architectural design and construction. More important, conscientious plan review will result in a knowledge and understanding of the building project that can not be gained in any other way. The time spent will be richly rewarded by the sense of participation and the increased depth of knowledge of the building's most complex and intimate details.

APPENDIX A

ESTIMATED SPACE REQUIREMENTS FOR VARIOUS ITEMS OF FURNITURE AND EQUIPMENT

THE FOLLOWING guidelines are suggested as a means for approximating space requirements for various library components. Actual space will depend on many factors including layout realities, variations in dimensions among manufacturers, and the amount of "circulation" space allowed around each piece of furniture or equipment (see Appendix B). These guidelines have been gathered from a number of sources and are based on current practice. As Keyes Metcalf admonished, "Estimating space requirements of a library . . . is a bit of the problem that must be faced when a new building is planned. If a completely satisfactory formula could be provided for such estimates, the task would be greatly simplified, but experience suggests, rather, that the first rule should be: *Beware of formulas.*"[1]

Shelving Capacities

Capacity is generally understood to be "working capacity," which can be interpreted as meaning that a portion of each shelf is available to accommodate the normal expansion/contraction cycle imposed on shelving by circulation and acquisition activities. Metcalf, who has written more extensively on this subject than perhaps anyone else, suggests that "working capacity" is exceeded when the average vacant space per shelf is less than 5 inches; at such a point, he considers shelving to be 86% full.[2] The following guidelines are usually recognized as quantifying this premise.

Calculating Shelving Capacities

Trade books generally can be shelved at the rate of 8 volumes per lineal foot of shelf: each 3-foot shelf will then contain 24 volumes.

1. Keyes D. Metcalf, *Planning Academic and Research Library Buildings* (New York: McGraw-Hill, 1965), p. 157.
2. *Ibid.*, p. 155.

Ninety-inch-high shelving: Assuming seven shelves per single-faced section, (SFS), each single-faced unit will contain up to 168 volumes. Assuming 14 shelves per double-faced section (DFS), each double-faced unit will contain up to 336 volumes.

Sixty-inch or 66"-high shelving: Assuming five shelves per single-faced section, each single-faced unit will contain up to 120 volumes. Assuming ten shelves per double-faced section, each double-faced unit will contain up to 240 volumes.

Forty-two-inch-high shelving (Counter height; may also be 48" high): Assuming 3 shelves per single-faced section, each single-faced section will contain up to 72 volumes. Assuming 6 shelves per double-faced section, each double-faced section will contain up to 144 volumes.

Exceptions: Reference books should be calculated at 5–7 vols. per lineal foot; use only 5–6 shelves for single-faced sections and 10–12 shelves for double-faced sections. Bound periodicals may be calculated at the same rate as reference books. Art books should be calculated at the rate of 6–7 vols. per shelf foot using a maximum of 5–6 shelves per single-faced section or 10–12 shelves per double-faced section.

Children's books: Easy books (primers) and picture books: assume ½" per title = 24 vols. per lineal foot. General fiction & nonfiction: assume ¾" per vol. = 16 vols. per lineal foot.

Audio-visual materials: Space requirements for audio-visual materials vary greatly depending upon the kind of shelving or display equipment selected. Use manufacturer's recommended capacities.

Note: The amount of space required for shelving is a combination of the space occupied by the shelving unit and the adjacent aisle(s). The basic arrangement assumes that each double-faced section will measure approximately 36" wide × 24" deep (6 square feet), to which must be added the adjoining aisle measuring 3' wide by 3' long (9 square feet). Thus, the total square feet per double-faced section is 15 square feet. If aisle width is greater than the minimum of 3', the total square footage for each double-faced section must be increased. For example, a 4' aisle results in 18 square feet per double-faced section. A single-faced section of shelving occupies 3 square feet plus 9 square feet of adjoining aisle space: total is 12 square feet. Because the number, width and length of transverse aisles are products of design, the space they will require cannot be accurately estimated. Therefore, the building program should note this omission and indicate that transverse aisles are to be considered as a part of the gross square footage. The number of double-faced sections that can be joined together as a range will be determined in part by the dimensions of the space to be occupied. Usually 5–7 double-faced sections forming ranges 15–21 feet in length are considered optimal. However, more economical use of space may dictate consideration of ranges containing up to 10 double-faced sections, creating ranges 30 feet in length. Space occupied by shelving and other items of furniture and equipment is indicated below:

Shelving

Note: No allowance has been included for transverse (cross) aisles; a base depth of 12" has been assumed for single-faced shelving and 24" for double-faced shelving.

Approx. Ft² Allowance

A 3 ft-wide section of single-faced shelving with a 3 ft aisle	12
A 3 ft-wide section of single-faced shelving with a 4 ft aisle	15
A 4 ft-wide section of single-faced shelving with a 3 ft aisle	16
A 4 ft-wide section of single-faced shelving with a 4 ft aisle	20
A 3 ft-wide section of double-faced shelving with a 3 ft aisle	15
A 3 ft-wide section of double-faced shelving with a 4 ft aisle	18
A 4 ft-wide section of double-faced shelving with a 3 ft aisle	20
A 4 ft-wide section of double-faced shelving with a 4 ft aisle	24

To produce a rough estimate of space required for collections based on the total number of volumes to be housed, assume:

- 15 volumes per ft² for circulating books
- 10 volumes per ft² for reference and bound periodicals
- 20 volumes per ft² for children's books
- 1 current magazine per ft² (display shelving)

For a preliminary estimate of space required for public seating, allow 30 ft² per seat. For a preliminary estimate of space for offices and workrooms, allow 150 ft² per staff member. For conference rooms (group seating around a table) allow 20–25 ft² per person; actual space required will depend on the dimensions of the rooms, size of table, etc. For multipurpose meeting rooms, allow 10'–12' per seat (includes aisles but *not* platform, projection booth, table and chair storage, or food preparation space.

Seating

Table with four chairs including circulation space on all sides	100 ft²

Note: Space allowance includes approximately 3' surrounding the perimeter of a 4-place table (3' × 5') providing room for chairs and their occupants: two tables back-to-back would have 6' between them with a side aisle of 3'.

Lounge (informal) seat	30–40 ft²
Couch (multiseat) per seat provided	30–40
Chair at table	25
Single study carrel with chair (depending on size)	25–30
Media carrel with chair (depending on size)	25–35
Public access terminal (stand alone)	15–25
Personal computer with printer on table or desk	25–35
Typing carrel	30–35
Seat at microfilm reader	25–30
Seat in multipurpose room	10–12
Seat at conference table in conference room	20–25
Fixed seat in auditorium (*not* including aisles, platform, lobby, stage, projection booth, etc.)	8–10 ft²
Movable seat in a multipurpose room	8–10

Files

Standard file cabinet (letter)	10
Standard file cabinet (legal)	12

Lateral file (30″ wide)	15
Lateral file (36″ wide)	18
Lateral file (42″ wide)	21
Jumbo (picture file)	15
Flat files (maps, etc.), depending on dimensions	30–40
Card catalog (72-drawer unit)	20
Microfiche file	10
Microfilm file	13

Miscellaneous Library Furniture and Equipment

Note: Items preceded by an * include space for user but not for aisles or circulation on either side or at back.

*Free-standing dictionary stand	10
*Free-standing atlas case	17
Index Table 4′ × 6′ (2 seats on each side)	110
Index table 4′ × 90″ (3 seats per side)	140
*L.P. record bins with 4 compartments (18″ × 39″)	25
Spinner rack for paperbacks, cassette tapes, etc. Two-side exposure to users	36
Four-side exposure to users	80
Book truck (16″W × 32L) empty	4
filled	6
Book truck (18″W × 42L) empty	5
filled	7

Offices and Workrooms

Note: The amount of space required for a work station or office is determined by: 1/ the furnishings and equipment to be housed, 2/ supplementary space for aisles and access, 3/ the shape of the space and 4/ any structural elements that must be accommodated. In the space estimates which follow, space includes aisle on one side only; automated work stations tend to require more space. *Not* included in these estimates is space in workrooms for shelving, counters, files and other items that may be shared.

Work stations at public desks (circulation, reference, etc.) allow for planning purposes	150
60″ desk and posture chair	50
72″ desk and posture chair	60
72″ desk with posture chair and credenza	70
Small office containing 60″ double pedestal desk, typing return, credenza with shelving above, side chair, letter file	100–110
Office with 72″ desk with conference top and two side chairs, letter file, credenza with shelving above, typing return	125–150
Office with same furnishings plus a conference table for 4	150–200
Executive office	250+

APPENDIX B

HOW CIRCULATION SPACE IS CALCULATED

WHEN estimating space requirements it is necessary to include space for the movement of people as well as for furniture, equipment, etc. The estimated space requirements in Appendix A, which are to be used only for making needs assessment studies and building programs, include a certain amount of the space needed for this purpose. This appendix indicates how circulation space is calculated (Figure B-1). Generally, circulation space is interpreted as the amount of space required for people, book trucks, etc., to move around a fixed object such as a table, or space required to work at a desk, counter, etc. Needless to say, figures for a given object are subject to a variety of conditions which cannot be included here. For this reason, many sources for this information tend to provide ranges of figures rather than a single number for some items. Whether the amount of space is 100% accurate or not is less important, however, than consistency in its use.

Two Examples with Circulation Space shown in white:

      Double Faced Section of Shelving with 3´ or 4´ aisles

      4-place 60" Table

Note: Figures are NOT to scale

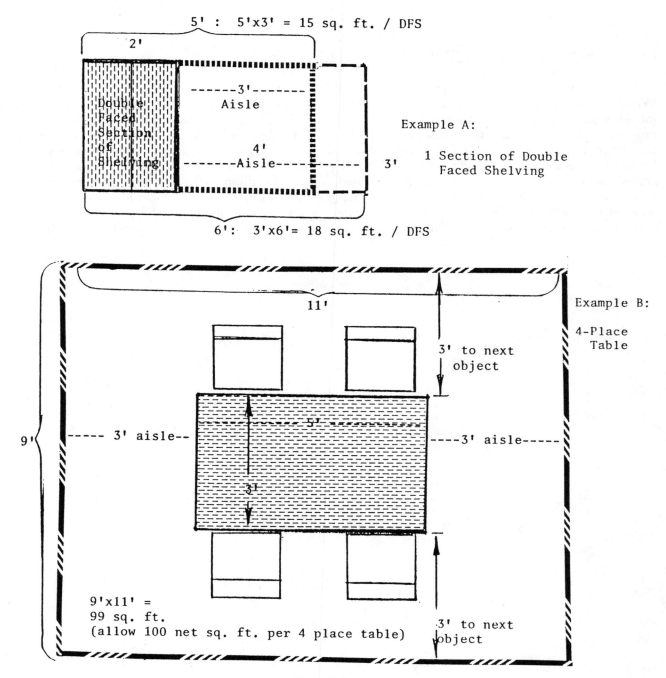

Example A:

1 Section of Double Faced Shelving

Example B:

4-Place Table

Figure B-1
How Circulation Space Is Calculated

APPENDIX C

MATRIX FOR PRESENTING FACILITY OPTIONS

FACILITY options explored during the needs assessment process can often be presented most clearly if a matrix is used. The following matrix format is suggested as one such approach. Obviously, it will need to be tailored to each situation. Most important is the fact that information covered in the narrative needs assessment report can be capsulated and presented in a concise, comparative format. The number of options to be shown will vary, of course, with each project.

SUGGESTED FORMAT FOR A MATRIX TO COMPARE FACILITY OPTIONS

Factor	Option 1 (remodel)	Option 2 (remodel & add)	Option 3 (new bldg.)	Option 4 (convert existing bldg.)
1. *Physical condition*				
Mechanical				
Plumbing				
Lighting				
Power				
2. *Site and location*				
Size				
Accessibility				
Traffic				
Parking				
Orientation				
Adjacent uses				
Visibility				
3. *Usefulness of space*				
Amount of space gained				
Quality of space after construction				
Potential impact on users				
Impact on staffing				
4. *Effect on future space needs & expansion*				
(Compare with long-term goals)				
5. *Provisions for the physically handicapped*				
(Indicate major barriers and possible solutions)				
6. *Interim conditions*				
(Describe impact on existing library operations during remodeling or expansion)				
7. *Estimated costs*				
(Indicate source of estimate)				
Site acquisition				
Remodeling				
New construction				
Other related work				

SUGGESTED FORMAT FOR A MATRIX TO COMPARE FACILITY OPTIONS (*continued*)

Factor	Option 1 (remodel)	Option 2 (remodel & add)	Option 3 (new bldg.)	Option 4 (convert existing bldg.)
Total initial cost				
Site				
Construction				
Total				

8. *Estimated cost impact on 20-year facility needs*

Total for 20-year program

Initial

Future

Total for 20 years

(Compare cost of a short-term solution with one adequate for at least 20 years)

9. *Miscellaneous information, observations, & relevant comments*

APPENDIX D

OUTLINE FOR A BUILDING PROGRAM

As DISCUSSED in Chapter 4, the content of a building program must describe requirements in detail. While the order of presentation may vary from program to program, the following outline indicates the major topics to be considered. (While this program outline is for a public library building, the general outline can be modified for use with any type of library.) This is, by no means an exhaustive outline. Rather, its purpose is to provide a partial framework. Most libraries will find it necessary to augment this outline with a variety of other topics.

Consider the building program to be the primary source book for the project: when in doubt, it is preferable to include information rather than to leave it out. Finally, remember to focus on the information needs of the design professionals for whom the building program is the major reference tool. The more comprehensive the program, the more likely that the design professionals will understand and appreciate your library's needs.

I. Introductory Statement

A/Very brief statement of the nature of the project: type of library (academic, public, school, institutional, etc.), estimated size (gross square feet), whether a new building, addition, remodeling, conversion, etc.

B/Character and size of the service area population including significant factors affecting library services and facilities.

C/Brief history of the library in the community or academic institution.

D/Brief history of the existing library building with identification of previous architects, dates of construction, etc.

E/Overview of the library's major functions, services, collections and special activities to be affected by the building project.

F/Discussions of the impact new technologies are expected to have on library collections and services, including distribution of power, data transmission, wire management, and future space needs.

G/Indicate how much, if any, of the space called for in the building program can be satisfied by one or more future additions; note the specific areas that are most likely to need more space.

H/Description of the basic concepts which have governed the preparation of the building program, such as:

1/ Creating flexible space which can be reorganized as conditions change, including the addition of new collections, services, staffing patterns, etc.;

2/ Maximizing staff utilization and productivity;

3/ Use of integrated systems for library operations and services;

4/ Minimizing staffing required primarily for supervision of public areas, responding to routine directional questions, etc.;

5/ Creating a building which can accommodate future expansion either through creation of unfinished space or through additions.

I/Indicate special problems such as the needs of the physically handicapped, energy conservation, security and building maintenance.

J/Describe, in generic terms, the major requirements that apply throughout the library, such as those relating to lighting, acoustics, power, data transmission, graphics, ceiling heights, floor load, etc.

K/Describe the general ambiance to be created by the building's interiors by indicating how the building should be perceived by its users and staff: friendly, efficient, inviting, etc.

II. Exterior

A/Describe the site to be used for the project including salient characteristics, adjacency to streets, adjoining land uses, possible soil conditions (if known) and any other pertinent data; include a site map if one is available.

B/Describe the importance and specifics of the following as they relate to the overall siting and exterior design:

1/ High visibility;
2/ Positive identification as a library;
3/ Easy and safe ingress and egress routes for vehicles, pedestrians, and bicycles;
4/ Provision for buses (if applicable);
5/ A single street-level entrance for the public—no steps;
6/ Entrance to be obvious, easily approached, inviting;
7/ Delivery/staff entrance relationship to site, parking, use by library vehicles, etc.;
8/ Appropriate on-site signage;
9/ Provisions for parking;
10/ Provisions for passenger drop-off;
11/ Safety precautions including lighting, ice-free non-slip surfaces, low shrubs;
12/ Landscaping design; security and maintenance considerations.

C/Explanation through bubble diagrams and narrative of the basic relationships of the exterior and the entrances to the building.

III. Foyer and Public Entrance

A/Use bubble diagrams and narrative to explain relationship of entrance to major public functions inside the building; special attention to this area as a transition space.
B/Purpose of the foyer to serve as a weather lock:
1/ Describe any weather factors such as possible orientation to avoid prevailing wind and storm patterns;
2/ Indicate possible use of foyer for location of foot mat to remove soil from shoes at entry.
C/Type of entry doors to be used: automatic or manual, etc.
D/Functions to be contained in the lobby or related thereto.
E/Special equipment such as public telephones, display cases, pamphlet distribution racks, bulletin boards, building directories, etc.
F/Specific concerns such as energy conservation, transitional lighting, acoustics, security, etc.
G/Public restrooms (if located here), drinking fountain, access to meeting rooms for after-hour use, etc.

IV. Circulation Desk Area

A/Description by bubble diagrams and narrative of the Circulation Desk functions and their relationship to other major spaces.
B/Brief description of the circulation control system and its requirements as they relate to space needs and functional layout.
C/Brief description of each major process such as check-in, check-out, registration, collection of fines/fees, pick-up of interlibrary loan books, reserve books, and any other material located here for that purpose: indicate equipment used, number of staff involved, typical handling patterns, etc.
D/Description of all other activities carried out in this area—ILL, Reserves, etc.; note especially the number, use and movement of book trucks.
E/If a collection security system is to be used, describe the equipment involved, the necessary traffic patterns, staff response, etc.
F/Indicate the maximum number of staff likely to be at the Circulation Desk at peak periods.
G/Indicate the maximum number of users likely to be at the check-out stations at peak periods.
H/Describe the use of any equipment that might be located adjacent to the circulation area for public use such as coin-op copy machines, typewriters, microcomputers, etc.; indicate how it is to be housed and supervised.
I/Discuss any other issue relating to the circulation area such as traffic, noise, lighting, supervision.

V. Public Service Areas

A/Using bubble diagrams and narrative description, indicate the major public service areas to be accessible from the Circulation Desk area; where necessary, prioritize the services that should be given precedence in their accessibility.
B/Indicate functions which have a negative relationship to the Circulation Desk area and can therefore be located elsewhere.

VI. Children's Services Area

A/Brief description of the major functions provided in the Children's Services area; note age group to be served and any philosophical background.
B/Indicate basic relationships of the Children's Services area to other parts of the Library:
1/ Circulation
2/ Young Adults
3/ General Adult Collections
4/ Reference Services
5/ Staff office/workroom for Children's staff
6/ Programming space
7/ Other.
C/Describe the atmosphere to be achieved in the Children's Room.
D/Indicate the number and location for the card cata-

log or the public access terminals; note the number of terminals needed and whether they are to be on tables or counters.

E/Indicate the relationship of the Children's Reference Desk to collections, seating and other functions; indicate the number of staff to be at this desk at any one time and describe the equipment needed here.

F/Describe print collections for the Children's Services area in terms of numbers of volumes to be shelved, division into various sub-collections (Easy Readers, Picture Books, Board Books, Reference, Magazines, Fiction, Nonfiction, and any other categories); indicate usage patterns.

G/Describe non-print collections for children, indicating the quantity of each type of material to be housed, type of shelving or other equipment to be used; describe how in-house use (if any) will occur and be supervised—what kinds of equipment will be involved, etc.

H/Describe how microcomputers, CD/ROM equipment will be used, numbers of machines, etc. and their location relative to the Children's Services Desk.

I/Indicate number of seats to be provided by type of seating: lounge chairs, chairs at tables, carrels, listening/viewing carrels or tables, etc.

J/Describe and quantify any other equipment, materials, etc., that must be housed (pamphlet files, picture files, atlas cases, dictionary stands, etc.).

K/Describe any requirement for display cases, bulletin boards, or other exhibit needs; indicate sizes and relationships to other functions.

L/Describe programming activities and the kind of space needed for story hours, class visits, and other programs; include average number of children participating (not the maximum number expected for special programs, end of summer reading, etc.).

M/Indicate desirability of separate restrooms for children located adjacent to the Children's Room.

N/Describe office/workroom requirements:
1/ Office for Children's Services Librarian (if needed)
2/ Workroom for Children's Services Staff (if needed)
  a/ Location
  b/ Number of work stations
  c/ Activities to occur there
  d/ Shelving needs
  e/ Other requirements.

VII. *Young Adult Services Area*

A/Describe the library's philosophy in working with the young adult; indicate age range for this group, special interests, etc.

B/Collection requirements:
1/ Hardcover
2/ Paperback
3/ Magazine
4/ Nonprint.
C/Seating Requirements:
1/ Lounge seating
2/ Chairs at tables
3/ Study carrels
4/ Other.
D/Activity space, if any (describe fully).
E/Other equipment to be available here:
1/ PAC terminals
2/ Microcomputers
3/ AV listening/viewing stations
4/ Bulletin Boards
5/ Other.
F/Staffing requirements.
G/Special concerns such as acoustics, traffic, supervision, etc.
H/Office/workroom needs, if any.

VIII. *Adult Browsing Area*

A/Purpose of the Browsing Area in terms of user access, with description of atmosphere to be achieved.

B/Relationship to Circulation and other major adult areas.

C/Contents of the Browsing Area (List and quantify in terms the number of volumes to be on shelf):
1/ New books
2/ Paperbacks
3/ Special interest displays
4/ Newspapers and magazines (if not in a separate area)
5/ Other.
D/Desirable shelving/display techniques, arrangement and equipment.
E/Seating accommodations:
1/ Lounge seating
2/ Chairs at tables
3/ Other.
F/Indicate which desk will be responsible for supervision.
G/Bulletin boards or other equipment.

IX. *Newspapers and Magazines (if these are in a separate area)*

A/Using bubble diagrams and narrative, describe the relationship of this area to other major services in terms of adjacency priorities, traffic flow, and supervision.

B/Describe uses made of newspapers and magazines and identify the major groups of users.

C/Indicate the contents of this area and how each type of material is to be shelved:
  1/ Magazines
  2/ Newspapers
  3/ Backfiles
  4/ Other.
D/Supervision and service aspects: discuss which desk will be responsible.
E/Seating:
  1/ Lounge
  2/ Chairs at tables
  3/ Study carrels.
F/Description of any other furniture or equipment to be located here; indicate the atmosphere desired.
G/Other issues.

X. *Public Catalog/Public Access Terminals*

A/Using bubble diagrams and narrative, describe the relationship of the public catalog and/or public access terminals to other major adult service areas and functions.
B/Indicate the number of catalog cabinets and/or public access terminals to be accommodated now and in the future.
C/If public access terminals are to be used, describe wire management needs and indicate how many are to be on stand-up counters and the number to be at sit-down height; note the number of printers and how they are to be arranged.
D/Indicate who will provide assistance to users.
E/Discuss any other relevant issues such as traffic, acoustics, lighting and glare, etc.

XI. *General Adult Collections*

A/Using bubble diagrams and narrative, describe the relationship of the general collections to other adult library functions.
B/Describe the book collections in terms of:
  1/ Numbers of volumes in each category to be separately shelved or otherwise identified
  2/ Any special display needs for collections.
C/Indicate seating requirements and describe how seating is to be related to collections:
  1/ Lounge seating
  2/ Chairs at tables
  3/ Study carrels
  4/ Individual and/or group rooms
  5/ Other.
D/Indicate whether there is to be a separate Adult Services or Readers Advisory Desk; if so, describe its functions and the furniture/equipment needed.
E/Describe other furniture and equipment to be provided such as:

1/ Atlas stands
2/ Dictionary stands
3/ Index tables
4/ Copying machines
5/ Book display shelving such as "A" frames, book troughs, etc.
6/ Other.
F/Describe any special interest niches or collections desired, such as:
  1/ Consumer education
  2/ Business
  3/ Careers/employment
  4/ College preparation
  5/ Other.
G/Describe any other needs pertaining to this area.

XII. *Reference Services*

A/Using bubble diagrams and narrative, describe the relationship of the Reference Services area to other major areas of the library.
B/Describe the atmosphere that is to prevail in the Reference Services area.
C/Describe the Reference collections including any special groupings of materials and indicate the numbers of volumes to be shelved.
D/Describe any special shelving needs such as:
  1/ Use of counter-height (42"–48"-high shelving)
  2/ Locked cases
  3/ Other.
E/Indicate any requirements for catalogs or public access terminals.
F/Indicate the number of index tables needed and how they should relate to other parts of the Reference Services area.
G/Indicate quantities of other furniture and equipment needed such as:
  1/ Public Access Terminals
  2/ CD/ROM terminals
  3/ Microform cabinets
  4/ Microform readers and reader/printers
  5/ Pamphlet files
  6/ Picture files
  7/ Map files
  8/ Atlas cases
  9/ Dictionary stands
  10/ Copy machines
  11/ Other.
H/Indicate seating requirements:
  1/ Lounge seating
  2/ Chairs at tables
  3/ Study carrels
  4/ Other.
I/Describe the Reference Desk, the number of staff that might be located there at any one time, indicate size and desired location of a ready reference

collection if one is to be used, note location requirements for the desk as it relates to other parts of the Reference Services area, describe furniture and equipment needs including terminals for on-line access.

J/Discuss the accommodation of microform indicating how its use relates to other reference functions, space needed, lighting, acoustics, traffic, etc.

K/Discuss other issues such as:
1/ Lighting
2/ Acoustics
3/ Traffic
4/ Supervision
5/ Other.

XIII. Audio-Visual Services (Non-Print Media)

A/Describe the library's philosophy of dealing with non-print media in terms of their separation or integration into the other service areas, capability for in-house use, and similar issues.

B/Using bubble diagrams and narrative, describe the desired relationships to be achieved for non-print materials.

C/Indicate the quantity of each type of non-print material and the preferred method of housing it.

D/Describe the seating requirements for the Audio-Visual area:
1/ Lounge seats
2/ Chairs at tables
3/ Listening/viewing stations
4/ Group viewing rooms, if any.

E/Discuss whether or not public-use microcomputer terminals will be located here; if not, where.

F/Indicate the source for supervision of this area and any furniture and equipment requirements if a public desk is to be used.

G/Describe other equipment needed:
1/ AV equipment for playback
2/ Catalogs or Public Access Terminals
3/ Other.

H/Discuss other issues considered pertinent:
1/ Accommodation of future media
2/ Acoustics
3/ Lighting
4/ Security
5/ Other.

XIV. Local History/Genealogy Rooms

A/Describe objectives of the Local History/Genealogy Room, indicating purpose, usage, etc.; describe atmosphere to be achieved; indicate whether the room is to have a special name that might lend character.

B/Using bubble diagrams and narrative, indicate the relationship of the Local History/Genealogy Room to other functions.

C/Describe the collections to be housed, indicating numbers of volumes, types of shelving (open shelf arrangement, locked cases, etc.).

D/Indicate amount of supplemental materials:
1/ Pamphlet files
2/ Map files
3/ Picture files
4/ Audio-visual materials files including oral history tapes, video tapes, slides, etc.
5/ Microform files
6/ Microform reader/printers
7/ Other.

E/Seating:
1/ Lounge seats
2/ Chairs at tables
3/ Study carrels
4/ Assignable studies
5/ Other.

F/Miscellaneous equipment:
1/ Catalogs and Public Access Terminals
2/ Copy machines
3/ Map table
4/ Microcomputer terminals
5/ Display cases
6/ Bulletin Boards
7/ Other.

G/Indicate the furniture requirements for the Reference desk which will serve the Local History/Genealogy Room.

H/Local History/Genealogy Office/Workroom:

If the Local History/Genealogy area is to have its own office and/or workroom, these facilities should be described in terms of their requirements and relationships to the public area.
1/ Office furniture and equipment needs
2/ Workroom
a/ Number of work stations
b/ Storage requirements
c/ Materials preservation requirements
d/ Storage vault
e/ Darkroom (if collection contains numerous historic photographs that require restoration, preservation and/or reproduction)
f/ Microcomputer for producing indexes related to local history and genealogy.

XV. Meeting Rooms and Other Special-Purpose Areas

A/Describe the various types of meeting rooms that the library wishes to provide; indicate numbers of people to be accommodated, type of programming, and other salient features.

B/Using bubble diagrams and narrative, describe the relationship of the various meeting facilities with other library functions, with emphasis on relationship to the public entrance, lobby, etc.

C/Describe furniture, equipment and special requirements such as projection facilities, access to kitchens, storage for chairs, tables and platform furniture, etc.

D/Describe any special requirements such as fixed seating on a sloped floor, movable partitions, projection booths, stages, dressing rooms, etc.

E/Describe any other special services, rooms or functions, giving full details of activities, space requirements, furniture and equipment, etc.
1/ Individual instruction rooms (Tutorial rooms)
2/ Typing and/or microcomputer rooms for the public
3/ Video production facilities
4/ Special materials and services for the physically handicapped
5/ Non-print production facilities for public use
6/ Other.

XVI. Staff Offices and Workrooms

A/Using bubble diagrams and narrative, identify and describe each of the major staff areas in terms of functions, numbers of staff, relationships to public areas and to other facilities.

B/Provide a detailed current staff organization chart which delineates the number of positions involved in each major division of the library.

C/Describe each major staff office/workroom area, giving attention as relevant to:
1/ Functional relationships of the division to other divisions and library functions
2/ Number of staff to be provided
    a/ Offices
    b/ Work stations in workrooms
3/ General descriptions of work flow including required space, furniture and equipment
4/ Storage needs
5/ Equipment and furniture needs
6/ Shelving
7/ Counters
8/ Sinks
9/ Other.

XVII. Public Services

A/Describe the general purpose and nature of offices and workroom(s) to be provided for Public Services staff; use bubble diagrams and narrative to indicate internal relationships as well as relationships to other offices/workrooms.

B/Describe any offices needed because of supervisory or other special duties.

C/Describe workroom requirements, indicating:
1/ Number of work stations
2/ Description of generic work station (if applicable)
3/ Specialized work stations (if needed)
4/ Use of automated equipment (whether at individual desks and/or grouped for shared use)
5/ Shelving requirements
6/ Counter space (if any)
7/ Supply storage
8/ Other.

D/Describe any special work areas that need to be created, such as:
1/ Telephone reference room
2/ Interlibrary Loan work area
3/ Other.

XVIII. Extension Services (Branches, Outreach, Etc.)

A/Describe the library's extension services program in terms of objectives, number of staff, major requirements, use of vehicles, use of Delivery Room and/or other spaces.

B/Using bubble diagrams and narrative, describe the internal relationships of Extension Services staff work spaces as well as their relationship to other library functions, collections, storage, delivery, etc.

C/Describe any offices required for Extension staff, including furniture and equipment.

D/Describe any workrooms to be shared by Extension staff, including:
1/ Number of work stations
2/ Description of work stations
3/ Shelving requirements
4/ Counter space
5/ Other.

XIX. Technical Services

A/Describe the nature of activities to be carried out in Technical Services, indicating work flow in narrative and by diagram.

B/Describe relationship of the Technical Services area to other staff and library service areas, using bubble diagrams and narrative.

C/Describe any offices required by staff because of supervisory or other specialized duties; indicate furniture and equipment.

D/Describe the Technical Services workroom using flow charts and/or other diagrams to clarify internal relationships of work stations to the various processes; include:

1/ Number of work stations
2/ General characteristics
3/ Specialized work stations (if any)
4/ Shelving needs
5/ Use of book trucks including typical number at each work station and in any holding area
6/ Where terminals are to be located: at individual work stations? grouped for shared use? other arrangement?
7/ Supply storage needs
8/ Other.

XX. General Shared Staff Facilities

A/Describe the nature of shared staff facilities, for instance: lunch room, lounge, restrooms, lockers, mail boxes, bulletin boards, conference room, other.
B/Using bubble diagrams and narrative, indicate how the shared staff facilities relate to the arrangement of offices and workrooms and to the entrance to be used by staff.
C/Describe each shared staff function in terms of its particular requirements including accessibility, space, furniture, equipment, numbers of staff to be accommodated, etc.

XXI. Miscellaneous Spaces

A/Delivery Room: Using bubble diagrams, indicate relationship of the Delivery Room to other library spaces and describe work flow, furniture and equipment, security, etc.
B/Custodial Services: Indicate space required for custodial services including janitorial closets on each level as well as a main custodial services area for staff, supplies, equipment, etc.; describe how custodial services will be handled: number of staff, scope of duties (cleaning, general maintenance, minor repairs, etc.).
C/Storage: The library's need for storage space deserves careful detailing as to purpose, amount of space, and relationship of the storage area to those functions it supports; use bubble diagrams and narrative to describe purpose, uses and work flow; give separate consideration to storage for:
1/ Collections
2/ Supplies
3/ Open floor storage for equipment, furniture, other large objects
4/ Other.

XXII. Conclusion and Space Summary

Provide a brief conclusion which includes a space summary for all areas of the library.

APPENDIX E

SAMPLE OF AN AREA DATA SHEET

AREA DATA SHEET 3300
REFERENCE SERVICES

Net Sq. Ft.	3,360
Function	Provides area for reference materials and their use by staff and public.
Relationships	Primary relationship to Adult Services, Index & Bibliographic Center and Magazines; occasional need to get materials from storage area, especially magazine backfiles older than those in the Magazine area.
Special Requirements	Atmosphere suitable to longer periods of concentrated work; use alcove or other arrangement to provide identification of Genealogy Collection, and Reference Collection.
Seating	12 seats near business indexes; 8 seats for Genealogy Collection; 36 seats for general reference; divide seating between 48″-wide carrels and chairs at wide tables.
Collections	Reference = 12,000 volumes Indexes and directories for business = 1,000 vols. on two index tables Genealogy = 1,800 volumes Pamphlets = 10 4-drawer lateral files (legal) Maps = 1 plan file (3 5-drawer sections + base).
Staff	Reference services desk for three staff working simultaneously; bibliographic terminal with printer on desk or sideboard; shelving for 300 ready-reference volumes; credenza for storage of bibliographies; 2-drawer lateral file (legal).

Furniture & Equipment	For collections, users, and staff as noted above:
	
	Genealogy = 8 90″ DFS
	Reference = 60 90″ DFS
	Index Tables = 2 90″ wide w/2 shelves
	Pamphlet files = 10 4-drawer lateral (L)
	Maps = 1 plan file w/3 5-drawer
	   sections
	Copying machine = Table top w/4′ counter
	   for assembling pages.

Casework	May develop casework for partial enclosure of copy machine station.
Lighting	Ambient: 100 cf, unless task lighting is used for carrels and reading tables, in which case ambient = 50 cf and task lighting 100 cf; also 100 cf at staff Reference Services desk with shielding of CRT from direct light and glare.

Power	Duplex receptacles as required for equipment above; signal wire as needed for terminal.
Automation	Library system bibliographic terminal at staff desk; may have printer; automated data base searching to be done in Public Services workroom.
Communications	3 telephones at Reference Desk; PA speakers.
HVAC	As appropriate.
Acoustics	To be a quiet area—aim for 30 dBA; location must not intercept traffic to other areas.
Finishes	Carpet.
Plumbing	None.
Signage	Attention-getting signage to identify Reference Services desk; signage to identify various collections within Reference area.

APPENDIX F

QUESTIONS TO ACCOMPANY A REQUEST FOR QUALIFICATIONS OR A PROPOSAL FOR ARCHITECTURAL SERVICES

THE FOLLOWING questions are typical of those that might accompany a Request for Qualifications (RFQ) or Proposal (RFP) for architectural services. Questions should be phrased to elicit information and opinions helpful in comparing and evaluating several firms; questions that can be answered with a "yes" or "no" should be rephrased. Unless design professionals are required to respond to such questions, the information gathered by the RFQ or RFP may be too general or routine to be helpful in distinguishing desirable qualifications.

1/ Based upon your understanding of contemporary public library service, in what ways do you think future building requirements can best be anticipated for the next 10–20 years?

2/ In what ways and to what degree have you familiarized yourself with the details of our project?

3/ How well do you feel the library's building program responds to your requirements for information and what additional information do you believe is necessary?

4/ What do you consider to be your firm's major strengths in design? Please illustrate with examples from your work.

5/ Approximately what proportion of your firm's time would you expect to allocate to the following:
a/ pre-schematics
b/ schematics
c/ design development
d/ construction documents (working drawings and specifications).

6/ Based upon your current knowledge of the project, what do you see as the major design issues you must cope with?

7/ For the areas of specialization listed below, please indicate:
a/ Those you feel unconditionally qualified to furnish within your own staff; indicate qualifications and experience;

b/ Those services you feel qualified to provide for routine situations but not for more complex situations;

c/ Those areas for which you would expect to use outside assistance.
Specialized concerns:
• energy conservation
• lighting
• acoustics
• graphics and signage
• communications technology and systems
• automation
• non-print media (audio-visual, video, etc.).

8/ How will fees for outside specialists be covered?

9/ If you anticipate requiring the services of outside specialists for any of the above, whom would you recommend and what are their qualifications?

10/ What supervision services does your firm normally provide during construction? Are these included in your base fee?

11/ Describe the procedures your firm would use to minimize the necessity for change orders during construction.

12/ What would be the extent of your on-site inspection responsibilities during construction and to whom would this be delegated? How often would site visits be made?

13/ At what times during the planning period and in what manner will your firm provide projected cost estimates for the project?

14/ If, in spite of the best efforts of all concerned, the project construction bids exceed available funds, how would your firm assist in determining the best ways of bringing the project within budget? How would such work be reflected in your fees? To what extent would you assume responsibility for the redesign of the project if required to reduce cost?

15/ At what stages of design and for what purposes does your firm use study models? Is construction of models covered by your standard fee quoted in your proposal? Are study models constructed in-house? How are they used with the client?

16/ If a separate interior design firm is selected for this project, how would your firm coordinate the design process to insure a harmonious end-product?

17/ What general design characteristics do you believe are shared by the various structures your firm has designed in the past 5–10 years?

18/ What criteria would you use in selecting exterior and interior materials and finishes?

19/ What would you identify as the single, unique characteristic of your firm and its practice that distinguishes it from others?

20/ If awarded this project, what other commitments does your firm have which would need consideration in establishing a project schedule?

APPENDIX G

TYPICAL QUESTIONS FOR DESIGN PROFESSIONALS' INTERVIEWS

QUESTIONS used in interviewing architects and interior designers will depend to some extent upon the evaluation of materials submitted with their respective proposals. Enough of the same questions should be asked each firm to provide a basis for comparison. However, the content of the proposals, and especially the responses to the questions submitted with the RFP, usually lead to individualized questions. As with any interview, there should be sufficient opportunity for follow-up questions which arise as a result of the interview process.

In addition to clarifying and elaborating on material submitted with the proposal responses, certain other questions may be asked, such as the following:

1/ Please describe the engineering and other specialized services your firm is prepared to provide as a part of its regular services.
2/ What specific experience has your firm had in the design of energy-efficient buildings of this type and size?
3/ What do you consider to be your firm's most important qualifications for this project?
4/ Please comment briefly on your firm's major strengths and achievements in design.
5/ What design characteristics would seem important in identifying this building as a library rather than some other type of facility?
6/ At what point do you consider the schematic phase to be completed?

7/ Approximately what percentage of your firm's effort will go into each phase:
a/ Schematics
b/ Design development
c/ Construction Documents
d/ Construction supervision
8/ How will the efforts of engineering be coordinated with architectural and interior design development?
9/ Will production of construction documents be completed in-house or contracted to another firm?
10/ How does your firm evaluate an evolving design in terms of life-cycle costs? Maintenance?
11/ How do you arrive at project cost estimates and at what times are these presented?
12/ In general, would you describe the design philosophy of your firm as tending toward the conservative end of the spectrum or directed more toward the innovative and experimental? Examples?
13/ What is your experience with the planning team approach on projects of this size and complexity?
14/ What do you feel are the key security issues facing libraries? How can these be addressed through design?
15/ How do you propose to handle the review of drawings at the various stages by City staff, Library staff and consultants to get comments and approval?
16/ What libraries do you use personally? When did you last use one and for what purpose?
17/ What is your perception of this community and how will that influence design concepts?

APPENDIX H

TYPICAL PLAN REVIEW COMMENTS

THE FOLLOWING review comments have been excerpted from an actual review of design development drawings. A portion of the sheet of drawings, Figure H-1, is included for reference. Note that comments are referenced by item numbers enclosed in hexagons inserted on the drawing.

Figure H-1

1/ This window could pose a security problem; please make certain that it and the adjacent elevator vestibule are included in perimeter security alarm system.

2/ Use of terrazzo, as noted in the finish schedule, creates a possible acoustical problem; how will this be handled? Arrows point to spaces where recessed mats should be provided to reduce the amount of dirt tracked into the entrance.

3/ The Circulation Desk is very tight for the amount of activity to take place here; some adjustments will be required.

4/ What is the purpose of this space? The dimensions vary from those on other sheets; which is correct?

5/ Can this space be consolidated with the space to the east?

6/ What is the purpose of this space? Can it be consolidated with Room 108?

7/ Compared to program requirements, this space for the Friends Book Store is too small; could walls be replaced by some sort of movable screen to increase visibility and flexibility?

7A. The shelving in the Browsing Area does not meet program requirements and seems to be too scattered to be useful; less than half of the programmed 5,000 volumes can be shelved, even using top and bottom shelves, which is to be avoided if at all possible.

8/ Finish schedule for all restrooms must be corrected as per program to require floor-to-ceiling ceramic tile on all walls.

9/ See item 8.

10/ Program requires 42"-high shelving for picture books and Easy books; 66"-high shelving will place much of the collection out of reach for pre-school and primary-aged children.

11/ See item 10.

12/ Program requires that all shelving in the Children's Services area be 66" or less in height; use of 90" shelving here, while increasing the capacity, will place many volumes out of reach and will entice youngsters to climb on the shelving to reach books on the upper shelves—a hazardous practice; moreover, use of such high shelving will create a feeling of density which will damage the ambiance of this part of the Children's Library.

12A. Shelving capacity in the Children's Room is estimated at 20,475 volumes (using the recommended shelving sizes), of which 16,800 will be in the stack area at the south end of the room.

13/ Should the Children's Desk be moved forward to occupy a more accessible location and provide better supervision?

14/ See item 8.

15/ See item 8.

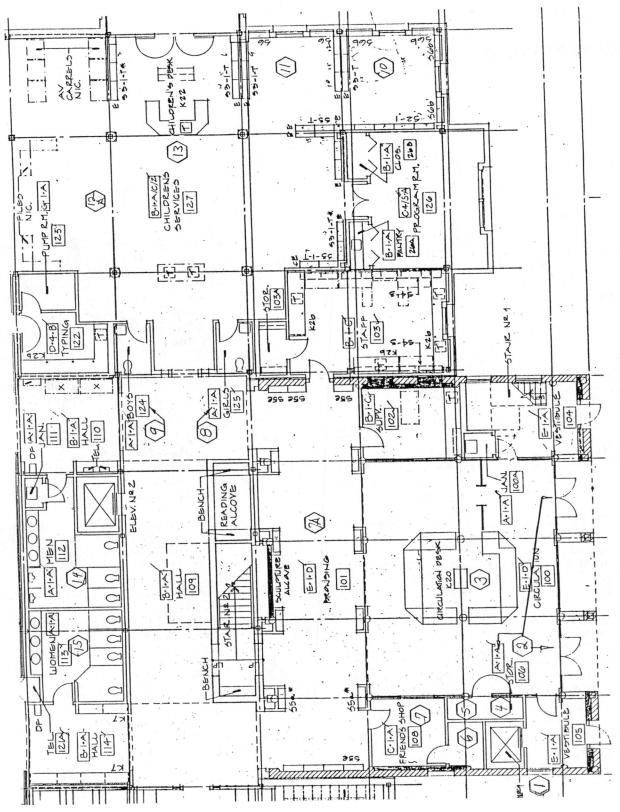

Figure H-1
How Review Comments Are Keyed to a Drawing

A BASIC BIBLIOGRAPHY ON PLANNING LIBRARY BUILDINGS

THE LITERATURE on library buildings includes a variety of books, magazines, and other sources. The titles included in this bibliography are among those most frequently referred to at this time. This is a selected, not a comprehensive, listing. Those who are currently engaged in, or preparing to be involved in, a building project will benefit from reading current issues of the journals listed in the final section of this bibliography.

The citations in this bibliography are divided among several broad topics as an aid in selection. Additional information on many building topics can be located through the various guides to periodical literature.

Those wishing a more comprehensive bibliography, especially for academic library buildings, are referred to:

Snowball, George J., and Rosemary Thompson. *Planning Library Buildings: A Select Bibliography*. 2nd edition. Chicago: Buildings for College and University Libraries Committee, Buildings & Equipment Section, Library Administration & Management Association, American Library Association, 1984.

General Materials for Planning, Programming, and Managing the Library Building Project

Cohen, Aaron, and Elaine Cohen. *Designing and Space Planning for Libraries*. New York: Bowker, 1979.

Dahlgren, Anders. *Planning the Small Public Library Building* (Small Libraries Publication - No. 11). Chicago: American Library Association, 1985.

Deasy, C.M. *Designing Places for People: A Handbook on Human Behavior for Architects, Designers and Facilities Managers*. New York: Whitney, 1985.

Fraley, Ruth A., and Carol Lee Anderson. *Library Space Planning: How to Assess, Allocate and Reorganize Collections, Resources and Physical Facilities*. New York: Neal-Schuman, 1985.

Holt, Raymond M. *Wisconsin Library Buildings Project Handbook*. Madison, Wisconsin: Wisconsin Department of Public Instruction, 1978.

_____. *Talking Buildings: A Practical Dialogue on Programming and Planning Library Buildings* (Proceedings of Building Workshops sponsored by the California State Library). Sacramento: California State Library, 1986.

"Library Buildings," *Library Trends*, Anders C. Dahlgren, Issue Editor. Bloomington, Ill.: University of Illinois, Graduate School of Library and Information Science. Vol. 36, No. 2 (Fall, 1987).

Lushington, Nolan, and Willis N. Millis, Jr. *Libraries Designed for Users*. Hamden, Conn.: Library Professional Publications, 1980.

Mason, Ellsworth. *Mason on Library Buildings*. Metuchen, N.J.: Scarecrow Press, 1980.

Metcalf, Keyes D. *Planning Academic and Research Library Buildings*. New York: R.R. Bowker Co., 1966.

_____. *Planning Academic and Research Library Buildings*. 2d ed., edited by Philip D. Leighton and David C. Weber. Chicago: American Library Association, 1986.

Myller, Rolf. *The Design of the Small Public Library*. New York: R.R. Bowker Co., 1966.

Nyren, Karl, ed., *L.J. SPECIAL REPORT #1: Library Space Planning*. New York: Bowker, 1976.

_____. *L.J. Special Report #8: New Public Library Buildings*. New York: Bowker, 1979.

_____. *L.J. Special Report 15: To Grow Or Not To Grow?* New York: Bowker.

_____. *L.J. Special Report #16: New Academic Buildings*, New York: Bowker.

_____. *L.J. Special Report #23: New Academic Buildings/II*. New York: Bowker.

_____. *L.J. Special report #25: New Public Buildings/III*. New York: Bowker, 1983.

Schell, Hal B., ed. *Reader on the Library Building*. Washington, D.C.: Microcard Editions Books, 1975.

Wheeler, Joseph L., and Alfred Githens. *The American Public Library Building*. New York: Charles Scribner's Sons, 1941.

The foregoing titles contain material ranging from general information to specific guidelines on planning, programming and managing the library building project. They vary widely in content but form a basic reference collection for those contemplating or engaged in a library building project whether it is a remodel, addition, new construction or adaption.

The Metcalf text, though for academic libraries, is by far the most thorough treatise presently available on library buildings. It is a very useful source of information, regardless of the size or type of building project. Rolf Myller's work is brief but helpful, especially as a point of departure. Although very much out of date, the Wheeler-Githens opus is still frequently cited.

Building Codes

Construction is regulated in most areas by building codes adopted by local governmental agencies. While such codes may be of local origin, most agencies adopt one of the major building codes, making such changes as they see fit. Building codes are usually revised every two or three years. However, their provisions do not become effective until the new edition is officially adopted by the local jurisdiction. While building codes contain highly technical information, it is important for the librarian engaged in a building project to be familiar with the code governing construction in the jurisdiction. A copy of the relevant code or codes should be available for immediate reference. The following general building codes are generally recognized as model building codes and are widely used throughout the country. However, each tends to be most heavily used in one part or another of the nation, as noted below.

Basic Building Code. Building Officials and Code Administrators International, Inc., Homewood, Illinois 60430. [Referred to as the BBC; used generally in the Midwestern States.]

National Building Code. American Insurance Association, New York: N.Y. 10038. [Referred to as the NBC and used widely, especially in the Eastern portion of the United States.]

Standard Building Code. Southern Building Code Congress International, Birmingham, Alabama 35213. [Referred to as the SBCC and used extensively in the Southern States.]

Uniform Building Code. International Conference of Building Officials, Whittier, California 90601. [Referred to as the UBC, this model code predominates in the Western States and is widely used elsewhere in the country.]

Other Sources for Codes, Standards, and Guidelines for Construction

In addition to the general building codes above, there are many others which are used in conjunction with them when dealing with specific areas such as electrical, heating and air conditioning, fire detection and suppression, plumbing, etc. These are often the products of such professional institutes and societies as the American Standards Institute (ANSI), the American Society of Heating, Refrigerating, and Air Conditioning Engineers (ASHRAE), American Society of Testing and Materials (ASTM), Illuminating Engineering Society of North America (IESNA), National Fire Protection Association (NFPA), and the Underwriters Laboratories, Inc. (UL). These are but a few of the many groups which offer codes, standards and guidelines for the construction industry.

Interior Design, Furniture, and Equipment

Draper, James, and James Brooks. *Interior Design for Libraries.* Chicago: American Library Association, 1979.

Gueft, Olga. "Perfectly Orchestrated Civic Core," *Interiors,* Vol. 89, No. 5 (December, 1976), pp. 60–63.

Klein, Judy Graf. *The Office Book: Ideas and Designs for Contemporary Work Spaces.* New York: Facts on File, 1982.

Pollet, Dorothy, and Peter C. Haskell. *Sign Systems for Libraries.* New York: Bowker, 1979.

See also the following titles listed under the heading "Institute Proceedings" in this bibliography:

- *Guidelines for Library Planners.*
- *The Library Environment: Aspects of Interior Planning.*
- *Library Furniture and Equipment.*
- *The Procurement of Library Furnishings: Specifications, Bid Documents, and Evaluations.*

Site Selection

"A Public Library Site Symposium," edited by Hoyt Galvin, *Library Space Planning* (LJ Special Report #1). New York: R.R. Bowker Co., 1976.

Rohlf, Robert H., and David R. Smith. "Public Library Site Selection," *Public Libraries,* Vol. 24, No. 2, Summer, 1985, pp. 47–49.

"Site Selection," *Library Buildings: Innovation for Changing Needs.* Chicago: American Library Association, 1972, pp. 152–163.

Wheeler, Joseph L. *The Effective Location of Public Library Buildings* (Occasional Papers No. 85). Urbana: University of Illinois Graduate School of Library Science, 1958.

——. *A Reconsideration of the Strategic Location of Public Library Buildings* (Occasional Papers No. 85). Urbana: University of Illinois Graduate School of Library Science, 1967.

The major work on locating public library buildings was done by Joseph L. Wheeler. More recent experience is reported in articles such as those noted above and in items which can be located through *Library Literature*.

The Consultant and Project Team

The Library Building Consultant, Role and Responsibility. Edited by Ernest R. DeProspo. New Brunswick, N.J.: Rutgers University Press, 1969.

"The Role of the Building-Planning Team," *Library Buildings: Innovations for Changing Needs.* Chicago: American Library Association, 1972.

Numerous articles in the proceedings of library building institutes and in library literature pertain to the role of the library building consultant.

Security

Protection of Library Collections, 1976 (NFPA No. 910). Boston: National Fire Protection Association, 1976.

Hopf, Peter S., ed. *Designers' Handbook of Building Security*. New York: McGraw-Hill Book Co., 1978.

Reber, Jan R. *Manual on Library Security*. New York: The Haworth Press, 1978.

Library of Archival Security. New York: The Haworth Press (Quarterly).

Security of people, collections, equipment, and facilities is an important but often overlooked aspect of library building projects. The foregoing citations should create an awareness of the subject and alert the members of the project team to explore the ramifications. Arson, vandalism, theft of materials, and various life-threatening situations are encountered with increasing frequency.

Blueprint Reading

Bellis, Herbert F., and Walter A. Schmidt. *Blueprint Reading for the Construction Trades*. 2nd ed. New York: McGraw-Hill, 1978.

Hornung, William J. *Blueprint Reading: Interpretation of Architectural Working Drawings*. Englewood Cliffs, N.J.: Prentice-Hall, 1961.

Huth, Mark W. *Basic Construction Blueprint Reading*. New York: Van Nostrand, 1980.

Palmquist, Roland. *Answers on Blueprint Reading*. New York: T. Audel, 1977.

Wallach, Paul I. and Donald Helper. *Reading Construction Drawings*. New York: McGraw-Hill, 1979.

The above titles are merely suggestions of a few among the many books written to assist those wishing to learn to read architectural drawings with some proficiency. Your architect and/or consultant can no doubt suggest others. Most libraries have one or more titles on this subject in their collections. The Hornung title noted above even has segments containing a few drawings of a small library building project as illustrations.

Additional Sources of Information

Institute Proceedings

The following items are citations for the various proceedings of institutes conducted by the Buildings and Equipment Section of the Library Administration and Management Association (formerly Library Administration Division) of the American Library Association. They are presented in alphabetical order by title.

An Architectural Strategy for Change: Remodeling and Expanding for Contemporary Public Library Needs. Edited by Raymond M. Holt. Chicago: American Library Association, 1976.

Guidelines for Library Planners. Edited by Keith Doms and Howard Rovelstad. Chicago: American Library Association, 1960.

Libraries: Building for the Future. Edited by Robert J. Shaw. Chicago: American Library Association, 1967.

Library Buildings: Innovation for Changing Needs. Edited by Alphonse F. Trezza. Chicago: American Library Association, 1972.

Library Environment: Aspects of Interior Planning. Edited by Frazer G. Poole. Chicago: American Library Association, 1965.

Library Furniture and Equipment. Chicago: American Library Association, 1963.

Planning Library Buildings for Service. Edited by Harold Roth. Chicago: American Library Association, 1964.

Problems in Planning Library Facilities: Consultants, Architects, Plans and Critiques. Edited by William A. Katz and Roderick G. Swartz. Chicago: American Library Association, 1964.

The Procurement of Library Furnishings: Specification: Bid Documents and Evaluations. Edited by Alphonze F. Trezza and Frazer G. Poole. Chicago: American Library Association, 1969. 150 pp.

Running Out of Space—What Are the Alternatives? Edited by Gloria Novak. Chicago: American Library Association, 1978.

Annuals

"Buildings," *The ALA Yearbook* . . . . Chicago: American Library Association.

"Public Library Building," *The Bowker Annual of Library & Book Trade Information*. New York: R.R. Bowker Co.

Architectural Source Books

The latest editions of these titles should be considered as essential reference tools for everyone involved in the design and construction of a library facility.

De Chiara, Joseph, and John H. Callender. *Time-Saver Standards for Building Types*. 2nd ed. New York: McGraw-Hill Book Co., 1980.

Ramsey, Charles G., and Harold R. Sleeper. *Architectural Graphic Standards*. 8th ed. Edited by John Ray Hoke, Jr. New York: John Wiley & Sons, 1988.

Reznikoff, S.C. *Interior Graphic and Design Standards*. New York: Watson-Guptill Publications, 1986.

Journals for Current Reading

Architectural Record. New York: McGraw-Hill Inc.

Contract: The Business Magazine of Commercial Furnishings and Interior Architecture. New York: Gralla Publications.

Interiors: For the Contract Design Industry. New York: Billboard Publications.

Library Journal (December 1 issue usually features library buildings with statistical data repeated in the *Bowker Annual*).

Progressive Architecture. Cleveland, Ohio: Reinhold Publishing.

INDEX